Kishwaukee College Library
21193 Malta Road
Malta, IL 60150-9699

Ambition and Division

Kishwaukee College Library
21193 Malta Road
Malta, IL 60150-9699

AMBITION AND DIVISION

Legacies of the George W. Bush Presidency

Edited by

STEVEN E. SCHIER

University of
Pittsburgh Press

Published by the University of Pittsburgh Press, Pittsburgh, Pa., 15260
Copyright © 2009, University of Pittsburgh Press
All rights reserved
Manufactured in the United States of America
Printed on acid-free paper
10 9 8 7 6 5 4 3 2 1

Library of Congress Cataloging-in-Publication Data
Legacies of the George W. Bush presidency / edited by Steven E. Schier.
    p.   cm.
  Includes bibliographical references and index.
  ISBN-13: 978-0-8229-6049-2 (pbk. : alk. paper)
  ISBN-10: 0-8229-6049-4 (pbk. : alk. paper)
   1. United States—Politics and government—2001–2009.   2. Bush, George W.
(George Walker), 1946–   I. Schier, Steven E.
  E902.L444 2009
  973.931092—dc22   2009024335

For President Robert A. Oden Jr.

and

Associate Dean Elizabeth J. Ciner

of

Carleton College

in thanks

for their unflagging support

of my scholarship

CONTENTS

Part III. Washington Governance

Part IV. Economic and Foreign Policy

Ambition and Division

INTRODUCTION
The Ambitions of the George W. Bush Presidency

STEVEN E. SCHIER

The peculiar circumstances surrounding the election of George W. Bush to the presidency in no way prepared Americans for the remarkable twists and turns of policy and politics that characterized his eight years in office. Elected with no public mandate whatever, Bush achieved surprising legislative success in his early months in the White House, winning passage of his two top priorities. These were a major tax cut—$1.35 trillion over ten years—and reform of education policy involving a new system of standardized testing of elementary and secondary school students (Barshay 2001). His public support remained reasonably strong during this period, given that he had won only a minority of the popular vote. The defection of Senator James Jeffords of Vermont to the Democratic caucus in mid-2001, however, gave Democrats control of the Senate and heightened the intensity of partisan conflict in Washington.

Then came 9/11—the terrorist attacks on September 11, 2001, that refocused his presidency on national security concerns and drove his public support to unprecedented heights. The political opportunity granted by strong public popularity revealed the grand ambitions underlying the Bush presidency. Bush gained a rare supremacy over national security

1

policy. Congress granted him war powers authority to initiate conflict with rogue regimes in Afghanistan and Iraq, granted the administration extensive authority over domestic surveillance in the USA-PATRIOT Act, and acquiesced to the administration's requests for additional military spending. Recurring partisan divisions in Congress in 2002 caused Bush gradually to adopt a more partisan approach in seeking congressional support. The president also took the unusual political risk of deploying his personal popularity in the 2002 elections, with considerable success. The Republican ascendancy in the Senate (a two-seat gain) and gains in the House (six seats) constituted the first such gain for a president in his first midterm since the Roosevelt New Deal sweep of 1934. The Bush administration then scored an important congressional victory in mid-2003 with passage of a bill cutting taxes $326 billion through 2013, aimed at spurring the flagging economy (Ota 2003). Although $326 billion was less than half the size of the tax cut originally proposed by his administration, Bush claimed a policy victory. Congress also considered another administration priority: an ambitious plan for prescription drug coverage for Medicare recipients costing an estimated $400 billion over ten years (Toner and Pear 2003). Perhaps the greatest risk of his presidency, the war with Iraq, produced a swift military victory but also spawned much international opposition and a troublesome and politically costly regime of military occupation.

As the Iraq occupation that began in 2003 dragged on into 2004, Bush scored a narrow reelection victory over Democratic nominee John Kerry, a senator from Massachusetts, drawing crucial support from voters concerned about national security (Taylor 2004). Republicans also picked up four Senate and three House seats, padding their slim majorities in Congress. The year 2005, however, proved to be another great turning point in the Bush presidency. As conditions deteriorated during the lengthy Iraq occupation and no weapons of mass destruction—a vital argument for the war—were found, public support for Bush and the GOP steadily eroded. Bush compounded his problems in 2005 by launching a futile campaign to fundamentally restructure Social Security, the largest and probably most popular domestic program of the national government. In August of that year, the sluggish governmental response to Hurricane Katrina's devastation further punctured the president's popularity. By 2006, a string of scandals involving the congressional GOP, combined with continuing bad news from Iraq, led to a Democratic takeover of both chambers of Congress.

The final years of Bush's presidency involved more of the same bad news for the president. Progress in Iraq slowly appeared after Bush fired Defense Secretary Donald Rumsfeld and replaced him with Robert Gates. In late 2007, Bush announced a change in Iraq strategy, which involved sending a surge of additional troops into the country. This approach, advocated by the new general in charge of Iraq operations, David Petraeus, did lead to a substantial reduction in American and Iraqi casualties, which permitted some steps toward political reconciliation in that battered nation. Public opinion, however, was slow to warm to the new approach, and by early 2008, a majority of Americans were telling Gallup pollsters they preferred military withdrawal either immediately or on a fixed timetable (Gallup 2008a). An unsteady economy, caused by excesses in the housing and lending sectors of the economy and rising oil prices, led to public pessimism about Bush's stewardship. Bush was able to withstand policy challenges by the Democratic Congress in 2007 and 2008 on Iraq war funding and federal spending. By the final year of his second term, though, Republicans were unpopular as a party and the GOP had dim prospects in the 2008 elections. Barack Obama's solid win in the presidential race coupled with Democratic gains in House and Senate contests delivered a final repudiation to Bush and his party.

The Grand Task of Regime Restoration

How do we make sense of these zigs and zags? Presidential scholar Stephen Skowronek provides several concepts that help us to understand the project at the heart of the Bush presidency. To Skowronek, the presidency is an inherently "disruptive" institution, a sort of "battering ram" used by presidents to alter the actions and results issuing from permanent Washington, that thick encrustation of interest groups, legislative specialists in Congress, and careerist federal bureaucrats. Permanent Washington has evolved through "secular time," which Skowronek defines as the historical medium through which power structures grow and change (Skowronek 1997, 30). The rise of lasting power relationships beyond direct presidential control proceeded apace throughout the twentieth century. This "institutional thickening" involved an "ever thicker" set of governmental and political arrangements in Washington that produce greater "institutional resilience" to attempts by presidents to alter established arrangements (Skowronek 1997, 413).

A new president seeks to create an alternative conception of government. Instead of merely acceding to the power patterns that develop in

3

secular time, presidents seek to rework those patterns to further their own purposes, as Nicol C. Rae notes in his chapter placing George W. Bush's presidency in historical context. In Skowronek's terms, presidents seek to create an alternative form of governmental operation by invoking "political time," the historical medium through which authority structures have recurred (Skowronek 1997, 30). That is, presidents frequently try to create political regimes supported by constitutional authority and popular approval. A successful political regime can order events according to its own schedule, displacing the ability of permanent Washington to order events through its residues of power. It is a battle between presidential authority and other traditional sources of power in Washington.

What constitutes a successful presidential "regime"? Robert C. Lieberman defines their various aspects: "Regimes appear at a variety of levels, from formal institutions (such as the structure of Congress and the administrative state) to the social bases of politics (such as party alignments and coalitions and patterns of interest representation); from ideas (such as prevailing beliefs about the proper role of government) to informal norms (such as patterns of Congressional behavior). Nested within these broadly defined institutional arrangements are commitments to particular policies that become the touchstone for political action and conflict for leaders and would-be leaders over the course of a generation or more" (Lieberman 2000, 275). From this definition, it is not difficult to outline the regime the Bush administration sought to entrench. Institutionally, the Bush administration sought control of Congress by reliable, partisan Republican majorities and enhanced presidential control over the executive branch through reorganizations spawned by national security concerns, such as the creation of the Department of Homeland Security. Politically, the administration pursued consistent Republican electoral majorities. The primary tactical imperative in this was maintaining high support among the party's core of activists through strong national security policies and tax cuts. James L. Guth notes in his chapter how Bush also cultivated Christian conservatives within his coalition with careful emphasis on particular social policies. A second primary tactic was the wooing of key elements of the electorate—suburbanites, rural residents, white Catholics, Latinos, working-class males—through artful public statements and emphasis on issues of particular interest to them (accountability reforms in education, farm price supports, stem-cell research, judicial appointments, steel tariffs) (Brownstein 2002, 2). Key ideas of the regime included a recurrent emphasis on tax cuts as the preferred engine of economic management and an aggressive new foreign policy involving military preemption of potential terror threats and distrust of recent international agreements such as those on global warming and the International Criminal Court. Informal norms included a personal distancing of the president from micropolitical dealing and renewed emphasis on partisan unity in Congress.

What lay behind all of these efforts? The primary project of the Bush presidency was the completion of the political reconstruction of national politics, government, and policy begun by Ronald Reagan in 1981. Examine the features of the second Bush regime, and you will find commitments, policies, and tactics consistent with those of Reagan and having as their ultimate end the lasting triumph of Reaganite rule in national government: military strength, tax cuts, enhanced executive power at the expense of Congress, and a stable electoral majority that prefers conservative Republicans. George W. Bush was centrally engaged in a project of political restoration through tactically innovative means.

Skowronek identifies such presidents as "orthodox innovators" who seek to "articulate" the commitments of a previous regime: "to fit the existing parts of the regime together in a new and more relevant way . . . they galvanize political action with promises to continue the good work of the past and demonstrate the vitality of the established order to changing times" (Skowronek 1997, 41). How did Bush seek to make the Reagan regime relevant to the early twenty-first century? He resurrected unsuccessful initiatives of recent GOP presidents, such as the privatization of Social Security, a missile defense system, educational vouchers, and less invasive environmental regulation. Bush employed the Reagan administration's concept of the "unitary executive," explained in Peri E. Arnold's chapter, in order to harness presidential power for his regime mission. His judicial appointments, analyzed by Nancy Maveety in this volume, sought to continue the approach to constitutional interpretation practiced by Reagan appointees. Bush varied from the Reagan policy agenda, however, by pursuing "magnet" issues that might broaden the regime's coalition of supporters through measures such as education reform and prescription drug coverage for Medicare recipients.

Bush also went beyond the previous regime in pursuing some of its original commitments. One example, assessed in detail herein by John Frendreis and Raymond Tatalovich, involves the supply-side economics of tax cutting. Ronald Reagan and his vice president and successor, George Herbert Walker Bush, both signed tax increases (in 1982 and 1990) in the wake of budget deficits. As deficits grew in 2003, George W. Bush instead

5

proposed large tax cuts totaling $726 billion through 2013, much to the delight of his coalition's antitax advocates, like Grover Norquist, head of Americans for Tax Reform. Another example is Iraq policy. The elder Bush tried to contain Iraq and hoped for a coup in the wake of the Gulf War in 1990–1991. George W. Bush followed a more aggressive approach of "regime change" and invaded the country. More broadly, as James M. McCormick notes in his chapter, Bush's foreign policy doctrine of military "preemption" with regard to international terror threats codifies in doctrine the earlier regime's pattern of situational uses of force overseas against perceived national security threats from Libya, Grenada, and Panama. Bush's national security policies adopted in the face of international terrorist threats, Stanley A. Renshon notes in his chapter, may be Bush's most enduring legacy.

In his mission of regime articulation, Bush resembled previous orthodox innovators of American political history. These presidents' innovations often involved aggressive foreign policies, given the constraints on domestic policy innovation presented by the established regimes with which they were affiliated. Democrat James K. Polk, a loyal Jacksonian Democrat nicknamed "Young Hickory," led the nation through a war with Mexico. William McKinley and Theodore Roosevelt, operating within the long-established Republican political regime of the era, greatly expanded America's diplomatic and military role in the world. Harry Truman and Lyndon Johnson, heirs of FDR's New Deal regime, committed American troops to long conflicts in Korea and Vietnam. George W. Bush, loyal to the commitments of the earlier Reagan-Bush regime, prosecuted international war on terror and invaded Iraq.

High Risk

The presidencies of many orthodox innovators came to a bad end because their innovations spawned dissension within the established political regimes with which they were affiliated. Polk's expansionist policies sparked controversies over the extension of slavery; he could not quell those controversies, and they ultimately destroyed the Jacksonian regime. Theodore Roosevelt's domestic progressivism caused a split in his party that led to the election of Democrat Woodrow Wilson in 1912. The interminable Korean War caused Truman to leave the White House as a highly unpopular president, succeeded by Republican Dwight Eisenhower. Johnson's disastrous Vietnam policy deeply spit his party and helped elect Republican Richard Nixon president in 1968. All three recent presidents—Truman, Johnson, and Bush—ended their presidencies with low popularity and depleted ranks of fellow partisans in Congress. David Mayhew notes that a war can bring electoral contests about whether it "should have been fought in the first place" and over the possibility of "incompetent management" (Mayhew 2005, 480). Both types of debate occurred in 2006 and 2008, to the disadvantage of Bush and the GOP.

The chief political strategist of the Bush White House, Karl Rove, looked for lessons in the presidency of William McKinley, the only orthodox innovator who presided over a major and lasting popular electoral realignment (Dubose, Reid, and Cannon 2003, 169; Dionne 2001, 1). John J. Coleman and Kevin S. Price note in their chapter how the Bush administration pursued partisan realignment as a governing strategy, hence McKinley's relevance for Rove. McKinley's term included a muscular new foreign policy and a popular foreign war (the Spanish-American War in 1898), as well as a domestic strategy that won additional working-class voters for Republicans through the promise of burgeoning industrial capitalism—the appeal of the "full dinner pail." Democrats veered from the mainstream by nominating the strident populist William Jennings Bryan, who ran against McKinley in both 1896 and 1900. The Bush White House hoped the Democrats would similarly vacate the center in 2004. Their dreams were realized by the nomination of a strong liberal, Senator John Kerry of Massachusetts. Even given that advantage, Bush won only a narrow reelection victory.

Bush's narrow margin underscored the great obstacles his administration faced in its attempt to entrench the Reagan regime. First, as Skowronek notes, the political reconstruction attempted by Ronald Reagan was far from complete. He describes it as largely "rhetorical rather than institutional" (Skowronek 1997, 32) because "institutional thickening" in national government had become steadily more prevalent over time (Skowronek 1997, 422). The firm relationships between a Democratic Congress, sympathetic interest groups, and career bureaucrats made domestic policy innovation difficult for Reagan after his initial success in cutting spending and taxes in 1981. These constraints encumbered his successor, George H. W. Bush, even more, leading him to raise taxes in a 1990 budget deal with the Democratic Congress, which splintered support among his conservative regime followers and contributed to his defeat in 1992. The Reaganite regime did reappear in the Republican sweep of Congress in 1994, led by the outspoken conservative Newt Gingrich (R-Georgia), who became House Speaker. But the Republican Congress had at best mixed results in dueling with Democratic president Bill Clinton. From 1993 to 2000, elements of the Reagan regime contested but in no sense dominated national policymaking and political appointments.

George W. Bush's accession to the White House, despite his losing the popular vote, and Republican losses of House and Senate seats revealed that the electoral coalition supporting a conservative policy regime had a far from secure grip on power. Bush nevertheless proved remarkably adept in winning congressional approval of his top agenda items in 2001. One, the large tax cut, served to consolidate his base, while the other, a reform of education policy passed with the support of leading Democrats, including Senator Edward Kennedy (D-Massachusetts), served to broaden his appeal among suburbanite voters not reliably part of his electoral coalition (Ornstein 2001). Bush's early success despite his controversial election victory lends support to Richard Pious's contention that adept use of the presidency's constitutional prerogatives is more central than short-term political factors "in determining what a president can accomplish" (Pious 1979, 16).

Ironically, 9/11 greatly boosted Bush's personal popularity and, for a time, public support for his party. However, by 2002, the president faced a highly competitive midterm election. The savvy political tactics of regime leaders in the White House and national Republican Party leadership, coupled with the president's risky decision to deploy his personal popularity on behalf of key Senate candidates, produced small but historically remarkable gains for Republicans. Republicans achieved narrow majorities in the House and Senate, but a close partisan division remained among the public. Superior GOP get-out-the-vote efforts in 2004 created an electorate with equal numbers of Republican and Democratic identifiers—37 percent (Barone and Cohen 2005, 25). But adverse events turned independents away from the GOP, and by 2006, there was a decline in Republican identification (Abramson, Aldrich, and Rohde 2007, 280). By 2008, Democrats enjoyed a 10- to 15-point lead in party identification in national polls (Pew Research Center poll 2008) that propelled them to solid victories in the presidential and congressional contests.

By the end of the Bush presidency, Republicans had failed to solidify a majority of voters around a conservative political regime. The GOP did make gains among rural voters, but they are a declining part of the electorate. It is true, as Coleman and Price note in their chapter here, that the fastest-growing counties in America voted increasingly Republican in 2000 (Barone 2001, 31). Yet, in the elections of 1992, 1996, and 2000, Democrats did quite well among female and professional voters. They maintain a huge advantage among African Americans. Latinos, the sleeping giant of American politics, also continue to favor Democrats by a substantial margin. Analysts John B. Judis and Ruy Teixeira find an emerging Democratic electoral majority in these trends that "reflects deep-seated social and economic trends that are changing the face of the country. . . . Today's Democrats are the party of the transition from urban industrialism to a new postindustrial metropolitan order in which men and women play equal roles and in which white America is supplanted by multiracial, multiethnic America" (Judis and Teixeira 2002, 6). The 2006 and 2008 elections lent credence to their analysis.

Bush's task, unlike that of previous orthodox innovators, involved the unprecedented challenge of finally installing a successful political regime, rather than merely maintaining its current dominance, which was the mission of Presidents Polk, McKinley, Theodore Roosevelt, Truman, and Johnson. It is harder to complete a major regime transition than to maintain one that has already transpired. The "indeterminate" regime situation in which Bush found himself was very evident in Washington politics during a time of "institutional thickening." Benjamin Ginsberg and Martin Shefter describe it as "institutional combat" in which national politicians use weapons of institutional power to fight over governmental direction (Ginsberg and Shefter 2002, 21). Elections are less conclusive, often resulting in narrow margins of control for the winning national party. Given the absence of an entrenched political regime, incentives for obstruction grow among leaders of both parties.

The frequently even partisan balance in government sharpens motivations to use institutional authority to disrupt opponents. Congress in recent years witnessed an abundance of such behavior. During the Bush presidency, party government has prevailed in the House during periods of both Republican and Democratic control. The Speaker and Rules Committee together structure the floor agenda to limit the potential of the minority party to prevail via amendments or procedural obstructions. This strategy facilitated Bush's agenda until 2007, when Democrats stifled it. A prime weapon of institutional combat during the Bush presidency was the Senate filibuster. Ironically, Republicans were the first to employ it effectively—against Bill Clinton's 1993 budget plan. From 2001 to 2006, Senate Democrats prevented several judicial nominations via filibuster. Republicans returned the favor in 2007 and 2008 by derailing Democratic legislation to curtail America's involvement in Iraq.

Hence the high risks for the Bush administration: it sought to entrench a conservative regime among a public beset by even partisan divisions and without a stable Washington governing coalition. Journalist John Harwood aptly termed the Bush incumbency a "low margin, party-line presidency" (Harwood 2003, 1). The Bush administration had limited room for maneuver, despite the windfall of public support after 9/11. George W. Bush played this national security "trump card" for maximum political effect from 2001 to 2003, but in terms of electoral and institutional politics, he faced considerable challenges as he completed his first term. Those challenges became larger after his reelection, putting an end to his administration's grand regime ambitions. The public came to disapprove of his economic stewardship and the difficult military occupation of Iraq. Dissension within his own party arose about a series of White House missteps—the Katrina response, the aborted Supreme Court nomination of Harriet Miers, and the administration's controversial Social Security and immigration reform plans.

Consider the fragility of several regime components during Bush's presidency. The 2000 popular coalition that elected Bush amassed about 48 percent of the vote, half a million votes fewer than Al Gore received. In 2004, despite a spike in turnout yielding more than 59 million votes for Bush, he won a popular vote victory by a margin of less than three percentage points. Neither Congress nor the Supreme Court fell securely under long-term conservative control under Bush. Conservatives held a narrow 5-to-4 majority at the end of his presidency that could be easily overturned by a single future court appointment. Business and ideologically conservative interest groups did not continuously prevail on major issues in Washington and were frequently outgunned on important issues by opposing liberal groups (Hacker and Pierson 2007; Smith 2000; Berry 1999). Most major new ideas and policy commitments came from the Bush White House; other components of the Reagan regime seemed content with a more conventional conservative agenda, one that did not seem to be growing in popular appeal (Abramson, Aldrich, and Rohde 2007, 272–79).

After 2004, the GOP regime fell into disarray. Republicans lost control of both congressional chambers in 2006 and seemed unlikely to regain control of them anytime soon. Bitter partisan contestation, chronicled here by John J. Pitney Jr., became the norm in Congress and throughout Washington. Bush himself suffered a big drop in popular approval, detailed by John Kenneth White and John Zogby in their chapter, which greatly curtailed his influence in Washington. The risks Bush undertook did not reward his regime with political preeminence.

Clinton the Preemptor

At the end of Bush's second term, Skowronek's politics of "permanent preemption" seemed an apposite description of contemporary national politics, in which presidents faced "the proliferation of interests and authorities throughout the government and the organizational resilience of the institutions that defend them" (Skowronek 1997, 443). In such a situation, regime construction or renewal is extremely difficult. A prudent presidential strategy in this situation is that followed by Bush's predecessor, Bill Clinton, in which presidents "build new, personal bases of political support outside of regular political alliances and often outside of institutional politics altogether" (Skowronek 1997, 44).

Clinton was tactically nimble (after his many political mistakes of 1993–1994), announcing domestic policies poll tested to appeal to swing voters and "triangulating" between Democrats and Republicans in his dealings with Congress. Clinton's project was not regime maintenance but rather, as is the mission of "preemptive presidents," tactically to master a difficult environment established by the hostile presidential regime that preceded him. The incomplete nature of Reagan's reconstruction lowered the cost of Clinton's improvisations until he laid himself low with scandal. Conservative forces in Congress and in the public forced him to pay the steep price of impeachment.

Though George W. Bush confronted a political environment similar to the one that Bill Clinton encountered, Bush's mode of governance differed from that of Clinton. The politics of preemption often involves personal attacks on presidents because no single regime is fully in control of government. Resurgent Republicans in the late 1990s, envisioning regime restoration, thus pilloried Clinton in harsh terms. Democratic politicians and activists loudly announced their low esteem of Bush, particularly after his aggressive use of his office to win, narrowly, the 2002 elections. That chorus only grew in volume and intensity as his presidency proceeded. Politics in a preemptive era usually produces little regime construction and a reduced policy legacy for incumbent presidents. That seems a fair thumbnail summary of the Clinton legacy. Bush, however, sought far more than the largely personal stamp on leadership and policy that Clinton pursued. As John F. Harris puts it in his chapter here, Bush sought primarily to win partisan victories as a "national clarifier," but Clinton sought to govern from the middle as a "national unifier," a position, he thought, of political strength. For George W. Bush, conservative regime restoration through electoral domination and a strong policy legacy were the measures of presidential success. This is a big ambition, indeed, and, as we have seen, it brings many political risks. Bush's experience suggests the prospects for success at this are limited in contemporary politics. Bush's successor Barack Obama and his supportive Democratic majorities in Congress will test those limits yet again.

Bush's Strategy and Tactics

The Bush presidency pursued its grand design with much adroitness in its early years. The initial task involved demonstrating presidential leadership in the absence of an electoral mandate. This Bush did very well, in part by adopting some preemptive tactics of his predecessor. He came into office stating that he wished to "change the tone" in Washington through pursuing personal, less partisan leadership. True to his word, he personally persuaded a handful of conservative Senate Democrats to pass his tax bill and worked well with liberal Democrats to get his education bill passed into law. At the same time, Bush kept unvarying party unity among congressional Republicans.

In the wake of his great popularity after 9/11, however, a more partisan style appeared, well documented in the chapters by Bertram Johnson and John F. Harris. Bush's 2002 campaigning was party based and unusually aggressive. At the center of his 2003 agenda were orthodox conservative items—a large tax cut and possible war with Iraq—and an innovative proposal for Medicare prescription drug coverage for seniors. Bush's success in Congress in 2003, as Bertram Johnson notes in his chapter, came primarily through party-line votes. The administration's 2004 reelection strategy also seems based on a central imperative of maintaining strong party unity behind the president. The strategy, as one White House aide put it, "has to be to hold what you start with and then change the dynamics of four percent or five percent total. It's not like you're trying to build sixty percent of the vote, but rather build to fifty-two percent" (Brownstein 2002, 1). The primacy of regime maintenance put a ceiling on Bush's likely vote, given the political weaknesses of the regime he sought to restore.

Despite this emphasis on regime maintenance, Bush consistently employed some of Bill Clinton's political tactics. Both White Houses sought to govern by campaigning, having the president "go public" in a "permanent campaign" seeking agenda domination (Kernell 1997; Mann and Ornstein 2000). The Clinton presidency became famous for shaping its policy agenda according to poll results (Harris 2000). Pollsters had a much less public presence in the Bush administration, and Bush paid much less personal attention to poll results than did Clinton. Still, Karl Rove, Bush's chief strategist, pored over polls regularly. Poll results ultimately played an important role in shaping Bush administration tactics, just as they had in previous administrations. Still, for all of the polling and campaigning, Bush failed to move public opinion in his direction on many issues (Edwards 2007). His governing agenda and personal advocacy efforts were unable to transform the entrenched and evenly balanced partisanship in American politics.

Similar tactics, dissimilar ends. The Bush administration engaged in a permanent campaign for public support, touted and traded on the personal popularity of the incumbent, targeted swing voters in the electorate with its appeals, and tactically emphasized issues that might boost its political prospects. The Clinton administration did the same. However, Bill Clinton after 1994 was protecting himself in a hostile political environment and did little to tie himself publicly to his congressional Democrats or to create lasting political advantages for his political party, which at times split internally in response to his great flexibility on issues. George W. Bush's pursuit of a lasting conservative policy regime was comparatively far more ambitious and risky a goal than that of his predecessor. Bush rode that approach to a narrow supremacy that adverse events quickly transformed into a political fall.

Bush's "regime" helps to explain his superior issue discipline compared to that found in Clinton's more personal politics. Clinton's improvisational style, ranging from issue to issue, stands in stark contrast to Bush's dogged focus on a few issues. If the issues are well chosen, limited focus can be a great tactical asset to a president. Given the large regime task Bush set for himself, such discipline was essential. The Bush White House pursued several issues in order to "take them away" from Democrats— by achieving credibility with the public on a number of issues on which Democrats have traditionally been more trusted. The great example of 2001 was education; in 2003, it was a Medicare prescription drug benefit. A similar attempt in 2005 on Social Security overreached and failed. The long-term gains of such tactics were quite limited. By 2008, strong majorities of the public preferred Democrats to Republicans on health care, education, and Social Security (Pew Research Center poll 2008). Bush's successor Barack Obama and his fellow Democrats enjoyed public backing on these issues as they began governing in 2009.

A Dangerous Opportunity

The 9/11 attacks gave George W. Bush considerable political capital. He spent much of it in the 2002 election, taking a risk that aggressive partisan campaigning would pay off. It did, narrowly. Still quite popular in early 2003, Bush took three other risks. First, he proposed to cut taxes by $726 billion through 2013, despite short-term deficit forecasts—that did not include the costs of the Iraq war—exceeding $300 billion per year. Second, he proposed a prescription-drug benefit for Medicare recipients that required them to enter managed-care plans to receive the benefit. Third, he pressed a war against Iraq despite widespread opposition from major allies. All of these risks fit his role as an orthodox innovator. The Iraq war and tax cuts fit the aggressive foreign policy and supply-side economic policy of Reagan. The Medicare plan attempted to neutralize one of the Democrats' best domestic issues for 2004.

Not all risks pay off. The Medicare plan eventually passed Congress by the narrowest of margins but failed to improve public perceptions of the GOP on health care. The Bush tax cuts produced large budget deficits that aided the GOP strategy of limiting spending by reducing revenues— "starving the beast"—but the deficits contributed to public disapproval of Bush's economic stewardship. The initial military success in Iraq boosted public approval of Bush and the GOP, but the turbulent military occupation of the country produced persistent problems for the administration. Bush's rocky tenure during his second term grew from the difficulty of the task he set for himself. Aiming to consistently "swing for the fences," he, like the proverbial power hitter in baseball, frequently struck out as events and opponents threw him difficult pitches. John F. Harris suggests here that Bush might have had more success by operating as Bill Clinton did, courting personal popularity in a Washington of even partisan balance and recalcitrant political institutions. But for Bush, personal popularity was merely a means to be used—and at times sacrificed—in the service of the greater end of conservative regime restoration.

The Bush presidency thus involved a grand paradox. A president must garner personal popularity in order to address other Washington institutions from a position of political strength. Yet Bush's fealty to a conservative policy regime required him to expend his political capital in its service, which put his personal survival at risk. This would have turned out well if that regime had received the lasting embrace of a majority of voters. However, it did not. George W. Bush took risks and spent political capital on a regime project that was unlikely to succeed in any event. If Skowronek is right, and Washington authority structures are so impervious to presidential change that regime construction is impossible, then political time—and the ability to build political authority structures that outlast any administration's time in office—has vanished. George Bush gambled that he could deploy the power of his office to resurrect political time. His presidency suggests, however, that political time is no longer with us. If political time does reappear, ironically for Bush it will be his successor Barack Obama and his fellow Democrats who will resurrect it.

History, Legitimacy, and Leadership

PART I

2

THE BUSH PRESIDENCY
IN HISTORICAL CONTEXT
The Limitations of the Partisan Presidency

NICOL C. RAE

George W. Bush's presidency was contentious from the moment that his election as president was confirmed by the decision of the U.S. Supreme Court in *Bush v. Gore*. The court's decision meant that Bush joined the list of three other U.S. presidents who owed their election to a victory in the Electoral College while finishing second in the national popular vote. The protracted and bitter post-election conflict over Florida's electoral votes not only raised further initial questions about the "legitimacy" of the Bush presidency (Dionne and Kristol 2001; Coleman and Price 2009) but also took place within a context of increasing partisanship in American politics. Unlike the three presidents referred to above, George W. Bush was narrowly reelected to a second term in 2004, but his narrow victory in a close and bitterly contested election only intensified the atmosphere of polarization that had already come to characterize his administration.

Despite losing the popular vote for president, Bush from the outset governed as if he had a clear mandate from the public for his strongly conservative economic, domestic, and foreign policy agenda (Frum 2003a; 2003b). So integral are the role of national agenda setter and the notion of a policy "mandate" to the modern presidency that these claims were generally accepted by both press and public, and several of the most significant items on the Bush agenda were enacted during his first term (Cochran 2002). Ironically, despite winning a popular vote mandate in 2004, Bush was to be far less successful in implementing his legislative agenda in his second term, despite his claim on the day following the election that his 51 percent popular vote victory over Democrat John Kerry had earned him "political capital" (Edwards 2007, 188).

George W. Bush's presidency was also characterized by his response to 9/11. The hijackings and terrorist attacks on New York and Washington marked a significant early turning point in the Bush administration, not only in the president's popularity, which soared temporarily in the wake of the tragedy, but also in the administration's focus and direction in foreign and internal security policy, including military action in Afghanistan and (more controversially) Iraq and strong domestic security measures and federal government reorganization (Keller 2003). Even as the U.S. military became bogged down in Iraq in 2003–2004, the "war on terror" was still apparently decisive in Bush's narrow reelection victory in 2004 (Jacobson 2007; Fiorina et al. 2005).

In the second Bush term, however, the continuing attrition of American lives and resources in Iraq coupled with the administration's politically ham-fisted reaction to the damage inflicted on New Orleans by Hurricane Katrina in August 2005 were the major factors contributing to the collapse of public support for the president in 2005–2006. These factors also contributed to the loss of Republican control of both houses of Congress in the 2006 midterm elections, which effectively ended the administration's ability to set the national domestic political agenda. The "base-plus" (united congressional Republicans with selective Democratic support) politics of the first term that had enabled the administration to pass important tax-cutting and education reforms proved ineffectual in rallying public support for the president's reform of Social Security in 2005, and Bush's bipartisan initiatives on immigration in 2006 and 2007 failed for lack of support within his own party. With the national economy also gradually moving into recession and the dramatic collapse of the nation's banking and financial system due to the home mortgage crisis in September 2008, George W. Bush would leave office generally regarded as a failed president, with some of the lowest presidential approval ratings in American history.

Bush was initially able to take advantage of the highly partisan and competitive American electoral politics at the turn of the twenty-first century as well as the natural authority that Americans bestow on the chief executive in times of perceived crisis in national security. The ultimate political fate of the administration seems to demonstrate, however, that a partisan approach to presidential leadership, while it can produce presidential successes in specific circumstances, does not render incumbents immune to the natural rhythms of the contemporary presidency.

Past and Present Problems of Presidential Legitimacy

George W. Bush's victory in the 2000 election was a reminder that American presidents are elected by the 538-member Electoral College, composed of blocs of electors (roughly proportionate to the population of each state) awarded on a winner-take-all basis (with the exception of Maine and Nebraska) to the plurality vote winner in each of the remaining forty-eight states and the District of Columbia. The original intent of the aristocratically minded framers of the U.S. Constitution was that each state would select the "best and the brightest" among its political elite to elect the federal chief executive (Ceaser 1979, 41–87). With the advent of party competition, however, and the increasing democratic pressures within American society, states began to choose their electors at large by direct popular vote, and the subsequent development of national political parties in the 1820s signaled the end of the Electoral College as an independent decision-making body (McCormick 1975).

These changes made the election of the president more of a popular contest but not completely, since states remain the key unit of election rather than the national popular vote. It is quite possible therefore not only that a president might prevail in the Electoral College with less than a majority of the popular vote but also that in a very close election a president might be elected—if carrying enough states with significant numbers of electoral votes by narrow margins—after finishing second in the overall national popular vote. In the wake of the 2000 election, the final awarding of Florida's 25 electoral votes to George W. Bush (based on an official statewide plurality of 537 votes) enabled him to eke out a 271-to-267 margin over Democrat Al Gore in the Electoral College while losing the national popular vote by some 540,000 votes (0.5 percent).[1]

1. Somewhat ironically, George Bush only narrowly avoided being the victim of an even greater Electoral College "misfire" in 2004. Had Democrat John Kerry been able to win the 20 electoral votes of the bitterly contested state of Ohio, which he lost by only 119,000 votes, Bush would have lost the presidency while still winning the national popular vote by a 3 percent margin.

Table 2.1. Presidents who failed to win a majority of the popular vote since 1824

Year	President	Popular vote (%)	Margin (%)	Electoral vote (%)
1824*	**J. Q. Adams**	**30.5****	**-13.1**	**32.2**
1844	Polk	49.6	1.5	61.8
1848	Taylor	47.4**	4.9	56.2
1852	Buchanan	45.3**	12.2	58.8
1860	Lincoln	39.9**	10.5	59.4
1876	**Hayes**	**47.9**	**-3.1**	**50.1**
1880	Garfield	48.3	0.1	58.0
1884	Cleveland	48.5	0.2	54.6
1888	**Harrison**	**47.8**	**-0.9**	**58.1**
1892	Cleveland	46.1**	3.2	62.4
1912	Wilson	41.9**	14.5	81.9
1916	Wilson	49.3	3.2	52.2
1948	Truman	49.5**	4.4	57.1
1960	Kennedy	49.7	0.1	56.4
1968	Nixon	43.4**	0.7	56.0
1992	Clinton	42.3**	4.9	68.8
1996	Clinton	49.2**	8.5	70.4
2000	**G. W. Bush**	**47.9**	**-0.5**	**50.4**

Source: Data from Mieczkowski 2001.

Note: Boldface text indicates data for presidents who lost the popular vote.

*The election of 1824 was the first with accurate data on the national popular vote.

**Minor party candidates gained more than 5 percent of the national popular vote.

Table 2.1 shows the eighteen (38 percent) of forty-seven presidential elections from 1824 to 2004 in which presidents have been elected despite having won less than a majority of the national popular vote. In four (8.5 percent) of those forty-seven elections, presidents have been elected despite losing the national popular vote: John Quincy Adams (1824), Rutherford B. Hayes (1876), Benjamin Harrison (1888), and George W. Bush (2000).

John Quincy Adams, Sixth President

In addition to being popular vote losers, George W. Bush and John Quincy Adams shared the distinction of being the only presidential offspring to ascend to the office. The younger Adams was an extremely distinguished public servant, having been a U.S. senator (1803–1808), ambassador to Great Britain (1815–1817), and secretary of state (1817–1825). His presidential candidacy in 1824, however, was engulfed by the new democratic fervor and political controversy sweeping the nation in the 1820s (Wood 1992, 287–305). The Jeffersonian Democratic Republican Party had become meaningless in the absence of serious competition, and the nomination of its congressional caucus ("King Caucus") was no longer decisive, as the 1824 caucus nominee, Treasury Secretary William Crawford of Georgia, attracted opposition from Adams (Massachusetts), House Speaker Henry Clay of Kentucky, and General Andrew Jackson of Tennessee, the hero of the 1815 battle of New Orleans and champion of states' rights against the federal government (Remini 1999, 99–117). Adams finished second behind Jackson in both the electoral vote (99 versus 84) and the popular vote (43 to 32 percent), but as no candidate had gained a majority in the Electoral College, according to the Constitution, the House of Representatives, with state delegations voting as units, had to choose the president from among the top three contenders: Jackson, Adams, and Crawford (41 electoral votes). Clay (37 votes) had been eliminated, but in the House, the Speaker threw his support to Adams, who won thirteen states, compared to seven for Jackson and four for Crawford. Three days later, Adams nominated Henry Clay as secretary of state (Milkis and Nelson 1999, 108–12).

Jackson's supporters accused Clay and Adams of having made a "corrupt bargain" to deny the presidency to the popular favorite (Remini 1999). The Jacksonians were further provoked when President Adams pursued an ambitious policy agenda that focused on internal improvements to be implemented by a vigorous federal government (Skowronek 1993, 110–27). Dogged by controversy over his election, Adams was unable to advance his legislative program. After the rampant Jacksonians took over Congress in 1826, his presidency was essentially at an end in policy terms (Milkis and Nelson 1999, 108–11; Hargreaves 1985), and Jackson easily defeated him in 1828. The circumstances of John Quincy Adams's election undoubtedly undermined his authority as president, and once in office, he lacked the political ability to escape the shadow of illegitimacy that hung over his presidency.

Rutherford B. Hayes, Nineteenth President

In contrast to John Quincy Adams, Rutherford B. Hayes, while losing the popular vote, actually did win a majority in the Electoral College, but he did so only after the House of Representatives intervened to resolve disputed electoral votes in his favor following another notorious political "deal."

Rutherford B. Hayes of Ohio was a typical Republican presidential nominee of the post–Civil War era. He had served as a major general during the Civil War and as a congressman and three-term governor of his home state (Hoogenboom 1995; DeGregorio 1997, 279–91). Hayes's reputation as a reformer also endeared him to Republican Party bosses concerned about the electoral fallout from the scandals that had marred the administration of incumbent Republican president Ulysses S. Grant (Sproat 1968, 88–103). The Democrats selected another reformer, Governor Samuel J. Tilden of New York, who won a narrow but decisive 51-to-48 percent popular vote majority on election day. Tilden also led Hayes 184 to 165 in the electoral vote but remained one vote short of an Electoral College majority, due to disputed election returns in Florida, Louisiana, South Carolina, and Oregon—the first three being former Confederate states still under occupation by federal troops (Mieczkowski 2001, 63–64). The Republican-controlled House of Representatives created a committee of ten members of Congress and five Supreme Court justices to resolve the issue. Coincidentally, this commission had an 8-to-7 Republican majority, which resolved the votes of all the disputed states in favor of Hayes, thus giving him the 185 electoral votes sufficient for victory. In exchange for Democratic acceptance of Hayes as president, the Republicans conceded that federal troops would be withdrawn from the former Confederate states and Reconstruction brought to an end (Ayers 1992).

With Hayes having been elected in such circumstances, it is no surprise that his legitimacy as president was clouded (Mieczkowski 2001, 64). But no matter how cynical the dealmaking that had led to his occupying the White House, Hayes was serious in his commitment to civil service reform (Hoogenboom 1995). He appointed the nation's leading civil service reformer, Carl Schurz of Missouri, as interior secretary (Sproat 1968, 100) and established an independent commission to investigate corruption in the New York federal customs house, where tariffs on imported goods (the main source of federal government revenue at the time) were collected (Milkis and Nelson 1999, 173–76).

The struggle over the customs house used up what little political capital Hayes possessed, and his administration achieved little else. Having alienated the party bosses, Hayes would have been an unlikely nominee in 1880 even had he wished to run for a second term. For all the murkiness surrounding his election, however, Hayes did succeed in restoring integrity to the federal government in the wake of the Grant administration scandals. In an era of limited federal government and a generally weak presidency, Hayes was not notably weaker, in fact, than any of his contemporaries who occupied the office during this period and whose elections were uncontroversial.

Benjamin Harrison, Twenty-third President

Like Hayes, Benjamin Harrison was a Republican president in an era of very limited presidential power. The Gilded Age (1876–1896) was a period of intense party competition and extremely close presidential elections. In the five presidential elections from 1876 to 1892, presidential "winning" margins in the popular vote were -3.1, 0.1, 0.2, -0.9, and 3.2 percent, respectively (see table 2.1). With the parties so closely matched, it is hardly surprising that half of the four instances in U.S. history of popular vote losers winning in the Electoral College were during this period.

Former Indiana senator Benjamin Harrison had not enjoyed a particularly distinguished political career prior to his 1888 nomination for president, but he was the great-grandson of Benjamin Harrison, a signer of the Declaration of Independence; the grandson of the ninth president, William Henry Harrison; and had served as a brigadier general during the Civil War. Harrison led a united Republican campaign against Democratic incumbent Grover Cleveland on the tariff issue, which stimulated a high level of Republican support from the northeastern business community (Marcus 1971, 101–50). While the incumbent secured a narrow popular vote plurality of 0.9 percent—which was, ironically, more than four times his winning margin in 1884—Cleveland lost the Electoral College vote 233 to 168 to Harrison because he narrowly lost the 36 electoral votes of his home state of New York (Mieczkowski 2001, 71–72).

Any possible lack of authority stemming from the 1888 election had little relevance for the presidency of Benjamin Harrison, since Harrison himself was so reluctant to use what little power the presidency did possess at the time, preferring to subordinate himself to Congress in terms of setting the national political agenda (Sievers 1968; Socolofsky and Spetter 1987). Indeed, the presidency was so ineffectual at this time that real national political leadership lay in the hands of House Speaker Thomas B. Reed of Maine (Strahan 1998; Peters 1990, 52–91). In the 1892 rematch between Harrison and Cleveland, again fought largely over the tariff issue, the Democrat won a comfortable Electoral College victory of 277-145-22 (the third candidate was the Populist Party's James Weaver) and a popular vote plurality over Harrison of more than 3 percent.

A Popular Vote Loser in the Modern Era

Perhaps the major difference between George W. Bush and the presidents who lost the popular vote during the nineteenth century was the vastly changed nature of the modern presidency in terms of both the degree and scope of presidential power. A century of expanded federal government in the domestic sphere and the United States' rise to global superpower status have made a contemporary presidency like that of Hayes or Harrison not only impossible but inconceivable. The president is the most visible symbol of the United States at home and abroad and is expected to display immediate and decisive leadership in times of national calamity or crisis. Of course, expanded presidential power in the case of national emergencies—particularly in the foreign policy sphere—was implicit in the Constitution of 1787, but because the United States was a peripheral power for most of the nineteenth century, this potential went untapped (with the notable exceptions of the presidencies of James K. Polk and Abraham Lincoln). When the United States rose to global power and then superpower status in the twentieth century, the latent power of the presidential office became evident (McDonald 1994).

In the domestic sphere, presidential power remains more circumscribed, particularly by Congress's strong constitutional power over the federal budget (Wildavsky 1975). The contemporary president is nevertheless expected to claim an electoral mandate from the voters and use that mandate to set the national policy agenda in Washington (Ceaser 1979, 170–212). Indeed, the president has almost come to resemble an institutionalized "charismatic leader" in Weberian terms, expected to render shots of democratic energy and adrenalin to a political system that is largely inert and incremental most of the time (Weber 1970, 245–52). The president roams the modern American political system like a "magnificent lion," in Clinton Rossiter's colorful phrase (Rossiter 1957, 52). By contrast, Richard Neustadt's classic, *Presidential Power and the Modern Presidents,* emphasizes the persisting constitutional constraints on presidential power in a separated system of government, even in the modern era (Neustadt 1990). Yet Neustadt's purpose was to show presidents how to accumulate political power within those constraints, because he was convinced that the modern American political system required strong and effective presidential leadership (Neustadt 1990, 152–63).

Following the failures of the Johnson, Nixon, and Carter presidencies, a recurring theme in presidential scholarship was the growing gap between the actual powers of the presidency and public—and presidential—expectations as to what the holder of the office can realistically achieve (Lowi 1985). At least since the time of Woodrow Wilson, who first thoroughly articulated the theory, most presidents have claimed that their election constitutes a "mandate," that is, an expression of the will of the American public regarding the course of public policy. Moreover, according to this view, as the sole nationally elected officeholder, the president is best placed to interpret and shape that popular will once in office (Tulis 2003). This has is turn given rise to an increasingly "plebiscitary" presidency that constantly campaigns for public support or "mandates" against the other branches of the system, a tendency, which, some scholars have argued, undermines the spirit and the authority of the Constitution and the American system of separated branches of government (Lowi 1985; Dahl 1990; Kernell 1997). One implication of enhanced presidential power contingent on popular support is that the authority of a contemporary president elected after losing the national popular vote might well be seriously undercut from the outset of the administration, with potentially deleterious consequences for a governmental process now so dependent on presidential power and authority.

Like other presidents who lost the national popular vote, Bush faced unrelenting hostility from core opposition party supporters that contributed to an atmosphere of polarization around his presidency from the beginning (Jacobson 2007). John J. Coleman and Kevin S. Price (chapter 3, this volume) argue that, in addition to the dependence of the modern American governmental process on presidential power, party polarization and increased party unity in contemporary American politics provided George W. Bush with opportunities to overcome this legitimacy problem that were not available to previous presidents in a similar situation. Realizing this, the Bush administration proceeded as if it did have a mandate and began to advance a highly conservative Republican policy agenda (Frum 2003a; 2003b). This was a shrewd political move since the notion of presidential leadership is so endemic to the modern American governmental process, and the president was thus able to implement a significant $1.3 trillion tax cut in 2001 with the support of several Senate Democrats. In the first months of his presidency, Bush was also able to pass the bipartisan "No Child Left Behind" education law that sought to improve school standards through increased use of standardized tests while also increasing federal aid to education. The Senate Democrats were still largely able to block the Bush policy agenda on other domestic issues in the spring and summer of 2001, however, particularly after they regained control of the Senate in May of that year following the defection of Vermont Republican senator James Jeffords. While the conservative Bush strategy alienated moderates like Jeffords, it did give direction and energy to his presidency and enabled him to solidify his support among the conservative Republican base (Keller 2003). Before 9/11, then, it appeared that Bush would be a highly partisan Republican president and that his administration would be characterized by the legislative gridlock and partisan strife typical of late-twentieth-century American politics. Even with his legitimacy still questioned by many Democrats, it was by no means obvious that Bush would lose this struggle if he chose his issues carefully—as in the case of the tax cuts—and kept his base mobilized (Brownstein 2002).

With 9/11, the political equation changed dramatically in favor of the administration. Remaining doubts about Bush's legitimacy faded into the background and the public rallied behind the president (Cook 2001). America's exposure to periodic national security crises since it became a global superpower has given modern presidents (regardless of how they got to the White House) a potential political advantage denied to most of their nineteenth-century predecessors. The airliner hijackings and attacks on New York and Washington demanded a firm presidential response, and Bush provided it with the successful American military operation against the Taliban regime in Afghanistan. The aftershock of 9/11 also enabled the administration to pass the USA-PATRIOT Act, which established the monitoring of potential terrorists, by a huge congressional margin and to carry out the largest reorganization of the federal executive branch since 1947 with the establishment of the new Department of Homeland Security.

Bush further parlayed the effectiveness of his response to 9/11 into victory for his party in the 2002 midterm elections as the Republicans regained control of the Senate and strengthened their grip on the House. Following the election, Bush submitted another huge tax cut proposal ($726 billion) to the new Congress (Brownstein 2003). The president ended up getting only $326 billion in tax reductions from Congress in May 2003 but still could claim a success in achieving another substantial federal tax reduction (Ota 2003). In April 2003, Bush, in defiance of several of America's traditional allies and the United Nations Security Council, led the United States into an initially successful "preemptive war" against Saddam Hussein's Iraq (McManus 2003). Despite the evident problems with the occupation of Iraq and the loss of more than two thousand American lives by November 2004, George W. Bush became the first popular vote loser to secure reelection as president, largely due to his stronger credentials with the voters regarding the ongoing "war on terror" in comparison with his Democratic opponent, Senator John F. Kerry of Massachusetts (Jacobson 2007).

The redefinition of the role of the president in modern American government thus provided Bush an advantage in the struggle to establish himself as a legitimate president, an advantage that was denied to the three nineteenth-century presidents who came to office in a similar political predicament. Even prior to 9/11, Bush was, with some success, using the power and authority of the office to establish a governing "mandate." The ongoing atmosphere of crisis both at home and overseas after 9/11 elevated the president's actual authority to an even higher plane. Like all modern presidents, however, Bush remained vulnerable to the "expectations gap" discussed earlier. Having raised public hopes concerning the effectiveness of "preemptive war" in neutralizing the dangers from international terrorism and rogue states and the efficacy of large tax cuts as the remedy for the sluggish domestic economy, the administration needed to produce substantive results on both fronts or face the prospect of loss of legitimacy from another and more electorally significant direction—policy failure. This by and large explained the president's increasing problem with the American public during his second term in office.

The Second-Term Nightmares of the Bush Administration

One of the cast-iron rules of presidential politics is that presidents who get elected to a second term in office inevitably suffer more problems during their second term than during their first. The Twenty-second Amendment to the Constitution, which limits the president to two terms in office, may have some impact here. Certainly it has meant that any president reelected since the amendment was ratified in 1951 has faced being an immediate "lame duck" due to the inevitable tendency on the part of relevant political actors to look ahead to the next presidential election. Yet presidents elected to second terms in the modern era prior to the implementation of the amendment—Woodrow Wilson, Franklin Roosevelt, and Harry Truman—also suffered from political setbacks in their second term in office.

Presidents who have won a second term following the passage of the Twenty-second Amendment have all struggled in their second terms, although the extent and character of the struggle have varied. Scandals have been a common denominator, with the Nixon, Reagan, and Clinton administrations debilitated by the Watergate, Iran-Contra, and Lewinsky scandals, respectively. Nixon was forced out of office, while Reagan and Clinton were able to recover from scandal and still end their presidencies highly popular with the public. The Republican Party suffered serious losses in Congress in the second-term midterm elections of the three Republican two-term presidents: 1958 (Eisenhower), 1974 (Nixon-Ford), and 1986 (Reagan), while Democrat Bill Clinton avoided the trend, partly due to public disapproval of Republican congressional efforts to impeach him in 1998 and the fact that the Democrats had already suffered serious congressional losses in Clinton's first midterm election, in 1994.

In terms of advancing their policy agendas, all four post–Twenty-second Amendment two-term presidents found more problems in their second term than in their first, although more of those problems were in the domestic than the foreign policy area. Eisenhower effectively lost control of the domestic policy agenda after the 1958 midterms, Nixon was hobbled politically by Watergate, Reagan's signal domestic political achievements took place in his first term, and aside from the 1997 budget deal, Clinton's second-term domestic initiatives fell by the wayside as he became preoccupied with political survival during the Lewinsky scandal. Two of the four presidents had more success in foreign and defense policy, reflecting the greater leeway given to the modern president in those policy areas. Reagan during his second term undertook the personal diplomacy with Mikhail Gorbachev that initiated the end of the cold war. Clinton's administration put together a formidable NATO coalition to essentially bomb the renegade Serbian regime of Slobodan Milosevic into submission over its maltreatment of the Kosovo Albanians.

From all of this, some ground rules can be deduced regarding presidential second terms. All administrations are likely to face problems following the reelection of the president. These arise for a variety reasons: the Twenty-second Amendment and the "lame duck" factor; the tendency of incumbent presidents to conduct bland, "feel-good" reelection campaigns, thereby depriving themselves of the opportunity to claim a mandate for a second-term political agenda; severe "sixth-year" midterm election losses for the president's party in Congress; and recklessness and/or complacency stemming from overconfidence, which leads to scandal and political ineptitude—the "hubris" factor. Three of the four post–Twenty-second Amendment second-term presidents—Eisenhower, Reagan, and Clinton—managed to overcome the scandals and stumbles and end their administrations on a high note in terms of public approval. Even in these instances, however, their ability to set the domestic political agenda had largely evaporated by their seventh year in office, although Reagan and Clinton still had significant foreign and defense policy achievements in the last years of their presidencies. Richard Nixon suffered the worst fate, as his administration got caught in a downward spiral of scandal, public disapproval, and policy ineffectiveness leading to his near-impeachment and resignation.

The pattern of George W. Bush's second term was somewhat different inasmuch as his public approval ratings went into a downward spiral in 2005 and never recovered (Jacobson 2007; Edwards 2007), but no scandal surfaced of sufficient extent to threaten his eviction from the White House. In this regard, Bush's second term is more similar to Harry Truman's than to his post–Twenty-second Amendment counterparts. But Bush was an outlier from the start due to the unusual nature of his reelection in 2004. A second term won by a margin as narrow as Bush's—3 percent—is very unusual. Of twentieth-century presidents, only Woodrow Wilson in 1916 experienced a similarly narrow reelection margin. FDR, Eisenhower, Nixon, Reagan, and Clinton, by contrast, all won landslide reelection victories. In general, presidents either are defeated running for reelection or they win big; in this regard, Bush is very much the exception.

Despite his narrow victory margin, Bush immediately claimed a mandate for this second term and announced it at a postelection press conference: "I earned capital in the campaign, political capital, and now I intend to spend it" (from Edwards 2007, 188). The issue that the Bush administration chose to focus on in its second term was reform of Social Security (Draper 2007), although this issue had not featured greatly in the 2000 or 2004 election campaigns. Bush campaigned hard on the issue in 2005, but his appeals fell completely flat as public opinion did not move in his direction (Edwards 2007; Jacobson 2007) and the Republican Congress felt no compulsion to address a highly troublesome issue. The administration suffered further attrition after March 2005, when the president and the Republican Congress moved the case of Terri Schiavo—a comatose Florida woman who was the subject of a legal dispute between her husband and her parents over maintaining life support—into the federal courts (Draper 2007, 308–9). The public was also singularly unimpressed by the administration's initial relief effort following Hurricane Katrina's devastation of New Orleans in August 2005, and this episode also took its toll in terms of public support (Draper 2007, 305–37). All of the above problems were accompanied by continuing casualties in the American effort to pacify post-invasion Iraq, and Bush's approval ratings continued downward, further impeding his ability to move his domestic agenda forward. In 2006, Bush was unable to persuade the Republican Congress to take up a major immigration reform bill because it included a guest worker program and a pathway to citizenship for illegal aliens, and he had to settle for merely tougher enforcement measures at the border. Administration efforts to open the Arctic National Wildlife Refuge to exploratory drilling for petroleum also failed to pass the Senate in 2005.

Bush's second term was not without some legislative successes, however. In 2005, the president did succeed in passing an energy bill that focused more on expediting oil and gas production than on conservation, and after a struggle, he got Congress to approve the Central American Free Trade Agreement (CAFTA). The major successes of Bush's second term in domestic policy, however, were the Senate confirmations of his conservative picks to fill vacancies on the Supreme Court, with John Roberts confirmed as chief justice in 2005 and Samuel Alito confirmed in early 2006. The Alito nomination to replace Justice Sandra Day O'Connor clearly moved the Court in a conservative direction, although Bush was forced to withdraw his original nominee—White House counsel Harriet Miers—after vociferous opposition from conservative Republicans (Draper 2007, 342–47).

Like his Republican predecessors Eisenhower and Reagan, Bush endured major losses for his party in Congress in the "sixth-year" midterm election that effectively put an end to his domestic policy agenda. An attempt at a bipartisan compromise on immigration reform with the new Democratic majority Congress again foundered due to Republican intransigence in the Senate. Like his two predecessors, Bush also found himself resorting to a defensive "veto strategy" to prevent passage of policy proposals from the Democratic Congress. Given the relatively narrow Democratic majorities in Congress, particularly in the Senate, the veto strategy was highly effective, as the congressional Republicans still invariably stood united (save for the immigration issue) behind their president, and only on a November 2007 federal water projects bill was the Democratic congressional leadership able to muster in each chamber the two-thirds majority necessary to override Bush's veto. In foreign policy, the president always has more cards to play as commander in chief, and Bush was successful in preventing Democratic attempts to force through Congress a change in Iraq policy and a plan to withdraw troops. The 2006 election defeats did produce changes in Iraq policy, however, as the president removed his controversial defense secretary, Donald Rumsfeld, and implemented a new "troop surge" strategy to retain enough support in Congress to block demands for an exit timetable.

The slowing national economy also added to Bush's woes during his second term, and the final blow to his prestige came with a Wall Street financial meltdown in September 2008 that necessitated a $700 billion federal bailout of the nation's financial institutions under the Troubled Assets Relief Program or TARP—the complete antithesis of the "small government" fiscal conservatism that the administration was supposed to represent.

Overall—with the obvious exception of the disgraced Richard Nixon— the Bush second term was perhaps the least successful of all the post– Twenty-second Amendment two-term presidents. The president could point to no signal second-term achievements at home or abroad beyond getting two conservatives on the Supreme Court, and his personal popularity and prestige continued to erode. The Bush second term contributed to the loss of the Republican majority in Congress that they had held since 1994 and a stalling of the conservative domestic and foreign policy agendas. Indeed, the massive federal financial bailout of 2008 estranged the president from his own party and represented a clear reversal of the so-called "Reagan Revolution" in economic policy. As usual, the second Bush term was afflicted by scandals—the deliberately blown cover of CIA officer Valerie Plame that led to the conviction of the vice president's chief of staff Lewis Libby, the firings of U.S. attorneys, the conflicting testimony and later resignation of Attorney General Alberto Gonzales, and the activities of lobbyist Jack Abramoff (although the last took a heavier toll on the congressional GOP than on the Bush administration). These scandals, together with the military stalemate in Iraq and the administration's inept response to Hurricane Katrina, all helped to derail the administration's policy agenda, but none was sufficiently significant to threaten the president personally. George W. Bush proved utterly unable to defy the second-term blues that characterize most two-term presidencies and suffered more than most, perhaps because the president himself had become such a polarizing figure.

George W. Bush and "Political Time"

Political scientist Stephen Skowronek (see also chapter 1) has suggested that presidents should be viewed from the perspective of their place in the development of a specific political regime or what Skowronek refers to as "political time" (Skowronek 1993; 2003). These regimes reflect the balance of power between political forces during a particular period, define the roles of political institutions, and set the national policy agenda. Skowronek classifies presidencies as presidencies of "reconstruction" (founding a regime), "articulation" (maintaining the regime), or "disjunction" (signaling the end of a regime and beginning the transition to a new regime). He also has a fourth category of "preemption," in which peculiar short-term circumstances might lead to the election of a president from outside the regime but who is ultimately unable to change it substantially (Skowronek 1993, 3–58).

If we take Ronald Reagan as the founder of the conservative Republican regime that began in 1981, then the most obvious classification for a Bush presidency would seem to be one of "orthodox innovation" or "articulation." This is the category in which Skowronek himself initially placed Bush (Skowronek 2003, 153–54). Bush has made no secret of his admiration for Reagan and adherence to the Reaganite values of a smaller federal government, major tax cuts to stimulate growth, social conservatism, and "standing tall" in defense of American interests abroad. Indeed, it appears that Reagan was more of an ideological and political model for Bush than the latter's own father, whose electoral defeat in 1992 helped instigate the son's political career and whose alleged mistakes in office he strove to avoid (Keller 2003; Nagourney 2003). Of course, as the elder Bush demonstrated, a presidency of articulation—or what Skowronek refers to as the "faithful son" (Skowronek 1993, 430)—does not guarantee political or electoral success, particularly if the president is being forced by the exigencies of political time into a role contrary to his personal political inclinations (Parmet 1997).

If, however, the conservative Republican regime had exhausted itself intellectually and its nostrums had become irrelevant to the changed circumstances of the nation at home or abroad in the first decade of the new century, then George W. Bush also might be seen as a president of "disjunction," representing the last gasp of a dying political regime. The end of the cold war that was so integral to the Reagan regime certainly appeared to have eroded the Republican grip on the presidency during the 1990s. And Bush's own slender and contentious election victory in 2000 and narrow reelection in 2004 compared with the Republican landslides of the 1980s might be adduced as additional evidence for regime decay. George W. Bush's post-9/11 foreign policy doctrine of "preemptive war" against rogue states left America isolated internationally, still vulnerable to international terrorism, and still enmeshed in civil strife in Iraq and Afghanistan at the conclusion of his presidency. The banking and financial crisis of September–October 2008 and the huge TARP bailout that resulted from it would legitimate the heavy dose of government interventionism that characterized the economic policy of the succeeding Democratic administration of Barack Obama. Depending on the success or otherwise of Obama's approach to the world economic crisis, it may well be that the failure of the George W. Bush administration marked the final demise of the post-1980 Reagan Republican regime of deregulation and limited government at home coupled with aggressive assertion of America's interests abroad.

A Partisan President in a Partisan Era

George W. Bush's presidency occurred during the most partisan period in recent American history. Most of the twentieth century had been characterized by party decline, and political scientists and historians have well documented the erosion of the party machines, the erosion of party loyalty in Congress, the rise of the primary system for choosing presidential candidates, and the loosening of party ties among voters (Wattenberg 1984). The major parties were at their nadir in the period from 1952 to 1980, when they appeared to be irrelevant to the dominant concerns of the country, such as civil rights and the Vietnam War (Nie et al. 1979). The civil rights revolution and the political turmoil of the 1960s, however, also generated a gradual realignment of electoral forces so that the two major parties gradually became increasingly ideologically homogeneous, particularly with reference to issues involving cultural cleavages—abortion, church/state relations, affirmative action, gun control, the environment, and gay and lesbian rights. With the dramatic decline in the numbers of "liberal northern Republicans" and "southern conservative Democrats," party loyalty rates in Congress have risen dramatically, and the two congressional parties have strengthened their leadership in an effort to implement a partisan policy agenda (Rohde 1991; Sinclair 1995).

Party competition in the United States today has not only become increasingly shrill; it has also been remarkably evenly balanced of late. The Republican dominance of the presidency and the Democratic control of Congress that prevailed for most of the 1952–1992 period have been replaced since the early 1990s by competitiveness at all levels. Margins of victory have been slight and tenuous, and elections have increasingly become a game of mobilization—getting one's own faithful troops to the polls—rather than a battle for the broad center ground of American politics (Schier 2000; Jacobson 2007). And while the number of "ticket-splitting" voters has declined from the high rates of the 1970s, there were still sufficient of them to lead to situations of divided government, with different parties controlling the presidency and at least one chamber of Congress, for all but a few months in the 1995–2002 period (Jacobson 2000). From the 1950s to the mid-1970s, the congressional parties were so amorphous and broad that divided government could be mitigated by cross-party coalitions—such as that which passed the Civil Rights Act of 1964. By contrast, the congressional parties of today are so polarized, so ideologically homogeneous, and the margin of control has been so slight, that there is little incentive for cooperation on either side (Sinclair 2006).

As we have already noted, the 2000 presidential election was characteristic of the preceding decade: exceedingly close and exceedingly partisan, with a highly controversial aftermath in Florida that left the parties more embittered and polarized than ever. George W. Bush's rise to the presidency took place within the context of this new polarized politics. Presidential nominations today are decided in relatively low-turnout primary elections where single-issue and ideological groups and activists aligned with the major parties exercise disproportionate influence (Schier 2000; Fiorina et al. 2006). In the 2000 election, Bush triumphed over his only serious rival, the maverick Arizona senator and Vietnam POW hero John McCain, because he secured the necessary money, endorsements, and activists from the conservative base of the Republican Party early in the campaign (Ceaser and Busch 2001, 49–76). McCain enjoyed some successes in early primaries largely due to the help of independents and Democrats in states where they could vote in the Republican presidential primary, but in the end, Bush easily overwhelmed him among mainstream conservative Republican primary voters on "Super Tuesday" (Mayer 2001, 34–37).

For the remainder of the 2000 campaign season, Bush did nothing to distance himself from conservative Republicans. While electoral strategy might have dictated the choice of a northeastern moderate as his vice presidential running mate, Bush instead chose a reliable Republican conservative, former congressman and defense secretary Richard Cheney (Ceaser and Busch 2001, 137–41). Bush's gestures toward the political center in the 2000 general election campaign were mainly cosmetic and rhetorical, such as the staging of the anodyne 2000 Republican convention and presenting himself as a "compassionate conservative" in an effort to reach out to the political center (Ceaser and Busch 2001, 116–17).

Governing as a partisan president in a partisan era is a skill that requires some degree of political dexterity. Bill Clinton demonstrated how it might be done in the last six years of his presidency through the agile use of the "triangulation" strategy pioneered by his 1996 reelection strategist—Dick Morris. Triangulation meant keeping the devoted loyalty of your own party's core voters while making strategic overtures to the political center on certain selected issues, such as the 1996 welfare reform and the Defense of Marriage Act in Clinton's case (Rae 2000). Even so deft a politician as Clinton was able to make "triangulation" work only intermittently, and, as the events of 1998 proved, it did nothing to reduce the intense Republican hostility toward him.

Since George W. Bush was evidently not a "preemptive" president in the Clinton mold and his personal authority clearly benefited from his response to 9/11, he was not required to demonstrate the same degree of political agility. Yet while the president's main political strategist, Karl Rove, publicly eschewed the idea of a Republican version of "triangulation" (Crabtree 2003), the Bush White House pursued a "base plus" strategy: seeking to reach out to key Democratic constituencies while fortifying the GOP's conservative base (Schier 2004, 10–13). Bush did not depart from a strict conservative Republican agenda in terms of budget policy, abortion, affirmative action, or in the highly vexed areas of court appointments, and his loyalty to the Republican base removed the possibility of debilitating intraparty challenges in 2004 (Nagourney 2003). At the same time, Bush made inroads into the political center by choosing his issues and his rhetoric carefully (as in the August 2001 presidential address on stem-cell research) and practicing his own version of "triangulation" on Democratic issues like education and prescription drugs (Brownstein 2002), for which the president earned plaudits from the architect of triangulation, Dick Morris (Morris 2003). The catastrophe of 9/11 and the subsequent wars in Afghanistan and Iraq made it easier for Bush to govern in a partisan era since that day and its aftermath focused political debate on the presidential terrain of national security. Democrats found it extremely hard to oppose the president vigorously in such a crisis atmosphere. This was demonstrated dramatically in the 2002 congressional elections when Democratic senators and Senate candidates suffered at the polls after the president and the Republicans had attacked them for failing to support legislation establishing the new Department of Homeland Security (Nather and Cochran 2002).

In Bush's second term, however, the shortcomings of the Rove strategy were revealed as Bush's domestic policy agenda stagnated due in large part to the refusal of congressional Democrats, particularly in the Senate, to continue to cooperate with him. Heightened partisanship and Bush's dwindling approval ratings due to the Iraq war made it easy for them to do so. The unremitting hostility of the Democratic base toward Bush made it politically almost impossible for Democrats to cooperate with him after 2004, as moderate Democratic senator Joseph Lieberman of Connecticut discovered when he lost his bid for reelection in the 2006 primary. After Republicans lost the congressional majority in 2006, Democratic cooperation with the president would be even less forthcoming. A partisan, term-limited president whose party does not control Congress is in a very weak position indeed, and the political failures of the second Bush term could be seen as demonstrating the limitations of the partisan presidency.

In his first term, Bush found that the mantle of defender of the nation thrust upon him by the 9/11 attacks enabled him to transcend polarized ideological party politics without conceding any substantial ideological territory to his political opponents. The strategy was contingent, however, on his continued ability to "deliver the goods" in terms of economic prosperity and the global war that Bush himself had declared against terrorism and rogue states. In the second Bush term, the military and political quagmire in Iraq helped to undermine political support for the administration's policy objectives at home and abroad. Bush's major domestic policy venture—Social Security reform—offered nothing politically to Democrats and did not capture the imagination of the public, and the bungled public response to Hurricane Katrina made the administration appear incompetent. By the time Bush turned to immigration reform, he had lost the confidence of his own party on the issue, and Democrats who were more sympathetic to his proposal ideologically had no political incentive to cooperate with him.

The federal bailout of the banks through TARP in response to the financial crisis in fall 2008 finally severed the relationship between the president and the congressional Republicans (who overwhelmingly voted against the program). It also damned the prospects of the 2008 Republican presidential nominee, Senator John McCain, whose inability to carry several key Republican-leaning states, such as Ohio, Florida, North Carolina, Colorado, Indiana, and Virginia, ensured a heavy 173-to-365 Electoral College loss to Democrat Barack Obama. McCain's defeat, coupled with further dramatic Republican losses in both houses of Congress in the 2008 elections, demonstrated that the partisan nature of the Bush presidency had ultimately backfired badly on his co-partisans, who clearly suffered at the polls from their close association with him in 2006 and 2008.

If the first Bush term demonstrated the possibilities of a partisan approach to the presidency in the modern era, the political failures of the second term amply demonstrated its limitations.

3

LEGITIMACY, LEADERSHIP, AND LONGING FOR REALIGNMENT

The Party Basis of the Bush Presidency

JOHN J. COLEMAN and
KEVIN S. PRICE

W hat started rocky, ended rocky. Elected under controversial circumstances, George W. Bush entered office with a legitimacy crisis on his hands. A significant proportion of the American public viewed Bush as a dubious president, in part because he was outpolled in popular votes by the losing candidate and in part because his road to the White House took several legal detours through the Florida courts and finally through a contentious Supreme Court decision. His legitimacy crisis may have ebbed when 9/11 recast his presidency, but it did not disappear. About 65 to 70 percent of Democrats questioned the legitimacy of Bush's election throughout his first term, according to CBS News/Gallup polls. The broader leadership question encased in the legitimacy problem remained: how can this president lead? Most observers thought his second-place popular vote finish made any claim to a mandate irrelevant. Accordingly, when Bush entered office, many expected the new president to have tremendous difficulty enacting his legislative agenda and leading the government.

The American party system, however, provides opportunities for presidents to establish legitimacy and exert leadership. Presidents seek to establish identities and political strengths independent of their party, but they remain dependent on party members to achieve many of their goals. Presidential leadership is connected to the party system in two important ways. First, the historical trajectory of the party system may be more or less favorable for the establishment of presidential leadership. That is, some presidents are simply in a more difficult position historically because of the strength or weakness of current party alignments. Second, presidents whose own victories were very narrow may face additional leadership challenges when their party's majority is also paper thin, but this situation can also create opportunities.

President Bush was in a strong position regarding the first point, the historical trajectory of the party system. Simply put, the basic dynamics of the party system—realignment, economic conditions, and decreasing ownership of issues by the Democratic Party—provided a relatively favorable environment for Bush's leadership claims. On the second point, Bush faced a challenge of legitimacy and leadership similar to that faced by many other presidents we classify as "plurality presidents"—those who receive less than half the popular vote and nonetheless win the presidency because of severe splits in the other party's coalition, reflected in the other major party's candidate losing significant vote share to third-party candidates—but Bush's situation was sufficiently different in that he had a distinctive set of advantages relative to other plurality leaders. Therefore, despite some similarities of their election victories, Bush started his term in a stronger position. The ingredients were in place for Bush to establish both legitimacy and leadership, even without the intervening events of 9/11.

For a long while, the president appeared to capitalize on this promise. Over his first six years, his support score in Congress—the percentage of times Congress voted in accordance with the president's position—was 81 percent. For eighteen months of those six years, Democrats controlled the Senate. As a measure, the support score has its weaknesses. For example, the votes in question might not reflect the president's agenda per se. And items on that presidential agenda that never made it to a congressional vote, such as the president's plans to reform Social Security, are not factored into the score. Still, the measure provides a rough sense that Congress was casting votes consistent with the president's wishes, to a degree that might be considered surprising in light of the circumstances surrounding the president's victory in 2000. The president felt compelled to uncap his veto pen only once in those first six years, a historically low record.

Despite this success, the president's fortunes began drifting downward in his first term. Within twenty-four months, all of the approval bounce of 9/11 had been depleted. The conflict in Iraq, along with growing economic uncertainty, ate away at the president's approval and became a large share of political dialogue and rhetoric in Washington. Room for the president's other hoped-for signature accomplishments, including reform of immigration and Social Security, was scant. The president won reelection, but relatively weakly for an incumbent. By 2006, control of Congress had been lost. In the end, it was not legitimacy concerns that dragged the president down and weakened his leadership success in his final years. The president's leadership ultimately suffered from a weakened Republican Party, the difficulties in Iraq, a revitalized liberal political infrastructure, failure to adapt to a shifting domestic agenda, and the difficulties inherent in a plurality presidency.

The Republican Ascendancy

When Bush became president, he inherited a party system that was well situated for his leadership efforts. Although Bush did not have an electoral mandate in 2000, the trends in the party system were largely favorable for his party and his presidency. First, although this is a matter of some controversy, it was plausible to say that the party system had shifted or perhaps even realigned in the Republicans' favor.

The concept of partisan realignment is an umbrella term covering distinctive varieties of political change. These varieties include secular realignment and critical realignment. Uniting these terms is an attempt to understand changes in the party system and how a party system moves from one type of competition to another (Stonecash 2005). In effect, realignment theory takes "before and after" photographs of the party system. The "before and after" might be from a period in which one party is dominant to a period in which the other party dominates, or from a time when a party has a particular coalition to a time when that party has a different supporting coalition, or from a period in which one party dominates to a period in which neither party dominates. No matter what type of change it is, significant policy departures accompany the party realignment.

Our analytical eye is often drawn to the dramatic and disruptive, but V. O. Key (1959) alerted scholars to the fact that significant political change often occurs gradually, with the accumulation of small, incremental developments. This variety of realignment is known as secular (i.e., steady, gradual) realignment. As a social group becomes more affluent, for example, its members might find the policy appeals of a conservative political party more to their liking. As one particular social group becomes better represented within a political party, other groups might gradually pull out of that party. Scholars have suggested that both of these developments have occurred in the party system over the past few decades. For example, as Catholics moved steadily into the middle class, they became less reliably Democratic. As African Americans gained a louder voice in the Democratic Party, whites, especially southern whites, increasingly supported Republicans. As religious and social conservatives played an increasing role in the Republican Party, Republican moderates found themselves increasingly likely to vote Democratic. Evangelical Christians moved from Democratic voting to Republican voting over time.

In the 1990s, secular realignment moved in a direction that tended to favor Republicans. Groups that were considered part of the Democratic New Deal coalition—organized labor, agricultural interests, urban ethnic groups, Catholics, Jews, the less educated, southerners, industrial blue collar workers, liberals—tended to support Democrats less strongly in the 1990s than in the 1940s (Mayer 1998). Indeed, if these groups had still been voting for Democrats at their traditional level, Democrats would not have lost control of Congress, state legislatures, and governorships in the 1990s. Still, Jeffrey Stonecash (2000) and Stonecash, Mark Brewer, and Mack Mariani (2003) have shown that class-based divisions between the parties were on the upswing in the 1990s, so the idea that Republicans represented those who were better off economically and Democrats, the less well off, still held true.

In the 1990s, the New Deal coalition could no longer cement Democratic victories, and that worked to the Republicans' advantage. By the 1990s a Democrat, particularly a Democratic presidential nominee, could no longer plan on winning by simply rounding up the old coalitional suspects. Even candidates who found that they did well with these traditional New Deal coalition groups—and most Democratic candidates did do reasonably well with them—would find that they needed to reach outside this cluster to ensure victory (Bartels 1998). This situation provided an opportunity for Republicans in general and George Bush in particular. Although Bush fared miserably among African Americans, in 2000 he eroded some of the Democratic advantage with other groups, such as

43

women, and co-opted some of the issues that were typically seen as owned by Democrats, such as Social Security and education. And in 2004, Bush gained among a majority of groups in the population.

The upshot is that the Republicans were poised to strengthen their majority status when Bush entered office, and his fellow partisans knew that. That gave them great incentive to cooperate with Bush, which they did at very high levels in roll call votes. Unlike Bill Clinton, whom many Democrats suspected did not have the key to future Democratic victories—and indeed, the party's presidential nominees cast a more liberal tone in 2008 than Clinton had in 1992 and 1996—Bush seemed to have had his fellow partisans believing he had unlocked the code to Republican dominance. Regaining control of both houses of Congress with the 2002 elections only reinforced that impression among Republican elites. As Philip John Davies put it when reviewing the results of the national and state 2002 elections, "It is almost a statistical tie—a shift of a few votes here and there would have changed the results. But the Republicans won this tie. In every case the small majority lies with the Republicans, and the combination is to give that party a very considerable, and interlinked, foundation for national political authority" (Davies 2003, 146).

With secular realignment, Republicans were at worst co-equal with the Democrats or were arguably the majority party. It had been a long time since Republicans controlled the presidency, House, and Senate simultaneously and an even longer time since they had won and maintained control of Congress for several consecutive elections (which they did from 1994 through 2004). Bush's presidency, though the result of an unusual election, benefited early on from its place in history. His fellow partisans in Congress proved willing to let him lead. This did not mean that he had the unconditional support of his party, but it did mean that Bush was seen by fellow Republicans as the person who could make the Republican majority, thin as it was, durable (Barone 2002; Brooks 2003; Meyerson 2002; Teixeira 2003). This forecast was shattered in the 2006 and 2008 elections.

Another form of historical change is known as critical realignment. Elaborated most importantly by V. O. Key (1955) and Walter Dean Burnham (1970) and vigorously challenged by David Mayhew (2002), realignment theory posits that some elections (either an individual election or a series of two elections in sequence) have enduring consequences for the party system. Rather than the gradual change at the heart of secular realignment, critical realignment focuses on sharp, quick transformations of the political landscape that have effects for a generation or longer. Typically, critical realignments bring a new majority party to power and have effects at the local, state, and national level. Scholars place the elections of 1800 (Jeffersonian Republicans), 1828 (Jackson and the Democrats), 1860 (Lincoln's Republicans), and 1932 (Roosevelt and the Democrats) in this category. Other realignments might keep the same majority party but create a new supporting coalition for that party, as in 1896 (McKinley and the Republicans).

Scholars such as John Aldrich (1995) and Walter Dean Burnham (1996) have argued that the 1968 election marked a critical realignment of a different type. This realignment was notable for its dealigning features: members of the public pulled away from their party loyalties, turnout began to drop, and control over government was usually divided between the two major parties. With this shared power, policy began to move in a more conservative direction after decades of nearly continuous Democratic control in Congress and Democratic presidents for twenty-eight of thirty-six years. The dramatic victory of Ronald Reagan in 1980, in this view, solidified the ongoing system rather than marking a realigning election in its own right. The Republican Party was strengthened by gaining control of the Senate from 1981 through 1986, and policy moved even more clearly in a conservative direction, but control of government in Washington remained divided and the Democrats remained the majority party in the states and cities.

The 1994 electoral earthquake had all the hallmarks of a traditional partisan critical realignment: issues were highly prominent, the political atmosphere seemed unusually energized, the election results tilted almost universally toward one party, institutional reorganization (especially in the House) was extensive, and policy changes (or attempts at policy changes) were numerous and, for the most part, ideologically consistent (Burnham 1996). It seemed that at last the Democratic era was over.

History, however, is rarely as neat and tidy as our models. In this supposed new Republican era, a Democrat won the presidency in 1996 and the Democrats pulled off the historical anomaly of gaining seats in the midterm election of 1998. Much of the conservative Republican agenda either failed or was watered down to ensure passage and the Democratic president's signature.

Still, with 1994, the Republican Party achieved parity with the Democrats throughout the country and at all levels of government. The period from 1968 to 1994 featured divided government that leaned toward Democratic control at most levels and in most offices but with generally increasing Republican success, notably in the 1980s. The 1994 election seemed to most Republicans to hold the promise that the balance of party power had tilted in their direction. By the end of 2005, Republicans had remained the majority party in Congress for six straight terms (with a brief deviation following the defection of Senator James Jeffords in 2001), something the party had not accomplished in nearly seventy years. Moreover, of the nineteen states where population growth from 1990 to 2000 exceeded the national average of 13.2 percent, Bush won fourteen of them in 2000. Republicans were doing best where the population—and the electoral votes it provides—was growing the most. This was apparent in 2004; if Bush simply won in 2004 the same states he won in 2000, his electoral vote margin would have increased from his four votes in 2000 to eighteen votes in 2004.

And the Republican Party's electoral fortunes remained strong during Bush's first term. The party picked up seats in the House and Senate in the 2002 midterm elections, a historical oddity at any time. In 2004, the Republicans picked up even more, partly as a result of the redrawing of congressional districts in Texas in 2003. Republicans, unhappy with a judicially created redistricting map for their state, opened a special session of the legislature to produce a new map, which ultimately would lead to seven new Republican-leaning districts. Democratic state senators went into hiding in Oklahoma, and then New Mexico, in protest. The U.S. Supreme Court upheld the legislature's right to redraw the map. The party also retained a lead in state governors and split evenly on the number of state legislators.

The 1990s and first Bush term also witnessed the partial demise of ideas that the American electorate was dealigning at the national level. In the 1970s and 1980s, a number of scholars pointed out that Americans seemed to be losing their partisan moorings, that attachments to the parties were not as deep or as permanent as they had once been. Rather than realignment, these scholars suggested, *dealignment* best described the new American electorate. To a large degree, these accounts were compelling descriptions of the electorate of those two decades. In the 1990s, however, this trend bottomed out and reversed. Most notably, the percentage of voters splitting their tickets between the two major parties—for example, voting for a House candidate of one party and a presidential candidate of another party—declined throughout the 1990s and in the 2000 election. In 2000, that percentage of vote splitters (14 percent) was the lowest it had been since 1964. Similarly, the percentage of districts electing a House member of one party while supporting a presidential candidate of another party in 2000 (20.2 percent) was at its lowest level since 1952. This figure dropped even further in 2004. Voters had become better "sorted" into the correct political party, with liberals encamped in the Democratic Party and conservatives in the Republican Party.

In both senses of realignment, secular and critical, the historical position of the party system was advantageous for George W. Bush. Republicans had, for the first time in many decades, a clear opportunity to become a durable majority party. Viewing the hard-right tactics of Newt Gingrich in the 1990s to have been a failure, the party was open to a different approach and somewhat different message. Bush capitalized on these openings and garnered tremendous loyalty from Republicans in Congress. Coming to office when he did, Bush was able to leverage his leadership opportunities to an unusual degree, certainly to an extent greater than his thin 2000 victory would suggest. His ability to exercise leadership, his Republican colleagues realized, would enhance his legitimacy credentials. This favorable environment would shift starkly after 2004.

We will mention other features of the historical trajectory—political time, economic conditions, and changing issue ownership—only briefly. First, Bush's leadership benefited Republicans because of his place in political time. As explained elsewhere in this volume, Bush entered office as an "orthodox innovator," in Stephen Skowronek's terms. Expectations are relatively low for such presidents, and their ability to lead is tied to the perceptions of the president they are linked to, the president whose agenda they are seen as eager to advance. In Bush's case, that would be Ronald Reagan. The reverence for Reagan among Republicans was and is substantial, and Bush found himself domestically in the role of fine-tuning and adjusting the Reagan legacy and agenda, not discarding it. For this, he was given substantial leeway to lead among Republican politicians and activists. His early passage of a large tax cut and his insistence on additional cuts proved his Reaganite credentials to both groups. By the end of his second term, however, Bush was widely criticized by conservatives for deviating from the Reagan philosophy.

Second, Bush inherited an economy that had grown strongly for years and generated budget surpluses. This situation allowed him to make the case for his tax cuts in 2001 despite, initially, any clear economic reason the economy required such stimulus. Early into his term, however, the economy began to slide, and the tax cut in the Economic Growth and Tax

Relief Reconciliation Act of 2001 could now be defended as reasonable and stimulatory. He could use the continuing troubles of the economy to push additional rounds of tax cuts in the Job Creation and Worker Assistance Act of 2002 and the Jobs and Growth Tax Relief Reconciliation Act of 2003. In his first term, the president was able to leverage economic conditions in pursuit of his ideological beliefs in a manner satisfactory to his base. This pattern would not hold out for long, however.

Third, Bush in 2000 rode the wave of the nationalization of the education issue, particularly as the link between education and financial well-being became ever more strongly entrenched in public assumptions. Both of these developments proved helpful for passage of major parts of the Bush campaign agenda. Because of his personal efforts, the Democratic ownership of the education issue had diminished markedly by the time Bush took office. The same was true of Social Security, though the collapse in the stock market following 2000 prevented Bush from making any early headway on his campaign promise to reform the pension system. And while Bush had weakened some of the Democratic ownership of key issues, he was able to reinforce issues on which Republicans had been strong. The tragedy of 9/11, in particular, provided a means to reinforce Bush's arguments during the campaign that American military and security readiness needed to improve. On issue ownership, too, Republicans would be worse off by the end of Bush's second term.

Avoiding a Legitimacy Crisis

We believe that "close matters," but it does not fully determine presidential success and public acceptance. For most Americans in 2001, President Bush's legitimacy would depend on his ability to achieve some measure of policy success. That success would depend on his ability to master the difficulties inherent in his controversial victory. Even after 9/11, it was not obvious or inevitable that Bush would escape questions about the legitimacy of his presidency, even if these questions might be asked in hushed tones.

Through most of the 2000 campaign, many Americans appeared unmoved by the leading presidential candidates and unconvinced that the upcoming election would make much of a difference in their lives. Indeed, Ralph Nader grounded his insurgent candidacy in the premise that a President Gore would differ from a President Bush only in the smallest details of program and rhetoric. Amid the unfolding drama of election night, however, many formerly uninterested citizens began to suspect that something vitally important was at stake. By the time the Supreme Court ended the suspense five weeks later, committed partisans on both sides had adopted scorched-earth tactics in pursuit of their preferred outcomes, and many of those who yawned their way through the official campaign now seemed certain that the extra-inning selection of their next president would be very consequential indeed (Dionne and Kristol 2001).

Submerged by the remarkable developments of the Bush years, the political problem of the forty-third president's legitimacy receded beyond recognition during his first term. What explains the rapid disappearance of legitimacy as a politically contentious characteristic of the Bush presidency? Credible questions of legitimacy could have plagued this president, especially given the deep partisan divides in American politics and the then–still-fresh memories of the Clinton impeachment. That they did not requires an explanation that situates George W. Bush in the ongoing flow of American party politics.

We begin with the simple notion that elections provide political information to winners and losers alike. Generally speaking, winners—and the journalists who play a central role in establishing the conventional wisdom after each election—will credit the victorious side's savvy tactical decisions, the general brilliance of the triumphant candidate, or, at times, the inevitability of the outcome. Losers, on the other hand, engage in postmortem analysis not simply to apportion blame but to develop a strategic plan for future contests. Not all presidents are elected in the same circumstances. Some win landslides. Others win comfortably. Others manage close wins. Some win despite having received less than half the vote. In this last category, some win largely because of the implosion of the opposition party. Presidents like Richard Nixon and Bill Clinton won, to a significant degree, because of the internal fractures within the opposition party that led to third-party candidates. It is this last type of presidential winner that we refer to as a plurality president.

The central intrigue of the plurality presidency is that it fuses the analytical frames of the winner and the loser into a single act of political interpretation. After all, plurality winners have indeed triumphed, and they are thus entitled to use the authority of the presidency, but the unconvincing nature of their victory compels them and their teams to search for more reliable footing in the shifting sands of American politics. This prospective project—a fusion of the winner's rationalization and the loser's retooling—captures the basic outlook of the plurality presidency. Moreover, this dynamic process connects elites and voters in an ongoing process of party definition in which elites offer voters a choice, voters choose, and elites interpret that choice with an eye to the next round of electoral competition.

As party politicians assess their prospects, the best guide to an upcoming election is the most recent one. In other words, potential candidates (including incumbents) look ahead by looking back. In search of a winning formula, candidates in the just-defeated party assess the political terrain and build an electoral blueprint based on the best available information. A defining characteristic of a plurality election is that its winner must engage in effectively the same analysis as the losers of most other elections. The key difference is that the winners of these elections conduct such assessments from the White House. To put it another way, plurality presidents engage in something like a loser's analysis from a winner's position of power.

To understand the plurality presidency, one must understand what it is not. First, it is not an automatic result of multiparty elections. Third- and fourth-party insurgencies have played significant roles, but other notable multicandidate contests have not produced plurality presidencies as we define them. Consider the 1948 election, in which Democrat Harry Truman fell just short of a popular majority at 49.6 percent of the vote. We do not regard Truman as a plurality president because the minor-party candidates who held him short of a majority—Dixiecrat Strom Thurmond with 2.4 percent of the vote and Progressive Party candidate Henry Wallace with 2.3 percent—broke from the Democratic orbit.

Truman won the presidency *despite* a split in one of the major parties. Plurality presidents, on the other hand, win in part *because* of a split in one of the major parties. Elites will derive little political information from the simple fact that a candidate does not reach 50 percent. Instead, elections that reveal the winning side's persistent weakness in the party system generate useful political information. If Truman could succeed even when his party suffered two breakaway movements, he would perceive electoral vindication for the orthodox Democratic formulas of the New Deal and Fair Deal. Victory in such a contest would thus embolden its winner, suggesting little need to revise basic party positions.

Now consider the contrasting message of the 1912 election, in which Woodrow Wilson won largely—if not exclusively—because of Theodore Roosevelt's challenge to incumbent Republican William Howard Taft. In nearly eight years as president, Roosevelt forged a distinctly progressive identity for himself and, by extension, for the Republican Party. By siphoning substantial progressive support from Taft's Republican coalition, Roosevelt effectively guaranteed Wilson's victory. The political upshot of this election turned on what Wilson would do with the information conveyed by his election. In practice, Wilson's plurality election compelled him to pursue a new direction for the Democratic Party, which remained tied to the conservative impulses of the Bourbon South. The important point here is that plurality presidents (a category for which the winners in 1856, 1860, 1912, 1968, and 1992 clearly qualify) win under conditions that encourage them to reformulate their parties' respective identities.

If the plurality presidency is not just a function of multicandidate campaigns, neither is it a simple consequence of close races. The more relevant question is, what does a narrow victory suggest about the underlying state of party competition? It certainly suggests that it is *close* and that any given election can go either way. But narrow victories do not necessarily indicate that the winners prevailed in spite of their party's ongoing electoral weakness. In turn, narrow victories do not necessarily recommend that the winners and their party move in any particular ideological or programmatic direction in order to generate additional support in future contests.

All of this leads us back to the election of 2000. Did George W. Bush qualify as a plurality president? He may be the most difficult historical case to categorize. The 2000 election was indeed quite close. By winning nearly 48 percent of the popular vote, Bush did well enough to suggest that his party remained fully competitive, if not dominant, at the presidential level. In addition, continued Republican control of Congress suggested that the party was plenty viable at that level. Nevertheless, on one count—the nature of significant minor-party insurgencies—the 2000 results suggested that Bush would confront the challenges and opportunities of plurality leadership.

Given the razor-thin margins in key states where Ralph Nader hurt Al Gore, Bush may have won because of Nader's departure from the Democratic fold. It is true that Patrick Buchanan's share of the vote could be said to have denied Bush victories in some states, but Nader's vote totals in these states were often larger still. During the campaign of 2000, Bush fused appeals to his ideological base with self-conscious departures from party orthodoxy, which is a hallmark of savvy plurality leadership. The notion of "compassionate conservatism" fits comfortably within the basic premise of plurality leadership, which recommends subtle revisions to the presidential party's identity.

The Elections of 1824 and 1992

To get a clearer sense of Bush's legitimacy and leadership situation in historical perspective, one might look back to two other presidents. In early 1825, John Quincy Adams prevailed in the House of Representatives after no candidate in the effectively partyless contest of 1824 received a majority of the votes in the Electoral College. Immediately, a defeated Andrew Jackson railed against the "corrupt bargain" allegedly struck between Adams and the fourth-place finisher, Speaker of the House Henry Clay. The purported deal between Adams and Clay had the former agreeing to appoint the latter as secretary of state. When Adams did so, he added substantial fuel to Jackson's political fire. Jackson had won the popular vote by more than 10 percent, and he did not let Adams or the rest of the country forget it. In the ensuing four years, Jackson assembled a potent set of electoral claims rooted largely, though not exclusively, in the presumptive illegitimacy of the Adams presidency. Ultimately, those claims propelled Jackson to victory in 1828 and finally secured the enduring connection between the constitutional office of the presidency and the extraconstitutional domain of party politics.

One should not strain the comparison with more than it can bear, but the events of early 1825 are at least roughly analogous to the events of late 2000. In both cases, a popular vote winner was stymied not only by the Electoral College but also by the intervention of a co-equal branch of government and was ultimately forced to concede the election to a bitter rival. For our purposes, however, two key distinctions are more instructive than the similarities between the cases. First, where Andrew Jackson protested his defeat unrelentingly in the mid-1820s, the defeated Al Gore did nothing of the sort in 2000. Second, where John Quincy Adams had no viable, reliable party organization to which he might turn for support, George W. Bush enjoyed the effectively unanimous backing of a vigorous Republican apparatus before, during, and after the Florida controversy. Though it is tempting to think of the latter as a matter of course, the unbridled enthusiasm with which Republican elites advanced Bush's claims in the postelection period requires some elaboration and explanation. Moreover, Gore's dignified concession attracted substantial praise at the time, but, following Jackson's (admittedly remote) precedent, he might have protested a bit more loudly. Why did all of this turn out the way it did? Why, in other words, did Bush encounter so little trouble with the problem of legitimacy in the aftermath of such a hotly contested, highly controversial victory? To begin to answer these questions, one might turn to a more recent election for a second point of comparison.

In 1992, Bill Clinton won a classic plurality election. With a comfortable majority in the Electoral College, the Arkansas governor was the first Democrat to win a presidential election in sixteen years. After more than a decade in the presidential wilderness, many Democrats anticipated a productive era of harmonious unified government. Lost amid the celebration was the essential characteristic of Clinton's triumph: he carried only 43 percent of the popular vote. Like other plurality presidents before him, such as James Buchanan (45 percent in 1856), Abraham Lincoln (40 percent in 1860), Woodrow Wilson (42 percent in 1912), and Richard Nixon (43 percent in 1968), he won in spite of his party's continuing weakness in presidential politics. More to the point, his election confronted him with three related dilemmas.

First, Clinton encountered an abstract dilemma of legitimacy. This is admittedly an expansive concept, and it lacks clear empirical referents, but Bob Dole, the Republican Senate minority leader, seemed to know it when he saw it. As soon as the day after Clinton's 1992 election, Dole offered a telling interpretation of that victory. "Fifty-seven percent of the Americans who voted in the Presidential election voted against Bill Clinton," Dole intoned from the Senate chamber, "and I intend to represent that majority on the floor of the U.S. Senate" (from Tumulty 1993). Dole soon adopted a more conciliatory tone (in his public rhetoric, at least) after critics objected to his "rancorous" partisanship, but one can scarcely imagine a more resounding declaration of plurality politics.

Second, Clinton faced a practical dilemma of governance. Notwithstanding his lifelong ambitions, Clinton ran in 1992 for reasons larger than his own power prospects. He had in mind a number of ideas for improving the performance of the national government and, of course, the lives of American citizens. But he recognized that the constitutional system separates institutions and distributes lawmaking authority horizontally among branches and vertically between the federal government and the states. He hoped to enact measures that might give practical meaning to his rhetorical vision, but his limited victory rendered that task uncertain. How would Clinton make this fragmented system do what he wanted it to do? If nearly every member of Congress won a larger share of the popular vote than he did, how might he lead the national legislature with any authority?

Third, Clinton confronted a political dilemma of reelection. Perhaps he ran for reasons larger than simple ambition, but the old congressional maxim that one needs to save one's seat before one can save the world also applied to Bill Clinton as he assumed the presidency. Clinton clearly intended to run again in 1996, but he could not assume that the peculiar circumstances of his initial victory—especially the significant minor-party insurgency of Ross Perot—would repeat themselves in his bid for reelection. Clinton had to wonder: if he won only four in ten voters the first time, how might he expand his support on the road to reelection?

Though each of these dilemmas related to a specific dimension of presidential politics, they combined to encourage Clinton—just like most of his plurality predecessors—to swim upstream against the prevailing ideological and rhetorical currents of his party. In Clinton's case, of course, this incentive structure confirmed the incoming president's inclination to pursue the identity of a "New Democrat." One should note, of course, that Bill Clinton was present at the creation of the centrist Democratic Leadership Council (DLC) in 1985, later chaired the group, and invoked the New Democrats' holy trinity of opportunity, responsibility, and community as a central theme of his 1992 candidacy (Baer 2000). In a sense, then, the election of 1992 did not turn the incoming president into a New Democrat, but what it did was hugely important: it made a would-be New Democrat the incoming president, placing him at the vital center of the American party system. In addition, it set the stage for an intraparty struggle between Clinton and his centrist allies on the one hand and an array of unreconstructed liberals in Congress and their supporters on the other (Price 2002).

Contrast Clinton's treatment after the 1992 election—outright claims of his illegitimacy from conservatives who could not abide the new president and an uneven welcome from liberals who were unmoved by all the talk of New Democratic politics—with the reception George W. Bush received after his victory in 2000. In the latter case, the incoming president encountered congressional Democrats who were relatively docile and congressional Republicans who were both deeply supportive and broadly unified. Why the difference?

First, and most important, Bush encountered a Republican majority in the 107th Congress that was both narrower and shorter-lived than its

Democratic analog of the 103rd. While many congressional Democrats resisted Bill Clinton's reformist party project, in part because they had little reason to suspect in 1993 that their own electoral prospects turned on the success of that project, many Republicans had plenty of reason to believe in 2001 that the preservation of their tenuous congressional majorities would depend on the new president's vindication in office. One might note here that the Democrats had gained House seats in every congressional election since 1994; in the Senate, meanwhile, the Democrats had forged a 50-50 tie by erasing the Republicans' four-seat advantage in the elections of 2000. In this context, what would demonstrate Bush's legitimacy more clearly than a congressional majority rallying immediately to his side?

The primary point here is that the congressional Republicans of 2001 interpreted George W. Bush's 2000 election differently than the congressional Democrats had interpreted Bill Clinton's 1992 election. In the earlier case, Clinton's party was certainly pleased that he had prevailed, but many of his putative allies remained largely unmoved by the New Democratic formula during the 103rd Congress. In Bush's case, on the other hand, Republican elites moved quickly to bolster the new president. One can now place the Bush experience in context alongside these two points of comparison. Where John Quincy Adams had no real party to which he could turn in 1825, and where Bill Clinton could turn only to a divided (and in some ways recalcitrant) party in 1993, George W. Bush found in his fellow Republicans just what he needed in 2001.

A second factor could be that Republican elites endowed Bush with the legitimacy that flows from unified partisan support in part because the outcome of the 2000 election was so indeterminate, because the Court's decision in *Bush v. Gore* was likely to be perceived by some observers as partisan, and because the entire episode had produced such deep cynicism on all sides. Because potential charges of illegitimacy were so plausible, and thus the risk of illegitimacy so acute, Bush and the Republicans moved quickly to nullify such charges before the Democrats could get them off the ground. In the aftermath of *Bush v. Gore,* in other words, the Republicans may have suspected that the Democrats would hammer away at the uncertain legitimacy of the incoming Bush administration. To counter that would-be challenge, they circled the partisan wagons and denied that anyone could question the legitimacy of the outcome without treading on treasonous ground.

But a third element in this story remains to be explained: the fact that neither Al Gore nor the vast majority of elite Democrats questioned, at least publicly or loudly, the legitimacy of the Bush presidency. The only notable elite-level protest of the outcome took place when members of the Congressional Black Caucus walked out on the vote-counting ceremony in the House of Representatives. Unlike John Quincy Adams, who faced a bitterly determined Andrew Jackson and a budding Democratic juggernaut in the 1820s, and unlike Bill Clinton, who faced a conservative movement that simply never accepted his legitimacy, George W. Bush encountered a relatively quiescent Democratic opposition. Democrats had mobilized behind Gore during the Florida recount, of course, but once the Court stopped that process, they folded the battle flag. Why were the Democrats so reluctant to depict President-elect Bush as somehow less than fully legitimate?

When Gore conceded in a nationally televised address on December 13, 2000, he enjoyed a generous reception in the political press. At the conclusion of the wrenching process in Florida, the conventional wisdom suggested that the country could not take any more scorched-earth politics. If the country suffered from "Florida fatigue," this line of thinking went, Al Gore had only one choice once the game was up: concede like a gentleman and move on. Indeed, we suspect that the weight of journalistic opinion, which implied that the only thing less legitimate than a Bush presidency would be an ongoing Democratic protest of same, led Gore and his fellow partisans to choose to simply concede. They decided that playing the legitimacy card would prove more costly than beneficial, in part because establishment opinion simply would not tolerate it.

Another factor in the Democrats' relative quiescence after *Bush v. Gore* was the fact that some congressional Democrats ran and won in states and districts where George W. Bush had done quite well, and with the balance of power in Congress so precarious, "some" often equals "enough." Such Democrats figured they had little to gain from a sustained challenge of the fundamental legitimacy of the Bush presidency. Again, the contrast with John Quincy Adams and Bill Clinton is instructive. In the former case—where Adams won only 31 percent of the popular vote—members of Congress who might challenge the president's legitimacy had little to fear in their own states and districts. In the latter case—where Clinton won with 43 percent of the popular vote—few Republicans hailed from states or districts where Clinton had outpolled them in 1992. In 2000, however, Democrats such as Senators John Breaux of Louisiana, Ben Nelson of Nebraska, Tim Johnson of South Dakota, and Max Baucus of Montana had more to lose than to gain from making aggressive, partisan charges of illegitimacy against the new administration.

Unraveling the Best-Laid Plans

We have suggested that George W. Bush entered office facing significant challenges of legitimacy and leadership. We have argued, however, that Bush was well positioned to make the best of these challenges despite his controversial victory, and, we suggest, this would have been true even without 9/11. Our argument has essentially been that Bush, given his dilemma, benefited from being on favorable historical ground. First, the currents of partisan realignment were favorable to Bush and gave him the kind of support from congressional Republicans that he dearly needed. Second, although Bush's victory resembled those of other plurality presidents, he was able to read a different meaning from his victory than his immediate plurality predecessor, Bill Clinton, could divine from his.

By the time of his second inauguration, in 2005, Bush could look back and see gains for Republicans in the House and Senate. He owned a re-election victory that was more comfortable than his initial victory, though thin by historical standards. Urged on by his chief strategist, Karl Rove, the president thought big, believing he could forge a durable Republican realignment. He unapologetically claimed a mandate and famously noted that he had earned "political capital, and now I intend to spend it." But midway through 2005, observers were already noting that the president seemed to be failing on several policy fronts and that Republicans were growing more restless (Baker and VandeHei 2005). By 2006, Republicans had lost their House and Senate majority. And by 2008, the Democratic presidential nominating contest drew a historically large turnout and Republicans braced for the worst in congressional races. The November election results served up precisely what Republicans had feared: a victory by Barack Obama in many states won by Bush, a drop in vote percentage in nearly all states and among nearly all social groups, the first Democratic presidential candidate to finish with significantly more than 50 percent of the vote since Lyndon Johnson in 1964, and the loss of yet more seats in the House and Senate, bringing the Senate Democrats very close to the magic number of sixty needed to defeat any Republican-led filibuster. The hope for a Republican political era was dashed, and many analysts speculated that the party would be in the political wilderness for some time.

What went wrong? Simply put, virtually all of the political infrastructure supporting Bush in 2000 disappeared. We highlight several contributing factors.

First, Bush's strategy of straddling Democratic issues and positions—which emerged centrally from his plurality status, as well as from his experience in Texas—led to disappointment among conservatives. In his first term, Bush followed a two-path strategy. He appealed to conservatives with substantially lower taxes, higher defense spending, an increased role for faith-based organizations, the elimination of "partial-birth" abortions, and business-friendly deregulation in some areas. On these issues, Bush needed to hold on to every Republican vote he could in the highly partisan atmosphere in Washington. His successes on these matters pleased Republicans and angered Democrats. Bush's second path was to move in on Democratic turf, on issues such as education, campaign finance reform, and Medicare drug coverage. Conservatives expressed anger about all three policy initiatives—and Democrats were not happy about having to share credit on their signature political issues—the first because it advanced a huge new federal role, the second due to its free-speech implications, and the third because it created an expensive new federal entitlement. That the *National Review,* the stalwart periodical on the right, printed an editorial in its July 23, 2003, issue titled "Left Turn: Is the GOP Conservative?" gives some sense of conservative unease at these developments. The *Review* noted that it never expected Bush to be a solid conservative on issues like small government, racial preferences, or immigration but believed that he would act conservatively on most matters. Granting Bush a passing grade for national security, judicial appointments, and tax cuts, the *Review* viewed him as unable to deliver on the rest of the conservative agenda. Moving into his second term, Bush's compassionate conservatism became, to many, simply "big government conservatism." The response to Hurricane Katrina weakened the Republican brand label's claim that it was the party not of big government but well-run government. The president's proposed immigration reform seemed to many to be too soft on illegal immigration and went down to defeat. His disastrous nomination of Harriet Miers for a Supreme Court seat perplexed his conservative supporters.

Second, some of the favorable issue ground inherited by Bush shifted, without accompanying shifts by the president or party. While one could certainly make a plausible argument that, in many respects, life in the United States had never been better (Easterbrook 2008), the political reality was that vast swaths of the public felt uneasy and vulnerable to economic insecurity (Hacker 2006). The positive economic conditions of the late 1990s gave way to more troubled times. Unemployment, inflation, gasoline prices, mortgage foreclosures, and the federal budget deficit mushroomed. Trade deficits grew, while the relative value of the dollar fell. Health care costs continued to climb, while the percentage of the workforce covered by company retirement pension plans continued to decline. Virtually none of these issues elicited a forceful or vocal response, whether market oriented or otherwise, from the president and his fellow partisans. Whether this failure to grasp the shifting landscape was due to preoccupation with the Iraq war, poor political calculations, or some other factor, it surely contributed to the overall public clamor for a change in direction in Washington and to the fact that nearly 80 percent of the population in mid-2008 said the country was on the wrong track.

Third, the very fact of being a plurality president presents some difficult obstacles to establishing a durable partisan victory. Previous plurality presidencies did not end well. James Buchanan, elected in 1856, was the last Democrat elected to the presidency for twenty years. Woodrow Wilson, elected in 1912 and reelected in 1916, carried a Democratic majority with him to Washington, but divided government was in place by the beginning of his second term and a unified Republican government by the end of that term. Richard Nixon, elected in 1968 and 1972, contributed to massive Democratic gains in the 1974 election and the Democrats' return to the White House in 1977 following Gerald Ford's short tenure in office. Bill Clinton's problems culminated in GOP victories in 2000. Standing alone among the plurality group is Abraham Lincoln. Though he met personal tragedy, Lincoln would by most standard accounts be considered a successful president, and his party prospered under the unique conditions of Reconstruction. The point here is not that Bush was doomed to failure but that the plurality presidency is an inherently difficult one. Derailment is all too possible.

Fairly or not, the long, difficult war in Iraq became the centerpiece of Bush's presidency and dramatically affected every other aspect of it. The president's time and attention were focused there, even as the public's focus shifted to domestic matters. Federal spending for the war was not available for other purposes, such as giving voters further tax breaks. Disappointing developments in Iraq combined with economic difficulties to drag down the president's popularity.

All of these circumstances had opposite effects on the two parties. Focused around the president's war and anti-terror agenda, the Republican Party failed to craft a compelling domestic agenda. The party base recoiled from what it saw as the congressional party's comfort with big government, key constituencies such as social conservatives felt neglected, independents who had supported the party grew tired of scandals involving individual members of Congress, and the increasing unpopularity of the Iraq war sapped the enthusiasm of all but the most ardent party supporters.

For the Democratic Party, however, the war was a singular organizational boon. The war was deeply unpopular among party activists. Like the think-tanks, magazines, and radio talk shows that vaunted conservative ideas in the 1970s and 1980s, the Democrats were winning the battle for Internet supremacy during the Bush presidency. The disputed election of 2000 set the stage for the growth of left-leaning political commentary on the Web. But it was opposition to the war that was the spark that turned these embers into roaring partisan flames. The liberal blogosphere exploded during Bush's first term and continued apace in his second term. Opposition to the war was the glue unifying this movement. Gary Jacobson (2007) shows that support for the Iraq war was more divided by party than was true of any other conflict after World War II. Moreover, opposition on Iraq translated into distrust of and opposition to President Bush on other issues. Perhaps more than at any point since the early 1970s, the liberal political infrastructure had been revitalized. The new centrism of the Democratic Leadership Council had receded to the point that it was nearly institutionally invisible during the 2008 nomination process. Blogs and social networking sites provided forums for policy and political analysis, discussion of candidates, organization around the country, and massive fund-raising. Meanwhile, the Republican Party lagged well behind this new organizational curve.

The net impact of these four factors—dissatisfaction among conservatives and Republicans, a shifting domestic agenda, the inherent difficulties of plurality leadership, and the Iraq war and its attendant revival of the liberal political infrastructure—combined to thwart the president's leadership. To be sure, Bush continued to use the unilateral powers at his disposal, but where he needed congressional cooperation, his leadership stalled. In 2007, the president's support score in Congress was as low as Bill Clinton's in 1995, and both of these were the lowest since *Congressional Quarterly* began computing such scores in 1945.

The four factors also pushed in a Democratic direction. On party identification, Democrats gained nationally while Republican identifiers declined, and the Democratic gains among those age eighteen to twenty-nine were especially dramatic. Given highly partisan voting—about 90 percent of party identifiers will tend to vote for their party's candidate—this created a stiff headwind against Republican victories. Democrats were favored on virtually every issue by 2008. A survey by the Pew Research Center for the People and the Press in February 2008 showed Democrats were thought likely to do a better job on the environment, energy, health care, education, reforming government, the economy, taxes, morality, Iraq, foreign policy, and immigration. Republicans led only on handling terrorist threats. These trends continued throughout 2008. Overall, the issue landscape was bleak for Republicans. Democrats once again owned traditional Democratic issues and had muscled Republicans aside on many issues typically owned by Republicans.

Over his two terms, President Bush's leadership overcame potentially debilitating legitimacy concerns but ultimately came apart on the rocks of a rapidly shifting political landscape. With substantial losses in 2006 and 2008, the Republicans' hoped-for durable realignment was derailed, and there was little ground for optimism that it could be revived anytime soon. To many analysts, the electoral crash resembled those of other wayward presidents and parties: Herbert Hoover and the Republicans in 1932 and Jimmy Carter and the Democrats in 1980. Each of those defeats inaugurated a dramatic and lasting shift of public policy in the new presidencies of Franklin Roosevelt and Ronald Reagan, respectively, and the early months of the Obama administration suggested to many observers that the new Democratic president was hoping to follow in the footsteps of those role models.

4

BUSH AND CLINTON
Contrasting Styles of Popular Leadership

JOHN F. HARRIS

N ear the midpoint of George W. Bush's administration, the editor of
this volume collected a series of first appraisals of the president's political style and governing impact. Steven E. Schier aptly titled his
compendium *High Risk and Big Ambition.*

At the time of that volume's publication in 2004, and for at least a year
afterward, much American political and academic commentary viewed
Bush through the prism of his outsized ambitions. Bush and his team—
most notably Vice President Dick Cheney and chief strategist Karl Rove
—signaled early in the administration that they were not motivated primarily by the drive for short-term political success. They were striving
for historic change on multiple fronts. Around the world, they sought to
impose a new doctrine of "preemption," including the option of preventive war, against national security threats. In Washington, the administration was determined to assert the supremacy of the executive branch
and to reverse what Cheney, in particular, viewed as a dangerous weakening of the powers of the presidency in the decades since Watergate. Bush
was similarly expansive in his political ambitions: he wanted to create the
conditions that would permit lasting dominance for conservative ideas,

with the national Republican Party serving as the essential vessel for these ideas.

Big ambitions, indeed. What was most striking for a long while was that Bush seemed to be succeeding in his aims. Brushing aside the inconvenient fact that he lost the popular vote to Al Gore in 2000 and required the intervention of the Supreme Court to win office, the new Republican president moved quickly to pass the tax cuts that were the centerpiece of his economic agenda. Empowered by a surge in public support for an aggressive national security policy after 9/11, he launched wars in Afghanistan and Iraq. Certain that he could win any contest in which he could position himself as the candidate of strength and clear thinking, he ran a reelection strategy that ignored Clinton-era assumptions about the primacy of swing voters and the imperative of capturing the center with soft-edged, nonideological policies. In 2004, many classic indicators, such as presidential approval ratings and the percentage of Americans saying the country was on the "wrong track," suggested that Bush was headed for defeat. When he prevailed over John F. Kerry on election day, even many Democrats seemed ready to concede that Bush had managed to create a new model for the modern presidency—and that his big ambitions looked quite likely to be fulfilled.

Days after Bush's reelection, tens of thousands of Democrats convened in Little Rock, Arkansas, for the dedication of Bill Clinton's presidential library. Following tradition, Bush was on hand for the occasion—as was Rove, who moved through the crowd like a conqueror. At the time, many Democrats said what their party needed was their own version of Karl Rove—a political practitioner who could energize liberals as Rove had done with conservatives and use even narrow political margins to power large policy gains. Even Clinton bounded over to Rove, to say, "I want to talk politics with you. You just did an incredible job and I'd like to really get together with you, and I think we could have a great conversation" (from Halperin and Harris 2006, 138).

Soon enough, it would become apparent that Bush and Rove had not repealed the laws of political gravity. The second term brought a nearly unrelieved string of policy and political setbacks. A growing majority of Americans believed that the Iraq war, the signature project of Bush's administration, had been a mistake. What was intended to be his transformational domestic policy achievement, a plan for the partial privatization of Social Security, was a flop that not even Bush's Republican allies on Capitol Hill wished to be associated with. And, after the 2006 elections, there were a lot fewer of those allies: a dozen years of GOP dominance in Congress evaporated in a Democratic rout. Bush's own approval ratings hovered at Nixonian lows throughout 2007 and 2008, with fewer than 30 percent of Americans backing his presidency, as John White and John Zogby note in their chapter here. Democratic electoral triumphs in 2006 and 2008 marked a final repudiation of Bush's big plans.

Little wonder that the attention of the political, academic, and media communities analyzing Bush's presidency shifted away from his big ambitions and on to his high risks—and the enormous costs that came from his inability to navigate those risks.

As he limped to the end of his presidency, it strained memory to recall that, just a few years before, even Democrats looked with envy at Bush—not for his policies but for the way he marshaled political power.

The Problem of Polarized Politics

Bush's early successes, and his later failures, came within a distinct context: the polarization that has marked American politics for a generation. There is an underappreciated aspect of Bush's presidency: he, Rove, and Cheney had clear notions—a theory of the case—about how to survive amid polarized politics and indeed how to use the ideological and cultural divisions in American life to advantage.

An aside, given that most readers of this volume will do so in an academic setting, seems relevant here. It is not intended as an insult—but, alas, no compliment either—to note that the Bush administration was more influenced by the thinking and analytical methods of political scientists than any modern presidency. Recall that Dick Cheney did graduate work in political science. Karl Rove taught a class at the University of Texas, and journalistic visitors to his office learned to expect expositions on historical voting trends and realignment theories—replete with ostentatious citations to the work of assorted academics.

The abstract views about elections and executive power at the top of the Bush White House closely complemented a more gut-level feeling: disdain for Bill Clinton. It is scarcely possible to overstate the antipathy of people in the Bush White House for their immediate predecessors. This was not merely (or even mainly) disapproval of Clinton's personal failings and scandals. It was a contempt for his governing style, which Bush and his team regarded as weak and focused on short-term political prosperity at the expense of lasting achievements. In public, Bush nodded toward this view in his acceptance speech at the 2000 Republican convention:

"The path of least resistance is always downhill." In private, Bush political operatives would invariably cite Clinton and his political style when making a point of what they were trying to avoid.

What the Bush operatives were reluctant to acknowledge is that Bill Clinton, too, had a theory of the case about how to prosper in a polarized electorate—one that informed the sometimes random-seeming excursions and improvisational efforts of his presidency. Clinton's theory about the causes of the polarized electorate was quite different from Bush's. From these different theories flowed two different styles of presidential power.

In the wake of the 2004 election, Mark Halperin and I undertook an effort to understand the similarities and differences in the political methods of the forty-second and forty-third presidents and their implications for the future. We conducted several lengthy interviews with key characters in the story, including Bill Clinton, Dick Cheney, and Karl Rove.

The Way to Win: Taking the White House in 2008 (2006) argued that the two presidents had created two distinct brands of politics: Bush Politics and Clinton Politics. Even casual followers of politics usually have at least some familiarity with the differences between these two brands. People know that Clinton Politics was obsessed with the pursuit of ideologically moderate "swing voters." Bush Politics, by contrast, was obsessed with energizing the "base" of conservatives and maximizing their turnout at the polls.

What these superficial understandings—correct, as far as they go—typically do not appreciate is that there was a more profound disagreement at the root of these two political styles: why is American politics so polarized?

Clinton's Unifying Leadership

Clinton Politics has one answer to this question. The answer is that the American people—as opposed to American politics—are not particularly polarized. Bill Clinton believes that the divisions in our politics are echoes of the great debates of his youth in the 1960s and early 1970s—over the Vietnam War, over civil rights, over women's rights and the sexual revolution. These were profound matters at the time. But most Americans have come to terms with—and reached a sensible balance—over these issues. Voters, Clinton believes, are not ideologues but synthesizers. For instance, lots of people are not comfortable with excessive sex and violence in popular culture, but they also do not wish to return to 1950s-era values about the role of women or treatment of homosexuals. They think the move toward racial equality was a good thing, and they will support affirmative action—so long as it is not a rigid system that promotes racial quotas and diminishes merit. Voters are suspicious of foreign trade and overseas military entanglements, but with the right kind of education from political leaders, voters are clear-headed about, and even supporters of, the reality of globalization. Regarding their fellow citizens, Clinton believes, most Americans want unity and are willing to extend a measure of tolerance. Regarding politicians, he believes, most Americans want them to eschew ideology in favor of practical solutions that will affect real problems in people's lives. People have moved on from the old sixties-era battles. Consensus, not division, describes the reality of the American electorate.

Given this, why is American politics still so fractious? Clinton and practitioners of Clinton Politics believe it is because a generation of political operatives has a vested interest in conflict. These operatives thrive by ruthlessly identifying and exploiting the narrow range of issues where Americans have not yet reached a consensus: gay marriage, for instance, or the regulation of guns. (Clinton believes these techniques of exploiting voter fears exist primarily on the Right, but this plainly reflects his own experience and preoccupations. Conservatives will have their own examples of Democratic operatives exploiting divisions for advantage.)

If you believe, as Clinton does, that the divisions within the electorate are more artificial than real, a particular style of presidential leadership follows naturally. The goal is to aggressively lay claim to the political center by transcending partisan rancor and uniting the large majority of Americans who want to be united. This is accomplished by blurring, in most cases, ideological lines and by a relentless focus on high presidential approval ratings.

A president who believes in Clinton Politics knows that effective politicians must be constantly focused on weak links in the administration's political flanks and be engaged in constant reassurance. In his conversation with us, Clinton cited his determination to talk about gun control in 1996 in New Hampshire—a state where the gun issue had made Clinton unpopular.

"Our guys in Washington thought I was crazier than the March Hare, you know," Clinton explained. "I said, 'I'll go up there and I want to meet with the deer hunters.' . . . And they said, 'Well, you don't want to talk about this.' I said, 'Oh, yes I do'" (from Halperin and Harris 2006, 104–5).

By engaging the issue directly, Clinton said, he could soften perceptions that his policies were hostile to hunters rather than narrowly focused on the problem of urban crime. In the same conversation, Clinton was critical of 2004 Democratic nominee John F. Kerry for not focusing more on white, married evangelical voters—even though there was no prospect he would win a majority of this bloc. "You know, if you want to run this country, particularly if you are a Democrat and you're going to push for change, you have to be able to talk to everybody," he said. "We give other people permission to define us if we don't even enter the conversation" (from Halperin and Harris 2006, 105).

From this position of strength in approval ratings, Clinton believed, a president can marginalize the opposition as extremists out of touch with the mainstream. This brand of politics, though, never securing him a popular vote majority in 1992 or 1996, did allow him to frustrate his Republican opponents, who were convinced that if they could only expose Clinton's personal failings they could drive him from office. During the Monica Lewinsky uproar, as Clinton's job approval rating continued to climb, Jay Leno joked that Clinton was doing so well that he was already planning his next sex scandal.

For all the chortling, Clinton's political techniques rested on a serious idea: that successful presidents must be national unifiers.

Bush's Clarifying Leadership

George W. Bush believed something different: that successful presidents must be national clarifiers. This is the essence of Bush Politics: The divisions in the electorate are not artificial. They are genuine. Bush, and certainly Rove, believed that there are legitimate differences on which Americans were powerfully, and narrowly, divided. In the culture, the battle is between those who support a secular culture and those who find this culture, particularly as expressed by the mass media, to be coarse and unfulfilling. Nationally, there is an authentic divide over the size of the federal government and the taxes necessary. Abroad, there is an equally authentic divide over the proper response to an age of terrorism and the proper balance between force versus diplomacy, between unilateral action and coalition building.

If you believe, as Bush and Rove do, that polarization flows from real divisions rather than manufactured ones, and from central questions rather than marginal ones, a particular style of presidency is logical.

Rather than blurring lines, Bush was quite willing to illuminate and even exaggerate them. Rather than trying to reassure opponents, Bush was willing to antagonize them—at least on issues in which he believed he could excite his own supporters in even greater measure.

A supreme example was national security. Many Democrats and media commentators expected that, after 9/11, this was an issue above politics. They were infuriated when Rove, in a 2002 speech to the Republican National Committee, made plain that it was not. "We can go to the country on this issue because they trust the Republican Party to do a better job of protecting and strengthening America's military might and thereby protecting America," Rove said (from Edsall 2002). Terence McAuliffe, the Democratic National Committee chairman, sputtered in response, "If the Bush White House now politicizes the war, that would be nothing short of despicable" (from Edsall 2002). Rather than high approval ratings, Bush and Rove sought voter intensity. Rather than focusing on reassurance and speaking to voters who disagreed, Bush focused on speaking to voters who already agreed. The Rove-McAuliffe exchange set the tone for the partisan wars that would follow throughout the Bush years—on the war, on civil liberties, on the response to the Hurricane Katrina disaster, on Supreme Court nominees.

Bush Politics, when it was succeeding, was aided by two closely intertwined trends. The first was the proliferation of conservative media platforms—on talk radio and the Web—that had blossomed over the preceding years as alternatives to the so-called "mainstream media." It was no surprise that, while often shunning establishment organs like the *Washington Post*, Bush and Cheney gave regular interviews to such commentators as Laura Ingraham and Rush Limbaugh. The second trend consisted of the technological advances that allowed much more precise targeting of conservative voters—identifying them through polling and consumer data and mobilizing them through the Web and e-mail, and supplementing those virtual efforts with carefully coordinated in-person contacts.

During the Kerry campaign, the candidate and his Democratic allies achieved every one of their turnout targets in the critical swing state of Ohio, which decided the 2004 election. In that state and nationwide, Kerry won significant majorities of independent voters—the very people that Clinton courted so ardently. But Bush won Ohio by bringing the turnout of conservatives to even higher levels. It was the signature triumph for Bush Politics.

There are caveats and qualifications to Bush Politics and Clinton Politics. There were of course times when Clinton made public gestures to mobilize his base in the fashion of Bush Politics. There were times when Bush, in the fashion of Clinton Politics, tried to soften his image and make inroads with the opposition, such as with his courting of Hispanic voters. In the main, however, Bush believed in a dramatically different model of power than Clinton. The differences between Bush Politics and Clinton Politics are real. And they centered on precisely the question Schier identified in 2003—the willingness to accept risk in the pursuit of his political and policy ambitions.

Bush believed great presidents must be willing to divide Americans on large questions. Only by dividing Americans—as Franklin D. Roosevelt did and as Ronald Reagan did two generations later—can large goals be accomplished and Americans be reunited around new assumptions and levels of understanding. Great presidents are unifiers only in retrospect.

Initial Verdicts

Presidents willing to risk big are sometimes going to lose big. There is no ambiguity about the initial verdict on Bush Politics: his presidency was a political failure. Far from building a long-term Republican majority, Bush presided over the steady disintegration of Republican rule in Washington. Far from using early victories as a lever to achieve further gains, Bush's early victories—most notably, on lowering marginal tax rates for upper-income earners—were nearly his only lasting ones. (The exception looms large: his two successful Supreme Court nominees in the second term.)

The Democrats who envied Bush and Rove after the 2004 election now know better. The logic of Bush Politics was that the president might have a low ceiling of support, but, thanks to loyal partisans, he would enjoy a high floor. But the floor turned out to be lower than Bush and Rove supposed. In early November 2008, on the eve of the election of his successor, his approval rating measured 25 percent, its record low. This is about the same number that Richard Nixon had to endure through most of 1974, the year he was forced from office. It is only a few points higher than Gallup's all-time low for any president, the 22 percent recorded by Harry Truman in February 1952 (Gallup 2008b). Indeed, in his second term, Bush surpassed Truman as the longest serving president since World War II without a majority of the public's approval (Langer 2008).

Gallup's numbers also plotted the devastating deterioration in Bush's public support among all groups. In January 2002, still buoyed by the rush of support after 9/11, Bush enjoyed 98 percent approval among Republicans, 83 percent approval among independents, and 73 percent approval

69

among Democrats. By the end of October 2008, those figures were 61 percent among Republicans, 20 percent among independents, and 5 percent among Democrats.

Some remained unfazed by these astonishing numbers. In an interview with ABC News, when asked about poll numbers showing deep opposition to the Iraq war, Vice President Cheney replied, "So?"

"You don't care what the American people think?" responded interviewer Martha Raddatz.

"You can't be blown off course by polls," said Cheney. "This president is very courageous and determined to go the course. There has been a huge fundamental change and transformation for the better. That's a huge accomplishment" (from Venkataraman and Brady 2008).

Low public approval, legislative defeats, political defeats—at least at first blush, Bush Politics was a failure.

Might first-blush looks be misleading? The political models described by Bush Politics and Clinton Politics are not restricted to parties. There are Republicans who practice something like Clinton Politics. At least in some moods, John McCain, with his instinct for crossing partisan lines and his appeal to independent voters, was one of them. What's more, there are liberals who believed that the antidote to eight years of Bush Politics was to have a Democratic president who shared Bush's willingness to draw sharp lines and engage in partisan combat. *New York Times* columnist Paul Krugman stood out among liberal columnists for his early coolness to Bush's successor, Barack Obama—a skepticism that flowed in part because he believed Obama was naïve about the fight for power. "Mr. Obama, instead of emphasizing the harm done by the other party's rule, likes to blame both sides for our sorry political state," Krugman complained. "And in his speeches he promises not a rejection of Republicanism but an era of postpartisan unity" (Krugman 2008).

Some conservatives, meanwhile, note that what happened to Bush was not a failure of his political model but a consequence of his policies. The Iraq war did not go well, and when it foundered, so did his presidency. If it had gone well, according to this line of thinking, he would have engineered the kind of transformational presidency he sought and Bush Politics would have been vindicated. If, in history's view, the Iraq war comes to be seen as a more successful venture than it looks now, Bush Politics might ultimately be vindicated.

At this writing, that day looks far away. In the here and now, the evidence is that Clinton Politics—for all its frustrating compromises and line blurring and even pandering—is a more successful model for the modern presidency. The problem with Bush Politics is that it works only when it works: it leaves too narrow a margin of support when events and political fortunes go astray. What's more, it leaves its practitioners almost by design living in isolation—talking to one another, reinforcing each other's views, viewing people who disagree not simply as opponents but as mortal foes. That is an unpromising formula for a democracy—particularly in an increasingly pluralistic nation living in an increasingly interconnected world. A successful president must constantly balance the imperative of rallying supporters with the political and even moral imperative of persuading skeptics and must forever harness his or her grand ambitions to a deeply rooted sense of reality.

Popular Politics

PART II

5

A PUBLIC DEATH

The Failure of the Bush Presidency and the Future of American Politics

JOHN KENNETH WHITE and

JOHN ZOGBY

n 2004 we wrote the following words concerning the relationship between the American public and George W. Bush: "Ever since the hor-
rific events of September 11, 2001, George W. Bush has ranked among
the most popular of American presidents. Americans admire his
strong leadership, especially in the tension-filled days following the terrorist attacks. Just three weeks after Osama bin Laden and his al Qaeda
network recreated a twenty-first century Pearl Harbor on American soil,
Bush's job approval rating soared to an astronomical 90 percent, exceeding the previous record of 89 percent posted by George H. W. Bush during
the Persian Gulf War" (White and Zogby 2004, 79; Moore 2001).

How times change! Beginning in January 2006 and continuing to the
dismal end of his tumultuous presidency, when Americans were asked by
pollsters to rate Bush's job performance, the numbers of those approving
were stuck between the upper twenties and low thirties. By election day
2008, only about 27 percent of voters liked the job Bush was doing—one of
the lowest approval ratings ever recorded. While 89 percent of those who
approved of Bush voted for Republican John McCain, 67 percent of those
who *disapproved* of Bush's performance in office supported Democrat Ba-

rack Obama (Edison Media Research and Mitofsky International exit poll, November 4, 2008). In many ways, the 2008 election was all about George W. Bush. And the unfavorable light in which voters saw the incumbent all but ensured the election of the first African American president.

How Bush was transformed from the "fifty-something" percentage president we described in 2003 into a "twenty-something" president by 2008 is a fascinating tale. It is a story of woe, from the chaos that descended upon Iraq, an inept federal response when Hurricane Katrina drowned the city of New Orleans, to a financial crisis that shook Wall Street institutions to their core (leaving some venerable companies, including Lehman Brothers, bankrupt). The cumulative effect of these disasters was to hollow out George W. Bush's presidency and subject him to a kind of public death. Simply put, from 2006 until he left the White House on January 20, 2009, Americans had given up on the forty-third president. Even those closest to Bush expressed doubts. Matthew Dowd, who served as Bush's pollster in 2000 and 2004, told the *New York Times* that Bush had lost his "gut-level bond with the American people," including Dowd himself (Rutenberg 2007). As Bush was preparing to leave the White House, Dowd told *Vanity Fair*'s editors that the headline of the Bush presidency was "MISSED OPPORTUNITY, MISSED OPPORTUNITY, MISSED OPPORTUNITY" (Murphy and Purdum 2009). For many, it is not just the poor implementation of policies both at home and abroad but the missed opportunities to pass much-needed legislation (particularly immigration reform) after 9/11 that constitutes the tragedy of the Bush presidency.

Of course, George W. Bush's reduced public standing did not diminish the institutional powers of the office he held. Until the moment he left the White House, Bush could still veto legislation, issue pardons, name Cabinet officers and other officials, issue executive orders, and pursue the wars in Iraq and Afghanistan (as he did in 2007, when thirty thousand soldiers were deployed to Iraq thanks to a new "surge" strategy). Moreover, Bush's diminished public standing did not impede his ability to appoint Supreme Court justices, as he did in 2005 when he selected John Roberts and Samuel Alito. Indeed, Bush's reshaping of the Supreme Court is one of his most important legacies. But the fact remains that the only thing George W. Bush could *not* do for much of his second term was govern with the consent of the governed.

The failure to find weapons of mass destruction in Iraq, an inept and clumsy response to Hurricane Katrina, and an economic crisis led to a crisis of confidence. Americans judged both Bush and his fellow Republicans to be inept stewards, a dramatic reversal of the confidence voters once placed in the GOP as a party of government. In 1980, the year Ronald Reagan won the presidency, voters saw the Republicans as "better able to manage the government" by a margin of 42 percent to 29 percent (CBS News/*New York Times* poll, August 2–7, 1980). Even when George H. W. Bush ran into strong political headwinds in late 1991, two-thirds still associated the word "Republican" with "competence" (ABC News/*Washington Post* poll, October 24–29, 1991). But by 2007, the public was evenly split on the question of George W. Bush's competence: 46 percent thought he was competent; 49 percent disagreed (Opinion Research Corporation poll, March 9–11, 2007). As one Republican professional noted after the Katrina disaster, "We're supposed to be the party of competence. When we look incompetent, it's a real problem" (Cook 2007). Peggy Noonan, a former speech writer for Ronald Reagan and George H. W. Bush, believes that George W. Bush "destroyed the Republican party, by which I mean he sundered it, broke its constituent pieces apart, and set them against each other. He did this on spending, the size of government, war, the ability to prosecute war, immigration and other issues" (Noonan 2008).

The policy failures and missed opportunities made Bush not just an unpopular president but one who became the object of public scorn. In a 2007 opinion survey, 42 percent told pollster John Zogby that they were "ashamed" to have Bush as their president (Zogby International poll, May 17–20, 2007b). Other polls showed a public believing Bush had sundered the Constitution itself: 64 percent thought Bush had abused his presidential powers (American Research Group poll, November 9–12, 2007) and 31 percent favored the impeachment of either President Bush or Vice President Cheney or both (Zogby International poll, August 23–27, 2007a). On the eve of Barack Obama's inauguration, 75 percent said they were glad Bush was leaving the White House (CNN/Opinion Research Corporation poll, December 19–21, 2008). CNN senior political analyst William Schneider likened the Bush presidency to a "failed marriage," adding, "As President Bush prepares to leave office, the American public has a parting thought: Good riddance" (CNN broadcast 2008). When pollsters asked people in late 2008 (Pew Research Center poll, December 3–7, 2008) to use one or two words to describe their impressions of George W. Bush, the responses received were particularly devastating:

Incompetent, 43 percent

Honest, 24 percent

Idiot, 21 percent

Arrogant, 18 percent

Good, 15 percent

Failure, 12 percent

Honorable, 12 percent

Stupid, 12 percent

Ignorant, 11 percent

Selfish, 10 percent

Mediocre, 9 percent

Ass, 7 percent

Ineffective, 7 percent

Inept, 7 percent

Integrity, 7 percent

Many historians came to share the public's view that the Bush presidency is headed, in the words of Princeton University's Sean Wilentz, "for a colossal historical disgrace" (Wilentz 2006). George Mason University political scientist James P. Pfiffner contends that Bush's excesses—e.g., suspending the Geneva Conventions and interrogating prisoners using harsh methods; creating military tribunals to try terrorist suspects; permitting warrantless wiretapping; and deciding which laws he will enforce (and which ones he will not)—endanger democracy itself: "Even if President Bush was a noble defender of freedom, the authority that he claims to be able to ignore the law, if allowed to stand, would constitute a dangerous precedent that future presidents might use to abuse their power" (Pfiffner 2007). Columbia University political scientist Eric Foner maintains that Bush "has managed to combine the lapses of leadership, misguided policies and abuse of power of his failed predecessors," concluding that "there is no alternative but to rank him as the worst president in history" (Foner 2006). Yale University political scientist Stephen Skowronek believes that Bush's abuses institutionalized a monarch-like presidency that can be easily torn asunder whenever its inhabitants possess imperial-sized ambitions (Skowronek 2008, 150–66).

One President, Two Images

In the television age, presidencies are remembered by the images associated with them. Often, the pictures resemble a split television screen: on one side, there is a flattering photograph; on another, a darker visage.

Thus, there are the images of John F. Kennedy's vigor in 1960 as he became the youngest person to be elected president, and the horror of his assassination three years later. There is Lyndon B. Johnson's mammoth 1964 victory and his haggard appearance upon leaving office in 1969. There is the newly elected Richard M. Nixon admonishing Americans to "lower our voices" and "stop shouting at one another" (Nixon 1969), and a woeful, teary-eyed Nixon announcing his resignation in 1974. There is a happy Gerald R. Ford toasting his English muffins in 1974, and a grim-faced president announcing the Nixon pardon one month after assuming office. There is the erstwhile peanut farmer Jimmy Carter arguing in 1976 for a government that was "as good, honest, and decent" as its people (Carter 1979), and an aged Carter three years later declaring a "crisis of confidence." There is a triumphant George H. W. Bush following the Gulf War in 1991, and a befuddled president standing in front of a new-model grocery scanner one year later, seemingly out-of-touch. Only Ronald Reagan escaped this bifurcated television screen that became the fate of so many modern-day presidents.

George W. Bush, on the other hand, fits the prevailing pattern. Like his predecessors, Bush has two distinct images that have become embedded in the mystic chords of public memory. The first is his 2001 stance atop the ruins of the World Trade Center following the 9/11 attacks, bullhorn in hand and telling a crowd of firefighters, "I hear you, the rest of the world hears you, and the people who knocked these buildings down will hear all of us soon" (Bush 2001d). A second set of darker images surrounded the forty-third president as he left office: tragic scenes of people wailing for help after Hurricane Katrina while a seemingly indifferent president flew overhead on Air Force One; daily images of roadside bombings, carnage, and casualties in war-torn Iraq; and a financial meltdown that gave a jittery public the economic shivers.

One reason why Bush came to be held in such low esteem during his second term is the manner in which he won reelection. In 2004, Bush captured a huge majority of Republicans and forgot about everyone else. To wit: Bush received 93 percent of the GOP vote but won only 11 percent of Democrats' votes. Bush also received just 48 percent of his support from independents and only 45 percent backing from moderates. These results contrast sharply with Bush's immediate GOP predecessors. In 1980 and 1984, Ronald Reagan won the votes of one in four Democrats; in 1988, George H. W. Bush received one in five Democratic votes. As a result, Democrats were placed on the defensive, as the party stewed over how to win back the so-called "Reagan Democrats." But after the 2004 election, there were virtually no "George W. Bush Democrats." So when Bush ran into serious political difficulties, he was already in a weakened position among Democrats, independents, and moderates. Thus, by the end of Bush's second term, only 8 percent of Democrats and 20 percent of independents gave him a positive job approval rating (Zogby International poll, December 10–13, 2008).

There is an old maxim in politics that says, "How you win determines how you govern." For eight years, Bush's governing base relied *exclusively* on Republican backing. But even the solid Republican backing Bush once enjoyed cracked during his second term. In December 2008, only 49 percent of Republicans backed Bush, a far cry from the 93 percent Republican backing he received in 2004 (Zogby International poll, December 10–13, 2008; Edison Media Research and Mitofsky International exit poll, November 2, 2004).

Even among Republican elites, Bush's once-formidable standing has been vastly reduced. In a provocative 2008 work entitled *Comeback: Conservatism That Can Win Again,* conservative Republican and former Bush speech writer David Frum wrote that the Bush presidency was a conservative catastrophe: "So many mistakes! And such stubborn refusal to correct them when there was still time! So many lives needlessly sacrificed, so much money wasted, so many friends alienated, so many enemies strengthened" (Frum 2008, 2). Former American Enterprise Institute scholar Bruce Bartlett concurred, writing that Bush was a "pretend conservative" who masqueraded as a "partisan Republican" (Bartlett 2006, 1, 16).

The Failed Presidents

Upon assuming the presidency in January 2009, Barack Obama inherited a dispirited and disillusioned country. Two years earlier, the Gallup Organization took stock of faith in government and found a widespread public disenchantment not seen since the dark days of Richard M. Nixon's Watergate scandals:

- 51 percent trusted the federal government to handle international problems, the lowest level recorded since 1972
- 47 percent trusted the federal government to handle domestic problems, the lowest percentage since 1976

- 43 percent trusted the executive branch of government, just above the 40 percent expressing support in April 1974, four months before Nixon resigned the presidency
- 50 percent trusted the legislative branch, a decline from 62 percent in 2005
- 55 percent trusted "the men and women in political life who are seeking office," matching the lowest percentage that was recorded in 2001 (Jones 2007).

One of this chapter's authors, John Zogby, found that two-thirds believed that the United States was facing a "very serious crisis." As Zogby stated on the eve of the 2008 election, "The public mood is not just dark. What's darker than dark? The mood is getting ugly" (Zogby 2007). That darkness prevented Bush's presidency from enjoying any public revival in 2008, an outcome that was ensured by the financial crisis that beset the country that October. As a hospital doctor might have put it, "The patient is on life support."

It is instructive to look at other presidents who, like George W. Bush, also failed to recoup their public standing. Since the advent of public polling in 1937, there are six presidencies that have been judged by the people of their time as failures, that is, there was a substantial period in which the president's approval was well below 50 percent, with no hope of recovery: Harry S. Truman, Lyndon B. Johnson, Richard M. Nixon, Gerald R. Ford, Jimmy Carter, and George H. W. Bush. In 1952, Harry Truman saw his approval rating fall to a mere 22 percent after he became mired in the Korean War (Gallup poll, February 9–14, 1952). Day after day, U.S. soldiers battled North Korean and Chinese troops for control of one small hill after another, with neither side winning a decisive victory. Americans quickly tired of Truman and concluded that he had no plan for resolving the Korean conflict. Frustrated, they turned to Dwight D. Eisenhower, especially after the former World War II general reassured voters by promising, "I shall go to Korea" (from White 1997, 97).

Lyndon B. Johnson suffered a similar fate, as he saw his 1964 landslide victory melt away in the tropical heat of Vietnam. A Gallup poll taken in August 1968 found just 35 percent gave him positive marks (Gallup poll, August 7–12, 1968). Johnson's job approval ratings suffered from the unpopular war in Vietnam and racial riots, and they made it nearly impossible for his vice president, Hubert H. Humphrey, to win in 1968—a predicament similar to the one that befell John McCain forty years later, when an unpopular president proved to be his undoing. In many ways, LBJ foresaw his own political demise, telling columnists Rowland Evans and Robert Novak after his overwhelming win in 1964, "I was just elected by the biggest popular margin in the history of the country, fifteen million votes. Just by the natural way people think and because Barry Goldwater scared the hell out of them, I have already lost two of these fifteen and am probably getting down to thirteen. If I get into any fight with Congress, I have already lost another couple of million, and if I have to send any more boys into Vietnam, I may be down to eight million by the end of the summer" (from Evans and Novak 1968, 514–15).

In 1973, Richard M. Nixon's presidency was caught in the web of Watergate. Opinion polls showed Nixon with a dismal approval rating of 30 percent (Gallup poll, October 5–8, 1973). Repeatedly, the beleaguered president tried to change the public focus, even admonishing Congress in 1974, "One year of Watergate is enough" (Nixon 1974). But the disclosure of the Watergate tapes only intensified the media scrutiny of Nixon's wrongdoings. By the time he left office, just 24 percent of his fellow Americans approved of his performance (Gallup poll, August 2, 1973).

Gerald R. Ford, too, suffered a crippling blow to his public esteem. With a breathtaking 71 percent job approval upon taking office, his support dropped 21 points after he granted a pardon to Richard Nixon little more than a month later (Gallup polls, August 16–19, 1974, September 27–30, 1974). Declaring that Watergate had been "an American tragedy" and "someone must write the end to it," Ford hoped the pardon would turn attention away from Nixon and toward more pressing matters—especially high energy prices and a stubbornly persistent inflation rate (Ford 1974). But 60 percent said Ford was wrong to issue the pardon, and 62 percent thought it condoned two standards of justice: one for the rich and powerful, another for the ordinary citizen (Louis Harris and Associates poll, September 23–27, 1974). Ford could not escape the political fallout: a 1976 exit poll found 14 percent cited Watergate and the Nixon pardon as important issues, and an overwhelming percentage of these disenchanted voters backed Jimmy Carter (CBS News exit poll, November 2, 1976).

Jimmy Carter was the fifth president to suffer a fatal collapse in public support. Upon entering the White House, Carter received a 66 percent job approval rating (Gallup poll, February 4–7, 1977). But three years later, Carter's positive ratings plummeted to 29 percent (Gallup poll, June 1–4, 1979). In response, Carter delivered his famous "malaise speech" and proclaimed a "crisis of confidence" in government (Carter 1979). Voters disagreed, believing that the constitutional mechanisms established by the framers still worked and that nothing was wrong with their character. The voting public thought something was decidedly wrong with Carter, however, and they ousted him in a landslide. So great was the distaste for Carter that public disdain for him persisted long after his presidency ended; a 1988 Harris poll, for example, gave Carter the dubious distinction of being first (with 46 percent) in the category "least able to get things done" (Louis Harris and Associates poll, November 11–14, 1988). Only in more recent years has Carter recouped his standing, thanks to an unusually effective post-presidency (see Brinkley 1998) and a longing for truth-in-government that powered one of his books, *Our Endangered Values: America's Moral Crisis,* to the top of the *New York Times* best-seller list (Carter 2005).

George H. W. Bush suffered a similar fatal fall in public esteem. Shortly after the successful Persian Gulf War, the elder Bush had an 89 percent approval rating (Gallup poll, February 28–March 3, 1991). But Americans are a restless people, and after the quick war, a floundering economy became a primary concern. In 1992, voters thought Bush was inattentive to their economic worries, and he received a dismal 37 percent of the vote in his reelection bid—a percentage that corresponded exactly to his approval rating in a preelection Gallup poll (Gallup poll, October 22–23, 1992).

What unites these six failed presidencies is each man's inability to change the subject. Harry S. Truman could not get the public's mind off the Korean War. Lyndon B. Johnson could not get people to focus on anything except Vietnam and race riots. Richard M. Nixon could not erase the airing of the Watergate tapes (even as he tried to erase them in fact). Gerald R. Ford could not ameliorate voter anger over the Nixon pardon. Jimmy Carter became identified with his malaise speech and the American hostages in Iran. And George H. W. Bush was a foreign policy president at a moment when voters could not have cared less.

George W. Bush shared the fate of his failed predecessors for precisely the same reason: he could not change the subject. Bush could not shift the public's focus from his errant judgment regarding the presence of weapons of mass destruction in Iraq and his postwar failure to secure that country (even though the troop surge did much to curtail violence and bring some semblance of order there). Similarly, Bush could not take the public focus away from the devastation that crippled New Orleans after Hurricane Katrina and his government's inept response to it. Finally, Bush could hardly hope to alter the public's attentiveness to the financial meltdown that turned into the most severe economic crisis since the Great Depression. Whenever Bush tried to refocus attention elsewhere, voters answered with a resounding "NO!" Early in his second term, one poll found 62 percent disapproving of George W. Bush's proposals to privatize Social Security (CNN/*USA Today*/Gallup poll, July 22–24, 2005). At his final White House press conference, Bush acknowledged that his focus on Social Security had been a "mistake" (*New York Times* 2009).

Iraq, Hurricane Katrina, a credit crunch, plunging stock markets and 401(k) retirement savings plans, and a prevailing sense that George W. Bush did not know how to use the levers of government all became the dominant themes of his second term. While there was some good news during the Bush years—for example, effective presidential speeches following the 9/11 attacks and the capture of Saddam Hussein by U.S. forces in Iraq—even with each successive positive development, Bush's "bounce" in the polls got smaller. Indeed, the various "Bush bounces" were akin to that once-famous 1960s-era Wham-O Superball, whose initial bounce attained great heights and then dribbled into smaller bounces until the end inevitably came.

What Comes Next

In 1980, Ronald Reagan taunted Jimmy Carter and the Democrats by asking, "Can anyone look at the record of this administration and say, 'Well done?'. . . Can anyone look at our reduced standing in the world today and say, 'Let's have four more years of this?'" (Reagan 1980). By 2008, the many Democratic presidential candidates, including Barack Obama, were effectively quoting Reagan's words, but in reference to George W. Bush and his fellow Republicans. At one Democratic debate, for instance, Bush's name was invoked forty-seven times (all of them negatively), while at a comparable Republican debate Bush was referenced just twice (and one of these mentions was uncomplimentary [Nagourney 2007]). Even when Democrats Barack Obama and Hillary Clinton took swipes at each other, Democratic voters remained focused on attacking George W. Bush. Typical was Hillary Clinton's first television advertisement, which made Bush (and not her fellow Democratic candidates) her primary target:

HILLARY CLINTON: As I travel around America, I hear from so many people who feel like they're just invisible to their government.

ANNOUNCER: Hillary Clinton has spent her life standing up for people others don't see.

HILLARY CLINTON: Now if you're a family that is struggling and you don't have health care, well, you are invisible to this president. If you're a single mom trying to find affordable childcare so that you can go to work, well, you're invisible, too. And I never thought I would see that our soldiers who serve in Iraq and Afghanistan would be treated as though they were invisible as well. Americans from all walks of life across our country may be invisible to this president, but they are not invisible to me. And they won't be invisible to the next president of the United States. (http://www .hillaryclinton.com, September 11, 2007)

During the general election, Barack Obama criticized the Bush-Mc-Cain record so often that it seemed that John McCain's first name had been changed to "Bush." Typical was Obama's oration at the Democratic national convention: "John McCain has voted with George Bush 90 percent of the time. Senator McCain likes to talk about judgment, but, really, what does it say about your judgment when you think George Bush has been right more than 90 percent of the time? . . . Tonight I say to the people of America, to Democrats and Republicans and independents across this great land: Enough" (Obama 2008).

It is often said that every president gets one line in the history books. Thus, for George Washington, "He was the Father of his Country." For Abraham Lincoln, "He saved the Union and freed the slaves." For Franklin Roosevelt, "He launched the New Deal and fought World War II." For Ronald Reagan, "He helped end the cold war." For George W. Bush, the line is not fully formed, but these words are likely to appear: "Iraq," "terrorism," "September 11," and "financial meltdown."

In many respects, today's Republican Party stands in a spot similar to the one where the Democratic Party stood back in 1968. The former president and party icon is held in disrepute, its governing coalition is fractured, it is ideologically is spent, and it has no real reason for holding on to power other than to keep the opposition party out of the White House. Just as no Democrat would have shouted "Four More Years!" in 1968, no Republican could holler "Four More Years!" forty years later. Just three weeks prior to election day in 2008, John McCain admitted as much, running a television advertisement in which he stated the obvious: "The last eight years haven't worked very well, have they?" (from Kurtz 2008). Instead of defending Bush, McCain tried to persuade voters that his administration would be "Four Different Years"—a hard case to make to disillusioned voters but one he nearly succeeded in making until he made a disastrous vice-presidential pick in Alaska governor Sarah Palin and the credit crunch and home foreclosures contributed to the financial crisis that dominated the fall headlines.

After eight years of George W. Bush, the country was emotionally exhausted, but in 2008, voters did not choose to take a breather by giving John McCain the keys to the White House. Rather, they wanted the nation to move in a radically different direction—thus delivering a mandate that Barack Obama recognized and began to fulfill during his first days as president when he issued executive orders reversing several prior Bush decisions. No matter how President Obama and the nation fare over time, one thing is certain: the failed George W. Bush presidency has set the parameters for what comes next in our country's political story.

6

BUSH AND RELIGIOUS POLITICS

JAMES L. GUTH

F ew of George W. Bush's Yale fraternity brothers would have predicted his rise to the presidency, despite his distinguished political heritage. Even fewer would have expected his administration to be the "most resolutely 'faith-based' in modern times" (Fineman 2003). In fact, the first "insider" book on Bush's tenure in office opened with an anecdote about religious life in the White House and closed with a Bible story (Frum 2003b). By the last year of his tenure, books and articles linking the president's actions to his personal religious beliefs or those of his political constituency were too abundant to enumerate, and the vast majority of those works were critical on both counts.

How did religion shape the Bush presidency? Some saw it as a central theme pervading the administration's policy and emphasized by its personnel (Kengor 2004b); for others, religion was a mere political stratagem, cynically employed to sell programs designed to meet purely secular goals (Marsh 2007). The truth lies somewhere between these extremes. Faith did play a crucial role in Bush's life, giving him the sense that he had a calling, and this faith had an impact on his drive for the presidency and his actions in office. In the eyes of his friends, this faith was a source of strength, but to critics it was something dangerous. The religious configuration of the electorate was never far from Bush's calculations (or those of adviser Karl Rove), and his policies offered new roles for religious institutions. Key personnel in his administration, as well as their decisions, often reflected the actively religious members of the GOP's constituency.

Religious Groups in American Politics

Any assessment of American politics must consider two competing interpretations of religious alignments. *Ethnoreligious* theory emphasizes the historic European religious groups that migrated to America and often multiplied upon reaching its shores. Nineteenth-century party politics consisted largely of assembling winning coalitions of contending ethnoreligious groups (Kleppner 1979). Well into the twentieth century, the GOP represented historically dominant mainline Protestant churches, such as the Episcopalian, Presbyterian, and Methodist denominations, while Democrats spoke for religious minorities, primarily Catholics, Jews, and evangelical Protestants (especially in the South). By the 1980s, these configurations had shifted as mainline Protestants dwindled in number, evangelicals moved toward the GOP, the long-term Catholic-Democratic alliance frayed, and African American Protestants became a critical Democratic bloc. Growing religious diversity added Muslims, Hindus, Buddhists, and others to the equation, usually on the Democratic side. Still, even today many analysts think in ethnocultural terms, referring to the "evangelical," "Catholic," "Jewish," or "Muslim" vote.

An alternative view is the *culture war* or *religious restructuring* theory, introduced into political parlance by James Davison Hunter's *Culture Wars: The Struggle to Define America* (1991). Hunter saw new religious battles emerging *within* the old traditions, based on theological differences: for example, "orthodox" believers accept "an external, definable, and transcendent authority" and adhere firmly to traditional doctrines, while "progressives" replace old religious tenets with new ones based on personal experience or scientific rationality (Hunter 1991, 44). The progressives are joined by secular Americans who reject religion entirely but view morality through the same personal or science-derived prism. These religious divisions quickly congealed around political issues such as abortion, feminism, gay rights, and the role of faith in public life, but there was soon evidence that they were underlying elements for other political attitudes as well.

Although Hunter's thesis captivated some scholars and pundits, most analysts concluded that his dualist model was too simplistic, that moral battle lines shifted from issue to issue, and that most citizens were non-combatants (Williams 1997; Fiorina et al. 2005). Some scholars have confirmed, in part, the political cleavages Hunter envisioned (Layman 2001), but old markers of religious tradition still retain considerable electoral influence. Thus, understanding the complex religious politics of the Bush era requires both the ethnoreligious and the restructuring perspectives.

George W. Bush and Religious Politics

Although the young George W. Bush had joined in his family's dutiful Presbyterian/Episcopalian observance, he experienced a dramatic religious rebirth as an adult, perhaps in response to business reverses and drinking problems. Bush renewed his faith in 1986, joined a Bible study group, and reassessed his life—experiencing one of those "moments that set you on a different course." Thereafter, he read the Bible and prayed regularly, spoke often of his faith, and gave generously to religious causes. Although Bush's later critics routinely characterized him as a "fundamentalist," his own Christian theology was both too fuzzy and too ecumenical to fit that rubric. He later joined his wife Laura in attending United Methodist services, but he clearly inhabited the conservative wing of that mainline Protestant denomination (Carnes 2000, 37).

These new religious interests soon proved useful politically. During his father's 1988 presidential campaign, his own contest for governor of Texas, and his race for the White House in 2000, Bush honed a religious strategy that remained remarkably consistent throughout his presidency. The first element was his strong appeal to evangelical Protestants, especially Southern Baptists, Pentecostals, and members of nondenominational suburban megachurches, which together constituted about one-quarter of the public. By upbringing and affiliation Bush was a "mainliner"—his Episcopalian, Presbyterian, and Methodist roots put him squarely in the "old" GOP religious coalition, but by experience, belief, and sensibility, he was "evangelical," speaking fluently the language of "new" party constituencies. Bypassing well-known but controversial Christian Right figures such as Pat Robertson, James Dobson, and Jerry Falwell, he relied instead on a "kitchen cabinet" of less prominent evangelical leaders, such as Richard Land, of the Southern Baptist Convention, who vouched for his religious credentials. Indeed, Bush's associations with Christian Right leaders never measured up to his easy rapport with local evangelical clergy and church-goers.

89

This "evangelical strategy" complicated Bush's pursuit of traditionalist Catholics, who shared conservative social views with evangelicals but also a long history of mutual animosity. Bush's 2000 campaign appearance at fundamentalist Bob Jones University before the crucial South Carolina primary angered Catholics, but he quickly countered with a public apology and ensured that Catholics—preferably with clerical collars—were highly visible during the fall campaign. Once in office, Bush consulted frequently with Catholic activists, addressed issues dear to traditionalist Catholics, visited Catholic churches and schools, quoted frequently from the writings of Pope John Paul II (Guth 2004), and met with both him and his successor, Benedict XVI. Indeed, a key aide noted that Bush's domestic agenda was "inspired, at least in part, by Catholic social teaching" (Gerson 2007, 164). Such efforts were warmly received by many Catholics, who thought of Bush as "the second Catholic president" (Lloyd 2008). And despite occasional friction, Bush maintained strong ties with the Vatican throughout his years in office.

Bush fared worse with his own ancestral religious tribe, the mainline Protestants. Although its adherents are now fewer in number, mainline Protestantism still retains some of its historic political importance, counting national leaders among its own far out of proportion to its membership. Bush's appeal to mainliners was secular: many are classic economic conservatives, prominent in the business and professional worlds, and receptive to his pro-business policies and tax cuts. But they are often moderate or even liberal on social issues, such as abortion and gay rights. And the leaders of mainline churches, whether in denominational lobbies or the National Council of Churches, invariably take "progressive" stances on national policy questions, domestic or international.

Not surprisingly, then, the Bush White House pointedly ignored mainline lobbyists, a decided change from Bill Clinton's practice (Guth 2000; Tipton 2007). Even officials of his own United Methodist Church were persona non grata. Nevertheless, he sought to reassure mainline church-goers that he was not a prisoner of the Christian Right and that he was advancing cautiously on a pro-life agenda, avoiding anti-gay rhetoric, and generally staking out moderately conservative positions on social issues. Nevertheless, Bush could not restore the GOP's historic dominance among mainline Protestants.

Even less successful was Bush's signature effort to cut into the large Democratic advantage among religious minorities. Although he cultivated relationships with prominent African American pastors and hoped that "faith-based programs" might build ties between the GOP and black clergy, this strategy was undercut by Congress's rejection of such proposals and the encroachment of international issues on the agenda. In a similar vein, Bush's appeal to both Jewish and Muslim voters met only equivocal success. The Bush outreach did produce increased support among Latino Protestants, but not among Latino Catholics, and even the gains among Protestants were lost as congressional Republicans resisted Bush's call for a moderate policy on immigration reform. (For a detailed review of Bush's 2000 religious coalition, see Guth 2004.)

Rhetoric and Personnel

Once in the White House, Bush set a distinctive example of religious practice and rhetoric. Although inaugurations are often infused with the rituals of "civil religion," the 2001 Bush ceremonies went beyond the usual parameters. The religious ambience was set by a pre-inaugural prayer meeting at St. John's Episcopal Church and inauguration prayers by evangelist Franklin Graham, heir apparent to his father Billy Graham's evangelistic organization, and by Kirbyjohn Caldwell, a black Methodist who was a friend of Bush. The inaugural address oozed religious symbolism, and soon after taking the oath of office Bush designated the next Sunday as a "national day of prayer." Many liberals criticized the conservative Christian tone of these events, but traditionalists applauded.

Bush maintained the public posture of a religious presidency, albeit an ecumenical one. He kept to a daily regimen of prayer and Bible reading, as well as regular Sunday worship (increasingly "in house" at the White House or Camp David), and met frequently with clergy, particularly those from religious groups vital to his electoral and policy concerns. Evangelical leaders were seen as crucial not only because they were critical links to that large constituency but also because they might prove crucial to achieving administration proposals. Black Protestant clergy who had a special interest in faith-based programs were frequent White House visitors, as were Roman Catholic bishops, providing further evidence of Bush's ongoing efforts to woo those voting blocs (Guth 2004).

Almost from the start, fierce debates raged over Bush's religious rhetoric. To some, he merely replicated the "civil religion" practiced by previous chief executives, albeit with "principled pluralism" (Gerson 2007, 106). To others, Bush's rhetoric was more frequently religious and sectarian, thus eroding the separation of church and state. Although polemics over his rhetoric outran analysis, eventually scholars concluded that

Bush's religious language did indeed have distinctive characteristics. David Domke and Kevin Coe (2008) found that use of "God language" in presidential addresses rose during the Reagan years and remained high through the next three administrations, including George W. Bush's. Although each president after Eisenhower was more inclined than his predecessor to speak in religious venues, Bush set the record. And he was also more likely to make explicit Christian references in "holiday" greetings to the nation. No doubt this behavior reflected both the president's personal faith and the clear expectations of his religious constituency (see Guth 2004, 125–26; Guth et al. 2006, 233).

Bush's White House staff also represented the GOP's new religious coalition more fully than did earlier administrations. Traditionalists were pleased that so many staffers were religiously observant, albeit from different backgrounds. Chief speechwriter Michael Gerson, a devout evangelical, would be responsible for many of Bush's memorable lines over the next six years, often drawing on religious themes; he later recruited William McGurn, a conservative Catholic, to assist him. Another speechwriter, Peter Wehner, soon became director of strategic initiatives and a key Bush adviser (Gerson 2007). Chief of staff Andrew Card's wife was a Methodist minister, and counselor Karen Hughes was a Presbyterian elder. Condoleezza Rice, who was national security adviser and later secretary of state, was a devout Christian and the daughter of a Presbyterian pastor, and evangelical Tim Goeglein served as a vital liaison to conservative religious constituencies. Kay Coles James, a black activist for the Christian Right, directed personnel matters. Speechwriter David Frum, who was Jewish, famously captured the evangelical ambience of the White House, "where attendance at Bible study was, if not compulsory, not quite *uncompulsory,* either" (Frum 2003b, 3–4). Even staff from minority traditions, such as Judaism, tended to be devout.

Bush liked to start Cabinet meetings with prayer (although Gerson complained they were often "overly scripted" [Gerson 2007, 221]) and preferred executives who could offer them without discomfort. Although his initial Cabinet ran the gamut of Christian communities, it favored the faithful. From Secretary of State Colin Powell, an active Episcopalian, to Education Secretary Rod Paige, a Baptist deacon, to Commerce Secretary Don Evans, a devout Methodist and Bush's old Bible study partner, many had strong religious credentials—sometimes too strong. John Ashcroft's nomination as attorney general aroused controversy as pro-choice liberals doubted that a fervent Pentecostal could enforce the Freedom of Access to

Clinic Entrances Act (1994), while evangelicals saw his confirmation as a test of Bush's moral commitment.

Later, Ashcroft's own prayer groups at the Justice Department were criticized as violations of the establishment clause, and he remained a lightning rod for liberals while not always moving fast enough for social conservatives (Toobin 2002). His successor, Alberto Gonzales, attended the same evangelical Episcopal parish as speechwriter Gerson (Goldberg 2006). Indeed, for Christian conservatives, the Justice Department was a haven where they could attack religious discrimination, pornography, and other traditionalist concerns (Lewis 2008; Lithwick 2007; Shenon 2007). The Office of the Solicitor General pursued establishment and free-exercise cases before the Supreme Court, in stark contrast to the Clinton administration's avoidance of such issues (Lewis 2008). And to a remarkable degree, government briefs echoed those of conservative Christian litigators (Kasniunas and Rossotti 2007).

Traditionalist Catholics held Cabinet posts as heads of Housing and Urban Development (HUD), Health and Human Services (HHS), and Veterans Affairs (VA). HUD secretary-designate Mel Martinez occasioned a stir among conservatives when his religious reflections about his nomination were "censored" from transcripts in some national papers. Tommy Thompson, the pro-life former Wisconsin governor and HHS secretary, had not always followed Catholic teaching in political decisions, but his feuds had been with Catholic liberals. Catholic traditionalists were especially numerous at second- and third-tier posts, joining many evangelicals, such as Wade Horn, assistant secretary for children and families in HSS, and James Rogan, a former California congressman, head of the Patent Office. Bush also named one pro-choice Catholic, Tom Ridge, to the Cabinet (as secretary of Homeland Security), after having passed him over as a vice-presidential possibility in 2000.

Although there is no systematic information available, religious conservatives also held a significant number of second- and third-tier posts during Bush's first six years in office. Many were evangelicals, but others were conservative Catholics or mainliners. At one point, Pat Robertson's Regent University claimed that 150 graduates worked in the administration, while conservative Catholic publications regularly featured coreligionists serving with Bush. Even at the lower end of the hierarchy, traditionalists abounded: Patrick Henry College in Virginia, an evangelical school specializing in public affairs, was said to have more of its students interning at the White House than any other college. Although such staffing trends alarmed liberals, experienced observers noted that the numbers of religious conservatives did "not seem incommensurate with their political importance to the president" (Robinson and Wilcox 2007, 222).

Although Bush's first Cabinet was notably lacking in Jews, Jewish groups enjoyed surprising access to the White House, in part because of the receptiveness of evangelical staffers (Frum 2003b, 246–60). Eventually, Jewish Republicans appeared in important posts, as when Josh Bolten moved from the Office of Management and Budget to replace White House chief of staff Andrew Card in 2006, and Michael Mukasey, an observant Jew, took over Justice in 2007. In replacing his original Cabinet, however, Bush tended to downplay recognition of his religious coalition in favor of loyalty and administrative experience, although some appointees, such as Treasury Secretary Henry Paulson, were religiously devout. At the second and third tiers of management, Bush continued to recognize his religious constituency by giving important posts to individuals with strong religious backgrounds.

Policy and Politics in the First Term

During his first term, Bush sought to make public policy mesh with his own values and those of his religious coalition. Indeed, specific examples are almost too numerous to list. He pushed for marriage incentives in welfare reform legislation, allowed federal funds to be used to restore historic houses of worship, challenged state medical marijuana and euthanasia laws, responded to persecution of Christians abroad, proposed dramatic initiatives to fight AIDS in Africa, and emphasized abstinence in pregnancy prevention programs, to name only a few. In these instances, the GOP traditionalist coalition united behind administration policies. But the most visible religious politics involved three major fields: abortion and stem-cell research, the faith-based initiative and educational vouchers, and international policy after 9/11.

For traditionalists, abortion represented the litmus test for Bush. Despite his pro-life sympathies and rhetoric, he had always moved cautiously. He had chosen a pro-life running mate, Dick Cheney, but refused to exile pro-choice Republicans from his entourage or, later, his administration. The First Lady publicly opposed reversal of Roe v. Wade, and Bush himself doubted that public opinion was ready for that change without the growth of a new "culture of life." Nevertheless, he implemented pro-life policies within existing opinion by reinstating Reagan's "Mexico City rule," which prohibited agencies from funding international organizations that promote abortion; by supporting the Unborn Victims of Violence Act (2004); and by advocating medical coverage for unborn children under the Children's Health Insurance Program (Jelen 2007). Bush also promoted a ban on "partial birth" abortion, signing a bill that passed Congress in 2003 and successfully defending its constitutionality in the courts. Even during the final days of his administration, the Health and Human Services Department issued rules requiring all recipients of department funds to certify that they did not force health care workers to engage in providing abortions against their conscience.

Bush's ultimate contribution to the pro-life cause may have been his early federal court nominations of many sympathetic jurists, often traditionalist Catholics or evangelicals, such as noted church-state law expert Michael McConnell (Silverstein 2007). Although most of these nominations cleared the Senate, a few vocal pro-life nominees were held up by Democrats on the Senate Judiciary Committee, including Texas Supreme Court justice Priscilla Owen, former Clinton Justice Department official Miguel Estrada, and Alabama attorney general William H. Pryor Jr. The hearings for Pryor, a devout Catholic, erupted into full-scale warfare when Republican senators charged Democrats with anti-Catholic bias, eliciting angry responses. Meanwhile, pro-choice and pro-life groups prepared for a future Armageddon over Supreme Court vacancies.

While partial birth abortion and judicial nominations united pro-life forces behind Bush, his prolonged deliberation over embryonic stem-cell research divided them. Many scientists saw such research leading to new treatments for disease, but most pro-life groups and the U.S. Conference of Catholic Bishops (USCCB) wanted a total ban on federal funding because the research destroyed human embryos. Pope John Paul II himself lobbied Bush, but some conservative religious leaders were not as adamant, sensing perhaps the growing public support for research, even among evangelicals and Catholics. Bush had endorsed a ban during the 2000 campaign, but HHS Secretary Thompson kept the issue open, and as some conservative religious leaders reconsidered their position, so did Bush. After long consultations with scientists, clergy, and ethicists, he rendered a Solomonic decision allowing funding for "existing lines" of stem cells but not for any produced by future destruction of embryos. The president's decision disappointed fervent pro-lifers but met with surprisingly positive responses from most evangelical leaders and even from some Catholic traditionalists (although the USCCB complained). In the end,

95

Bush avoided a serious rupture with pro-lifers while partially accommo-dating researchers' demands (Frum 2003b, 106–10; Jelen 2007). Moreover, Bush continued to support a total ban on human cloning and promised to veto any legislation expanding federally funded embryonic stem-cell research. By the 2004 election, pro-life groups were again firmly aligned behind the White House.

The faith-based initiative and educational vouchers presented even more complicated constituency problems. To some extent, these questions divided religious leaders along culture war fractures, with traditionalists leaning toward the president and modernists and secularists opposing him. But battle lines were more complex. The Catholic Church, with long experience in providing social services, was generally supportive. Some religious minorities, such as black Protestants, also favored allowing reli-gious institutions to deliver public services but were often suspicious of an "illegitimate" Republican president. Evangelicals were deeply split: many endorsed the idea enthusiastically, but some feared federal money would compromise their religious mission or produce unacceptable government regulation.

Despite these crosscurrents, Bush plunged in. On January 29, 2001, he announced an initiative to foster cooperation between religious groups and federal agencies, created the White House Office of Faith-Based and Community Initiatives (OFBCI) and satellite offices in five Cabinet de-partments (HHS, HUD, Education, Labor, and Justice), issued executive orders removing some barriers to religious participation, and proposed legislation to lower others. The legislative issues proved too difficult to re-solve quickly, however. John DiIulio, the Catholic scholar who headed the White House OFBCI, found the whirlpools of religious politics too strong to navigate. After a public feud with evangelical leaders, DiIulio resigned and was replaced by Jim Towey, a committed Catholic with consider-able legislative and administrative experience. Although Bush's proposal cleared the House, it foundered in the Senate over provisions allowing religious group beneficiaries to restrict hiring to those within their faith. Such provisions were demanded by most traditionalists but rejected by religious liberals and church-state separationists, who feared discrimina-tion on the basis of race, gender, or sexual preference. The lack of strong support and continuing attention from the White House itself (aside from the president's) was also an obstacle to resolution (Black, Koopman, and Ryden 2004; Gerson 2007, 169–71). Similarly, the cautious Bush commit-ment to educational vouchers was soon reduced to rhetoric praising parochial—especially Catholic—schools and providing modest political support for voucher experiments, most notably in Washington, DC.

Bush finally settled for legislation encouraging charitable contributions but continued to insist on religious groups' right to hire within the faith when using public funds. Meanwhile, the administration issued new regulations allowing religious groups to qualify under existing law. Seven Cabinet agencies created offices on faith-based services, funded pilot projects, and conducted outreach to encourage participation by religious institutions. Critics (including some inside the administration) saw these ventures as a cynical play for electoral support from black and Latino Protestants or as a device to channel funds to politically helpful clergy (Kuo 2006).

In normal times, one might expect that Bush's interactions with religious groups would center on "life issues," charitable choice, and other social policies. Ironically, Bush's religious strategy was subjected to the most intense scrutiny as a result of a national security crisis. The 9/11 attacks, the Afghanistan war, the invasion of Iraq, and renewed engagement with the Israeli-Palestinian conflict brought the president's own personal faith and handling of religious issues into sharp relief. Indeed, by 2008, a cottage industry had appeared to mass-produce arguments that American foreign policy was distorted by Bush's religious worldview and/or that of his supporting religious constituencies (for examples, see Guth 2006).

The 9/11 attacks had evoked even more religious rhetoric from Bush than was typical of presidents during national crises. Whether in memorial services, speeches to Congress, or public statements, the president gave voice to religious themes, drawing meaning from the crisis. Although his language was often Christian in origin, Bush spoke in the most ecumenical vein possible, especially after an incautious reference to a "crusade" against evildoers angered Muslims. Nevertheless, to critics his rhetoric smacked of Christian dualism, painting the war on terror as a pure struggle between good and evil (Domke 2004). Many even saw Bush's policy driven by apocalyptic "end-times" thinking, central to some evangelical theologies, although this assertion is clearly mistaken (Robinson and Wilcox 2007, 230; Gerson 2007, 99).

Although 9/11 united most religious communities behind the president in classic "rally 'round the flag" fashion, there was the special problem of dealing with the American Muslim community. Here, the president initially got high marks, as he forcefully reminded Americans that the war on terror was not directed at Islam. Bush invited Muslim clerics to

97

participate in the national memorial service for 9/11 victims, visited a Washington mosque, met Muslims in the White House, and hosted an Id al-Fitr there on November 19. In highly publicized events, the president invoked interreligious harmony, despite pointed barbs from some Christian allies.

The united religious front broke down, however, as Bush instigated hostilities abroad. Afghanistan began the erosion, as liberal Catholic and mainline leaders worried about the scope of the military campaign and the prospect of civilian casualties, while evangelicals, as well as leading Catholic traditionalists, quietly supported the president. When Bush moved against Iraq, however, a full-blown religious dispute erupted, as mainline denominations and the National Council of Churches protested. Although the press depicted a united Protestant front against the president, including his own United Methodist Church, Bush drew strong backing from evangelicals, including officials from the Southern Baptist Convention and Assemblies of God. Jewish organizations were divided and stood apart from the religious debate (Goodstein 2002; 2003), but anti-terrorism policies quickly antagonized American Muslims, who had actually provided some electoral support for Bush in 2000.

Perhaps the most visible debate occurred among Catholics, always of strategic concern to Bush. As Pope John Paul II warned against military action, American bishops argued that Bush's arguments for invasion had not met the criteria for a "just war." Catholic traditionalists were torn between affection for the president and respect for religious authority. Some traditionalists such as Deal Hudson and Michael Novak argued that "just war" criteria were in fact met and that, in any event, such prudential judgments were for political, not religious leaders. Novak even visited Rome to press Bush's case with church officials, without effect (Allen 2003). The impact of all of this elite religious agitation on public opinion was unclear. The press reported extensive discussions among conflicted Catholics and observed heated debates in mainline churches. Polls showed that churchgoers heard much about Iraq from the pulpit, usually in line with the dominant position of their tradition: evangelical clergy backed the war, while Catholic and mainline and black Protestant pastors opposed it (Pew Forum 2003; Marsh 2007). But critics of the war soon lamented their impotence, as people in the pews rallied behind the president.

As criticism of the Iraq engagement grew over the next few years, the loudest critique continued to come from mainline leaders, while many evangelical officials stood behind the president (Tipton 2007). In the mass public, evangelicals remained the president's staunchest defenders, followed by other traditionalists. On the other hand, modernists, secularists, and most religious minorities registered growing opposition to the Iraq involvement (Guth 2006; Baumgartner et al. 2008).

Religious debate over the Israeli-Palestinian conflict overlapped that on the evolving Iraqi situation. Since 1948, evangelicals have joined American Jews as fervent supporters of Israel; their recent prominence in the GOP has bolstered Israel's position, especially in Congress, where evangelicals dominated House leadership from 2001 to 2006 (Oldmixon, Rosenson, and Wald 2005). Mainline and Catholic churches, for various reasons, have sympathized more with the Palestinians. During Bush's first term, the pro-Israel coalition praised his "tilt" toward Israel but mobilized effectively on signs of wavering. His later "road map" for peace, however, was praised by mainliners and Catholics and criticized by evangelical and Jewish leaders. Despite this temporary reversal, the president soon returned to a pro-Israeli line that persisted, with few exceptions, into his second term. And this policy was staunchly backed by the evangelical core of his religious coalition and by other religious conservatives (Baumgartner et al. 2008). In fact, the same religious pattern held on most Bush foreign policies (Guth 2006). Only on the administration's efforts to foster religious freedom in China, end the war in Darfur, and fight AIDs in Africa did the religious coalition expand in scope.

Although Bush's domestic and foreign policies had considerable appeal to traditionalists, even Karl Rove probably did not foresee the addition of gay marriage to the 2004 campaign agenda. But when the U.S. Supreme Court in *Lawrence v. Texas* (2003) struck down state sodomy laws and the Massachusetts Supreme Court subsequently legalized gay marriage in that state, conservatives demanded that the president take a stand. Although Bush hesitated, seeking a centrist solution, he soon endorsed a constitutional amendment defining marriage in traditional terms (for White House deliberations, see Wells and Cohen 2007, 139–44). Meanwhile, his reelection campaign sought to ride the wave of thirteen state referenda to amend state laws or constitutions to prohibit same-sex marriage. These campaigns obviously attracted the same voters that the Bush reelection effort needed.

The 2004 Election and Religious Politics

As a result of all of these issues, religion played an important role in the 2004 campaign. As one account put it, Bush "showed himself willing to use religion forcefully to sharpen partisan divisions and highlight his own qualities as a leader," while John F. Kerry "faced obstacles in using religious rhetoric, in appealing to religion to underscore his qualities as a leader, and in benefiting from the political organization of religious groups." Religion, this analysis concluded, "was at the heart of the campaign" (Muirhead et al. 2005, 222).

Both candidates had a religious strategy, but Bush's was well developed and consistent while Kerry's was reactive and erratic. Chastened by Bush's failure to win the popular vote in 2000, Karl Rove sought to maximize the impact of religious traditionalists, especially evangelicals and conservative Catholics. Bush had presented himself as part of the conservative religious community, using religious rhetoric and themes to an extent arguably unparalleled for any president. Policies on abortion, stem-cell research, and same-sex marriage had been shaped with an eye toward attracting their support. Nominees for executive and judicial posts provided unprecedented recognition for these religious groups. Even Bush's actions on seemingly nonreligious issues, such as the war on terror and tax cuts, had substantial appeal to traditionalist voters (Guth 2004). Using these advantages, party officials assiduously cultivated religious leaders and sought to link their institutions to GOP machinery (Hudson 2008).

Senator Kerry, on the other hand, fruitlessly sought effective entree to America's religious communities. Although a practicing Catholic, Kerry was reticent about his faith, which he considered a private matter. Criticism from several bishops for his pro-choice stance often prevented him from attending mass while campaigning and kept him on the religious defensive. Kerry eventually tied his liberal Catholicism to Democratic policies on social justice and spent more time in religious settings, especially African American churches, often quoting scripture, but the effort seemed strained. Similarly, his campaign staff attracted some religious liberals from mainline and Catholic bodies, and, along with the Democratic National Committee, he sought institutionalized links with these groups. But these efforts foundered; they could not effectively compete with the vast array of other religious and secular groups represented among Democratic activists (Sullivan 2008).

How then did America's religious constituencies react to the first Bush administration and the 2004 campaign? Table 6.1 provides information on these questions, dividing the electorate into the major and minor American religious traditions and the three major traditions into four categories based on their position in the theological culture wars or religious structuring. First, note the variation in evaluations of Bush's job performance by religious group. Although his overall approval had dropped after the 2002 elections, the 2004 religious patterns still mimicked those of two years earlier (see Guth 2004). Despite modest differences in Bush's overall job rating and specific evaluations on foreign policy, social issues, and economic policy (with his scores declining in that order), his best evaluations came from religious traditionalists, especially evangelicals and Latter-day Saints, as well as Catholics, Latino Protestants, and to a lesser extent, mainliners. On the other hand, religious modernists, nominal members of the major traditions, the unaffiliated, and most religious minorities were critical of his performance (compare Olson and Warber 2008).

How did this affect the vote? Table 6.1 also compares Bush's performances in 2000 and 2004 among religious groups. First, note that the voting patterns are fairly consistent across time: Bush did best among evangelicals, much less well among white Catholics, and basically split mainliners with Kerry. Within all three traditions, Bush won the votes of most theological traditionalists and did worst with nominal adherents, but this pattern hid important changes from 2000 to 2004. Bush gained strongly among evangelicals outside their large traditionalist contingent (who could not be more Republican), lost ground among *all* mainliners, especially modernists and nominals, and gained traditionalist Catholics while slipping among modernist and nominal Catholics. He also advanced among unaffiliated but religious voters, while declining substantially among secular and nonbelieving contingents. Among smaller groups, Bush drew almost unanimous Latter-day Saint support, improved among Latino Protestants, added to his small Jewish and miniscule black Protestant totals, but slipped among voters from "other," mostly non-Christian, faiths.

The president also benefited from higher turnouts among some religious groups, although this effect is muddied by the campaign focus on "battleground states." As Rove hoped, evangelicals boosted their turnout across the board, but this was especially true of centrist evangelicals. Traditionalist mainliners and white Catholics saw a dramatic increase in turnout, benefiting Bush, but there was also a smaller countermovement among nominal mainliners and Catholics that helped Kerry. On the other hand, black Protestant turnout declined from its 2000 level and seculars

Table 6.1. Bush job performance ratings and 2004 presidential vote by religious group

	Percent-age of voters	"Excellent" or "good" job performance				Bush vote		
		Overall	Foreign policy	Social policy	Economic policy	2000	2004	+/-
Total	100.0	48	45	43	37	49.5	51.2	+0.7
Latter-day Saints	2.0	88	79	92	76	94	97	+4
Evangelical Protestants								
Traditionalist	13.6	85	71	86	71	87	88	+1
Centrist	8.5	62	49	58	49	63	70	+7
Modernist	2.6	55	34	36	34	42	58	+16
Nominal	1.4	50	36	25	36	44	55	+11
Latino Protestants	2.1	63	52	64	46	29	63	+34
Mainline Protestants								
Traditionalist	5.5	57	58	57	45	76	66	-10
Centrist	6.8	46	45	35	29	52	49	-3
Modernist	3.9	43	42	29	27	56	43	-13
Nominal	2.5	28	29	11	24	51	31	-20
White Catholics								
Traditionalist	5.4	70	68	73	54	61	74	+13
Centrist	7.7	48	45	43	39	50	52	+2
Modernist	3.8	40	36	29	24	40	38	-2
Nominal	2.4	27	27	14	27	38	29	-9
Latino Catholics	3.2	42	33	38	13	29	31	+2
Black Protestants	7.7	15	17	23	16	4	17	+13
Followers of other faiths	3.3	18	14	16	27	37	18	-19
Jews	2.7	33	28	22	26	23	27	+4
Unaffiliated voters								
Believers	2.9	27	27	32	21	28	37	+9
Secularists	8.0	25	23	11	18	42	30	-12
Atheists/agnostics	4.0	17	16	13	10	31	20	-11

Source: Fourth National Survey of Religion and Politics, University of Akron, 2004.

Note: (N=2730)

Table 6.2. Issue preferences of religious voters in the 2004 presidential election

	Believe Iraq war justified	Favor Israel over Arabs in Mideast	Support more restric- tions on abortion	Oppose gay marriage and civil unions	Favor charitable choice	Favor Bush tax cuts
All voters	57.3	40.5	44.4	50.6	45.1	49.0
All Bush voters (+)	35.0	18.5	19.6	17.9	10.6	24.5
Latter-day Saints	31.8	13.1	43.3	34.5	-5.0	26.1
Evangelical Protestants						
Traditionalist	32.5	32.0	45.8	39.3	10.5	22.2
Centrist	18.0	11.7	12.2	17.6	4.7	11.9
Modernist	0.6	0.1	-6.9	10.1	0.3	6.2
Nominal	-1.1	10.3	-28.0	-16.8	-13.7	0.6
Latino Protestants	14.0	14.6	28.7	35.8	5.2	11.9
Mainline Protestants						
Traditionalist	12.1	4.9	12.3	17.4	13.0	-4.3
Centrist	1.1	-4.7	-13.4	-11.2	-3.7	0.8
Modernist	-6.5	-14.5	-29.2	-18.1	-11.3	-1.4
Nominal	-16.5	-16.7	-35.2	-35.9	-18.5	-7.9
White Catholics						
Traditionalist	21.2	2.2	40.3	21.5	15.3	8.0
Centrist	2.2	1.1	-1.1	-11.5	2.1	3.6
Modernist	-12.2	-12.9	-23.2	-27.6	-4.2	-21.5
Nominal	-11.6	-18.1	-31.6	-33.2	-17.9	-14.9
Latino Catholics	-17.5	-13.4	-0.2	-4.9	-0.8	-5.4
Black Protestants	-23.1	-21.2	-4.7	19.2	-0.7	-3.6
Other faiths	-30.5	-16.3	-34.7	-40.8	-21.9	-22.8
Jews	-20.8	35.7	-30.7	-31.3	10.7	-8.9
Unaffiliated						
Believers	-14.8	-30.1	0.3	-11.6	0.9	-4.9
Secularists	-23.1	-13.2	-32.0	-35.0	-21.1	-19.1
Atheists/agnostics	-39.1	-21.5	-38.4	-38.2	-28.6	-24.7

Source: Fourth National Survey of Religion and Politics, University of Akron, 2004.

Note: (N=2730)

did not improve on their 2000 performance, depriving Kerry of needed votes (see Green et al. 2007 for more details on religious turnout). Generally, the president's supporting religious coalition exhibited even higher turnout in battleground states, where it really counted in the Electoral College (data not shown).

How did issues influence religious voters? With a divisive war, economic uncertainty, and social issues such as abortion, stem-cell research, and gay marriage all on the agenda, interpreting Bush's reelection victory is a complex task. When exit polls showed that voters cited "moral issues" more often than any other concern as the crucial factor in their choice, journalists seized upon this to explain Bush's victory. This instant analysis was soon challenged by those arguing that terrorism and the Iraq war were bigger factors. Although we cannot resolve this controversy here, it is important to remember that religious voters differ on many issues, not just "moral" ones. Table 6.2 reports how religious groups stood on six salient issues in 2004: the Iraq war, Mideast policy, abortion restrictions, gay marriage and civil unions, faith-based initiatives, and the Bush tax cuts. The table reports three items of interest: (1) the percentage of all voters supporting the Bush position; (2) the percentage by which Bush voters deviated from the national average; and (3) the extent to which religious communities differed from that national average.

Religious groups varied dramatically on Bush's signature policies. Evangelical traditionalists were by far the most supportive across the board, with Latter-day Saints, traditionalist Catholics, Latino Protestants, and evangelical centrists close behind. In each major tradition, support for his policies drops as one moves from traditionalists to nominals. In mainline and white Catholic communities, support from modernists and nominals was far below the national average. With occasional exceptions (such as Jewish approval of Bush's policy toward Israel), religious minorities and unaffiliated Americans (especially secularists and atheists) were in deep, consistent disagreement with the administration.

Clearly, religion differentiated the way that Republican and Democratic voters responded to many issues, not just "moral" ones, making it very difficult to assess the full impact of religion on the campaign. Despite the mountains of paper devoted to this effort, we may never have a definitive answer. Indeed, there is much dispute about which issues influenced different religious communities (see Guth et al. 2006 and Campbell 2007, for a sample of perspectives). Nevertheless, there can be little doubt that religious factors structured the outcome in 2004.

The Second Bush Term and Religious Politics

After his reelection, Bush renewed support for his faith-based initiative, vetoed legislation expanding federal support for embryonic stem-cell research, and continued various pro-life policies. But his administration was fighting the "second-term blues" (Fortier and Ornstein 2007) as the Iraq war dragged on, Hurricane Katrina presented Bush with a political disaster, scandals embarrassed the GOP, and the president's Social Security initiative went down in flames. Nevertheless, Bush persisted in actions important to his religious constituency, with success in some instances but failure in others.

The president ran into repeated resistance when he attempted to appoint religious conservatives to important second-tier administration positions, most notably that of surgeon general (Harris 2007). In this instance (and others), critics charged that Bush had overridden the recommendations of his career staff to promote health policies sponsored by traditionalists and now was attempting to put traditionalists in direct control. Although these controversies attracted little public attention, the opposite was true of Bush's intervention in the Terri Schiavo case. Schiavo was a Florida woman in a persistent vegetative state and the subject of prolonged legal controversy between her husband, who wanted to end life support, and her parents, who did not. A Florida court granted the husband's petition, but the state legislature, at the instigation of Governor Jeb Bush, attempted to block this action by passing "Terri's Law," subsequently struck down by the Florida Supreme Court and denied review by the U.S. Supreme Court. Pressured by pro-life groups, the Congress then passed a bill giving Schiavo's parents access to the federal courts; Bush signed the bill with great public flourish, flying back to Washington from his Texas vacation to do so. The federal courts still refused to interfere, and Schiavo died on March 31, 2005.

The episode was a public relations disaster for the GOP. The prominent role played by Republican congressional leaders, Governor Jeb Bush, and the president identified the federal legislation with the party, although many Democrats had voted for it as well. The press coverage was generally hostile, and many Americans instinctively disliked political intervention in what seemed a tragic private decision. Public opinion polls showed overwhelming disapproval of actions by the GOP Congress and White House (Jelen 2007). The president's own religious instincts and his response to his electoral constituency had proved politically dangerous.

The president had better luck with judicial nominations. The long-awaited Supreme Court vacancies finally appeared in the summer of 2005 when Sandra Day O'Connor retired and Chief Justice William Rehnquist succumbed to cancer. Bush's choices to replace these Court fixtures revealed his determination to appoint jurists who were advocates of judicial restraint, adherents of traditionalist social policy, and representative of his religious coalition. But the vacancies occurred immediately after protracted battles between Bush and Senate Democrats over other judicial nominations. Although the conflict was ostensibly about nominees' qualifications and judicial philosophy, Christian conservatives suspected that the jurists' traditionalist religious views were really at issue. Christian Right groups pushed Senate Majority Leader William Frist to invoke the "nuclear option" and held massive rallies to force the Senate's hand. The eventual compromise from the bipartisan "Gang of Fourteen" allowed most Bush nominees to go through, but it did not please Christian conservatives, who abhorred any concessions to liberal senators.

Thus, Christian Right groups were primed for battle. And Bush's choice of John Roberts for the chief justice's seat renewed religious controversy. Roberts, a devout Catholic, was praised by conservative Christian leaders but greeted with "concern" by the religious and secular Left for the same reason: he was thought to be a skeptic on *Roe v. Wade* (his wife was active in Feminists for Life) and an accommodationist on church-state issues. Although speculation on how his faith and his views on abortion and church-state questions might influence his rulings was rampant during confirmation hearings, Roberts's intelligent and good-humored responses failed to give opponents much ammunition. He was easily confirmed, although some of his answers evoked conservative fears that he might be "another Souter," that is, a Republican who turns "liberal" once on the Court (Singer 2005).

Bush's replacement of O'Connor proved more difficult. To avoid controversy, he first nominated his White House counsel and longtime aide, Harriet Miers, who had virtually no judicial experience and thus no track record on issues. Despite White House assurances that her attendance at an evangelical church proved that she thought correctly about social issues, most Christian Right groups soon lined up against her nomination. Lacking strong support from any quarter and not impressing senators in private visits, Miers soon had her nomination withdrawn. As Mark Silverstein concluded, "Social and religious conservatives . . . had dealt the president a harsh and totally unexpected setback" (Silverstein 2007, 217).

Bush quickly recovered by nominating Court of Appeals judge Samuel Alito, an experienced jurist with a solid conservative record. A devout Catholic like Roberts (and an opponent of abortion rights), Alito was the beneficiary of massive lobbying by conservative religious groups, who then celebrated his confirmation (which came with a narrow 58-to-42 vote), calling it "a turning point for our nation" (from Kirkpatrick 2006). And their expectations about Roberts and Alito seemed fulfilled over the next two years, as the "Roberts Court" (with its new "Catholic" majority) upheld the 2003 partial birth abortion ban, limited challenges to federal expenditures on establishment clause grounds, and upheld a 2003 statute curbing child pornography on the Internet. In retrospect, Bush's federal court choices gave Christian conservatives some of their most important advances. (For an excellent inside account of religious lobbying on these nominations, see Desmond 2006.)

The Bush Administration and the Future of Religious Politics

George W. Bush's tenure in office had several enduring effects on religious politics. First, his administration consolidated partisan ties between evangelical Protestants and the GOP, a process that took place over many years (Green et al. 2007). In rhetoric, appointments, and policy, Bush provided recognition for that religious community and in return, received his strongest support. Even in the "bad" Republican year of 2006, Democratic congressional candidates made few inroads among evangelical voters (Green 2006). As the 2008 campaign began, they were still the largest religious group in the GOP and strongly identified with the party, although not numerous enough to dominate without aid from other traditionalists.

Of course, by 2008, many evangelicals had joined the national criticism of Bush's performance, had split their votes among the aspirants in the GOP presidential primaries, and generally lacked enthusiasm for Senator McCain, the eventual nominee. In the end, very few deserted to the Democrats, although evangelical turnout was well below that of 2004 (Green 2009). On the entire range of issues—social, foreign, or economic—dividing the parties, evangelicals, especially the numerous traditionalists among them, are the religious group most supportive of GOP policy. Thus, McCain's fervid search for evangelical allies for the fall campaign was understandable, although too close an embrace may have been dangerous, as his political dalliance with Pentecostal pastor John Hagee and, perhaps, his choice of Alaska governor Sarah Palin for a running mate quickly proved.

While attracting many religious traditionalists, the Bush administration drove toward the Democrats various other religious groups, including modernists, nominals, and some centrists in all the Christian traditions; non-Christians and other religious minorities; and especially secular voters. As a result, Bush administration policies intensified the "culture war," at least in its political manifestations, producing major divisions in the 2004 elections along the lines of religious affiliation, observance, and belief. The misguided popular and academic debate over the role of "moral" issues largely obscured the deeper religious divisions revealed by the contest—divisions that ran along the lines of most ideological differences between the parties.

If some academics doubted that religion mattered in 2004, Democrats drew a very different conclusion, seeking ways to "speak religiously" to the electorate (Sullivan 2008). Constrained by the diversity of their religious (and secular) coalition, Democrats made some progress in reversing the GOP's gains among Catholics, Latino Protestants, and others in the 2006 elections, in part by running candidates whose religious profile looked "more Republican" (Green 2006). And both Democratic finalists in the 2008 presidential primaries cast their platforms in moral or religious terms, appealed to religious voters, and sought to reclaim territory lost to Republicans. Still, that protracted contest revealed tensions in the Democratic religious coalition, as Methodist Hillary Clinton attracted Catholics and the dwindling cohort of other Democratic traditionalists, and Barack Obama, an active member of a African American congregation in the mainline United Church of Christ, appealed strongly to black Protestants, religious modernists, upscale mainliners, and secular Democrats. As suggested by the prolonged debate over the views of Jeremiah Wright, Obama's pastor in Chicago, religious entanglements can pose pitfalls for Democrats as well as Republicans. What was remarkable in the end was how little the basic religious alignments set in 2000 and 2004 actually shifted (Green 2009; Guth 2009).

Although the 2008 presidential race proved to be a "maintaining election" in religious terms, there is always the possibility of "realignment." At least modest shifts in religious voting patterns might stem from the evolving religious makeup of the American public or from changes within religious communities. As a major survey in 2008 showed, the United States is ever more religiously diverse, perhaps benefiting the Democrats, but making the task of coalition building even more complicated (Pew Forum 2008). As minority religious traditions grow, as secular Americans increase in number, as citizens shift increasingly from faith to faith, and as major traditions are transformed from within, the issue agendas connected to religious values will change. But religion will never be far from the front page during the new presidential regime of Barack Obama.

Indeed, even as he was preoccupied with the economic crisis confronting the country, President Obama quickly applied his own religious style to the new administration. From his attendance at an unprecedented number of ecumenical worship services to his choice of clergy for inaugural prayers to his own address quoting the Apostle Paul, Obama showed his sensitivity to religious politics. Once sworn in, he complied with liberal expectations in reversing Bush's antiabortion "Mexico City" policy but also announced a "faith-based" initiative so close to Bush's that many church-state separationists blanched, and he appointed a religious advisory council, which included several prominent traditionalists, to advise him on ethical issues in a broad range of federal policies. Whether Obama can navigate the shoals of cultural politics will depend on his ability to construct a broad, supportive religious coalition, without at the same time antagonizing his strong secular constituency. That will be a formidable task.

7

THE CULMINATING POINT
Democrats versus Repubicans in the Bush Years

JOHN J. PITNEY JR.

O n the afternoon of November 2, 2004, Democrats thought that vindication was in their grasp. Two years earlier, the terrorism issue allowed President George W. Bush's party to pull off the remarkable feat of gaining seats in a midterm election. And for a while in 2003, it had seemed as if the military defeat of Saddam Hussein would ensure reelection victory for Bush. But on election day 2004, the Internet was abuzz with leaked exit poll numbers showing that Senator John Kerry would win.

As the votes mounted, though, it became clear that the early numbers were wrong. Democrats' joy turned into shock. Not only had their despised foe won a second term, but his party had gained even more seats in the House and Senate.

Mental health professionals soon reported that some Democrats were feeling traumatized. "Patients who I've had for a long time have come in absolutely devastated over the fact that the election went the way it did," said a clinical social worker in Madison, Wisconsin. "They were just terribly distraught and continue to be terribly distraught" (from Derby 2004). Some academics worried that the Republican hold on power threatened democracy itself (Hacker and Pierson 2005b). The 2005 annual conference of the American Political Science Association actually included a panel titled "Is It Time to Call It Fascism?"

Two years later, Bush's popularity was near Nixonian lows. In November 2006, Democrats won majorities in the House and Senate, and two years later they reclaimed the White House as well. In hindsight, it is clear that the 2004 election was not the start of permanent GOP dominance, much less a partisan dictatorship.

What happened? A Marine Corps handbook explains that every conflict has a culminating point: "We advance at a cost—lives, fuel, ammunition, physical and sometimes moral strength—and so the attack becomes weaker over time. Eventually the superiority that allowed us to attack and forced our enemy to defend in the first place dissipates and the balance tips in favor of our enemy" (U.S. Marine Corps 1994, 33). Something comparable happened in the party warfare of the second Bush term. Republicans reached this culminating point, and their advance turned into retreat.

In the 2002 midterm, the Republicans had achieved unified party control of the federal government, and they strengthened it in 2004. That goal had eluded them for nearly half a century, apart from a few months in 2001. Unified control has obvious advantages, such as the ability to move legislation and attract campaign funds. Less obvious are its hazards. Power invites abuse and complacency; the moral strength that led to victory may give way to the temptation to disregard ethics. And unified control means unified responsibility. When things go wrong, the party in power gets all the blame.

Another military analogy is useful here. In the nineteenth-century classic *On War,* Carl von Clausewitz described how things can go wrong: "Friction can arise both from minor mishaps and great disasters." Every war, he wrote, "is rich in unique episodes. Each is an uncharted sea, full of reefs" (Clausewitz 1976, 119, 120). During the second Bush term, the Republican battleship hit several reefs.

The Paper Elephant

The reversal of fortune during Bush's second term seemed so dramatic in part because many observers had overrated Bush and the national GOP. Republicans did have real strengths, yet they lacked the demonic powers that critics attributed to them. Robert Jervis put it well: "Domestic groups in conflict see the other side as more unified than it is. In local labor-management disputes each side is apt to believe incorrectly that the other is controlled from above. Both Democrats and Republicans in the House of Representatives see the other party as the one that is more organized and disciplined" (Jervis 1976, 327).

A Hill Divided

As the Jervis passage suggests, Capitol Hill is a good place to start a search for what went wrong. A common assumption has long held that congressional Republicans are inherently more unified than Democrats. At first, *Congressional Quarterly*'s party unity scores seem to reinforce the image of a GOP monolith. Between 2001 and 2006, the House Republicans always averaged a unity score of at least 92 percent. Their Senate colleagues had a score of 87 percent, slightly lower but still impressive (Stanley and Niemi 2008, 225).

At the same time, Democrats in both chambers achieved unity scores very close to those of their GOP colleagues: the difference in averages never exceeded single digits. And this minor gap stemmed less from inherent party distinctions than from the natural benefits of majority status. The last time the Democrats had enjoyed unified control of the government (1993–1994), their lawmakers had slightly higher party unity than the Republicans.

These data tell only a partial story. Party-line votes measure unity within each chamber, but they do not reveal anything about relations between the chambers. Instead of a single unified army, the congressional GOP was an uneasy alliance of House and Senate Republicans. Senators represent more diverse constituencies and operate under rules that give leverage to the minority party. They tend to favor compromise more than House members, who often come from politically homogeneous districts and whose procedures usually give the majority its way. "People are frustrated. They really are," said Representative Tom Price (R-Georgia), whose conservative voters wondered why unified control had disappointing results (from Weisman 2006).

Another limitation of party unity scores is that they do not distinguish roll call votes by their significance. Some legislative battles matter more than others. Bush won key victories during his first term, especially on tax cuts. In the second term, he wanted to advance into policy areas that held the promise of long-term political gain. This ground would prove more treacherous.

In the 2004 campaign, Bush spoke of an "ownership society" in which government would help Americans gain property instead of keeping them dependent on public expenditures. The policy rationale was that this approach would foster prosperity and reduce poverty. Reportedly, the political motivation was to expand the ranks of investors and landowners, who in turn would support the GOP in the decades ahead (Hamburger and Wallsten 2005). "It will be good for the party if we can continue to foster greater participation in the free market," said Ed Gillespie, who had chaired the Republican National Committee (from Keen 2005, 1A).

As a step toward the ownership society, Bush proposed letting workers put part of their Social Security contributions into individual investment accounts. Polls quickly registered wide disapproval. Although the idea had seemed politically viable a few years before, three things had changed. First, stock values had plunged with the dot.com bubble and 9/11. Although the market was recovering, the gyrations reminded people that stocks go down as well as up. Second, accounting scandals had undercut confidence in financial institutions. Third, the plan involved huge transition costs, since billions would go into personal accounts instead of government coffers. Several years earlier, when revenues exceeded spending, it was plausible to argue that budget surpluses could cover such costs. With the budget in the red, private accounts promised to worsen the deficit.

For congressional Republicans, the question was whether they would risk near-term political heat for the party's long-term benefit. Many thought that Bush was asking too much. "Why stir up a political hornet's nest . . . when there is no urgency?" asked Representative Rob Simmons of Connecticut. "When does the program go belly up? 2042. I will be dead by then," Simmons said. According to Representative Jack Kingston of Georgia, "Just convincing our guys not to be timid is going to be a big struggle" (from VandeHei and Allen 2005). House Republicans were reluctant to cast a dangerous vote only to see the measure die in the Senate, so they wanted the other chamber to move first. But nearly every Democratic senator opposed the plan, making it impossible for Senate Republicans to overcome a filibuster (Rosenbaum 2005).

The privatization plan never came to the floor. Its failure emboldened the Democrats, who could now see that the Republican "juggernaut" was vulnerable. And even though Republicans avoided the frightening Social Security roll call, Democrats attacked them on the issue anyway. One of their targets was none other than Rob Simmons, who would go on to lose his seat in 2006.

The Democrats' united front illustrates an important point about minority status in unified government: they never came together on a comprehensive proposal to preserve the system's solvency. There was no mystery about it; any realistic plan would include benefit cuts or tax increases. Some Democratic thinkers argued that their party's lawmakers had to take that risky step in order to show that they were "for something" (Balz 2005). Those urging such a move forgot that the Democrats had no responsibility for governing, so they could pick their issues. After all, the House Republicans' 1994 "Contract with America" skipped Social Security reform as well as such contentious social issues as abortion. In this sense, a congressional minority under unified government is like a guerrilla army. While it lacks some important resources, it has freedom to maneuver. Without the need to administer territory, it can choose its targets at will.

Just as Bush was urging major changes in Social Security, he also proposed an immigration reform that would set up a temporary-worker program and enable undocumented workers to seek legal status. As with Social Security, both policy and politics drove the idea. Bush described his policy as a humane way of enforcing the law and bringing aliens into the mainstream economy. Politically, it was a way to appeal to (or at least appease) the fast-growing Hispanic electorate (Gillespie 2006).

Many GOP senators joined with Democrats to pass a bill liberalizing immigration law. The view from the House was different. Mostly representing conservative constituencies with relatively few Hispanic voters, House Republicans preferred to step up enforcement (Fletcher 2005). They passed a tough bill that was hard to reconcile with the Senate measure. Instead of seeking a compromise in conference, they held forums to rally opinion against the Bush-backed Senate approach (Sandler 2006).

Democrats had their own divisions. But since Republicans controlled all branches of government, they bore the burden of resolving the issue. Democrats could focus on the GOP's inability to deliver. The Democratic National Committee made the point in a Spanish-language radio ad: "Now Republicans are lying to us. They control Congress and the White House, and in five years have done nothing. They've failed. If they wanted comprehensive immigration reform and to protect our borders, they would have done it already. But what Republicans and President Bush supported was a plan that would criminalize immigrants, families, doctors, and even churches just for giving communion" (Democratic National Committee 2006). The ad inaccurately depicted GOP stands and the House bill's specifics. (It would not have banned Holy Communion.) Politically, however, such details did not count.

Republicans once again dashed into political pincers. Bush and the Senate GOP had alienated the party's grassroots constituency, while the House Republicans' hard line yielded little political gain and may have hurt them. GOP House candidates won few of the toss-up races in which the issue was prominent (Dorval and LaRue 2006). It was the main cause of at least one GOP defeat. In the race to succeed Representative Jim Kolbe (R-Arizona), the National Republican Congressional Committee (NRCC) backed a moderate candidate, who lost the primary to hard-liner Randy Graf. Independents and Democrats spurned Graf, who went down to a double-digit defeat in November. Nationwide, Hispanic support for GOP House candidates fell about 10 points from 2004. Although other issues came into play, immigration contributed to this drop (Leal et al. 2008).

Bush faced another Republican revolt when the administration approved a Dubai company's planned management takeover of six U.S. seaports. Responding to constituents who saw the deal as an open door to terrorism, GOP lawmakers vowed to fight it. With great understatement, a White House spokesman acknowledged, "This is one where we probably should have consulted with or briefed Congress on sooner" (from Vande-Hei and Weisman 2006). The company withdrew its plan, but the damage lingered.

These episodes suggest that the Bush White House was not the disciplined political apparatus that many had imagined. One senior Republican senator told journalist Robert Novak, "I have been around a while, and this is the worst administration at congressional relations that I have ever been associated with" (from Novak 2005).

The much-touted GOP campaign "machine" had its problems, too.

Campaign Combat

Ken Mehlman, who chaired the Republican National Committee during the 2006 cycle, was very skillful. Under his leadership, the committee maintained its customary fund-raising lead over the Democratic National Committee. Even so, the latter's chair proved to be a worthy opponent. Former Vermont governor and presidential candidate Howard Dean carried out a "fifty-state strategy" to build party organizations across the nation. The strategy was controversial, igniting arguments with other party figures. In spite of the internal disagreement, Dean's strategy evidently boosted the party's vote (Kamarck 2006).

The Democrats had effective commanders at their congressional campaign committees. As Adam Nagourney of the *New York Times* put it, "Representative Rahm Emanuel of Chicago and Senator Charles E. Schumer of New York are loud, garrulous urban brawlers: a blur of endlessly quotable attack lines, opportunistic legislative proposals, relentless fund-raising and big-shoulder tactics" (Nagourney 2006b).

Emanuel and Schumer outgunned their Republican counterparts. Senator Elizabeth Dole of North Carolina had a long history in Washington but was unprepared for the intense political combat of 2006. Critics faulted her for passivity in fund-raising and candidate recruitment (Cottle 2007). Representative Tom Reynolds of New York not only faced the distraction of a tough race in his home district, but it later turned out that the GOP committee treasurer was embezzling hundreds of thousands of dollars. The Democratic committee chairs used all available media to pummel Bush and the GOP. In fact, it was Schumer who initially leaked the story of the Middle Eastern port deal (Sullivan 2006). The Republicans, by contrast, were on the defensive and sounded like it.

Moreover, the Republican congressional committees were losing ground in campaign finance. The Democratic committees nearly matched them, raising a combined $261 million to the Republicans' $268 million. In fact, the Democratic senatorial committee outraised the Republican committee by $121 million to $89 million (Corrado and Varney 2007).

The Democratic financial surge in contributions involved more than their comparative strength in leadership. Economic interest groups started to reckon that the Democrats might take control of Congress, and they shifted their giving accordingly. Charles Rangel (D-New York) joked to the *Los Angeles Times,* "I don't think meeting with the chairman of General Electric has anything to do with my taking over Ways and Means; I just never realized how much they loved me" (from Simon 2006).

Moreover, Internet fund-raising helped Democrats to expand their pool of small donors. Democratic committees raised about $130 million in small donations, more than doubling their 2002 take. Republicans raised $180 million—more than the Democrats' take but only a 10 percent increase from 2002 (Corrado and Varney 2007). An NRCC spokesman acknowledged a financial culminating point. Republicans had focused so much on direct mail that they had "maximized our potential return" (from VandeHei 2006).

Democrats also enjoyed the help of labor unions and other groups outside the formal party organization (Greenhouse 2006). "Netroots" orga-nizations such as Moveon.org and ActBlue raised and spent millions in support of Democratic candidates. Despite Democratic progress on fund-raising, Republicans still hoped that they could exploit their technological advantages in other areas (DeFrank and Bazinet 2006). They resembled a losing army that was counting on the last war's "secret weapons."

Using costly databases, Republicans amassed detailed statistics on millions of households. They precisely targeted voter appeals, sending one message to snowmobile owners, another to Krugerrand investors, and so on. GOP operatives claimed that this "microtargeting" had helped tip close states to President Bush in 2004 (Hamburger and Wallsten 2005). But under new leadership, Democratic party organizations and their al-lies were adapting. "We've caught up to, if not passed [the Republicans] on the technological level," said the head of one microtargeting firm working with Democrats (from Hoover 2006).

In any case, there were questions as to whether microtargeting lived up to its billing. One popular book explained that the technique drew on the kind of market research that had brought success to Applebee's res-taurants (Sosnik, Dowd, and Fournier 2006). But as the book was hitting the shelves, the restaurant chain was having economic problems. In the next year, it sold out to the International House of Pancakes. In a post-election article, a Republican consultant said that political microtargeting can work under the right circumstances. In an unfavorable setting—such as Republicans faced in 2006—the data become unreliable. He worried that GOP efforts may have backfired by inadvertently turning out Demo-cratic voters (Stutts 2006).

Another GOP "secret weapon" was redistricting. The House district lines that followed the 2000 census did protect incumbents, but some commentators exaggerated their effect. Over time, shifts in population and political leanings can weaken any redistricting scheme. The *Wall Street Journal* reported that gerrymandering efforts backfired in Texas, Florida, and Pennsylvania: "Republican leaders may have overreached and created so many Republican-leaning districts that they spread their core supporters too thinly. That left their incumbents vulnerable to the type of backlash from traditionally Republican-leaning independent vot-ers that unfolded" (Cummings 2006).

Democratic fears of unbreakable House GOP control proved over-blown. Jacob Hacker and Paul Pierson (2005b, 125) cited one estimate that the Democrats would need 57 percent of the congressional vote to win a majority in the House. In fact, the Democrats won 53.6 percent of the seats with just 52.8 percent of the total vote (Stanley and Niemi 2008, 46).

Communications

In politics, as in war, propaganda is a weapon. In his popular 2004 book *Don't Think of an Elephant,* linguist George Lakoff argued that Republicans had gained the upper hand in framing political debate. He gave several examples: "The Clear Skies Initiative. Healthy Forests. No Child Left Behind. . . . This is the use of Orwellian language—language that means the opposite of what it says—to appease people in the middle at the same time as you pump up the base" (Lakoff 2004, 21–22).

Lakoff was correct that Republicans had tried to present their ideas in the most appealing form and that they had scored some successes. For instance, they rebranded the estate tax as the "death tax." But Lakoff erred in at least two ways. First, he suggested that GOP tactics were something new. In fact, politicians had always used such techniques; one can read about them in Aristotle's *Rhetoric.* More important for our purposes, Republican language often failed to change minds. In discussing his Social Security proposal, President Bush spoke of "personal accounts" instead of "private" ones. Consultant Frank Luntz, whom Lakoff hyperbolically depicted as the GOP's language guru, approved of Bush's word choice. "'Private' is exclusive. . . . 'Personal' is encompassing. It's individual. It's ownership. In the end, you need the combination of 'personal' and 'security'" (from Toner 2005). Some polls did show that people liked "personal" better than "private" (Nohlgren 2005). But in the end, reality trumped semantics: voters simply did not like what Bush wanted to do.

The president was similarly unable to work verbal magic on the immigration issue. No matter how many times he spoke of a "path to citizenship," GOP conservatives countered that he was talking about "amnesty."

Some analysts have claimed a Republican bias in the mass media. The traditional media, they say, strive for balance while talk radio tacks to the right (Hacker and Pierson 2005b, 179–81). Different analysts have reached different conclusions about the political leanings of the press, but there is reason to doubt that Republicans dominate the media. In 2005, the University of Connecticut polled journalists on how they had voted the year before. Among those willing to answer, 68 percent said they had voted for Kerry, while only 25 percent had voted for Bush (University of Connecticut 2005). A *Washington Post* editor acknowledged, "We're not very subtle about it at this paper: If you work here, you must be one of us. You must be liberal, progressive, a Democrat. I've been in communal gatherings in *The Post,* watching election returns, and have been flabbergasted to see my colleagues cheer unabashedly for the Democrats" (Kurtz 2005).

Talk radio, conservative magazines, and other alternative media continued to matter, though they were increasingly critical of the GOP. Meanwhile, the blogosphere became an important medium. Liberals and Democrats ruled this cyber-turf: the two top political blogs were the Huffington Post and the Daily Kos (Blogger Central 2008). Markos Moulitsas, creator of Daily Kos, agreed that the liberal blogosphere resembled the conservative talk radio movement: "Yeah, absolutely. I think it's a very apt analogy. The idea being that here, finally, we have a place where good, strong, progressive voices can get together, and we can talk, and we can motivate each other, and we can organize, and we can do and plan the kind of hard work that it takes to win elections" (NBC 2006). On another occasion, he used a military metaphor: "I look at this as [training] armies. It's training our troops how to fight rhetorically" (from Brownstein 2007, 336).

Passion and Issues

Political success, like victory in combat, depends in part on the troops' morale. During the second Bush term, Republicans began to suffer from demoralization. In one poll just before the 2006 election, 52 percent of registered Democrats said that they were more enthusiastic about voting than usual, while only 39 percent of Republicans felt that way. Thirty-seven percent of Republicans were less enthusiastic than usual, compared with just 29 percent of Democrats (Lemonick 2006).

High morale stems from devotion to a cause. Republicans had long campaigned as the party of limited government and family values. Until they controlled all branches of the federal government, they still had something to fight for. Once they reached this goal, they faced a dilemma. On the one hand, they could break their promises and disillusion their supporters. On the other hand, they could do as they had said and risk taking their own issues off the table. In different ways, they did both.

Under Bush, Republicans cut taxes, just as they had pledged, but they hesitated to cut spending. One book suggests that the resulting deficits were part of a grand scheme to "starve the beast" of big government and force an eventual "day of reckoning" when huge cuts would be necessary (Hacker and Pierson 2005b, 103–4). The Republican record supplies no evidence for this notion. In 2005, Tom DeLay, the House majority leader, declared an "ongoing victory" in the fight to cut spending. When a reporter asked if the government were already running at peak efficiency, he said, "Yes, after 11 years of Republican majority we've pared it down pretty good" (from Fagan and Dinan 2006).

DeLay's remarks drew derision. As an analyst for the libertarian Cato Institute later wrote, "Since his election, Bush has presided over the largest expansion of government spending since Lyndon Johnson initiated the Great Society. Domestic spending has increased by 27 percent during his presidency. More people now work for the federal government than at any time since the Cold War. Not a single federal program has been eliminated" (Tanner 2007, 2). Republican lawmakers included billions of dollars of earmarks in appropriations bills. Though accounting for a very small share of federal spending, the earmarks generated bad publicity for the GOP and laid the groundwork for scandals.

Conservative voters blamed the White House and the Republican Congress for the runaway spending (Fournier 2006). As the 2006 election approached, conservative organizations and activists held a lively discussion over whether victory was even desirable (Antle 2006). *National Review* senior editor Ramesh Ponnuru wrote that a GOP victory would leave "the congressmen even less interested in restraining spending, reforming government programs and revamping the tax code" (Ponnuru 2006). He concluded that a loss of power "would make the Republicans hungrier and sharpen their wits." Former Delaware governor Pete du Pont, head of a conservative think tank, said of congressional Republicans, "Conservative principles seem to have faded away, and ethical principles have weakened—names like DeLay, Ney, and Foley make the point" (du Pont 2006). He was actually arguing *for* a GOP victory: though Republicans deserved to lose, he said, Democrats were worse.

On social issues, the picture was slightly different. Conservative Republicans did win victories, but it was at the expense of muting some of their rallying cries. For decades, Republicans had warned that liberal politicians and judges would undercut family values. After several years of conservative leadership at the Justice Department, and particularly after the Supreme Court appointments of John Roberts and Samuel Alito, the prospect of a liberal social offensive seemed remote.

Social conservatives had long been seeking a federal law banning "partial birth abortion." This side of the abortion controversy gave conservatives the political high ground, as 70 percent of Americans agreed with them (Ray 2003). When President Clinton vetoed such measures, he energized antiabortion activists to work even harder. In 2003, President Bush signed the ban. With this success, the activists had advanced about as far as they could go. The public was ambivalent about the underlying issue of abortion, and politicians were wary of stronger action.

In 2004, ballot measures against gay marriage may have helped increase Republican turnout in key states. There was little talk about gay marriage in the 2006 campaign, and for two simple reasons. To say the least, it seemed unlikely that the Roberts Court would impose gay marriage by judicial fiat. And thanks in part to the 2004 measures, most states had already limited marriage to the union of a man and a woman (National Conference of State Legislatures 2008). Constitutional amendments banning same-sex marriage were on the 2006 ballot in eight states, but all eight already had statutory bans. Voters approved seven of these measures, without any sense of urgency. Late in the season, the New Jersey Supreme Court ruled that same-sex couples should enjoy the same legal rights as heterosexual couples. Though some Republicans tried to rally the base, the decision came too late to make a mark.

Meanwhile, the issue environment had the opposite effect on Democratic leaders and voters. The stands of the Bush administration and the Republican Congress angered and mobilized party activists. The Terri Schiavo case proved to be crucial. Schiavo was a severely brain-damaged Florida woman whose husband sought to remove her feeding tube. Her parents fought the move, and the case went through the state courts as well as the Florida legislature. On March 21, 2005, Congress passed a law giving the parents another chance, this time in federal district court. Polls showed that most demographic and political groups disapproved of congressional intervention. In a *Wall Street Journal*/NBC poll, 39 percent of Republicans thought that removing the tube was the right move, while 48 percent said it was wrong. About 18 percent said that they had lost respect for Bush on the issue and 41 percent lost respect for Congress (Harwood 2005). Democrats were even more likely to question the motivations behind the measure (Jacobson 2008, 221). And opposition to congressional intervention was more intense than was the support (Langer 2005).

Commentary on liberal blogs showed that the Democratic Party's activist base was angry about the case. Though Democratic politicians were initially skittish about the issue, the blogs and the polls helped galvanize them against Republican positions on social issues. Representative Debbie Wasserman Schultz (D-Florida) said, "The Terri Schiavo case literally was the thing that, from that point forward, brought our caucus together and gave us the ability to become more unified" (from Allison and Kumar 2005). Virginia Republican Tom Davis agreed with the assessment: "They've just got to remember that what's happening with the Democrats is there's a stiffening resistance on these issues not to give us any help" (from Allison and Kumar 2005).

Enemies

"Politics is battle," wrote Richard Nixon, "and the best way to fire up your troops is to rally them against a visible opponent on the other side of the field. If a loyal supporter will work hard for you, he will fight twice as hard against your enemies" (Nixon 1991, 285). In this respect, the Bush years saw the advantage shift from Republicans to Democrats. During the 1970s and 1980, Republicans had rallied against Speaker Thomas "Tip" O'Neill and Senator Edward Kennedy. In the 1990s, their "visible opponent" was Bill Clinton (Pitney 2000). But by the turn of the twenty-first century, O'Neill was long dead, Kennedy was aging, Clinton was fading into the past, and Democrats were out of power. Senator Tom Daschle (D-South Dakota) made a convenient foil during his brief stint as majority leader, as did Senator John Kerry (D-Massachusetts) during his presidential campaign. But the value of those high-profile Democrats as "visible opponents" for the GOP was fleeting. Republicans controlled the government, so they could not effectively run against it.

Democrats could, however. In part because of the controversy surrounding the 2000 election, a hard core of Democrats loathed Bush right from the start. Most came from the "blue states," so they can be dubbed the "blue-hots." Yet anti-Bush sentiment did not quickly catch fire beyond their ranks. "Soon after George W. Bush took office, I'd occasionally see someone with a 'Hail to the Thief' poster, referring to Election 2000," wrote journalist Martha Brant in the spring of 2002. "But during the height of the war in Afghanistan, I rarely saw any protesters outside 1600 Pennsylvania Ave" (Brant 2002). Moreover, the president and his supporters initially proved skillful in containing the opposition. For instance, the administration worked closely with Senator Kennedy and other Democrats to pass the No Child Left Behind Act.

By Bush's second term, the environment was different. Not only did the president's job approval ratings drop, but Americans turned against him personally. Feelings split according to partisan lines. While Republicans still liked the man they had elected, a 2006 poll (Jones 2006) found that most Democrats had unfavorable opinions of President Bush (90 percent) and Vice President Cheney (83 percent). The ranks of the blue-hots had grown.

Liberal blogs reflected and reinforced such attitudes. They attacked Bush and Cheney with great zeal and sometimes with poor taste. Some, like whywehatebush.com and smirkingchimp.com, did nothing else. On the Huffington Post, "humorist" Tony Hendra offered a Thanksgiving wish for Cheney's death: "O Lord, give Dick Cheney's Heart, Our Sacred Secret Weapon, the strength to try one more time!" (Hendra 2006).

As Bush's popularity sank, his value to Democratic strategists soared. In 2006, Democratic attack ads often tied Republican congressional candidates to him. "In certain districts he's exactly who we want to pivot off," said Rahm Emanuel, chair of the Democratic Congressional Campaign Committee (DCCC). "I tell all the candidates: Him and his agenda are on the ballot this year" (from Nagourney 2006c).

Bush's troubles stemmed from more than unified government. Over the course of American history, periods of one-party control had not always ended so badly. What set Bush apart was the extraordinary friction that he and his party encountered midway through his tenure.

Friction from Iraq, Corruption, and Katrina

In the 1952 presidential election, Republicans distilled their case against the Democrats into three words: Korea, communism, and corruption. In 2006, the Democrats' message was just as simple: Iraq, corruption, and Katrina. (Somehow, they neglected to exploit the resulting acronym—ICK.) The three issues blasted Bush and the Republicans where they had once been strong. Bush came to office as the first president with an MBA, and some early accounts pictured his administration as a model of organizational effectiveness (Kettl 2003). Bush also promised to set high standards for openness and ethics. For a while, even most Democrats saw Bush as trustworthy (Jacobson 2008, 148–49). As a result of the three issues, however, more and more people perceived a toxic brew of incompetence and dishonesty.

Iraq

For much of 2003, it appeared that the invasion of Iraq would be a winning political issue for the GOP. But after the insurgency began and the Abu Ghraib scandal erupted, polls showed that most Americans disapproved of Bush's handling of Iraq. In the summer of 2006, the DCCC summed up the line of attack with a controversial Internet video. "Things have taken a turn for the worse," it began. Amid other painful images, it featured shots of a burning tank, a planeload of flag-draped coffins, and a soldier praying over a fallen comrade. "Washington Republicans have sold America out," read another title, along with photos of Bush, Cheney, Rove, and House Majority Leader Tom DeLay (R-Texas). Republicans sharply criticized the "coffin ad," but they only managed to draw more attention to it, prompting thousands to visit the DCCC Web site and provide their e-mail addresses (Bendavid 2007, 147–48).

The November exit poll showed that Iraq hurt the Republicans. But the poll showed another issue that hurt them even more: corruption.

Corruption

During Bush's first term, Democrats hoped that corporate accounting scandals might bring down the GOP. Democratic strategists James Carville, Stanley Greenberg, and Robert Shrum wrote, "Enron has the potential to shape the entire political environment for 2002" (Carville, Greenberg, and Shrum 2002).

It never happened. In an election-eve poll by CBS News, only 4 percent of respondents cited "corporate reform" as their key voting issue (Pollich 2002). Three things blunted the issue's impact. First, Democrats had failed to prove serious wrongdoing by major administration officials. Second, the issue was not neatly partisan. Although Enron executives favored the GOP, they gave significant sums to Democrats, including Daschle. Third, Bush co-opted the reform issue by signing the Sarbanes-Oxley Act, which improved corporate accounting standards, and the McCain-Feingold Act, which banned soft-money contributions to political parties.

By Bush's second term, Republicans were getting into more trouble. Their problem was not that they had suddenly turned evil. Rather, power had put temptation in their path. And as the scandals mounted, no one could miss their distinctly Republican bouquet:

- After former ambassador Joe Wilson questioned President Bush's claim that Iraq had shopped for uranium in Niger, an administration official told journalist Robert Novak that Wilson's wife, Valerie Plame, worked for the Central Intelligence Agency. Some Democrats referred to the leak as an act of treason. Although Deputy Secretary of State Richard Armitage was the official who leaked the information, the case led to a 2005 perjury indictment for Cheney's chief of staff, I. Lewis "Scooter" Libby. A jury convicted Libby in 2007.

- In 2005, a Texas grand jury indicted House Majority Leader Tom DeLay on a charge of illegally using corporate money to back Republicans in state elections. Republican conference rules forced him to step aside from the leadership. He later resigned from Congress.
- Representative Randy "Duke" Cunningham (R-California) resigned in 2005 after pleading guilty to taking huge bribes from defense contractors. A sentencing memo revealed that he had written out a "bribe menu" detailing what he expected for contracts of various sizes.
- In January 2006, lobbyist Jack Abramoff pleaded guilty to conspiracy, fraud, and tax evasion. News stories revealed his close ties to DeLay and other leading Republicans. In October, Representative Bob Ney (R-Ohio) pleaded guilty to taking Abramoff's bribes.

A survey found that most Americans saw the Abramoff case as evidence of "widespread corruption in Washington" (Morin and Deane 2006). Wherever they could, Democratic candidates highlighted their GOP opponents' links to Abramoff. Such a connection was especially damaging to Senator Conrad Burns (R-Montana), who would narrowly lose to Jon Tester. Abramoff also had a cameo in the DCCC's "coffin ad."

By itself, the Abramoff case did not seal the GOP's doom. Most voters were hazy on its specifics, and it did not pack the emotional firepower of an issue such as Iraq. Late in the campaign, another corruption issue had more impact. Representative Mark Foley (R-Florida) resigned shortly after ABC News reported that he had exchanged sexually explicit e-mails and instant messages with House pages. Questions soon arose about why Republican leaders had not acted on earlier reports of Foley's conduct. In one survey, 79 percent of respondents said House GOP leaders were more concerned about their political standing than about the pages' safety (Nagourney and Elder 2006). The DCCC encouraged Democratic candidates to raise the Foley issue against their opponents.

This scandal was different and more powerful. Few Americans know what lobbyists do. Everybody knows what sexual predators do.

Katrina

Fairly or unfairly, Americans believed that the federal government had badly botched its response to Hurricane Katrina. Democrats seized the opportunity:

"I think Katrina just did us a really big favor, to be crass about it," Emanuel said. He called Bill Burton, his communications director at DCCC, and ordered him to find out which Republican congressmen from the Gulf region had voted to cut the budget for the Army Corps of Engineers. The Corps was responsible for New Orleans levees, and given the levees' fate, such a vote would now look reckless. "Hey, look, if the AP doesn't do it, let's see if either the [*New Orleans Times*] *Picayune* would do it or we can go to a blog," Emanuel said. "No fingerprints," he added curtly, meaning the news item should not be traceable to the DCCC. (Bendavid 2007, 53)

Howard Dean later visited New Orleans. "I hate to be partisan at a time like this," he said, "but this is why the Republicans are going to be out of business." Democratic strategist Donna Brazile explained, "We're highlighting the incompetence of the government" (from Nagourney 2006a).

Besides highlighting the competence issue, Katrina also wrecked Bush's effort to reduce African Americans' hostility to him and the GOP. He tried hard in his 2000 campaign to avoid offending blacks. The Republican national convention pushed images of diversity to the point of self-parody. Bush finessed the issue of affirmative action, instead praising "affirmative access." During the 2002 midterm election campaign, Republicans stepped up minority outreach efforts, buying ads in radio markets catering to blacks and delivering messages that touted GOP ideas and attacked the Democratic record. Liberal commentator John Judis offered a cynical but accurate explanation: "The idea is not so much to win votes but to deprive the opposition of a bogeyman against whom they can turn out the vote" (Judis 2002). Two years later, Bush continued his effort at minority outreach by speaking at churches with predominantly black congregations and seeking support from black pastors. Although he gained only slightly in black support between 2000 and 2004, that small increase might have tipped the crucial and closely contested state of Ohio. In July 2005, Republican National Committee chair Ken Mehlman spoke to the NAACP in an apologetic tone: "Some Republicans gave up on winning the African-American vote, looking the other way or trying to benefit politically from racial polarization. I am here today as the Republican chairman to tell you we were wrong" (from Benedetto 2006).

When Katrina struck, so did Democrats. "George Bush is our Bull Connor," Representative Rangel told a cheering audience at a Congressional Black Caucus town hall. "And because of the Bull Connors," he added, "the American people said enough is enough." Rangel said that Connor, the Birmingham official who used attack dogs against civil rights demonstrators in the 1960s, "woke up the country in terms of racism, and maybe the indifference of Bush can wake up the country in terms of not having tax cuts but ending poverty" (from Clyne 2005).

A few weeks later, one poll found that Bush's approval rating among blacks stood at 2 percent (Froomkin 2005).

After the Culminating Point

In January 2007, Nancy Pelosi (D-California) became Speaker of the House and Harry Reid (D-Nevada) became majority leader of the Senate. They enjoyed early success. House Democrats won 90 percent of the party-unity votes in 2007, a record for either party in either chamber. Senate Democrats won 67 percent of the time, a very respectable level for a chamber in which the minority party can thwart so much of the action (Richert 2008). The Democrats passed crowd-pleasing bills to raise the federal minimum wage and lower interest rates on student loans. They burnished their image as reformers with tighter rules on congressional ethics. Meanwhile, their incumbents and congressional campaign committees did spectacularly well with campaign finance.

Conversely, Bush and the Republicans felt the sting of retreat. Their poll numbers and fund-raising worsened. The scandals continued: one GOP senator visited prostitutes and another solicited sex in an airport men's room. Under Democratic chairs, congressional committees probed cases of abuse and mismanagement, including poor care at Walter Reed Army Medical Center.

Janet Hook of the *Los Angeles Times* used military metaphors to describe Bush's reaction to the changing battlefield: "Rather than turn tail for his last two years in the White House, Bush has used every remaining weapon in his depleted arsenal—the veto, executive orders, the loyalty of Republicans in Congress—to keep Democrats from getting their way. He has struck a combative pose, dashing hopes that he would be more accommodating in the wake of his party's drubbing in the 2006 midterm voting" (Hook 2007). The Democrats remained on the offense. In 2008, they won 93 percent of party-unity votes in the House, an all-time record (Zeller 2008). Their lower success rate in the Senate—54.1 percent—redoubled their determination to win something close to a "filibuster-proof" majority of sixty votes in the 2008 elections.

Though he was not on the ballot in 2008, President Bush exerted a profound effect on both parties. Barack Obama won the Democratic nomination in part because he had been an earlier and more consistent opponent of Bush policies than Hillary Clinton had been (Ceaser, Busch, and Pitney 2009). The Republicans nominated John McCain, the maverick who had supported Bush on Iraq and immigration but had parted company with him on other issues. Antipathy to Bush helped congressional Democrats in their recruitment and fund-raising efforts, which also benefited from their majority status. Congressional Republicans recognized that Bush's unpopularity had severely damaged the GOP "brand," and they tried to separate themselves from him.

The "ICK" problem continued to weigh them down. Although the troop surge in Iraq apparently was working, the war remained unpopular. Just before the election, a jury convicted Senator Ted Stevens (R-Alaska) of concealing graft, which not only put his seat at risk but also gave national Democrats a new occasion to decry the "culture of corruption." And as the GOP convention began, another hurricane bore down on Louisiana. This one did far less damage than Katrina, but it did revive memories of the earlier disaster. For Republicans, the hurricane did bring one small consolation: it prompted President Bush to cancel his appearance at their national convention.

For a short time after the convention, it seemed that Republicans might be coming back. Some polls showed McCain with a lead and congressional Republicans with a narrowing disadvantage. Then came the financial crisis, which destroyed any chance the GOP may have had.

On election day 2008, the wheel turned full circle. Democrats would now control the White House and enjoy enhanced majorities on Capitol Hill. This victory gave President Obama a chance to enact sweeping legislation and leave a lasting mark on American public policy. It also posed potential problems for the Democratic Party. For years, hostility to President Bush had been a unifying principle. If Democrats disagreed on what they were *for*, they could at least agree on what they were *against*: Bush. Once he left the scene, old tensions and animosities would resurface. As the Republicans had learned a few years earlier, total control means total accountability. Someday, in the future, the Democrats would reach their own culminating point.

Washington Governance | PART III

8

SHIFTING SANDS

President Bush and Congress

BERTRAM JOHNSON

P resident George W. Bush had a mercurial relationship with the legislative branch. At times, the president seemed to be getting what he wanted out of Congress. On May 31, 2003, he stated, "I'm proud of the United States Congress. The Congress is focused on results, and they have delivered tremendous results for the American people. . . . No, this Congress, instead of endless bickering and needless partisanship, has focused on . . . doing [what's] right for the American people" (Bush 2003). Bush's top two legislative priorities—education reform and tax cuts— were taken up quickly and passed within six months of his inauguration. Subsequent presidential initiatives, including the USA-PATRIOT Act's antiterrorism measures, a bill creating a new Department of Homeland Security, further tax cuts, and Medicare reform, all met with favorable treatment on Capitol Hill. If one defines presidential success in terms of Congress doing what the president wants, Bush ranks near the top of the list of modern presidents for his first term (Jones 2003).

After his reelection, however, Bush did not fare as well. Shortly after Bush declared that he intended to make vigorous use of the "political capital" that the 2004 vote had bestowed, key senators and representatives

131

started parting ways with him. Social Security reform faltered in mid-2005; Hurricane Katrina prompted a chorus of congressional outrage that same fall; and, in 2006 and 2007, Bush pushed for immigration reform, to no avail. On October 30, 2007, he complained that "Congress is not getting its work done. We're near the end of the year, and there really isn't much to show for it. The House of Representatives has wasted valuable time on a constant stream of investigations, and the Senate has wasted valuable time on an endless series of failed votes to pull our troops out of Iraq. And yet there's important work to be done on behalf of the American people" (Bush 2007). As if to punctuate this reversal of fortune, the president's closest congressional allies turned against him during the greatest economic crisis in decades, nearly killing the massive bailout of the financial industry in September 2008.

But is there anything unusual about this pattern? After all, most presidents achieve their biggest successes early in their first terms and begin to drift after reelection (Nelson 1998). Franklin Roosevelt's first one hundred days are the standard by which historians measure presidential achievement, but in his second term Congress rebuked him over a failed attempt to reshape the Supreme Court. Ronald Reagan slashed taxes in 1981, but by 1986 scandals and congressional investigations distracted him. Sooner or later, most presidents lose whatever cordiality might have existed between them and the lawmakers at the other end of Pennsylvania Avenue. What's more, as one commentator put it, second-term presidents may fail to persuade Congress because "they and their people are exhausted, shellshocked, and out of good ideas" (Ponnuru 2007).

There is indeed something unprecedented about the Bush experience. No modern president has scaled such heights in his relationship with Congress and fallen so far, so fast. This is no coincidence—the factors behind the first-term victories are the same that lie behind the second-term defeats. The president's leadership style was well adapted for an environment in which he could serve as the agenda setter, moving first and then allowing Congress to react to his proposals. In addition, the polarized political context affecting both the president and Congress has increased the potential for sweeping (albeit narrow) victories but only when president and co-partisans share key policy preferences. When the president's party controls the House of Representatives, as Republicans did from 2001 to 2006, the potential for victories is especially great. The Senate, controlled by Republicans in the first part of 2001 and then again from 2003 to 2006, is more difficult to master.

Bush was most successful in achieving his goals on tax policy, and he used a "stake in the sand" strategy that relied on quick passage of a favorable bill by the House of Representatives, followed by more labored negotiations with key senators. On other domestic policy issues, Bush fared worse because his Republican allies were more divided. On oversight, Bush lost control of the agenda, and he faced repeated crises and embarrassments—especially once Democrats gained control of Congress after the 2006 elections.

The Bush Record

Measuring presidential success and failure is more difficult than it seems. Each measurement method has its flaws. For example, some observers may view a president who vetoes many bills as strong and successful, arguing that the frequent exercise of a constitutional power indicates strength. Others would say that frequent vetoing signals weakness, arguing that if a president has been unable to stop Congress from passing unappealing legislation, the president must not be very effective. President Bush vetoed only one bill (on stem-cell research) when the House of Representatives was under Republican control. Once Democrats took the reins in 2007, he used the veto eleven more times. This pattern might seem to suggest that the president grew weaker after the Democrats won control of Congress, a conclusion that squares with common sense. But Congress mustered the two-thirds majority in both houses required to override his veto only four times. Does this signal weakness or strength?

Despite the drawbacks of any single measure of presidential strength, one key measure does a good job of demonstrating the distinctiveness of the Bush years. Congressional Quarterly Inc.'s presidential support score, calculated annually by the staff of *CQ Weekly*, represents the percentage of the time that the House and Senate voted the way the president wanted them to, on bills for which the president or an official spokesperson had expressed a clear preference. There are therefore two components to this score—the numerator, representing the number of presidential "wins" on votes, and the denominator, representing the number of times the president took a position. The president can increase the support score by either increasing the number of victories or decreasing the number of positions the administration takes.

An examination of CQ support scores shows that the Bush administration is clearly unusual. In the first six years of the Bush presidency, Congress supported him, on average, slightly more than 80 percent of the time. Not since the support scores were first calculated in 1953 had a president sustained such a long period of high support from Congress. Lyndon Johnson, the only previous president to come close, had an average of nearly 83 percent approval from Congress during his five-year presidency (*CQ Weekly* 2008c). Ronald Reagan hit Johnson-like support levels during his first year in office but quickly lost support as Democrats in Congress grew restless and recession gripped the country. Nixon did well for several years, too, but faded as Watergate began to dominate his presidency. Only Bush was able to command such consistently solid support from Congress for so long.

But the fall from such a great height was precipitous. After Democrats won control of Congress in the 2006 elections, Bush's support score plummeted. In 2007, Congress voted his way only 38 percent of the time, a low rarely equaled in presidential history. What is more, when previous presidents have hit lows, it was not usually so soon after the highs. The year-to-year decline of more than 42 percent in the CQ support score that Bush experienced from 2006 to 2007 was exceeded only once in the previous five decades: between 1994 and 1995, during President Clinton's first term. Bush's luck improved only slightly in 2008; his support ratings from Congress remained among the lowest recorded (*CQ Weekly* 2008a).

It is the unprecedented and consistent success of Bush's first six years, followed by the dramatic decline thereafter, which makes his relationship with Congress unusual. The reasons for this distinctive record concern Bush's uncompromising leadership style and the polarized political context in which he used it.

Presidential Leadership

It is tempting to see Bush's early successes as triumphs of presidential leadership. After all, Bush advertised himself in a 2000 presidential campaign debate as someone who knew "how to lead" and had "shown the ability to get things done" (*New York Times* 2000). The dramatic shift between 2006 and 2007 ought to give us pause in accepting this theory, however, and it should remind us that leadership is a complex phenomenon. Political scientists have long been skeptical about whether presidents have the ability of unilateral command (Neustadt 1990). Instead, presidents are constrained by a number of factors that are largely beyond their control, including public opinion, the political parties, and the composition of Congress. In navigating this thicket, presidents do make meaningful choices, but "the range of maneuvering on these choices is often quite limited" (Peterson 1990, 266). As George Edwards has argued, presidential leadership operates "at the margins" of an existing political environment (Edwards 1989).

This is not to say, however, that presidential leadership is unimportant. In politics, often a "marginal" push in one direction can make the difference between the success and failure of a policy proposal. This analysis does, however, illuminate what effective presidential leaders do: they recognize the constraints that they face and they make the best of them. As Richard Neustadt argues, "a President's own prospects for effective influence are regulated (insofar as he controls them) by his choices of objectives, and of timing, and of instruments, and by his choice of choices to avoid" (Neustadt 1990, 90).

President Bush's leadership style has been variously described as aggressive, bold, reckless, stubborn, or uncompromising. With respect to his relationship with Congress, it is fair to say that his strategy has been to pick a few major issues of concern to him, to stake out a clear position, and to reiterate his position consistently and regularly. Bush's domestic policy team, headed for most of his time in office by senior presidential adviser Karl Rove, set a clear policy agenda, which was then shepherded through Congress by a series of experienced congressional liaisons, including Nicholas Calio from 2001 to 2003, David Hobbs from 2003 to 2004, Candi Wolff from 2005 to 2007, and Dan Meyer in 2007 and 2008. Each of these staffers had significant experience on Capitol Hill, working with and for members of the House and (in Wolff's case) the Senate.

In the past, the White House Office of Legislative Affairs has at times become almost a congressional outpost in the executive branch, with staffers accused of being overly sympathetic to Capitol Hill (Collier 1997). This was not the case in the Bush administration, however. On the contrary, members of Congress from both parties became increasingly vocal about not being consulted on new legislative initiatives. Furthermore, top White House aides declined to defer to the liaison office on legislative matters. Rove, Vice President Dick Cheney, and other top officials (later including presidential counsel Ed Gillespie) often had their own communication channels to congressional leaders without operating through the liaison office. Although the chief congressional liaison was always a person with ample experience and skill, the office was seldom charged with taking a leading role in policy formulation. Rumors in 2006 that the liaison office would be given new life with the appointment of an experienced former member of Congress failed to materialize (Baker and VandeHei 2006).

Rove and the rest of the Bush team made judgments about policy direction with an eye to the issues' appeal to key sections of the American electorate, and they saw these priorities as related to electoral mandates. They seldom based decisions about policy direction on the intricacies of congressional coalition building. In the first term, for example, tax cuts and education reform were two of a handful of major issues that Bush touted in the campaign and that he therefore pushed hard for once in office (Fortier and Ornstein 2003, 10–11; Brownstein 2001). In the second term, Bush pushed for Social Security reform because, as he put it, "This is what the people want" (from Draper 2007, 294).

When it came time to approach Congress, the Bush team kept to a well-defined strategy. They sought to discipline themselves by advancing a small number of ambitious proposals in order to avoid the confusion and overreaching that can occur when presidents try to do too much. As Calio pointed out in an interview, "The notion that we have this big broad agenda that we can force through Congress is a fallacy" (from Auster 2002). In fact, Bush took the fewest number of positions on House roll call votes in his first six years in office of any president since Eisenhower. The year 2001 was the first year a president had taken a position on fewer than fifty House votes since 1972. Bill Clinton typically held a position on between seventy-five and one hundred House votes; George H. W. Bush took a stand on slightly more (*CQ Weekly* 2008b). But George W. Bush remained silent on many more House votes, speaking out only on his top policy priorities.

After the Democrats took control of Congress, the president immediately began taking more positions on issues. After voicing an opinion on only 40 issues in 2006, the president nearly tripled his number of positions, to 117, in 2007. The entire increase was attributable to domestic policy, rather than foreign, economic, or trade policy, and of these domestic policy positions, more than 90 percent resulted in defeats. This was a steep drop for a president with an 80 percent support rating from the previous Congress. This decline in success suggests, at a minimum, that the president could no longer count on the House for support. The increase in positions taken suggests that House Democrats, rather than the president, had begun to set the agenda.

Political Context

If the political environment can make the difference between a successful and an unsuccessful presidency, it is important to characterize the environment that faced George W. Bush. The most important elements of this environment are broad trends that began before Bush entered the White House and continued during his tenure there. Three factors are most important: recent increases in party polarization in Congress, solid control of the House of Representatives by the majority party leadership, and the greater agreement within the Republican Party on economic issues rather than other issues.

Party Polarization

Parties in Congress are more united today than in decades past. One simple illustration of this is that members of the same party in Congress vote together more often. It might seem odd to modern Americans to think that the political parties did not always march in lockstep, but as late as 1968, votes in which a majority of one party voted against a majority of another made up only about one-third of all votes in the House and Senate. Since then, such "party unity votes" have been increasing steadily, until, in 2007, according to Congressional Quarterly Inc., these votes made up more than 60 percent of all votes in Congress. Reinforcing this trend is the tendency of parties to approach unanimity when party unity votes occur. In the early 1970s, the typical party unity vote attracted only around 70 percent of party members, whereas today the number is often 90 percent. Party-line voting has clearly been on the upswing in the last few decades.

Scholars disagree about why this polarization has occurred. Battle lines may have hardened because of more ideologically consistent voters (Jacobson 2000), an isolated and extremist activist class (Fiorina et al. 2005), greater socioeconomic inequality (McCarty et al. 2006), or some combination of these factors. Whatever the reasons, members of the same party have been voting together in Congress at increasing rates, making it easier to build a coalition on an issue that unifies one party or the other and tougher to persuade members of either party to cross party lines.

Leadership Power in the House

Both the House and the Senate have become more partisan since the late 1970s. In the House, however, the leadership has the power to structure the rules of debate in such a way as to minimize the impact of individual dissenters within the party. This power has increased since the early 1990s. From the 1940s until the 1970s, the House was dominated by powerful committee chairs, many of them from the South, who ruled their domains with near-total power. In the early 1970s, newer members of Congress began to undermine the power of these committee chairs, demanding more opportunities for less senior legislators to shape the agenda. As these efforts became more successful, there appeared a power vacuum into which the House leadership—the Speaker, the majority leader, the whip (chief vote counter), and others—could step. When Republicans gained control of the House in 1994 for the first time in decades, Speaker Newt Gingrich moved swiftly to establish himself as one of the most powerful Speakers in nearly eighty years (Aldrich and Rohde 1997; 2000). Many of the powers that Gingrich assumed (though not all) remain with the speakership.

A powerful House leadership has several critical tools at its disposal with which to shape the agenda. The Rules Committee (controlled by the leadership) can write restrictive rules governing floor debate, committee chairs can be selected based on their loyalty, and plum committee assignments can be withheld from recalcitrant partisans. The overall effect is that the minority party has a very difficult time making its voice heard in the House. It is even harder for one or a few members of Congress (in either party) to disrupt proceedings if they hold preferences contrary to the leadership's. One illustration of this situation is that when the Democrats took over the House in early 2007, a few left-wing members mounted a brief effort to impeach President Bush. Nancy Pelosi, the newly elected House Speaker, said bluntly that impeachment was "off the table," and that was that.

The Senate, on the other hand, operates by a different set of rules, designed to give each senator ample opportunity to shape the course of events. Rather than the agenda being determined solely by the leadership, for example, most bills are brought to the floor by "unanimous consent agreements." Astonishingly, a unanimous consent agreement is exactly what it sounds like: every senator must agree that a bill should come to the floor if it is to do so. If a single senator wishes to block, delay, or add extraneous amendments to a bill, then the leadership cannot easily prevent such action (Binder and Smith 1997). Far from dictating the course of events, party leaders in the Senate spend most of their time negotiating with other senators.

The increasing party polarization since the 1970s has made it easier for party leaders to command consistent majorities in both chambers, but only to a point. In the Senate, if even a few members disagree with the majority position, they can delay, block, or otherwise cause headaches for the majority. Even in the House, a powerful leadership can guarantee only that a given bill will be placed on the agenda. Once a bill comes up on the floor, members generally vote their preferences (Krehbiel 2000). Party discipline is not consistently powerful enough to force members of Congress to approve of policies that they do not prefer in the first place. When faced with an issue upon which there is disagreement within a party, the party leadership will be unable to compel conformity to a particular alternative.

Although any president would rather be backed by a united party than a disunited one, unity is less useful when the president's party is not in control of Congress. Furthermore, in circumstances in which parties are unified, it is much more advantageous to control the House of Representatives than the Senate. This is because the rigid, less flexible rules of the House serve to magnify the power of the chamber's leadership, while the less organized, less hierarchical Senate rules serve to elevate the importance of individual senators. If the president's party controls Congress, therefore, the key to passing the president's agenda is bold action in the House of Representatives.

Agreement on Economic Issues

Once an issue appears on the agenda, intraparty agreement is critical to a party's ability to move issues forward. It is therefore important to identify the issues on which each party's members most often agree. A comparison of interest group ratings of Republican members of the House of Representatives shows that economic policy issues unite the Republican Party more readily than other issues. Many interest groups rate each member of Congress on a scale from 1 to 100, based on their votes on issues of concern to that interest group. Two such groups are the National Taxpayers Union (NTU), which concerns itself with economic policy, and the Christian Coalition, which focuses on social policy. The NTU ratings of Republican members of the House cluster together more than do the ratings of the Christian Coalition. The vast majority of Republicans receive mildly favorable ratings from the NTU, but Christian Coalition ratings are spread out in a lopsided way, with a large number of Republicans scoring very positively but a significant minority scoring around 50 percent or lower. If disagreement among substantial groups of congressional Republicans occurs, it is unlikely to be on economic issues.

The Bush Strategy

In addition to restricting themselves to a few top priorities, members of the Bush administration adopted an aggressive Capitol Hill strategy that relied heavily on the House of Representatives. The strategy may be roughly summarized as follows: first, drive a metaphorical "stake in the sand" by pressing for swift passage of a House bill that is close to the president's ideal proposal; second, place pressure on pivotal senators to toe the administration line; and third, be willing to compromise if necessary, especially with respect to noneconomic issues.

In cases involving taxes, the Bush administration was able to secure significant victories by staking out a clear position, relying on the House to enact most of its plans, and, finally, bargaining with the more moderate Senate from the position of strength that the House bill established. In other policy areas, Bush took more moderate stances earlier because of divisions among House Republicans.

Tax Policy

Tax cuts were a centerpiece of George W. Bush's campaign for the presidency. In a debate with Vice President Al Gore in October 2000, Bush said, "I want to have a tax relief for all people who pay the bills in America because I think you can spend your money more wisely than the federal government can" (Federal Document Clearing House 2000). President Bush delivered on his tax cut promises, pushing major tax cut bills through Congress in 2001 and 2003. In doing so, he relied on the unity of House Republicans, who quickly passed plans that approximated his administration's initial proposals. Bush then went to work on the Senate, persuading just enough moderates there to pass plans that, while not as ambitious as the House plans, were acceptable to him. Finally, in an extended rear-guard action, Bush spent the remainder of his presidency defending his tax cuts from Democrats who sought to undo them.

Bush's first tax cut plan, which the Office of Management and Budget (OMB) calculated would cost $1.6 trillion over ten years, called for cuts in individual income tax rates, increases in the child tax credit, expanded educational savings accounts (special bank accounts that are not taxed as long as the money is used for education expenses), an end to inheritance and gift taxes, and expanded deductions for charitable contributions (Nitschke 2001).

Less than forty-eight hours after the president proposed the cuts in his first address to Congress, the House Ways and Means Committee (which has principal jurisdiction over tax issues) passed most of the Bush plan on a party-line vote. There was perfunctory debate on the measure, little or no consultation with Democrats, and no witness testimony (Kessler 2001). Within a week, the tax cut had passed the House with support from every single House Republican as well as from a handful of Democrats.

The bill was about to hit a series of roadblocks on the Senate side, however, and to help the bill along, the president began a visible public campaign to pressure lawmakers into adopting the cuts. In a move that one senator criticized as "tacky," Bush traveled to North Dakota, South Dakota, Louisiana, and Florida, to stump for his plan and urge voters to contact their senators, all Democrats, in support of tax cuts (Dewar and Balz 2001). "You're just an e-mail away from making a difference in somebody's attitude," Bush told a crowd in South Dakota, Senate Democratic leader Tom Daschle's home state (from Lacy 2001).

In April, the Senate agreed to a $1.2 trillion blueprint that trimmed Bush's proposed reductions by more than $400 billion in favor of spending on education and debt reduction. Democrats saw this as a significant setback for the administration, but if this was true, Bush and his aides were not admitting it. White House counselor Karen Hughes called the Senate vote "a great victory." "What we've really done," she said, "is pour in concrete the tax cut and set it anywhere between almost 1.3 and 1.6 [trillion dollars]" (from Kessler and Milbank 2001). Bush himself seemed pleased. "It's going to be a heck of a lot bigger than anybody thought," he told reporters (from Kessler and Milbank 2001).

The final bill, negotiated between the House and Senate by Representative William M. Thomas (R-California), chair of the House Ways and Means Committee, as well as Senate Finance Committee chair Charles Grassley, Senator Max Baucus (D-Montana), and Senator John Breaux (D-Louisiana), cut taxes $1.35 trillion over ten years. The core elements of the Bush proposal remained, in addition to an immediate tax rebate of $300 for individual taxpayers (Rosenbaum 2001). A triumphant President Bush said of the bill on May 26, the day of its passage, "Today, for the first time since the landmark tax relief championed 20 years ago by President Ronald Reagan and 40 years by President John F. Kennedy, an American president has the wonderful honor of letting the American people know significant tax relief is on the way" (from Kornblut 2001).

Victory would have been sweeter, however, if it had not come at the same time as a major loss for the Republican Party. Near the end of the tax-cut negotiations, Vermont senator James Jeffords announced that he would leave the Republican Party, become an independent, and caucus with the Democrats, upsetting the 50-50 balance in the Senate and placing control in Democratic hands. Jeffords was upset by the White House's failure to set aside $180 million in the tax bill for special education funding, and he had warned Bush not to disregard the concerns of moderate senators (Shepard 2001; Lancaster 2001). Bush's strategy of staking out a clear position in the House had won the tax battle, but it had (at least temporarily) cost his party control of the Senate.

In December 2002, as most of the world's attention focused on diplomatic efforts to determine the fate of Iraq, President Bush's economic advisers worked quietly, preparing a new round of tax cuts as part of an effort to boost the economy and advance the Republican domestic policy agenda. As the economic package took shape, the administration leaned toward making a cut in taxes on corporate dividends the centerpiece of the plan. By Christmas, administration officials were telling members of the press that the president would likely propose to cut dividend taxes by "about half" as part of an economic package that would cost around $300 billion over ten years (Andrews 2002a).

Two weeks later, in a dramatic shift, President Bush announced a plan that would not just reduce but would entirely eliminate taxes on corporate dividends paid to individuals. Democrats balked at the cost, protesting that it unfairly benefited the rich. House Democrats, led by Minority Leader Nancy Pelosi, announced an alternative $100 billion proposal, focusing on short-term tax rebates, aid to states, and an extension of unemployment benefits. Senator Baucus, the top Democrat on the Finance Committee, produced a similar $135 billion plan (Barshay 2003). Senator Breaux, a moderate, assured reporters that Bush's plan would be "replaced, and/or dramatically scaled down" (from Barshay and Ota 2003). By March, revised estimates pegged the cost of the plan at $726 billion over ten years. Some Republicans saw this large figure as cause for concern, but their skepticism did not slow down the bill's progress in the House. Tom DeLay (R-Texas), the new House majority leader, was a firm proponent of the Bush initiative, and he pressed for an even larger tax cut than the one Bush had proposed. Asked if he had an upper limit in mind, DeLay mused, "Who knows? . . . A trillion dollars?" (from Barshay and Ota 2003).

Meanwhile, in the Senate, moderate Republicans were concerned. "I won't take it as it is," Senator Olympia Snowe (R-Maine) bluntly told the press (from Hook 2003a). "Our government is in deficit and we have large expensive challenges ahead," said Lincoln Chafee (R-Rhode Island), announcing his opposition to the package (from Barshay and Ota 2003).

In mid-April 2003, each house voted on a budget resolution, the first step in determining the size and structure of the budget for the next fiscal year. The House included provisions for a ten-year tax cut of $550 billion—lower than the president had proposed but still substantial. Senate Republicans set a $350 billion limit, however, in a deal made to satisfy the concerns of moderates Snowe and George Voinovich (R-Ohio). Outraged House leaders claimed they had not been informed of the Senate's plans and felt betrayed. DeLay accused Senate Republicans of endangering the two houses' ability to work together. "We will continue to press for tax relief that will stimulate more than some senator's ego," he said (from Hook 2003b).

The final bill, passed in May, amounted to a $350 billion measure that included $20 billion in aid to financially distressed state governments. The White House declared victory. Calling it "bold legislation," Bush argued that the new law was "adding fuel to an economic recovery" (from Stevenson 2003). The president had good reason to be pleased—after all, $350 billion was the approximate goal the administration had started with five months earlier, and it was far larger than what Democrats had wanted. "Many Democrats were saying they would not support anything in excess of about $100 billion, as a temporary one-year tax cut," White House press secretary Ari Fleischer pointed out (from VandeHei 2003). Although it was much smaller than Bush's February proposal, the new law nevertheless enacted the third largest tax cut in U.S. history.

In the case of both tax cuts, then, the administration counted on near-unity among House Republicans to ratify a starting position that favored the administration. After the House passed a sweeping bill, the Senate chipped away at it but never whittled it down to levels that were truly disappointing for the Bush administration. Later, when Democrats regained control of Congress, Bush and a united House Republican caucus repeatedly blocked plans to repeal or significantly alter the tax cuts. Indeed, the call to make the tax cuts (many of which were set to expire in 2011) permanent became a rallying cry for Republicans in the 2008 presidential race.

Other Domestic Policy

Bush was not as successful in other domestic policy areas, in large part because Republicans in Congress were not as united on these issues as they were on fiscal matters. Even in the case of his signature domestic policy victory, the No Child Left Behind Act, Bush had to make significant concessions to satisfy critics on both sides in order to build a coalition that would pass the bill. On Social Security and immigration reform, Bush was forced into retreat in the face of vocal dissension from within Republican ranks.

In the same speech before Congress in which Bush outlined his tax-cut plans, he also proposed major education reforms. Calling education his first priority, he set forth a plan to tie increased funding for education to a new system of national testing. Children in grades three through eight would undergo standardized tests selected and administered by the states. Schools and states in which students did poorly for three years running would be punished with cuts in some federal grant money, while the best schools and states would be rewarded. Although the core of the administration's proposal was the testing, it also included a provision offering students in poorly performing public schools vouchers that could be used to pay tuition at private schools (Schlesinger 2001).

House Republican leaders introduced a bill close to the Bush plan, including the voucher provision, but signaled their willingness to compromise. "I think there's a lot of common ground on this issue," said Representative John Boehner (R-Ohio), chair of the House Committee on Education and the Workforce (from Mollison 2001). In early May, the committee dropped the voucher provision and sent the bill to the floor.

The White House recognized that the education bill might divide Republicans. The Christian Coalition, for example, worried that the state-based testing system could turn into a nationalized testing system, thus undermining local control of education (Nather 2001b). This and other reservations among conservatives threatened to create an alliance between some Republicans and liberal Democrats to defeat the measure. On the House floor, Representatives Peter Hoekstra (R-Michigan) and Barney Frank (D-Massachusetts) cosponsored an amendment to drop the testing provisions. After intense lobbying by White House chief of staff Andrew Card and strategist Karl Rove, the amendment went down to defeat on a vote of 173 to 255 (Nather 2001b). Although the House finally passed the bill on a vote of 384 to 45, this lopsided margin masked several such narrow escapes on amendments.

After the Senate passed its own version, the education bill languished at the conference committee stage, with conferees battling over overall funding levels, funding for special education, and the exact nature of testing standards (Nather 2001a). After months of delay, they arrived at a compromise plan that contained the core elements of Bush's proposal: state-administered tests for students in grades three through eight, and penalties for schools and states that failed to meet these standards.

Following a legislative journey similar to that of the education bill was Bush's plan for a new Medicare prescription drug benefit. Another Bush campaign promise, the Medicare overhaul was intended to modernize the entitlement program while at the same time winning the support of seniors by adding prescription drug coverage. In his 2003 State of the Union address, the president urged Congress to reform and strengthen the program.

As the White House lobbied for the proposal, Senators Grassley and Baucus crafted a compromise bill that would have established a privately run drug program with a government-run "fallback" program for seniors in rural areas not served by private companies (*Congressional Quarterly Almanac* 2004). Meanwhile, the House Ways and Means Committee under Chair William Thomas passed a much more conservative bill that would have relied entirely on private plans and that called for Medicare to enter into direct competition with private insurance by 2010. Representative John Dingell (D-Michigan) accused Republicans of plotting to let Medicare "wither and die" (from Pear and Toner 2003). Conservatives also began grumbling about the president's plan, calling it a major expansion of a costly government program.

Conservative discontent grew so problematic that when the full House held its vote on the measure, Republican leaders held the vote open for an unprecedented two hours and fifty-one minutes (rather than the prescribed fifteen minutes). As the vote dragged on past 4:00 A.M., Speaker Dennis Hastert, Health and Human Services Secretary Tommy Thompson, and even (by telephone) President Bush himself cornered, cajoled, and otherwise pressured recalcitrant Republican members to vote with the president. After the plan finally passed, by one vote, a disillusioned Republican called the stunt "an outrage" and accused it of being "profoundly ugly and beneath the dignity of Congress" (from Mann and Ornstein 2006, 3).

The final bill, negotiated by House and Senate Republicans, left Democrats unhappy and Republicans suspicious. It provided coverage for 75 percent of prescription drugs up to an annual total cost of $2,250, opened up the Medicare program to more competition from private plans, and created "health savings accounts" into which Americans could deposit some pre-tax earnings to withdraw when paying medical bills. Although

Bush hailed the measure as the "greatest advance in health care coverage for America's seniors since the founding of Medicare," many Democrats labeled it a giveaway to insurance companies (from Rosenbaum 2003). Budget-conscious Republicans had their own concerns: "The fiscal path this bill sets us on scares the heck out of me," said Representative Charlie Norwood (R-Georgia) (from Fagan 2003).

The successful passage of the No Child Left Behind legislation and the Medicare drug benefit, the two major domestic policy victories of the Bush administration, both hinged upon Bush's ability to build an ad hoc, bipartisan coalition to support his plans when his own party was not prepared to unite in support of him. The administration's two major domestic policy failures occurred because of Bush's inability to do the same thing.

Upon winning reelection, President Bush signaled that his top domestic policy priority would be Social Security reform. Nearly one-quarter of his State of the Union address in 2005 was devoted to the subject, and he called for personal retirement accounts into which Americans could deposit some of their Social Security payments as an alternative to paying into the Social Security system. That March, Bush and Vice President Cheney toured the country touting their plan, and Senate leaders suggested that a bill might make it out of committee by summer. But Democratic opposition to the measure hardened, and, even more importantly, Republican support was lacking. By April, polls showed a majority of Americans as being opposed to the personal accounts, and Republican opposition began to get more vocal.

In a bold attempt to save the plan and to address the substantial costs of transitioning to a system with personal accounts, Bush proposed a system of "progressive indexing" that would cut some Social Security benefits for all but the poorest recipients. Bush advisers also signaled that he would be willing to compromise on most aspects of the plan, as long as the resulting bill contained some kind of personal accounts system (Lambro 2005). It didn't work. Democrats protested more loudly, and moderate Republicans, concerned about costs and fearful of being punished at the polls, declined to offer the plan their support.

The Social Security issue may have occasioned some misgivings among fiscal conservatives, but the immigration issue prompted a full-blown revolt among House Republicans. Bush, owing to his (and to Karl Rove's) determination to secure more of the Latino vote for the party and relying on his previous practical experience with immigration policy as Texas governor, proposed a plan that would crack down on illegal border crossings but also establish a temporary guest worker program and a path to citizenship for many illegal immigrants. This reform, as Bush put it, would "address the issue of the millions of illegal immigrants already in our country, and honor America's great tradition of the melting pot" (from Lochhead 2006).

Senators John McCain and Edward Kennedy put together a bipartisan plan in mid-2006 that approximated the Bush proposal. But House Republicans would have none of it. Judiciary Committee chair James Sensenbrenner (R-Wisconsin) dismissed the Senate's proposal as unworkable and instead joined other House Republicans in a nationwide series of "field hearings" that highlighted problems with illegal immigration. Describing the citizenship program as "amnesty," the House Republicans rapidly dug a political grave for the Senate bill. The failed compromise plan dogged McCain for years, threatening his presidential candidacy in 2008.

In the domestic policy arena, President Bush was able to accomplish the most when he had a united House Republican caucus on his side. This unity was almost always present when tax cuts were on the table. In those cases, an audacious, extreme initial proposal of the type that the president found intrinsically appealing was most likely to plant a firm "stake" in the House and draw the more moderate Senate in his direction. Even after the Democrats regained control of Congress in 2007, the president was able to keep Republicans united in preserving his tax plans. In the case of social policies dealing with education, Social Security, Medicare, and immigration, the president either had to quickly moderate his initial proposal or face defeat, though altering the initial proposal sometimes failed to prevent defeat. The combination of context and leadership made for dramatic successes, but only under certain conditions.

Oversight

Oversight—Congress's monitoring of how the executive branch is performing its functions—has been on the decline in recent decades. As political scientist Joel Aberbach has found, oversight hearings have been decreasing in number since the early 1980s (cited Murray 2005). This decline continued for the first six years of the Bush administration. As Norm Ornstein and Thomas Mann explain, "Members of the majority party, including the leaders of Congress, see themselves as field lieutenants in the president's army far more than they do as members of a separate and independent branch of government" (Mann and Ornstein 2006, 155). That the period of declining oversight coincided with a period of partisan polarization is not surprising. If congressional party leaders agree with the president on fundamental issues, why complicate matters by probing too eagerly into how the administration is operating? Since the majority party controls when oversight hearings and investigations take place, the majority leadership can usually squelch these practices if they want to do so.

As a result, when oversight did occur between 2001 and 2006, it was usually the result of a major crisis that could not be contained. The 9/11 attacks, the Hurricane Katrina disaster, and the Abu Ghraib prison abuse scandal all prompted significant congressional inquiries. Some Democrats also tried to pursue oversight outside the halls of Congress. A group of members sued Vice President Dick Cheney (unsuccessfully) over the secrecy of his energy task force, for example. At times, Democratic members held "unofficial" hearings if House Republicans refused to hold regular ones. But these efforts failed to shape the agenda or prove to be a distraction to the president.

Once Democrats took control of Congress in 2006, oversight became a priority again, and a series of hearings on the Iraq war, intelligence-gathering procedures, the motives behind the Justice Department's firing of nine U.S. attorneys, and other major issues curtailed the president's ability to shape the agenda in Washington. The issue of the (possibly political) firing of the U.S. attorneys, in particular, dominated the news for months until Attorney General Alberto Gonzales finally resigned in mid-2007.

Oversight is just one example of how the Bush administration lost much of the control over the agenda that it had exercised prior to the 2006 elections. The White House found itself more often reacting to the Congress rather than the other way around. Hence, congressional Democrats directly challenged Bush's priorities in more bills and resolutions and thus forced the president to take many more positions on House votes than he had in prior years. The administration was also legally bound to react to a series of subpoenas, document requests, and committee inquiries.

Bush and Congress in Summary

The preceding accounts of Bush administration successes and failures illustrate the importance of three key factors in the Bush years: the intense ideological polarization of Congress; the greater agreement within Republican ranks on economic issues than on other matters; and the president's leadership strategy of staking out a strong position and letting House Republicans pull the congressional debate in his direction. Bush did best when introducing tax legislation to a Republican-controlled Congress. He was less successful in advancing his agenda on domestic policy issues other than tax issues and when a Democratic-controlled Congress held oversight hearings.

The increasing internal unity of the parties in Congress worked to the president's advantage, especially with respect to economic policy. In the tax policy cases described above, President Bush could count on much more united Republican support than a similar president could have dreamed of in decades past. While Lyndon Johnson, Jimmy Carter, and even Ronald Reagan struggled to keep their partisans in the fold, Bush found such efforts practically unnecessary in the tax-cut cases. The House voted on the 2001 tax cut less than two days after the president announced his plan and granted the president practically everything he asked for. In 2003, the House again moved quickly to provide the president a tax-cut blueprint that was more than $200 billion larger than White House insiders had thought possible a month before.

Education reform, Medicare, Social Security, and immigration policy illustrate the consequence of a disunited party. In contrast to the tax cases, splits in the Republican ranks on entitlements and illegal immigration killed two major bills. The Medicare prescription drug benefit passed by the narrowest of margins because loyal House leaders bent the rules, cajoling swing members into voting with the president. Even in the case of the No Child Left Behind Act, wavering support among Republicans forced the president to work with Democrats early in the process, and he had to swiftly discard a key component of his agenda: private school vouchers.

By exploiting Republican unity and control of the House of Representatives, George W. Bush was able to use his "stake in the sand" strategy to great effect in the first several years of his presidency, especially with respect to tax policy. He and his aides also recognized the inherent limitations of the office and therefore held to a limited legislative agenda over which they were willing to compromise. The president's leadership style was less successful when policy matters divided Republicans and when the president lost control over the congressional agenda during his last two years in office.

In the final months of his presidency, George W. Bush faced an unprecedented economic crisis. A collapse in the market for securitized debt left stock exchanges plunging and brought major financial firms close to insolvency. Ben Bernanke, chair of the Federal Reserve, and Treasury Secretary Henry Paulson told the president that, as Bush put it, "if we don't act boldly . . . we could be in a depression greater than the Great Depression" (Bush 2008a). The administration hastily proposed a $700 billion "rescue plan" for struggling financial institutions and begged Congress to act quickly. But House Republicans overwhelmingly voted against it, arguing that the bill represented a burden on taxpayers and an ill-advised interference in the private sector. The bill's defeat on September 29 sent the U.S. markets down nearly 7 percent, and a hasty renegotiation produced a successful bill—still with little Republican support—a week later.

Pundits called the episode a shocking defeat for President Bush. It was a defeat, certainly, but it was not all that shocking. House Republicans had simply remained consistent and (nearly) united on economic policy; the president's position had just moved sharply away from theirs. Four months later, House Republicans united to oppose President Barack Obama's economic stimulus package. Again, this Republican unity on economic policy was nothing new.

President Bush was able to accomplish a great deal on a slim mandate in his early years in office, but his success rate plummeted when Democrats captured Congress and the agenda became dominated by crisis events and by Bush's political opponents. Barack Obama and future presidents would do well to learn from Bush's example about the potential—and limitations—of the presidency.

9

AUTHORITY AND UNILATERALISM IN THE BUSH PRESIDENCY

PERI E. ARNOLD

George W. Bush's leadership in the White House presents a paradox between power and authority in the modern presidency. Bush pursued notably unilateral governance, evaded checks and balances, and finessed the Democratic opposition. From the beginning of his presidency, he seized executive power as if he had won an electoral landslide and as if energetic use of the presidency might obscure the memory of his clouded victory in the 2000 election. Yet, as we shall see in considering the uses to which he put unilateralism, the unbridled use of presidential power weakened this president, undermined his authority to govern, and left his policy agenda incomplete and vulnerable.

Power is "on tap," so to speak, for presidents from the Constitution, laws, and historical precedent. Presidents have strong incentives to use powers unilaterally to achieve their political and policy goals while avoiding the delay and compromises of the legislative process (Moe and Howell 1999). But power used without authority, a proper justification for action, is arbitrary and, ultimately, illegitimate.

President Bush relied on three different claims of authority at various times to justify his unilateralism. The first of these is the president's constitutional prerogative during crises, unleashed on September 11, 2001. The second authority claim was based in generating public approval for his actions through framing issues with "crafted talk" (Jacobs and Shapiro 2000). The third authority claim was based in a theory of the "unitary executive," which argues that the president, constitutionally, has virtually no limit in the uses and management of executive branch agencies, up to and including avoidance of the dictates of congressional legislation.

Republican Safety and Executive Energy

The Constitution established a constrained, checked-and-balanced government that could act decisively in a crisis. During normalcy, the presidency is constrained by checks and balances, and the president is constrained to faithfully execute the law. But in crises, the president can and historically has responded through broad, unconstrained executive power.

In the *Federalist Papers,* James Madison argued the importance of safeguards on government, writing that "the accumulation of all powers . . . in the same hands . . . may justly be pronounced the very definition of tyranny" (Hamilton et al. n.d., no. 48, 313). But Alexander Hamilton stressed a different ingredient of capable government, writing that "energy in the Executive is a leading character in the definition of good government." Executive energy ensures security, and on that point Hamilton approvingly cited occasions when the Roman republic took "refuge in the absolute power of a single man" (Hamilton et al. n.d., no. 70, 454). Checked government was normally well and good, but in an emergency, a single leader was necessary for security. Thus, the framers built the Constitution so that it contained both constraints on government and the possibility of singular or unilateral executive leadership. Yet the Constitution does not indicate when it is appropriate to trigger unchecked executive energy.

When should Americans seek "refuge in the . . . power of a single man"? Abraham Lincoln and Franklin Roosevelt help us answer that question. Both presidents' emergency leadership recognized that there were limits to emergency powers. As the Southern states seceded in 1861, Lincoln asserted, "I . . . consider . . . the Union is unbroken; and . . . I shall take care . . . that the laws of the Union be faithfully executed in all the States. . . . I trust this will not be regarded as a menace, but only as the . . . purpose of the Union that it . . . constitutionally defend and maintain itself" (Lincoln 1861). Between his inauguration in March 1861 and July 1862, Lincoln initiated war without calling Congress into session. He ordered a naval blockade, called up volunteers for the Union army, suspended habeas corpus, and spent monies without appropriation. However, in a July 1862 message to Congress, he carefully justified his actions and petitioned Congress to approve them.

In 1933, facing a grave economic crisis, Roosevelt said, "It is to be hoped that the normal balance of Executive and legislative authority may be . . . adequate to meet the unprecedented task before us. But it may be that . . . [the] need for undelayed action may call for temporary departure from that normal balance" (Roosevelt 1933). Roosevelt initially used the Democrats' congressional majority to push through his emergency agenda. Later, when the Supreme Court and an increasingly obstreperous Congress blocked him, he attempted to control the Court by "packing" it and sought expanded control over policy by centralizing his management of the executive branch (Arnold 1998, chap. 4; Milkis 1993, chap. 5).

Both Lincoln and Roosevelt invoked expansive executive power during crises. In doing so, both publicly justified the rationale for their actions *and* made clear that the exercise of broad executive power was temporary. Each president assumed inordinate powers while also publicly justifying his emergency actions (Goldsmith 2007, 82–85).

President Bush responded to terrorist attacks with a Hamiltonian assertion of executive energy. But his crisis leadership differed from the Lincoln and Roosevelt precedents. First, Lincoln and Roosevelt wielded weak executive resources compared to those available to modern presidents. The executive branch's growth since the 1930s, along with an expansive national security apparatus and presidential support staff, transformed presidents' capacities for policy management and public leadership (Burke 1992; Moe and Howell 1999, 135–39). Second, Bush's crisis presidency was fortified by his embrace of a novel theory of the unitary presidency that claimed unchecked presidential control over the executive branch of government, even under conditions of Madisonian normalcy (Kelley 2005; Krent 2008). In short, President Bush possessed tools to exert far more control over government than did either Lincoln or Roosevelt, and he asserted that control not as contingent on a temporary crisis but as a normal condition of executive governance.

Framing a Moderate Message and Pursuing Conservative Policy

Nothing in George Bush's 2000 campaign hinted at the trenchant conservatism and strong unilateralism he would exhibit in office. His campaign suggested a moderately center-right leadership attentive to middle-class

Americans. Bush disparaged President Clinton for dishonoring his office, and he pledged conventional morality in government (Neal 2000, A20). He promised a "humble" foreign policy eschewing foreign intervention and nation building (Commission on Presidential Debates 2000). About domestic affairs, he used a language of compassion instead of the anti-government rhetoric typical of Republican conservatism.

Bush's policy priorities in the campaign were tax cuts, education reform, and support for faith-based initiatives. He described the projected budget surplus as "not the government's" but "the hard-working people of America's money," implying that his tax cuts would benefit average Americans (Commission on Presidential Debates 2000). On education reform, he promised elevated standards and new funding so that poor and minority children would not "be left behind." As governor of Texas, Bush had sought increased taxes to equalize school funding between rich and poor communities (Weisberg 2008, 127). He also promised federal funding for religious groups serving the needy, unleashing the generosity of everyday Americans.

For many voters, the choice in 2000 between Bush and the Democratic vice president, Al Gore, seemed a matter of taste more than substance. E. J. Dionne observed that Bush and the Republicans "have been so successful in making themselves look unthreatening that among self-identified liberal Democrats . . . one in seven is willing to vote for Ralph Nader instead of Gore" (Dionne 2000, A35). Another reporter said of Bush, "He has charm, he's a moderate and he's run a state with success" (Milbank 2001, 84). Then Bush's loss of the popular vote in 2000 and victory by a 5-to-4 Supreme Court decision regarding the Florida recount suggested he would chart a moderate course. He assured Americans, "Our nation must rise above a house divided. Republicans want the best for our nation, and so do Democrats" (from Apple 2000, A1). Yet, through personnel appointments and specific policy initiatives, President Bush established an administration that was quite conservative and belied his moderate self-presentation. As Andrew Sullivan noted, "Despite losing the popular vote, Bush governed as if he had won Reagan's 49 states" (Sullivan 2007, 44).

From Movement to Government

Dana Milbank observed about the new administration, "Bush's appointments may surprise those who interpreted [his] soothing campaign rhetoric to mean that he was, if not a moderate, then a 'new kind of Republican'" (Milbank 2001, 84). President Bush chose his appointees from a personnel pool formed by the think-tanks, public interest legal organizations, media outlets, and foundations of the conservative movement (Saloma 1984). A new president fills about thirty-five hundred positions within the executive branch, and about five hundred of those appointments require Senate approval (Burke 2004). Personnel appointments are a means by which a president imposes control over government, seeking those who are politically loyal and, perhaps, competent as well. To maintain tight control of appointments below Cabinet level, Bush's White House Office of Personnel vetted the political suitability of every person available for those appointments, giving Cabinet secretaries three approved names for each opening (Barnes 2001; Weisberg 2008, 101).

Bush's upper-level appointments demonstrated the prominence of the conservative movement's constituent organizations. The Heritage Foundation contributed Elaine Chao, a foundation fellow, as labor secretary; Gail Norton, head of a Heritage-funded advocacy group, as interior secretary; Kay Coles James, a project director at the foundation (and dean at Pat Robertson's Regent University), as director of the Office of Personnel Management; and Alvin Felzenberg, a Heritage fellow, to Defense Secretary Donald Rumsfeld's advisory staff (People for the American Way). Those associated with the American Enterprise Institute (AEI) included John R. Bolton, deputy secretary of state; Douglas Feith, undersecretary of defense; Richard Perle, member of the U.S. Defense Policy Board; and the vice president's wife, Lynne Cheney. In a February 2003 speech, President Bush noted that he so admired AEI that he "borrowed" twenty of its members for his administration (Bush 2003a).

The Federalist Society, an organization of conservative lawyers, was especially prominent in the administration. Attorney General John Ashcroft and Interior Secretary Gail Norton were members of the organization, as were White House counsel Alberto Gonzales and Solicitor General Theodore Olson. Five of the eleven lawyers in the White House counsel's office were also members. Gonzales and his staff were responsible for the selection of candidates for judicial openings, and about 40 percent of those Bush nominated for the federal judiciary were Federalist Society members. The Bush administration also dispensed with the American Bar Association's long-standing nonpartisan role of vetting federal judicial appointees. Martin Garbus writes "that the Federalist Society was the employment center for judges" (Garbus 2003).

Ideological vetting of personnel also permeated the government's career ranks, especially in the Justice Department. The law school of Regent

University, founded by televangelist Pat Robertson, supplied about 150 of its graduates to the administration, many in career positions in the Justice Department as a consequence of changes in the method for selecting career (rather than politically appointed) personnel. Prior to 2003, civil servants in Justice screened applicants and recommended whom to hire, usually selecting graduates of distinguished law schools. In 2003, political appointees took on the role of hiring to fill career positions, and ideological bona fides became a prominent prerequisite for career employment in Justice (Savage 2007b, 296–97). That emphasis on partisan loyalty over professional qualifications appeared even where it is clearly illegal to take politics into account, such as the appointment of immigration judges by the attorney general and career attorneys in the Department of Justice's Office of Civil Rights (Goldstein and Eggen 2007; McQuilken 2009).

Appointees were also drawn from the K Street world of firms whose business is to lobby the departments of Interior, Agriculture, Labor, Commerce, Health and Human Services and the regulatory commissions (Confessore 2003; Mulkern 2004). Changes in the Interior Department's policies on the environment and land use illustrate the relationship between those appointments and policy. The new president rejected American participation in the Kyoto Protocol on global warming. Then the Interior Department issued rules loosening restrictions on water pollution by the mining industry. It reversed requirements that the industry pay for restoration of land after mining activity. The department ended the ban on snowmobiles in Yellowstone Park, and it reduced the size of wilderness preserves set aside by the Clinton administration. Describing Bush administration policies toward the environment, the *New York Times* editorialized that the Clinton administration's environmentally friendly appointees "have been replaced by the hard-edged advocates of development" (*New York Times* 2001, WK14). Consequently, in 2006, after examining decisions and practices in the Interior Department after five years of the Bush administration, its inspector general told a congressional committee, "Simply stated, short of crime, anything goes at the highest levels of the Department of the Interior" (from Andrews 2006).

Crafting the Message

Initially, President Bush's public narrative promised concern for average Americans and projected moderation. Lawrence Jacobs and Robert Shapiro observe that "politicians attempt to *stimulate responsiveness* by changing centrist opinion to support their positions" with "crafted talk" (Jacobs and Shapiro 2000, 44–45; original emphasis). Bush's promotion of tax cuts used this type of moderate message that was crafted to sell a conservative policy. His plan was based on supply-side orthodoxy—reducing marginal rates for high incomes, reducing the capital gains tax, and abolishing the estate tax or "death tax," as the administration rephrased it in a fine example of message crafting (Chait 2007, chaps. 1, 8). The administration justified tax cuts with arguments that a slowing economy needed stimulation and that a projected budget surplus should be returned to the taxpayers. President Bush ignored the contradiction that a slowing economy would reduce projected surpluses (Pianin 2001, 8).

The president promoted his tax cuts as benefiting average Americans. To prevent contradiction, the administration refused to release projections for how people of different income levels would benefit from the tax cuts. One tax expert said that what the department did release was "embarrassingly poor and biased" (from Hacker and Pierson 2005a, 43). In response to criticism that the cuts sharply favored the rich, Bush accused critics of fomenting class warfare. The Republican chair of the congressional Joint Economic Committee also refused to make public his committee's information about the plan's distributional effects, saying it "is hard to separate from the promotion of class warfare" (from Chait 2007, 136). In fact, by 2010, more than 50 percent of the bill's benefits would go to the wealthiest 1 percent of American households. Yet public opinion polls showed that the president's crafted message had found traction. At least 60 percent of Americans supported the 2001 tax cuts (Bartels 2005).

During summer 2001, President Bush's effort to appear moderate while governing to the right grew more difficult. Senator James Jeffords of Vermont left the Republican Party, decrying its extremism, and control of the Senate thus passed to the Democrats. The Congressional Budget Office forecast sharply reduced budget surpluses for the fiscal year, belying Bush's rationale for tax cuts. In March 2001, the surplus was projected to be $122 billion for fiscal year 2001, but by August, the surplus had shrunk to a trivial $600 million (Stevenson 2001, A1). At the end of the summer, President Bush was out of sight, vacationing in Crawford, Texas. Some Republicans complained that the White House political compass was askew (Berke and Bruni 2001, A11). At the end of June 2001, the president's public approval had declined to 55 percent, down from 63 percent in March (ABC/*Washington Post* poll 2001). In August it was announced that the president would flip a coin in the White House Rose Garden to open the National Football League's season. On September 9 the *New York Times* reported that "the man adores sports . . . and he prefers chatting about balls and strikes to the fuzzy math of the federal budget" (Van Natta 2001, 4:3). Two days later, everything changed.

A War Presidency

The 9/11 attacks made Bush a war president claiming authority to use unilateral national security powers to protect the country. He declared a new purpose for his leadership: "to answer these attacks and rid the world of evil" (Bush 2001b). His public approval spiked; 90 percent of Americans approved his job performance in the wake of 9/11 (ABC/*Washington Post* 2001). This was not only a "rally 'round the flag" response to the attack. It was a "rally 'round the presidency" at a time of crisis, validating Bush as a Hamiltonian president.

Bush's war presidency was reinforced by a claim that the president's authority over the executive branch is total or unitary. Since the 1980s, conservative legal theorists had argued that the Constitution gives presidents sole and unilateral power over the executive branch, a view they termed a theory of the unitary presidency (Krent 2008). The 1987 minority report of the congressional committee investigating the Iran-Contra affair was the "the Magna Carta of this combative ideology" (U.S. Congress 1987; Schwartz and Huq 2007). Vice President Dick Cheney cited it as a source for understanding that "the President of the United States needs to have his constitutional powers unimpaired . . . in terms of the conduct of national security policy" (Cheney 2005). That report had stated, "What President Reagan did in his actions toward Nicaragua and Iran were constitutionally protected exercises of inherent Presidential powers." The minority report concluded that no matter how flawed that action may have been, Congress cannot constitutionally interfere in the president's operation of the executive branch (U.S Congress 1987, 457).

Academic proponents of the unified executive claimed that Article II of the Constitution created "a hierarchical, unified executive" over which "the President alone possesses *all* of the executive power and that he therefore can direct, control, and supervise inferior officers or agencies who seek to exercise discretionary executive power" (Calabresi and Rhodes 1992, 1165). A more skeptical academic writes of the theory that it "assumes hostility in . . . [the president's] political environment and seeks to aggressively push the constitutional boundaries" (Kelley 2005, 11–12).

The Unitary Executive

While the administration trumpeted its unitary executive claim only after 9/11, Bush and his advisers actually embraced the idea from his first day in office. The day after inauguration, White House counsel Alberto Gonzales told the newly appointed lawyers in his office that the president expected them to aggressively expand presidential power (Savage 2007b, 73). After the terrorist attacks, that goal supercharged Bush's use of national security powers.

The unitary executive theory is a doctrine of institutional partisanship, favoring the presidency over Congress and the courts. In the Bush administration, institutional partisanship was joined with political partisanship. Since the 1980s, the Republican Party has identified with executive power, as if it is the natural party of presidential government. Conservative intellectuals have argued for strengthening the office, blaming Congress for intruding upon the president's rightful powers with the War Powers Resolution, the Budget and Impoundment Act, and reforms of the intelligence services. They also argued that the Constitution does not distribute power over national security, foreign and domestic, equally between the president and Congress (Schmitt and Shulsky 1987, 62). In these areas, the presidency was to be supreme.

The unitary executive claim justified virtually any presidential action under cover of national security. For example, in 2003, when Justice Department lawyers and White House lawyers discussed the utility of asking for congressional authorization for domestic surveillance of possible terrorism suspects, David Addington, counsel to Vice President Cheney and author of the Iran-Contra minority report, angrily asked, "Why are you trying to give away the President's power?" (from Goldsmith 2007, 124). Addington was present in virtually every important decision of the White House counsel's office, and he was an enforcer of the unitary executive principle. In one meeting, he expressed the Bush administration's approach to presidential power, saying, "We're going to push and push and push until some larger force makes us stop" (from Goldsmith 2007, 126). That quest for unchecked power is present throughout Bush's governance but is most obvious in matters related to the war on terror, such as claims of war powers, the administration's commitment to secrecy, and Bush's use of signing statements.

Presidential War Powers

For proponents of the unitary presidency, making the decision to go to war is inherently a presidential power. Although the Constitution states that Congress shall "declare war," "unitarians" have argued that the real meaning of this language is that Congress thereby recognizes when a state of war exists but does not make the decision to go to war. Should Congress wish to curtail the president's use of force, its power is through the denial of appropriations to support the use of force (Yoo 2005, 141–42). Expressing this view before the Persian Gulf War, Secretary of Defense Dick Cheney advised President George H. W. Bush against seeking congressional authorization for war because it was unnecessary and Congress "might well vote NO and that would make life more difficult for us" (from Goldsmith 2007, 88).

After 9/11, the White House found legal support for its broad claims of power from the Justice Department's Office of Legal Counsel (OLC). OLC opinions are authoritative within the executive branch. John Yoo, an academic lawyer and political appointee to the OLC, wrote several memoranda on war powers that gave Bush license to use force, control those detained in the war on terror, and spy on Americans. Yoo described the war power as "inherent" in the presidency. The president has "the constitutional power not only to retaliate against any person, organization, or State suspected of involvement in terrorist attacks on the United States, but also against foreign States suspected of harboring or supporting such organizations." Yoo's memorandum to the White House concluded, "In light of the text, plan, and history of the Constitution . . . we think it beyond question that the President has the plenary constitutional power to take such military actions as he deems necessary" (U.S. Department of Justice OLC 2001b, 115).

When Jack Goldsmith, another academic expert on war powers, became head of the OLC in 2003, he reviewed Yoo's memoranda and decided they had no basis in law. He later observed that "Yoo was a god-send" for Bush and his associates who sought maximum power for the executive branch in the war against terrorism (Goldsmith 2007, 98). Goldsmith's account of his experience reveals a driving spirit of unilateralism in the White House. Driven by an obsession with presidential power, the administration brooked no question of the need to consult Congress, seek legislative authority, or take into account the federal courts. As a case in point, the administration ignored the Foreign Intelligence Surveillance Act's requirement of judicial warrants for wiretapping as it pursued its large-scale surveillance of domestic electronic communications through the National Security Agency (NSA). Goldsmith writes that rather than seeking "indisputably lawful" authority, the administration "found it much easier to go it alone, in secret" (Goldsmith 2007, 182).

Bush's power claims became increasingly difficult to maintain in his second term. Neither the Iraq nor Afghanistan wars had fulfilled the president's promised goals. Osama bin Laden remained free in the border region of Afghanistan and Pakistan to plot against the United States. Bush's main domestic aim of privatizing Social Security had failed, and the president's public approval was declining. In that context, under political duress, the administration turned to Congress for legislation to authorize the secret domestic surveillance it had been conducting since 2002. With little resistance, a Democratic-controlled Congress passed the Protect America Act of 2007, creating a legal basis for what Bush had claimed as an inherent power of his office. At that point, one might have wondered if there was any benefit for the president in his extreme power claims, claims that his own ally, Republican senator Lindsey Graham of South Carolina, in 2008 admitted were "pretty aggressive, bordering on bizarre" (from Mahler 2008).

Executive Secrecy

After 9/11, the Bush administration "dramatically expand[ed] the zone of secrecy surrounding the executive branch" (Savage 2007b, 93). Broad claims of emergency presidential power do not by themselves necessitate secrecy. Lincoln and Roosevelt publicly justified their use of emergency powers to attain legitimacy for their actions. Nor does inordinate secrecy necessarily accompany broad executive power today. For example, Judge Robert Bork, a friend of unitary executive claims, proposed that presidents openly defy the other branches in order to legitimize unfettered presidential power. He writes that "the president must make a public issue of congressional attempts to control his legitimate powers, perhaps by refusing to accept . . . restrictions" (Bork 1989, xiv). However, the Bush administration paired its unilateralism with an obsession for secrecy in its deliberations and processes. That obsession was exhibited quite early in the task force on energy policy, led by Vice President Cheney.

Established in February 2001, the task force was a high-level effort to plan the administration's response to rising demands for the world's energy resources. The task force met with more than three hundred groups and individuals, largely from the petroleum, natural gas, and coal industries. Among these were major donors to the Bush campaign (Unger 2007, 202–3). When reporters and interest groups sought information about the task force's proceedings and those parties whom it consulted, the administration refused, claiming executive privilege. Ironically, the task force modeled its confidentiality claim on that of the Clinton administration's health care task force that Republicans had criticized in 1993 for its secrecy. The Bush administration went it one better, however. Thinking that the earlier task force had leaked information because of the group's unwieldy size, the Cheney task force was limited to a small group of highly placed individuals in the administration who worked closely with industry insiders (Milbank and Pianin 2001, A1). In April 2001, Democratic members of Congress requested information from the task force, and Vice President Cheney's office responded that Congress had no authority to require information from it (Dingell 2002, A27).

Members of Congress asked the Government Accountability Office (GAO), Congress's arm for auditing government activities, to examine the task force, and the administration rebuffed the GAO. In response to suits filed by the public interest groups Judicial Watch and the Sierra Club, as well as a separate suit by the GAO, to gain information from the task force, the administration indicated that because the task force was composed only of government employees, its confidentiality was protected under executive privilege. Critics countered that the task force worked so closely with industry executives that the executives were basically members of the task force. However, court rulings refused to force transparency upon the task force (Savage 2005, A3).

That episode was just the beginning of the Bush administration's appetite for secrecy. The president even sought to control history, so to speak. In November 2001, President Bush signed an executive order that gave him the power to prohibit the public release of any papers of past presidential administrations. That order preceded what would be the normal opening for public access of 68,000 pages of Reagan White House records, which could contain information embarrassing to members of the current administration, other leading Republicans, and the president's father (Bumiller 2001, A22). The administration was also intensely committed to maintaining secrecy for its current government documents, including the products of agencies dealing with domestic affairs. Access to government information is a principle of American democracy. However, the Bush administration fought to make government increasingly opaque. Between 2001 and 2006, the number of government documents annually classified and shielded from public access doubled, with more than 20 million documents classified in 2007 (Shane 2005, A14; Wood 2007).

The president ordered the heads of many domestic agencies, including the Environmental Protection Agency, the Department of Agriculture, and the Department of Health and Human Services, to classify more of its documents as secret. Commenting on the administration's propensity for secrecy, Thomas Kean, the former co-chair of the 9/11 Commission, observed, "You'd just be amazed at the kind of information that's classified . . . everyday information, things we all know from the newspaper" (from Shane 2005, A14). Thomas Blanton, director of the National Security Archive, a watchdog group concerned with government secrecy, suggested that the administration's practices had no other aim than "to enhance presidential power" (from Wood 2007, 45).

The self-defeating character of the administration's penchant for secrecy is revealed in its domestic spying program. In 2002, President Bush signed a secret order directing the National Security Agency to conduct surveillance of communication between persons within the United States and abroad. The president's order ignored the legal requirement that a warrant was required to conduct surveillance within the United States. The Foreign Intelligence Surveillance Court was established in 1978 to issue warrants for secret domestic surveillance. However, it seemed that what the president sought was not targeted surveillance of individuals but a broader "hunt for suspicious patterns and activities," an activity for which warrants were not obtainable (Leonnig 2006, A1). Among the officials who were aware of the spying program there were strong doubts about its legality. For example, in March 2004, Acting Attorney General James Comey refused to recertify the program's legality unless some changes were made (Lichtblau 2006, A1).

In the face of that internal opposition, the White House continued to insist the program was legal as an expression of the president's inherent powers. Members of the congressional intelligence committees were not briefed on the existence of the NSA program (Priest 2006, A1). Jack Goldsmith, head of the Office of Legal Counsel, was dismayed at the administration's refusal to go to Congress for supportive legislation to "put all its antiterrorism policies on a sounder legal footing." But Cheney and Bush resisted seeking legislation because they feared that it would be an admission that the president might not have total discretion in the national security arena (Goldsmith 2007, 29, 81–82).

The existence of the secret NSA spying program was published in the media at the end of 2005, based on leaks from both the NSA and the administration. Yet the White House refused access to information about the program to anyone but officials on the White House team. When the Office of Professional Responsibility in the Justice Department sought information about the role of government lawyers in approving what appeared to be a program of dubious legality, President Bush refused to give that office clearance to examine relevant documents (Lewis 2007, A14). However, in 2007, the administration, already beleaguered by its critics, submitted to the need for legislation to authorize the program.

Secrecy for the Bush administration was, in fact, as much a political weapon as a tool of national security. From the beginning, secrecy was a shield to hide the administration's use of government for partisan purposes, as appeared to be the case with Cheney's energy task force. In the administration's last months, secrecy shielded the White House from increasing pressure over the firings in December 2006 of nine U.S. attorneys. These officials, originally appointed by President Bush, were apparently removed for political reasons, such as unwillingness to serve Republican electoral interests through investigations and indictments of Democrats, insufficient energy devoted to cases against illegal border immigration, and, at least in one case, the energetic investigation of a Republican member of Congress suspected of corruption.

As congressional committees investigated the firings, the administration pulled a cloak of secrecy over the issue. When top aides to the attorney general, as well as Attorney General Alberto Gonzales himself, gave highly embarrassing testimony in committee hearings, the White House claimed executive privilege and refused to supply as witnesses those White House officials who were known to have been involved with the firings, including Bush's chief of staff, Joshua Bolten, White House counsel Harriet Miers, and Bush political adviser Karl Rove. In February 2008, the U.S. House of Representatives cited Bolten and Miers with contempt of Congress, the first time White House aides have been held in contempt by Congress. The law requires that congressional contempt citations be treated as indictments and be pursued by the U.S. attorney for the District of Columbia, but the Justice Department refused to pursue the case (Kane

2008, A4). What is revealing about the secrecy claims entailed in the U.S. attorney scandal is that this issue had nothing to do with national security but everything to do with the president's effort to use the executive branch agencies for partisan benefit.

The Signing Statement as a Line-Item Veto

Signing statements are issued by the White House to accompany the president's signature of a bill. Previous presidents have typically used such statements to comment about the legislation being signed. However, President Bush prolifically issued these statements to deny provisions of the legislation being signed and to declare some part of the bill unenforceable because of conflicts with the unitary executive's constitutional powers. In effect, Bush's signing statements aimed to function as a line-item veto (Cooper 2002, 7).

During the Reagan administration conservative lawyers in the Justice Department promoted aggressive use of signing statements to resist unwanted congressional policymaking. In 1986, then–Deputy Assistant Attorney General Samuel Alito (later appointed to the U.S. Supreme Court by President George W. Bush) wrote a memorandum suggesting a strategic use of statements to "ensure that presidential signing statements assume their rightful place in the interpretation of legislation [by courts]" (U.S. Department of Justice 1986). A 1986 memo from the Reagan Justice Department's Domestic Policy Committee called for the president to refuse to implement laws that encroach on executive prerogatives and to signal that stance through signing statements (Savage 2007b, 47).

In the White House, Vice President Cheney's aide, David Addington, reviewed bills coming to the president for signature. His task was to identify any provision conflicting with the powers of the unitary presidency and to prepare signing statements for the president's signature to deny the constitutionality of that provision (Savage 2007b, 23; Goldsmith 2007, 85; American Bar Association 2006). By the end of his presidency, President Bush had used such statements to declare more than a thousand provisions of law to be unenforceable (*Harper's Magazine* 2009).

The president used signing statements broadly, not only to challenge impingements on executive power but also to question congressional policy decisions, thus using the signing statement where an earlier president might have issued a veto message. For example, on April 1, 2002, President Bush issued a statement on the Bipartisan Campaign Finance Reform Act of 2002, noting that he thought several of its provisions presented "serious constitutional concerns," identifying the limits on individual contributions to parties in federal elections as one concern and a ban on issue advertising by groups prior to federal elections as another concern (Bush 2002b, 517–18). In other instances, signing statements would deny the constitutionality of congressional provisions for regular reporting information to Congress. Or, a statement might object to the constitutionality of a legislative designation of a specific qualification for an executive branch position. A particularly egregious example of using a signing statement to circumvent congressional intent was in the August 2005 energy bill, which offered protection for federal employees testifying about problems with federal nuclear power policy. President Bush issued a statement that the whistle-blower protections violated the president's comprehensive authority over the executive branch (Savage 2007b, 240).

Many of Bush's signing statements addressed his claimed discretion over national security activities. For example, in the case of the anti-torture provisions in 2005 legislation sponsored by Senator John McCain, President Bush's signing statement asserted that he would implement the act "in a manner consistent with the constitutional authority of the President to supervise the unitary executive branch and as Commander in Chief . . . of protecting the American people from further terrorist attacks" (Bush 2006, 1918). The breadth of the president's claim to power in the national security area was suggested by Solicitor General Paul Clement's statement to the U.S. Supreme Court in *Rumsfeld v. Padilla*. When the Court asked him about the constitutional limits of the president's power in war, Clement said, in effect, that there is no limitation on that power: "You have to recognize that in situations where there is a war, where the Government is on a war footing, that you have to trust the executive to make the kind of quintessential military judgments that are involved in things like that" (from Rudalevige 2006, 521).

Paul Clement's plea was to trust the president with unquestioned authority and broad power. In the war on terror, President Bush used constitutional powers and strong public approval to authorize unilateral leadership. The claim of a unitary executive accentuated unilateralism and defended it as a permanent characteristic of the presidency. However, there is a paradox within President Bush's rationale for and practice of unilateral leadership. The most important yet volatile foundation for his leadership was public approval in a time of war. And over time, his leadership in practice undermined his principled claim to a unilateral, Hamiltonian presidency.

The Paradox of Executive Energy and Declining Authority

President Bush's use of his office metaphorically put the Hamiltonian presidency on steroids. However, his claim to unilateralism greatly oversimplified the sources of authority for presidential power in the modern polity. Presidential authority is inescapably entwined with public approval; it is plebiscitary as well as constitutional (Lowi 1985). Even the Hamiltonian presidency today is ultimately dependent on public approval (Skowronek 2008, chap. 5).

In the short run, wars expand presidents' authority, but in the long run, wars enervate presidents and their public support. Woodrow Wilson's authority was sapped before the Senate rejected the treaty he negotiated after World War I. In the first congressional election after World War II, the wartime president's party was thrown into minority status in Congress. Presidents Truman and Johnson each abandoned contemplated candidacies for reelection as the Korean and Vietnam wars dragged on. War tests the electorate's patience and erodes trust in political leadership. President Bush's Iraq adventure similarly undermined his authority claims as a war president.

The Bush administration had worked assiduously to build and maintain public support for the Iraq war. After the terrorist attacks, the president used message framing to gain public approval for a strategy of preemptive military action. The administration explained to the public that an invasion of Iraq would be a main front in the war on terror. In speeches, the president and other officials implied that Iraq's government was supportive of al-Qaida (Gershkoff and Kushner 2005). But, in the words of one leading international security scholar, "Top officials knew what policy they intended to pursue and selected intelligence assessments to promote that policy based on their political usefulness, not their credibility" (Kaufman 2004, 9). As the Iraq war became protracted, with no end in sight, the administration re-crafted its public justifications for the war.

The war was originally explained to Americans in terms of Iraq's weapons of mass destruction (WMD), Saddam Hussein's propensity to use them, and his links to international terrorism. President Bush claimed Iraqis were developing "nuclear arms." The president's national security adviser, Condoleezza Rice, had said there might be some uncertainty but that "we don't want the smoking gun to be a mushroom cloud." By implication, Iraq's WMD were associated with the goals of al-Qaida to acquire such weapons for use against America. A mid-April 2003 poll showed that

66 percent of Americans agreed that the Iraq war was part of the global war on terrorism (CBS/*New York Times* 2003).

When no WMD turned up, President Bush's public justification for the war shifted to the goal of establishing democracy in the Middle East and then, later, to the goal of sticking it out because it was crucial that the United States achieve victory over terrorism. What would actually constitute victory remained vague. With an escalation of the number of American troops in Iraq in the summer of 2007, the level of violence declined in Sunni-controlled areas and in Baghdad. Still, little about Iraq's government, security forces, or economy suggested that, if the United States departed anytime soon, stability would prevail. In a major speech in mid-April 2008, President Bush assured Americans that the costs of the war in lives and treasure were justified. Then his message about Iraq shifted again, and he said the American war was justified because Iraq was "the convergence point for two of the greatest threats to America in this new century—al Qaeda and Iran. . . . If we succeed in Iraq . . . it [will be] a historic blow to the global terrorist movement and a severe setback for Iran" (Bush 2008b).

The Bush administration ran a sophisticated, covert program to shape domestic public opinion about the war and maintain support for the president. Gaining access through legal action to thousands of pages of Defense Department documents, the *New York Times* reported in April 2008 on a Pentagon initiative to achieve what an assistant secretary of defense termed "information dominance" of American public opinion (from Barstow 2008, A1). Beginning in spring 2003, the Defense Department programmed the views of retired military officers who worked as ostensibly independent "military analysts" for broadcast news outlets. The department held hundreds of high-level briefings for about seventy-five retiree/analysts and sent them on multiple trips to Iraq. The briefings and junkets were all structured to tell the story as the administration wished it to be conveyed to the public.

To ensure that its message would be accurately conveyed to the public, the Defense Department gave the analysts specific "on air" talking points. These military analysts' high-level access came with a condition: "Participants were instructed not to quote their briefers directly or otherwise describe their contacts with the Pentagon" (Barstow 2008, A24). A Pentagon contractor, Omnitec Solutions, closely monitored the military analysts' performance on the air. An analyst who strayed from the administration's story line received a quick, negative response. A tie binding the analysts to the Defense Department, beyond their military loyalties and ideology, was that virtually all of them were also connected to military contractors, and they gained potential commercial advantage from their high-level access to Pentagon and White House officials. The implied threat was that, were an on-air analyst to stray from the Pentagon story line, the defense contractor with which he was associated would be at risk of losing its contracts (Barstow 2008, A26).

There are limits to the efficacy of issue framing and information management. Nearly six years after the war began, events on the ground in Iraq and frustration with the war's costs and progress undermined the administration's information management and message crafting. By early 2009, more than forty-two hundred American lives had been lost in Iraq, and more than thirty-one thousand American troops had been wounded (iCasualties.org 2009). The war thus far had cost about $11 billion per month and carried potential costs as high as $3 trillion (Congressional Research Service 2008, 11; Stiglitz and Blimes 2008). In addition, daily news reports reminded Americans that for all the blood and money the United States had spent in Iraq, it was the Afghanistan/Pakistan border area that was the primary incubator of the world's terrorist threats. Pakistan seemed increasingly unstable. Afghanistan was mired in corruption, and the Taliban's power in both countries was expanding. Consequently, at the end of 2008, President Bush's approval rating among all polls averaged about 26 percent, the lowest of any post–World War II president (Pollster.com 2008). Numerous polls also showed that a large majority of Americans thought the war in Iraq was a mistake and had been mishandled by President Bush.

A war gone badly, accompanied by clumsy efforts at secrecy and unilateralism, eroded President Bush's authority. Without the proximity of crisis, and without public approval, Bush's claim to Hamiltonian energy was weakened and his project of unilateral leadership undermined. The Supreme Court has denied his unilateral control over detainees in the war on terror (*Hamdi v. Rumsfeld,* 548 U.S. ___ 2006). Officials in the Bush administration, some political appointees as well as careerists, pushed back against White House unilateralism. Military lawyers opposed detainee treatment and military commissions. Not least, the 2006 election gave Democrats a majority in both houses of Congress, ensuring increased congressional oversight of the administration's conduct and policies during Bush's last two years in office. Finally, a Democrat's winning of the White House in 2008 dashed Bush's hopes for extending Republican dominance.

The Endgame

Despite little public support and with Congress in Democratic hands, in the last months of his presidency Bush retained tools of executive power and unilaterally pursued his partisan goals. Having valued economic interests above environmental concerns throughout his presidency, right to the end of his tenure Bush fostered new administrative rules and issued executive orders to weaken restrictions on the uses of public lands, to reduce air pollution regulations, to lift rules protecting endangered species, and to end restrictions on coal mining. These orders were timed to be in effect when President Barack Obama was inaugurated on January 20, 2009; they would require a laborious process of review or legislative action to undo them (Zabarenko 2008). President Bush also used his appointment power to give last-minute rewards to a number of his loyalists, placing them in multiyear appointments on various minor government commissions and boards. White House spokesman Tony Fratto responded to criticism of the president's last-minute use of his executive powers. "We actually do have not just the authority," he said. "We have an obligation to do what we think is best for the country up until 11:59 A.M. on January 20" (from Rutenberg 2008).

At the end of his presidency, Bush's unilateral use of power looked very different than it had in his first term, after the terrorist attacks. After 9/11, he displayed what Alexander Hamilton had described as the necessary "power of a single man." But deep into his second term, Bush's unilateralism was exercised without public approval for either the man or his goals. Under the glare of a skeptical press, congressional investigative scrutiny, and citizen distrust, executive unilateralism looked less like Hamiltonian energy and more like partisan spoilsmanship.

Time and events diminished the Bush presidency and its unilateralism. What was once a bold stance of presidential prerogative became a holding strategy, the last line of defense by a politically vulnerable White House. Therein is the paradox of the Bush administration's muscular power claim. The administration gained its justification for unilateralism in the aftermath of terror attacks, but a striking commitment to unilateralism prevented the administration from building lasting support in Congress, establishing lawful grounds for its actions, and retaining approval for its policies from the public through accurate information and truthful arguments. Consequently, the most unilateral presidency in modern American politics ends as a lesson about the risks of unilateralism for presidents themselves and its dangers for American politics.

10

RICHARD CHENEY AND THE POWER OF THE MODERN VICE PRESIDENCY

MICHAEL NELSON

"**M**eteoric" is not the word that springs to mind when thinking of Richard B. Cheney. Nouns such as "gravity," "seriousness," and "prudence" may, along with such adjectives as "opaque," "subdued," "laconic," "taciturn," and "unflappable" (Hayes 2007, 260; Suskind 2004, 44, 46; Mann 2004, 97, 111). But "meteoric," with its connotations of energy, action, dazzle, and speed—probably not.

Yet consider. In 1968, twenty-seven years old and partly through his graduate studies in political science at the University of Wisconsin, Cheney accepted an American Political Science Association Congressional Fellowship in the office of Wisconsin Republican William Steiger. A year later he became special assistant to Donald Rumsfeld, whom President Richard Nixon had appointed to head the Office of Economic Opportunity. Two years after that, Cheney followed Rumsfeld to Nixon's price-controlling team, the Cost of Living Council, and then, soon after the president resigned in 1974, to the West Wing of the White House as deputy chief of staff to President Gerald R. Ford, serving directly under Rumsfeld. In 1975, when Ford appointed Rumsfeld secretary of defense, Cheney replaced his mentor as the president's chief of staff, the youngest person to occupy the position before or since. Cheney had been out of school for six years. He was thirty-four years old.

In 1978, two years after leaving the White House, when Ford lost his bid for reelection, Cheney was elected to the U.S. House of Representatives from his home state of Wyoming. In 1981, at the start of his second two-year term, Cheney's colleagues elected him chair of the House Republican Policy Committee; at age forty, he was the youngest member of either party's congressional leadership team in more than a century. In 1987, Cheney moved up a rung on the leadership ladder to become chair of the House Republican Conference. The following year, he was elected party whip. In all, after less than a decade in Congress, Cheney had risen from freshman member to the House GOP's second-highest position.

Having ascended close to the top in the White House and in Congress, Cheney became head of a major Cabinet department when President George H. W. Bush appointed him secretary of defense in 1989. He held that position during two wars, the relatively small incursion that deposed Panamanian dictator Manuel Noriega in 1990 and the massive offensive that drove Saddam Hussein's Iraqi army out of Kuwait in 1991. When Bush was defeated for reelection in 1992, Cheney hung his hat at the American Enterprise Institute as a senior fellow while preparing to seek the 1996 Republican presidential nomination. After campaigning widely for his party's candidates in the 1994 midterm election, he decided that he "really [did] not want to go do it" (Hayes 2007, 264). Cheney abandoned his candidacy in January 1995 and soon became president of the Halliburton Company, a massive international oil-services corporation based in Texas. Five years later, at age fifty-nine, Cheney was elected vice president in the 2000 election.

And so: meteoric. Not the word that comes instantly to mind in connection with Dick Cheney but perhaps the word that should. Within the span of a quarter century, Cheney occupied a host of important leadership positions as he advanced from youth to middle age, serving prominently in all but the judicial branch of government as well as in the corporate world.

The Modern Vice Presidency

The same less-than-obvious word may be applied to the vice presidency. For many years, the office was the butt of jokes and gibes. The first vice president, John Adams, called it "the most insignificant office that ever the invention of man contrived." A century and a half later, Vice President John Nance Garner said, "The vice presidency isn't worth a pitcher of warm spit"—or at least that's the G-rated version of what he said (from Nelson 1988b). In 1996, Cheney himself called being vice president "a cruddy job" (Hayes 2007, 268).

In truth, at about the same time Cheney was engaged in his meteoric rise, the vice presidency was experiencing its own steep ascent. The office's constitutional power has never been great, but during the late twentieth century, the vice presidency grew rapidly in influence and prestige. When Cheney became vice president in 2001, it was the furthest thing from a weak, vestigial, or risible institution. Instead, he inherited a strong office and, at least temporarily, made it stronger, even at the price of personal unpopularity.

The birth of the modern vice presidency can be dated to 1976, when Democratic presidential nominee Jimmy Carter selected Senator Walter F. Mondale as his vice presidential running mate, and 1977, when Carter and Mondale dramatically enhanced the vice president's role as a close and wide-ranging senior adviser to the president.

Carter established the modern pattern of vice presidential selection when, well in advance of his party's national convention, he began a careful search for a running mate (Nelson 1988a). In choosing Mondale, Carter gave the nod to someone with a longer résumé of public service than his own, as did Ronald Reagan when he chose George H. W. Bush in 1980, Michael Dukakis when he chose Lloyd Bentsen in 1988, Bill Clinton when he chose Al Gore in 1992, George W. Bush when he chose Cheney in 2000, and Barack Obama when he chose Joseph Biden in 2008. Once in office, Carter conferred on Mondale a host of institutional resources designed to allow the vice president to serve effectively as the president's leading adviser on many of the matters that crossed his desk. In addition to the large and professional staff and the weekly private lunch with the president already secured by Mondale's two most recent vice presidential predecessors, Gerald Ford and Nelson Rockefeller, Mondale was authorized to attend all of Carter's meetings, have full access to the flow of papers to and from the president, and occupy an office in the West Wing of the White House. Mondale's successor, George H. W. Bush, was heir to all of these institutional gains in roles and resources, as was the latter's vice president, Dan Quayle.

Gore's relationship with Clinton rivaled Mondale's with Carter for trust and responsibility. Gore was one of three or four people whose advice Clinton sought on virtually every important matter. Indeed, in 1998, a Clinton adviser was able to list several "areas where Al Gore makes the decisions—and the president rubberstamps[:] . . . science, technology, NASA, telecommunications, the environment, family leave, tobacco, nuclear dealings with the Russians, media violence, the Internet, privacy issues, and, of course, reinventing government" (Berke 1998, 47). Gore, like several other recent vice presidents, secured his party's presidential nomination at the end of the president's second term. His opponent was Texas governor George W. Bush.

The Cheney Vice Presidency

Governor Bush's decision to tap Cheney as his running mate in 2000 was in some ways consistent with recent patterns of vice presidential selection, but in other ways, it departed from them. In keeping with modern practice, the choice emerged from a long and careful search. A governor at the top of the ticket chose a Washington figure for the second spot, as did Carter in 1976, Reagan in 1980, Dukakis in 1988, and Clinton in 1992. A conservative chose a fellow conservative, eschewing the old-style ideological ticket balancing that characterized the pre-modern vice presidency.

Never before, however, had the person whom the presidential nominee appointed to head the vice presidential search process emerged as the candidate. In April 2000, with the Republican nomination locked up and months remaining until the convention, Bush invited Cheney to help him screen potential running mates. The two men were acquainted: when Cheney moved to Texas in 1995 to become head of Halliburton, he thought it made good business sense to get to know the governor, whom he had met only briefly during his father's administration. In late 1998, Cheney became part of a group of foreign policy experts who advised and to a large extent educated Bush about global affairs as he prepared to run for president. "He didn't speak a lot," Bush later recalled. "But the one guy that pretty much commanded, I felt, the respect of everyone around the table during these meetings was Cheney. And so he got my attention" (from Hayes 2007, 275).

Cheney told Bush several times that he was not interested in being vice president; four years earlier he had called the office "cruddy." Did he mean it, or was he coyly playing hard to get? The question arises because Cheney also persuaded Bush that the ideal running mate would have a record of prominent service in the White House, Congress, the private sector, and as head of an executive department. Cheney himself, of course, was one of the very few people who met this standard. None of the other finalists, including Senator John Danforth of Missouri and Governors Tom Ridge of Pennsylvania and Frank Keating of Oklahoma, even came close. Throughout the search process, Bush kept telling Cheney, joshingly at first and then seriously, "You're the solution to my problem" (from Draper 2007, 90). Finally, on July 3, Cheney agreed, but only after securing Bush's agreement that he was not going to be "the guy going to funerals." Cheney wanted "to be a real partner in helping . . . make decisions with regard to domestic and foreign policy" (Gellman 2008, 35). The tipoff to sharp-eyed reporters was that Cheney quietly changed his voter registration from Texas to Wyoming so that the presidential and vice presidential candidates would not be from the same state.

In an even more important departure from modern vice presidential selection, Bush chose someone who had no presidential ambitions. Although, as noted above, Cheney had tested the waters once, he found that he "was uncomfortable with the pressure to reveal his feelings and talk about his family" (Weisberg 2008, 170). Between 1978 and 1988, he had suffered three heart attacks. (He had another one two weeks after the 2000 election.) By temperament, Cheney was most comfortable outside the spotlight. His Secret Service code name in the Ford administration was almost comically apt: "Backseat." Of all the heroes to emerge from the Persian Gulf War, Cheney was the only one not to write a self-celebrating memoir.

Bush found Cheney's reticence enormously appealing. As Bush's first chief of staff, Andrew Card, later marveled, "The vice president is not looking to be president. Do you know how unusual that is? He is here to be an adviser and counselor to the president" (from Kessler 2004, 141). Bush knew he would never have to worry that his vice president's personal ambition was interfering with his commitment to the president's interests. "When you're getting advice from somebody," Bush said, "if you think deep down part of the advice is to advance a personal agenda, . . . you discount that advice" (from Hayes 2007, 307). For all Cheney's seniority, he always showed deference to Bush: "Yes, Mr. President," "No, Mr. President," or, when Bush wasn't around, "The Man," as in "The Man wants this" (from Woodward 2004, 430).

Bush frequently declared that in picking a running mate he was choosing a vice president, not just a candidate to help him win the election. "Mark my words," Bush said in July 2000. "There will be a crisis in my administration and Dick Cheney is exactly the man you want at your side in a crisis" (from Hayes 2007, 2). In truth, Bush's emphasis on Cheney's governing credentials doubled as a shrewd electoral strategy. Voters wanted to be reassured that the governor would have at his side an experienced Washington hand with a long foreign policy résumé. Cheney's presence on the ticket provided this reassurance. Exit polls in 2000 revealed that a majority of those who regarded foreign policy as the most important issue in the election voted for the Republican candidate, even though Bush's credentials in this area were far less impressive than those of his Democratic opponent, Vice President Gore (Nelson 2001, 72–75).

Famously, the 2000 election did not end with election day. The battle for Florida's twenty-five electoral votes prolonged the contest for another five weeks. Cheney asked Bush how he could be most helpful and was given a governing rather than a political assignment: to run the transition process, vetting prospective Cabinet and staff appointees on the assumption that the election would be resolved favorably. Although no previous vice president had run a transition, the decision to have Cheney run Bush's made sense. Cheney had participated in two previous transitions and served as a member of both the Cabinet and the staff. But, as with Bush's selection of Cheney as his running mate, the decision was politically astute as well. To the extent that Bush acted as though he had won the election during the recount process, the public was more likely to think of him as the presumptive winner and Gore as the challenger.

Bush had made clear during the campaign that he wanted Colin Powell to be his secretary of state, another effort to assure voters that his administration's foreign policy would be in good hands. Cheney did his best to offset the experienced, popular, and politically moderate Powell with a strong conservative counterweight by securing the appointment of his friend and mentor Donald Rumsfeld as secretary of defense. Indeed, Cheney was able to plant allies throughout the new administration. "Cheney people" were named as chief and deputy chief of the Office of Management and Budget, deputy national security adviser, undersecretary of state, deputy secretary of defense, and assistant or deputy assistant secretary in multiple Cabinet departments (Gellman 2008, 37–39). The vice president also was part of a small group that reviewed candidates for federal judicial appointments to appraise their conservative credentials (Toobin 2007, 260, 273).

In terms of the role he would play as vice president, Cheney brought a unique perspective to the office. He was the only vice president who had worked in close proximity to another vice president. As Ford's chief of staff, Cheney had seen Vice President Rockefeller thwarted time and again—often by Cheney—in his clumsy efforts to become the administration's dominant player in domestic policy (Hayes 2007, 110–11). Cheney was determined not to let that happen to him. To be sure, he pocketed the gains of other modern vice presidents, including the weekly private lunch with the president that Rockefeller had secured. But Cheney also obtained from Bush an unprecedented mandate granting access to "every table and every meeting" throughout the administration. This freed him to be active in "whatever area the vice president feels he wants to be active," affording a full outlet for his ambition to move public policy in a strongly conservative direction (Gellman and Becker 2007).

In forming his staff, Cheney signaled where his main policy interest lay. He appointed longtime associates I. Lewis "Scooter" Libby as his chief of staff and national security adviser and David Addington as general counsel. Both men had spent several years working with Cheney on foreign policy and defense matters when he was in Congress and the Defense Department. Cheney also doubled, from six to twelve, the size of the vice president's national security staff (Daalder and Lindsay 2003c, 59). Wise in the ways of Washington politics, Cheney secured an unprecedented seat at the table for all of his leading aides in meetings of the White House staff (Gellman 2008, 44–49).

Cheney before 9/11

After the al-Qaida terrorist attacks on New York and Washington, Cheney, like Bush, became consumed with fighting terrorists and their state sponsors in Afghanistan, Iraq, and around the world. But Cheney had taken an active interest in foreign affairs from the start. He met regularly not just with the National Security Council (NSC) but also, uniquely for a vice president, with the NSC's principals committee—that is, the NSC when the president is absent. Unlike previous vice presidents, Cheney exercised influence over foreign policy in small White House meetings rather than through overseas diplomacy. Early in the administration, former vice president Quayle had told him, "Dick, you know you're going to be doing a lot of this international traveling. . . . I mean, this is what vice presidents do. . . . We've all done it." Cheney "got that little smile," Quayle recalled, and said, "I have a different understanding with the president" (from Gellman and Becker 2007). Cheney made very few foreign trips as vice president.

Taking his cues from the president, Cheney's initial focus was on domestic policy. He joined Bush in scorning what he called the "bottled wisdom of Washington" about the election, which held that because they had won such a close, controversial victory, they should govern in a bipartisan manner. "That [idea] lasted maybe thirty seconds," Cheney said. "We had an agenda, we ran on that agenda, we won the election—full speed ahead" (from Woodward 2004, 28; Chafee 2008, chap. 1). An early test of their staunchly conservative approach to governing came in spring 2001 when Senator James Jeffords of Vermont, a moderate Republican, threatened to leave the party if Bush refused to support a proposal to spend more money on special education. Cheney helped persuade Bush not to yield, even though Jeffords's defection would mean that the Senate was no longer evenly divided between the two parties and, more to the point, that the vice president would lose his tie-breaking power as Senate president to award every committee and subcommittee chairmanship to a Republican (Becker and Gellman 2007).

From the start, Cheney played a vital role in making and promoting the administration's taxing and spending policies. He helped forge a compromise on Capitol Hill between the president, who wanted a $1.6 trillion tax cut, and Senate Democrats, who were willing to accept $1.25 trillion. The final figure was $1.35 trillion (Woodward 2004, 28–29). He chaired an annual budget review board to hear appeals from Cabinet members who thought the Office of Management and Budget had shortchanged their departments. In theory, these officials could go to the president if Cheney did not give them what they wanted. In practice, none did (Becker and Gellman 2007; Hayes 2007, 407–8). In addition to arranging for the taxing and spending bills, Cheney had all legislation passed by Congress go through his office so that it could be vetted before it reached the president's desk (Savage 2007b, 236). He attended most of the Senate Republicans' policy lunches, saying little but making himself available. "What I try to do is maintain those relationships when you don't need them so that they're there when you do need them," he explained (from Hayes 2007, 401). Senators appreciated the access, mostly because, as Bush often told people, "When you're talking to Dick Cheney, you're talking to me" (from Baumgartner 2007, 133).

Cheney also worked hard to advance pro-business, pro-development environmental policies throughout the executive branch. Widely connected in Washington, he was willing to reach deep into the Interior Department and Environmental Protection Agency to make sure, for example, that farmers in Oregon's Klamath Basin did not lose irrigation water for the sake of protecting two species of suckerfish (Becker and Gellman 2007). In March 2001, he made a successful end run around EPA administrator Christine Todd Whitman and Secretary of State Powell, persuading Bush to answer a letter from several senators by declaring that he had decided not to honor a campaign promise to reduce smokestack emissions from power plants. Cheney drafted Bush's reply, took it to him to sign, and personally carried it to Capitol Hill before Whitman and Powell (the latter worried about offending U.S. allies) could object (De-Young 2006, 326–27; Bumiller 2007, 148–49).

Cheney's most prominent assignment before 9/11 was to head a task force on energy policy, formally called the National Energy Policy Development Group. Concerned that the task force's deliberations remain confidential, Cheney followed counsel David Addington's advice that the membership consist entirely of government officials, thus freeing the task force from the open-government requirements of the Federal Advisory Committee Act. When Congress's investigative arm, the General Accounting Office (as it was then known), asked to review the task force's records, Cheney refused. He also rejected a House committee's request for a list of the task force's advisers and the times, places, and subjects of its meetings. Cheney's position was upheld by the U.S. District Court for the District of Columbia, which dismissed the GAO's lawsuit (Rozell 2004, 129–31; Savage 2007b, 85–89).

Cheney's strong stand was motivated less by any embarrassment about the task force's strongly pro-oil recommendations (these came as no surprise) than by his long-standing concern that presidential power was too limited and must be expanded. This concern dated back to his years in the Ford White House, when Congress was in a post-Watergate frenzy of reining in the "imperial presidency" with legislation and investigations. Right after Reagan was elected in 1980, incoming White House chief of staff James Baker sought Cheney's advice about how to do the job. Baker's notes of what Cheney told him include this statement, which Baker highlighted with six stars: "Pres. seriously weakened in recent yrs. Restore power & auth. to Exec Branch—Need strong ldr'ship. Get rid of War Powers Act—restore independent rights" (from Savage 2007b, 43; Gellman 2008, 101).

Even when serving as a congressional leader during the 1980s, Cheney opposed most restraints on the presidency. In 1987, he oversaw the writing of the minority report of the House committee investigating the Reagan administration's Iran-Contra scandal. The report targeted the wrong-headed (in Cheney's view) limitations Congress had placed on Reagan's policy of funding the anticommunist "contra" rebels in Nicaragua, limitations that provoked some White House staffers to fund the contras extralegally. "[T]he Constitution mandates the president to be the country's foreign policy leader," the minority report stated, and efforts by Congress to dilute that authority were improper (from Hayes 2007, 200). Four years later, having returned to the executive branch as secretary of defense, Cheney urged President George H. W. Bush not to seek Congress's endorsement of the Gulf War. "From a constitutional standpoint," he argued, "we had all the authority we needed" based on the president's authority as commander in chief (from Savage 2007b, 62).

Cheney's conservative ideology and expansive views of presidential power were interesting and mildly controversial aspects of his vice presidency before 9/11. Harnessed to the service of his long-standing ambitions to move public policy rightward, they became important and wildly divisive aspects afterward.

Cheney and 9/11

On the morning of September 11, 2001, President Bush was in Sarasota, Florida, visiting the Emma E. Booker Elementary School as part of his campaign to persuade Congress to pass the No Child Left Behind Act. Cheney was in his West Wing office when news reports arrived that large passenger jets had hit the twin towers of the World Trade Center in New York City. At 9:36, a Secret Service agent entered the vice president's office, told him that another rogue airplane, American Airlines flight 77, was headed for Washington, and, as Cheney remembered, "grabbed me by the back of my belt and propelled me out the door" and into the elevator to the Presidential Emergency Operations Center deep below the White House (from Hayes 2007, 333). At about 10:03, Cheney was informed that United Airlines flight 93, another commercial airliner loaded with passengers, was also en route to Washington. He and Bush subsequently told the 9/11 Commission that Cheney then called the president and secured authorization to order fighter jets to shoot down flight 93, a claim that the commission regarded with considerable skepticism (Shenon 2008, 264–67, 411–12; see also Gellman 2008, 119–25). Cheney issued the order at about 10:10, but flight 93 already had crashed in Pennsylvania. "He was very steady, very calm," the president's deputy chief of staff, Josh Bolten, said of Cheney. "He clearly had been though crises before and did not appear to be in shock like many of us" (from Hayes 2007, 338–39).

Cheney continued to make important decisions throughout the day.

He worked closely with Secretary of Transportation Norman Mineta to ground every civilian aircraft in the country. He arranged for the evacuation of congressional leaders to secure locations. He repeatedly urged Bush to delay returning to Washington until his safety could be assured. When Bush finally overruled him and came back to the White House to address the nation that evening, Cheney was choppered to Camp David after the speech so that he and the president would not be in the same location. During the 1980s, Cheney had participated in annual simulations designed to ensure that the federal government would continue to function, its line of succession intact, in the event of a nuclear war (Mann 2004, 138–45). Partly as a result of these experiences, "continuity of government" became a watchword of the vice president's after 9/11. He spent much of his time either at Camp David or, in a phrase that eventually became a running joke for late-night comedians, other "secure, undisclosed locations." No matter where he was, Cheney stayed in close touch with the president, his staff, and the NSC principals committee through frequent teleconferences.

On September 14 and 15, Cheney was joined at Camp David by the president and a host of other key advisers, mostly from the Departments of State and Defense, the CIA, the military, and the NSC staff. The president assigned to Cheney the development of a plan of defense against further terrorist attacks on American soil. Bush also decided to confine the initial U.S. military response to Afghanistan, whose Taliban regime had been sheltering al-Qaida. Although Deputy Secretary of Defense Paul Wolfowitz argued that the United States should target Iraq, Cheney joined Powell, Card, and CIA director George Tenet in demurring. (Rumsfeld abstained.) Cheney very much wanted to see Iraqi dictator Saddam Hussein removed from power, but for the moment he was more concerned about the risk of spreading the U.S. military too thin. "The longer it takes us to get al Qaeda, the greater our risk" from another attack, Cheney said. In addition, he said, "if we go after Saddam Hussein, we lose our rightful place as the good guy" (from Woodward 2002, 137, 165, 280).

Cheney's homeland defense assignment was critically important: in the aftermath of 9/11, additional attacks by suspected terrorist cells in the United States were widely expected and could possibly involve chemical or biological weapons. On September 16, Cheney told a national audience on *Meet the Press* that to fulfill his mission, the United States would have to work on "the dark side. . . . A lot of what needs to be done here will have to be done quietly, without any discussion, using sources and methods that are available to our intelligence agencies, if we're going to be successful" (from Kengor 2004a, 170; see also Mayer 2008).

In particular, Cheney believed that executive power would need to be exercised aggressively, with minimal checks from Congress and the courts. To an unprecedented degree, the vice president's counsel, David Addington, was integrated into the White House counsel's office (Goldsmith 2007, 76). In early November, for example, the vastly more experienced and personally forceful Addington pressured White House counsel Alberto Gonzales and lawyers from the Justice and Defense departments to accept his plan for handling captives in the Afghan war. Without consulting the State Department or the NSC staff, they drafted a four-page document authorizing the military to imprison and interrogate any "unlawful enemy combatants" suspected of terrorism, to hold them indefinitely, and to try them in military tribunals rather than in regular civilian or military courts. Cheney took the document to Bush at their lunch on November 13 and obtained his signature. The next day, Cheney told a chamber of commerce audience that such combatants do not "deserve to be treated as prisoners of war" protected by the Geneva Conventions. On February 7, 2002, twelve weeks later, Bush signed a document that made the vice president's statement official policy (Savage 2007b, 147; Mayer 2008, 79). In August 2002, a similar process produced a memo authorizing the use of extreme interrogation techniques (that is, torture) in seeking information (Bumiller 2007, 241).

Cheney and the War in Iraq

The rapid overthrow of the Taliban regime in Afghanistan (a new interim government friendly to the United States was in place by the end of 2001) did not reassure Cheney that al-Qaida had lost all state sponsorship. Like most U.S. officials, as well as intelligence agencies around the world, he was convinced that Saddam Hussein had for some time been stockpiling weapons of mass destruction: chemical, biological, and perhaps nuclear. Cheney frequently expressed to the president his concern that Saddam was sharing these WMDs with al-Qaida, which he was sure would try to use them against the United States (DeYoung 2006, 375). Although little in the way of reliable intelligence confirmed Cheney's suspicions of an Iraq–al-Qaida connection, he remembered from his years as secretary of defense how wrong the intelligence agencies had been in 1990 about Saddam's intention to invade Kuwait. These agencies also had not had any inkling of how close the Iraqi dictator was to developing nuclear weapons (Gordon and Trainor 2006, 126).

With victory in Afghanistan seemingly secured, Cheney's concerns about Iraq prompted him to push relentlessly for action to topple Saddam Hussein. In this effort he was closely allied with Rumsfeld, who since late 2001 had been pushing the military to develop an acceptable invasion plan. Powell, concerned about what he viewed as a rush to war, met with the president on August 5, 2002, to "make a pitch for coalition or UN action to do what needs to be done" (Woodward 2002, 333). If possible, Powell wanted to mobilize sufficient international diplomatic pressure to force Saddam to disclose and surrender his WMDs; if necessary, he was willing to support the invasion of Iraq. In any event, Powell argued, the United States would be going it alone if it went to war without first trying to disarm Saddam through diplomatic means. Such diplomacy must start with the United Nations, which Bush was already scheduled to address on September 12. Powell made his case persuasively to Bush, who was hearing the same thing from close friends of the United States, notably Tony Blair of Great Britain, John Howard of Australia, and José María Aznar of Spain.

Cheney disagreed strenuously with the diplomacy-first approach. He was certain that any effort to involve the UN would entail endless debate, compromise, and delay: "Wrap the whole thing up in red tape, . . . pass another resolution, call it good, everybody goes home and nothing happens" (from Woodward 2004, 156–57, 234–35). On August 26, in a much-publicized speech to the Veterans of Foreign Wars convention in Nashville, Cheney ramped up public support for war by declaring, "There is no doubt that Saddam Hussein now has weapons of mass destruction. . . . Time is not on our side. The risks of inaction are far greater than the risk of action." Sending UN weapons inspectors into Iraq, he added, "would provide no assurance whatever of compliance with UN resolutions" because Saddam would hide the weapons from the inspectors (Cheney 2002).

Within the White House, Cheney continued to argue against seeking resolutions from either the UN or Congress. Although he lost both arguments, he accepted the president's decisions, then tried to shape them. Reversing the sequence that preceded the Persian Gulf War, Cheney urged Bush to get Congress's endorsement for using force "as he [the president] determines to be necessary" before seeking the UN's endorsement—the former would strengthen the president's hand when he sought the latter. Congress, facing the November 2002 midterm election and a president with a near–70 percent job approval rating, passed a resolution of support by a 296-to-133 margin in the House on October 10 and, two days later, by 77 to 23 in the Senate. As for the UN, Cheney and Rumsfeld wanted a Security Council resolution authorizing "all necessary means" (that is, war) if Saddam did not disclose and disarm. Powell found no support on the council for such martial language, but on November 8, he was able to persuade all fifteen members to vote for a resolution that ambiguously vowed "serious consequences" for noncompliance (Woodward 2002, 351; 2004, 167, 174–76).

On December 7, when Iraq officially declared that it had no weapons of mass destruction, Cheney was alone among the principals in arguing that this denial was reason enough to go to war (Woodward 2004, 234–35). But when UN inspectors were unable to find any such weapons, Rumsfeld and, eventually, Powell added their voices to Cheney's, convinced that Saddam was subverting the inspections. On January 31, 2003, Tony Blair insisted that, for domestic political reasons, he needed Bush to try to get a second UN resolution explicitly authorizing war. Bush reluctantly agreed and then assigned Powell to make the case to the Security Council on February 5. Cheney pressured Powell to devote a large share of his presentation to arguing that there was a close Iraq–al-Qaida connection. When Powell declined, focusing instead on WMDs, Cheney threatened to give his own speech on Iraq's supposed ties with al-Qaida. He backed off when Tenet informed the president that the CIA would not be able to stand behind the charge. Bush told Cheney not to give the speech (Woodward 2006, 120, 135).

Although the Security Council refused to adopt a second resolution, Bush's effort to obtain one was enough to satisfy the leaders of Great Britain, Australia, Spain, and a few other allies. They were willing to defer to the president's claim that the threat of "serious consequences" in the first Security Council resolution was basis enough for war. Cheney had lost numerous skirmishes along the way, but he had won the battle; as Ivo Daalder and James Lindsay argue, Bush "decided to take Powell's route to Cheney's goal" (Daalder and Lindsay 2003c, 139). On March 19, Bush asked all of his closest advisers whether they thought he should go to war. All said yes. Bush then asked everyone to leave the room except the vice president. Cheney said to go ahead. In Bush's opinion, Cheney had been "a rock" throughout the entire process: "he was steadfast and steady in his view that Saddam was a threat to America and we had to deal with him" (from Woodward 2004, 420).

Reelection and the Second Term

Cheney's preoccupation with toppling the Iraqi regime did not distract him entirely from other matters. He took a continuing interest in regulatory policy, successfully pressuring the National Park Service in 2002, for example, to lift the ban on snowmobiling in national parks. He was instrumental in persuading Bush to seek an additional $350 billion tax cut in 2003, as well as in securing its congressional passage (Gellman 2008, chap. 10). In that same year, he prevailed over most of the president's economic advisers by persuading Bush to impose tariffs on imported steel. When securing the peace in Iraq proved much more difficult than winning the war, jeopardizing the president's chances for reelection in 2004, Cheney campaigned hard. His implicit theme was that, however disillusioned Americans might be with Bush, electing the Democratic ticket of John Kerry and John Edwards would be worse. "Only four senators voted for the use of force [against Iraq] and against the resources our men and women needed," Cheney charged. "Only four. Senators Kerry and Edwards were two of those four." Cheney also warned that if, on election day, "we make the wrong choice, then the danger is that we'll get hit again and we'll be hit in a way that will be devastating" (from Hayes 2007, 399–407, 447, 454; Suskind 2004, 216–21). His strong performance in the vice presidential debate helped to offset the losses incurred by the president's weak performance in his first debate with Kerry.

Although Cheney remained an active and influential vice president after the election, the second term went less well for him than the first, partly because it went less well for Bush, to whom his fortunes were inextricably tied. But Cheney contributed to his own problems. On May 31, 2005, he seemed wildly out of touch with reality on the ground when he said on *Larry King Live* that anti-American forces in Iraq "are in the last throes, if you will, of the insurgency." (More than a year later, in a June 2006 appearance before the National Press Club, he said the same thing.) Although Cheney lobbied strenuously on Capitol Hill against the anti-torture Detainee Treatment Act, which prohibited "cruel, inhuman, and degrading treatment or punishment" of captives held in American facilities at home and abroad, the bill passed the Senate on October 5, 2005, by a vote of 90 to 9 and the House on December 14 by 308 to 122. In the face of these veto-proof majorities, Bush signed the act against Cheney's advice, confining his objections to the signing statement that accompanied it. On October 28, the vice president lost his closest aide when Libby resigned after being indicted for lying and obstruction of justice in the leak of a CIA agent's name to the news media. Libby, who may have been protecting Cheney, was convicted on March 6, 2007 (Gellman 2008, 360–63).

On February 11, 2006, Cheney accidentally shot a hunting companion, Texas attorney Harry Whittington, in the face and was slow to inform the media that the incident had occurred. The event, minor in itself, became major because it symbolized existing public concerns that the vice president was both trigger-happy and overly secretive. On November 8, the day after the Democrats seized control of both houses of Congress in the midterm election, Cheney lost his closest ally in the administration when Bush fired Rumsfeld as secretary of defense. "I disagree," the vice president told the president after the decision was already made (from Woodward 2008, 205). More generally, according to the investigative reporter Bob Woodward, Cheney "felt like he was being pushed aside on the Iraq decision making" (Woodward 2006, 391), although he did play an important role in 2007 in promoting the "surge" strategy of sending in additional troops with a redefined mission (Woodward 2008, chaps. 28–37). In general, Cheney told the National Press Club in August 2008, Bush "has been absolutely true to his commitment to me, which was that I'd have an opportunity to be a major participant in the process, to be part of his government, to get involved in whatever issues I wanted to get involved in" (from Stolberg 2008b). Still, during the final days of the second term, Cheney was rebuffed again when the president refused his ardent and repeated pleas, both in person and over the phone, to pardon Libby (DeFrank 2009).

Cheney's approval rating in Gallup surveys, which had begun at 61 percent in April 2001 and remained above 50 percent throughout the first term, mirrored the growing political divisions he spawned as it dropped to 36 percent in 2006 and 30 percent in 2007, a record low for a vice president.

The Democrats' victory in the 2006 elections diminished even the vice president's relatively modest influence as president of the Senate. In 2005, when Senate Democrats had vowed to filibuster several of Bush's appellate court nominations, Cheney made clear his intention to rule that filibusters of judicial appointments could be ended by a simple majority vote rather than the customary three-fifths. The Democrats caved, agreeing to allow judicial nominees to be voted on in all but "extraordinary circumstances." But after the 2006 midterm, Senate Democrats had enough votes to overturn any ruling by the vice president.

A "Superlative" Career

Richard Cheney's tenure as vice president was marked by superlatives. He was the most influential vice president in history. One observer described Cheney's role in the administration as "war minister, uber diplomat, political adviser and consigliere to President Bush" (Schmitt 2001). Another noted that Cheney's voice was the last one the president wanted to hear before making any important decision. "What does Dick think?" Bush routinely asked (Page 2001). The historian Douglas Brinkley described Cheney as "the vortex in the White House on foreign policy making. Everything comes through him" (from Slavin 2002).

Certainly Cheney's influence was enhanced by the primacy of national security issues that marked the Bush presidency. But Cheney was an influential vice president even before 9/11. One reason is that, for all his ambitions to affect public policy, he was the least politically ambitious vice president in modern history. Cheney had served as White House chief of staff, congressional leader, and powerful Cabinet member. After suffering several heart attacks and testing the waters in 1996, he had abandoned any hope of becoming president. Vice president was the highest office to which he aspired. During his two terms in the office, Cheney spent no time thinking about the next step in his political career or about how his interests might be different from the president's.

Because Cheney's loyalty to the president was undivided by personal political ambition, Bush trusted him more—and assigned him more responsibility—than any other vice president in history. But the certain knowledge that Cheney's name would never appear on a ballot again sometimes made him reckless in his disregard for public opinion. In a March 2008 interview with ABC News, Cheney responded to correspondent Martha Raddatz's statement that "two-thirds of Americans say it's not worth fighting [in Iraq]" with a one-word answer: "So?" Few things are as likely to alienate public opinion as callous disregard of it.

Cheney's final superlative was to become the most unpopular vice president in modern history. This was partly an artifact of Bush's own second-term unpopularity, but only partly. Carter's approval ratings had sunk to a level as low as Bush's, for example, but Vice President Mondale remained popular. The difference was that the public regarded Cheney as being uniquely powerful but, with no concern for his political future, utterly indifferent to their opinions. They were right on both counts.

11

LOW RISK AND BIG AMBITION
Bush and the Judiciary

NANCY MAVEETY

Surprisingly, perhaps, for a president first elected with little excess political capital, George W. Bush made his appointments to the federal judiciary a high priority and spared no political expense to secure his patently conservative nominees' confirmation. His first-term clashes with the Senate, and the controversy over the Senate Republicans' spring 2005 "nuclear option" as retaliation for Democratic filibuster of certain circuit court nominees, heightened what was already an extremely politicized process. By the time of Bush's second-term confirmation face-offs to appoint two new members of the Supreme Court, his commitment to high-stakes judicial selection politics was evident. He seemed, by all accounts, to be the high-risk presidential operator scholars had predicted, one "seek[ing] to entrench a conservative regime among a public beset by even partisan divisions and without a stable Washington governing coalition" (Schier 2004, 9)

Nomination and confirmation of federal judges and, with presidential luck, Supreme Court justices, pits presidents desiring to leave a policy legacy beyond their administration against institutional and partisan forces. Within the matrix of nominee qualifications, presidential ideological preference, and contextual political constraints, chief executives struggle to select a suitable, if not desirable, candidate who is also confirmable. Thus enters the element of risk: how far should a president's reach threaten to exceed his or her grasp? As this volume maintains, George W. Bush has been what presidential scholar Stephen Skowronek calls an "orthodox innovator" (Schier 2004, 4). His judicial selections sought to articulate the commitments of the previous conservative regime—what new institutionalist scholars call the "New Right Constitutional Regime" (Clayton 2005, 8)—and "galvanize political action with promises to continue the good work of the past, and demonstrate the vitality of the established order to changing times" (Skowronek 1997, 41). He affirmed his commitment to appointing jurists like the conservative-loyalists Antonin Scalia and Clarence Thomas and his desire to continue and entrench GOP control of the federal courts. His avowed belief—stated on October 1, 2000, in the first presidential debate with Democratic opponent Al Gore—was in interpreting the Constitution strictly and not legislating from the bench, and his judicial candidates would believe the same. So, were his judicial candidates, in the last analysis, "risky"? Or does Bush deserve the distinction—distinctly undistinguished-sounding but perhaps begrudgingly admirable—of being known as "low risk and big ambition"?

This chapter contends that although Bush may have been an orthodox-innovator president, he was not really much of a risk taker in his judicial appointments. His most riskily aggressive behaviors backfired badly, and he backed down from asserting other bold moves in the face of likely and sustained resistance. Still, to say that he shied from risk is not to say that he was not successful in judicial staffing. Two reliably conservative and disarmingly palatable Supreme Court selections, and a cohort of like-minded, rightward lower federal court appointees, reveal that for the most part, George W. Bush's big ambitions for the judiciary at the time of his election in 2000 were realized—and through little real risk. Yet his ambitions, while fundamentally realized, nevertheless furthered divisions on the High Court and gaps in its development of the constitutional law of executive power. This chapter addresses how these seemingly counterintuitive propositions can coexist.

The Politics of Judicial Appointment

As Supreme Court confirmations scholar Mark Silverstein comments in the second edition of his volume *Judicious Choices*, "Both political and legal forces shape the selection of nominees to the [federal courts] and the process of their confirmation" (Silverstein 2007, 8). While nominees' legal experience and qualifications have always been central to their appointment, other factors regularly intervene. Lee Epstein and Jeffrey Segal (2005) see the appointment process in terms of two stages: presidential selection of candidates for the federal judiciary and the confirmation of those candidates by the Senate. At each stage, political actors make calculations about candidates' acceptability, based on nominees' legal, ideological, and demographic characteristics, about the political climate of executive-legislative relations, and about the balance of power in the judiciary and, especially, on the Supreme Court.

In the presidential calculation of whom to nominate, no considerations are more powerful than political ones. Presidents desire to leave a policy legacy in the federal courts—of their political party, certainly, and of their particular, personal vision, frequently. In selecting nominees who fulfill presidents' expectation of a certain legacy, several different political considerations affect presidential choice, but all can be thought of in terms of policy goals versus electoral goals. Policy goals stress the ideology, or manifested policy values, of the prospective nominee. Is the candidate reliably conservative/liberal, and does he or she have an established voting record as a lower court judge that demonstrates this reliability, particularly on legal policy issues important to the appointing president and his or her party?

Electoral goals turn a president's attention to other qualities in judicial nominees. Partisanship is the most obvious here, and it can also function as a surrogate measure of a candidate's commitment to an ideological position. Presidents overwhelmingly select same-party nominees to the federal courts. Such nominations are both the spoils of electoral victory and an effort to maintain electoral prowess by demonstrating to partisan constituents the value of holding office. Sometimes, geographic and demographic electoral considerations for the president's party exert pressure on the president in making judicial selections. Richard Nixon's nomination of Virginia Bar Association president Lewis Powell in 1971 was part of his Republican Party's "southern strategy" to capitalize on conservative southern Democratic discomfort with the liberal agenda of the national party. The nominee was an electoral overture to white southern voters. Similarly, presidents make considerations of demographic representation in their selection of judicial candidates, particularly for high-visibility Supreme Court positions. Candidates' religious, ethnic, racial, and gender characteristics are all operative in the nomination process and can be especially relevant when a president's party needs to appeal to a particular demographic or special interest group in the electorate. Ronald Reagan's 1981 nomination of Judge Sandra Day O'Connor, the first woman to sit on the Supreme Court, was such an appeal and an effort to close the electoral "gender gap" in the GOP's favor. Regional and demographic factors may mitigate ideological ones by constraining presidents' choices to certain "qualified" candidates within their political party.

The other powerful political consideration that affects presidential nominations to the judiciary is the candidate's confirmability. It is here that presidential risk—or, more specifically, the risk of failure—enters into the calculation. Presidents must balance who they want, politically, against who they can get through the confirmation process, politically. The latter is a matter of presidential political capital: presidential popularity, lame duckism, and power vis-à-vis the Senate. Generally speaking, the greater the political capital presidents possess, the greater the latitude they have to nominate the candidate they desire ideologically and politically. Presidents enjoying high levels of public support, in their first term, and with same-party control of the Senate have the freedom to pay back political favors, to bestow rewards on political cronies, or to put forward candidates whose ideological qualifications eclipse their legal ones. Lame duck or politically besieged presidents, on the other hand, must consider confirmability very seriously if they do not wish to suffer the defeat of a nomination and risk further loss of political capital. Presidents in politically challenging circumstances, therefore, must find candidates with impeccable legal credentials to bolster their qualifications and confirmability. In extreme circumstances, politically weakened presidents make cross-party or otherwise nonpartisan nominations to defuse potential ideological or political opposition.

Essentially, the presidential calculation in the judicial selection process is one of predictability and certainty: predictability of the nominee, in terms of the policy decisions rendered, and certainty of success, in terms of confirmation and ultimate appointment. This dynamic raises one final strategic ploy: the stealth candidate. Presidents may seek, through in-house screening or vetting, "predictable" nominees who nevertheless lack a paper trail that would allow opposition senators to detect their true ideological valence. The lesson here is of course the infamously unsuccessful Robert H. Bork nomination and confirmation battle of 1987. Ronald Reagan, seeking to further the agenda of the New Right, put forward Judge Bork, whose legal and scholarly credentials were as impressive as his political preferences and interpretive approach were outside the mainstream. Unfortunately for Reagan and Bork, both aspects of the latter's qualities were well established in a long trail of distinguished publications.

To avoid being "Borked," subsequent presidents—looking for ideologically satisfying candidates in politically constrained times—have opted for nominees without an ascertainable record of views that might be challenged by the political opposition. Of course, without such a record or paper trail of writings or prior judicial opinions, nominees are just as likely to fool their nominator as they are the Senate confirming them. One noteworthy example is Justice David Souter, who was plucked from obscurity in New England by George H. W. Bush on the strength of the recommendation of Republican aide and New Hampshire governor John Sununu. "Certified conservative" but without a manifest record to complicate proceedings, Souter was easily confirmed and went on to establish himself as part of the leftist coalition of the Rehnquist and then Roberts Court. To put it bluntly, the stealth option can backfire on the president who deploys it.

At other times, stealth equals success for a president—both in terms of appointee predictability and ultimate confirmability. In the case of George W. Bush's 2005 appointment of John Roberts, for example, Democratic senators seemed to know that they were being taken, even as the confirmation hearings and Roberts's testimonials about judicial restraint were occurring. To understand why the Senate minority allowed itself to be "Roberts'ed," we must examine the second stage of the federal judicial selection process—Senate confirmation of nominees—and the calculations and considerations affecting it.

From the beginning of U.S. constitutional history, the Senate has read Article II's phrase "by and with the Advice and Consent of the Senate" to mean that it must approve presidential judicial nominees by majority vote (Abraham 1999). And politics play an important role in the legislative branch calculus, as does the level of court appointment being made. Epstein and Segal sum up that calculus as follows: "While it is clear that the Senate plays a crucial role in Supreme Court appointments (if only by constraining the president to choose among confirmable candidates), custom imposes tighter limitations on presidential freedom of choice for judges of the lower courts, especially the district courts. As one senator once said, ' . . . judges of the lower federal courts are actually "nominated" by Senators while the President exercises nothing more than a veto authority'" (Epstein and Segal 2005, 21). That being said, three powerful considerations affect nominee confirmation: partisanship and interbranch power relations, nominee ideology, and interest group or public opinion politics. With respect to the first consideration, just as presidents consider their own popularity, lame duckism, and standing with the Senate, so too do senators weigh these considerations about the president. The two factors of greatest salience for Senate confirmation of presidential nominees are the partisanship of each branch and the president's midterm electoral coattails. When a majority of the Senate is held by the opposition party, the president must consider the political and ideology preferences of this majority in forwarding judicial selections. Yet if a president threatens to command a "coattail effect," and if midterm elections have yet to be held, Senate power in the appointment process—even that of an opposite-party Senate majority—is more tenuous. The Senate as a body enjoys any number of procedural strategies for thwarting or delaying judicial candidates, from outright defeat in a floor vote to filibustering to prevent a nomination from coming to a full vote by the Senate to the Senate Judiciary Committee declining to report a nomination out of committee (i.e., stalling indefinitely by "sitting on" a judicial candidacy). The face-off between Republican Senate Judiciary Committee chair Orrin Hatch and President Bill Clinton over the latter's appellate court nominations was a variant of this form. As committee chair off and on between 1995 and 2004, Hatch liberally used the Senate's "blue slip" procedure, allowing home-state Republican senators to quash Clinton's nominees by failing to return to the committee a positive blue-slip recommendation. When mixed with the volatile force of partisan politics, such separation-of-powers institutional maneuvers can preempt presidential choice.

Many political scientists who study the judicial appointment process argue that the ideology of the nominee—in interaction with the ideology of the median senator and median Judiciary Committee member, and the ideological balance on the Court/courts—is the most important consideration affecting confirmation of a president's candidates (Comiskey 2004). John Massaro (1990) acknowledges the critical role played by the nominee's perceived ideology while stressing the significance of presidential management of the confirmation process, which includes packaging of the nominee and anticipating and dealing with "adverse structural conditions" of a hostile Senate. In the end, then, good presidential management means being cognizant of the importance of ideology in confirmation success. Presidential failure to take account of competing ideological considerations in replacing a "swing" justice on the Supreme Court, for instance, cedes to the Senate both the opportunity and the power to make the nominee's ideology matter. There is, in addition, another interesting interactive effect, that of ideology and qualifications. Put crudely, the smaller the divergence between nominee and senatorial ideology, the greater the possibility that mediocrity—in terms of legal, scholarly, professional qualifications—can prevail. The greater the divergence in ideology, the more attentive a president must be to nominee quality. The greater the divergence, also, the more sensitive the Senate is liable to be to a nominee's relative youth and presumed longevity as a legal policymaker on the bench, although age has yet to doom a presidential choice. Older candidates, though, seem to be falling from favor generally, as recent presidents—including and especially George W. Bush—seek out younger nominees with potentially decades of judicial service ahead of them.

Finally, interest group politics and public reaction to nominees affect their confirmation. Since the Bork episode, interest groups have been actively involved in the evaluative debate over judicial candidates' suitability for their respective federal court positions. Their participation, and use of media ads, is especially pronounced in High Court confirmation proceedings and can galvanize public feelings of support or outcry. Senators, naturally, want to be reelected and view these intertwined barometric readings on a judicial candidate as indicators of their own political futures. This dynamic was especially pertinent in the 1991 confirmation struggle over Clarence Thomas. George H. W. Bush was nominating Thomas, an African American conservative Republican, to replace civil rights legend and LBJ appointee Thurgood Marshall, the Court's first black justice. Thomas's slender qualifications and suspected extreme right-wing ideology quickly came under attack, and his confirmation hearings then descended into political theater with the appearance of witness Anita Hill, a former federal employee and then–law professor who testified about the sexual harassment she experienced from Thomas during his directorship of the Equal Employment Opportunity Commission.

Despite what seemed a fatal confluence of negative factors and events, including opposition from liberal and civil rights interest groups, Thomas was narrowly confirmed—arguably because several southern Democratic senators, dependent on minority votes in upcoming and uphill reelection battles against GOP challengers in their states, defied their party and special interest groups and declined to vote against the African American nominee (Silverstein 2007, 188–89). Interest groups are surely part of the public relations mix when it comes to presenting and assessing judicial candidates, but the upshot of their presence is not straightforward. The twenty-four-hour news cycle means that candidate images, and imaging, are the product of a media dialectic that now includes the informational and participatory floodgate of the Internet (Comiskey 2006, 10). That dialectic and those images and imaging are a powerful force that can precondition or prejudice a nominee's confirmation.

A matrix of factors makes up the politics of judicial appointment. The appointment process is also a political chicken game. The principal parties at each stage of the process, the president and the Senate, assess the factors or considerations that are in play with each judicial vacancy and putative nominee. Presidents either take risks or do not, based on their intuition as to which factors or considerations are likely to prevail. High-risk presidential gambits "play chicken" with a potentially obstreperous Senate. Low-risk presidential options, conversely, almost guarantee that senators can "out-chicken" the president. Yet the game's outcome and its very identity depend on both parties accurately identifying high- versus low-risk presidential actions and acting accordingly. President Bush's successes, and his "big ambition" when it came to staffing the federal courts, lay in his ability to minimize risk while seeming not to, thus baiting his Senate opponents and galvanizing his conservative base. His failures, on the other hand, were old-fashioned blunders, in which he seemed to take a "risk-be-damned" view.

Bush's Lower Federal Court Nominations

George W. Bush inaugurated his presidency's federal judicial appointments on May 9, 2001, when he announced his first group of candidates for Courts of Appeals. Utilizing a publicized White House ceremony to make the announcement—a gesture previously reserved for Supreme Court nominees—Bush introduced eleven individuals, touting them as representative of what was to come. Their demographic variety and legal professional qualities seemed to promise a goal of diversity on the federal bench as well as a desire to reach consensus with the Senate (two of the nominees were previous Clinton selections). Yet what quickly became clear was that neither promise would be borne out and that ideological concerns and screening would repeatedly trump most other considerations in judicial selection during the Bush administration.

A large number of vacancies on the federal bench existed when George W. Bush took office in 2001: they numbered eighty-two, which was "quite a sizeable number by historic standards" (Carp et al. 2005, 113). This huge number of vacancies existed partly because his predecessor, President Bill Clinton, had experienced one of the lowest levels of confirmation of federal judicial candidates in history—although he was able to appoint two justices to the Supreme Court with relative ease. Clinton selected very well qualified, "compromise" candidates in both Ruth Bader Ginsburg and Stephen Breyer, having decided to use his political capital on issues other than judicial nominations in order to avoid protracted and bruising confirmation battles. Only 60.3 percent of his Courts of Appeals nominees were confirmed between 1997 and 2000, and the time between a nomination being received in the Senate to a nominee receiving a confirmation hearing grew from an average of 79 days during the first Clinton term to an average of 247 days in the 106th Congress (1999–2000) (Goldman et al. 2001). The Bush administration was determined to avoid Clinton's fate and achieve quick hearings for its candidates, and the president hoped to maximize the yield of nominees confirmed. The Bush plan even offered a desired timetable for the phases of the judicial selection process (Goldman et al. 2005, 89)

In Bush's first four years as president, he made thirty-six appointments to the federal appellate courts, meaning that, by 2005, more than one out of five sitting circuit judges were his nominees. Because of the few numbers of cases accepted for review by the Supreme Court, these lower federal court judgeships are among the most important and influential with respect to legal policy formulation that a president can fill. As Epstein and Segal note, "These figures demonstrate just how quickly a president can change the composition of the bench, and, assuming he selects carefully, the extent to which he can reap the benefits of such appointments during his tenure . . . in the form of a packed judiciary likely to support his policies" (Epstein and Segal 2005, 50). Bush was of course fortunate to have the opportunity to make so many lower federal court appointments, but he also made the most of this opportunity.

Against the backdrop of 9/11 and the war on terror, and the heightened presidential powers that ensued, it was the confirmation of federal judges that provoked partisan warfare and separation-of-powers rivalry. The reason for this conflict was that the new president did not hesitate to push ideologically charged judicial candidates and expend time, effort, and resources on transforming the bench, while his Democratic opponents in the Senate used every tactic available to the minority party to prevent GOP dominance of the federal courts. These appointment patterns set the stage, although not necessarily the tone, for what would follow in Bush's second term: two Supreme Court vacancies—one of them the chief justiceship, followed by loss of Republican control of the Senate in 2006 and a chastened and somewhat beleaguered Bush administration.

Of course, Bush had also set the tone for this debate with his campaign trail remarks about the priority he would give to getting "good conservative judges appointed to the federal bench and approved by the United States Senate" (from Steigerwalt and Johnson 2005, 18). In terms of operations in the Bush White House, White House counsel Alberto Gonzales (and later, Harriet Miers) was the president's "point man" on judicial selection, as the process was anchored in the Office of the White House Counsel beginning in the first term of the Bush administration. Traditionally shared with the Office of Legal Policy in the Department of Justice, decisions as to judicial nominations had been planted firmly under the control of the president and White House staff by previous GOP administrations. President Ronald Reagan, for instance, created the President's Committee on Federal Judicial Selection, which engaged in the systematic philosophical litmus testing of judicial candidates (Steigerwalt and Johnson 2005, 10; Maltese 1995, 123) and "glued" the Republican clientele, such as the Christian Right, to the party (Silverstein 2007, 202). Adding to the impression of policy vetting by a presidential administration, Bush took the dramatic step of unilaterally ending the semiofficial role of the American Bar Association's Standing Committee on Federal Judiciary in conducting prenomination evaluations of judicial candidates. ABA appraisal of judicial prospects was replaced with a revivified Office of Legal Policy, led by and searching out members of the conservative legal group the Federalist Society (Silverstein 2007, 202–3).

Despite the bonus of inheriting so many judicial vacancies and the intense focus on and organizational structure for judicial selection, the political atmosphere surrounding President Bush at the start of his first term was not especially promising. The central question was whether he had actually won the presidency. Despite ultimately winning the Electoral College vote, Bush had failed to prevail in the overall popular vote, pointing to a lack of mandate for his presidency. Bush also entered office with the highest public disapproval rating of an incoming president since the beginning of Gallup polling (Maltese 2003, 5). In addition, in terms of questionable political capital, he faced the prospect of an evenly divided Senate and little margin for error in the presidential calculation over judicial selections. His prospects worsened in July 2001 when Senator James Jeffords of Vermont defected from the Republican Party, causing the Senate majority to switch to the Democrats and Patrick Leahy, Vermont's other senator, to take charge of the Judiciary Committee.

Only 53.1 percent of Bush's circuit court candidates were confirmed during the 107th Congress (2001–2002); two candidates—Charles Pickering and Priscilla Owen—were defeated in committee vote, while a number of others struggled in other stages of the confirmation process. The climate became even more heated after the 2002 midterm elections, when Republicans regained a slight majority in the Senate, with the Judiciary Committee chair passing to GOP conservative Orrin Hatch. Bush promptly renominated those politically controversial candidates still pending confirmation, as well as the previously defeated Pickering and Owen. The minority party Democrats fought back in the 108th Congress (2003–2004), filibustering a record ten circuit court nominees on the Senate floor. (Those filibustered nominees were Henry Saad [Sixth Circuit], Janice Rogers Brown [DC Circuit], William Pryor [Eleventh Circuit], Charles Pickering [Fifth Circuit], Priscilla Owen [Fifth Circuit], William Myers [Ninth Circuit], David McKeague [Sixth Circuit], Carolyn Kuhl [Ninth Circuit], Richard Allen Griffin [Sixth Circuit], and Miguel Estrada [DC Circuit]— the last eventually withdrawing his nomination in 2003 following multiple failed cloture votes in the Senate.) This minority obstruction was in some ways payback for GOP and Senator Hatch's hindrance of Clinton nominees, but it was also triggered by Bush's nominations, which hued to his ideology and stuck a finger in the eye of the opposition. Pickering, for instance, came under fire for his voting as a federal district judge in civil rights cases and for his opposition as a Mississippi state senator to abortion rights and the *Roe v. Wade* precedent. Owen had been handpicked by key presidential adviser Karl Rove, despite some criticism for judicial activism from her own Texas Supreme Court colleagues. As a state appellate judge, she had routinely dismissed suits brought by workers for job-related injuries and unfair employment practices, and she ignored judicial bypass provisions in the Texas parental notification law in order to make abortions harder to obtain for pregnant minors. Such nominees engendered stubborn political ire in Senate Democrats like Edward Kennedy, who swore to mount a fight even if candidates could not be defeated, to make clear to the public what was at stake with judges.

As one scholar-observer summarized the dynamic between Bush and his minority party opponents, "The important pattern for judicial confirmations that emerged in Bush's first term was the continuing resolve of Senate Democrats to publicly fight—and thereby obstruct—the confirmation of judges perceived to be outside the mainstream, and the persistent decision by the Bush administration to fight these confirmation battles head on" (Steigerwalt and Johnson 2005, 19). In his lower federal appellate court nominations, Bush clearly prioritized policy and electoral goals, throwing caution to the wind when it came to their acceptability on an ideological basis. It was as if in acting with a sense of great presidential political capital, he could make it so. To some extent, he did. His doggedness in resuscitating the rejected would be repeated in his second term when, as a newly reelected but still pre-midterm elections president, he did possess the capital of popularity, coattails, and increased party control of the Senate.

The poisonous partisan atmosphere in the Senate caused by and exacerbated by the new politics of lower federal court judicial confirmations worsened after the November 2004 elections. Leadership of the Judiciary Committee had changed hands, with Orrin Hatch barred by term limits from continuing as chair and the moderate but suitably chastised Arlen Specter assuming control. The controversy within and agitation by the conservative base of the Republican Party over Specter's assumption of the chair, due to the fear that he would block pro-life judicial candidates, had effectively neutralized him as a possible impediment to Bush's nominees (Toobin 2005, 43). But the rules of the Senate remained another obstacle. The inflamed rhetoric around the Democratic filibustering and Republican angst because they still lacked the sixty votes necessary to control debate engendered discussion of changing Senate rules. Republicans wanted a rule that would allow a point of order to be raised and a majority vote taken to cut off debate and end a filibuster. This was the so-called "nuclear option" of spring 2005, first named by former majority leader Trent Lott (R-Mississippi) during GOP discussions in 2003. Conservative senators like Hatch and the new majority leader, William Frist of Tennessee, came to call it the "constitutional option" (Toobin 2005, 44) and to defend it as a more historically and systemically appropriate balance of authority between the executive and the Senate in the judicial confirmation process. However this option was labeled, Republican majority senators sought to debut it to chasten the Democratic minority before the full-scale political blowout of a Supreme Court confirmation battle.

The potential damage to the Senate as an institution and the further escalation of bitter partisan warfare threatened by the deployment of that "option" never occurred because of a truly remarkable parliamentary event—an event that ended up benefiting Bush's federal judicial ambitions.

A deal was brokered between seven moderate Republican and seven moderate Democratic senators to vote against any proposed change in filibuster rules as long as no floor vote on a judicial nominee was prohibited except in "extraordinary circumstances" (Silverstein 2007, 209–10). The "Gang of Fourteen" pact, as it came to be called, rescued Bush from himself and cleared the renominated Priscilla Owen, the ideologically suspect nominee, and also renominated William Pryor, and the extremely right-of-center African American judge, Janice Rogers Brown, to be confirmed and seated on the federal circuit court. Each was confirmed with barely more than the fifty-five votes wielded by Senate Republicans. A partisan-friendly and newly bipartisan Senate made possible Bush's successes—particularly striking in that both Pryor and Brown had received mixed "qualified/not qualified" ABA rankings subsequent to their original nominations.

With the war in Iraq continuing and worsening, and with mounting scandals in the Bush administration, GOP losses in 2006, the final midterm election of Bush's presidency, passed the Senate leadership back to the Democrats. Facing the 110th Congress (2007–2008) of new Senate Majority Leader Harry Reid (D-Nevada) and returning Senate Judiciary Committee chair Patrick Leahy, Bush withdrew from further consideration several judicial candidates left unconfirmed when the previous Senate adjourned. Senator Leahy's declaration that only "consensus candidates" would secure confirmation under the new Democratic majority was ringing true by July 2007, with only one half of 50 judicial candidates nominated since January 2007 approved. Still, after nearly seven years in the White House, Bush had successfully named 294 judges to the federal courts, giving Republican appointees a solid majority of the slots, including a 60-to-40 percent edge over Democrats on the U.S. Courts of Appeals. The Ninth Circuit Court was the last bastion of Democratic advantage, with the remaining regional circuits either closely split or dominated by Republican judges (Savage 2008). By October 2008, the number of Bush federal court nominees successfully confirmed had risen to 324, with 10 of the nation's 13 federal appellate courts "dominated by conservatives" (Eggen 2008).

A lame-duck, end-of-term, politically challenged president is rarely successful or a risk taker when it comes to judicial staffing decisions. Such a president has to take comfort in the triumphs of past tactical advances and in sound calculations about worthwhile risk made in more sanguine political times. As Bush's second term began drawing to a close, in late 2007 his Justice Department and Attorney General Alberto Gonzales became mired in scandal (over the warrantless eavesdropping on Americans in the war on terror) and incompetence (over the handling and disclosure of seemingly politically punitive dismissals of U.S. district attorneys) as well, distracting the administration from a judicial selection campaign already derailed by a disadvantageous political context. These distractions would eventually engulf even the White House counsel who succeeded Gonzales and had been put forward as a candidate for the Supreme Court: nominee Harriet Miers, who has the distinction of being one of the handful of persons whose name was withdrawn before it could be acted upon. Her selection tells a tale of how Bush turned his policy goals and political capital to staffing the High Court.

A Tale of Two Judges and One Revealing Blunder

Commenting on the Supreme Court's decisive vote in *Bush v. Gore* on the presidential election of 2000, law scholar Bruce Ackerman remarked with outrage that "the Supreme Court cannot be permitted to arrange for its own succession . . . [by] the right-wing bloc on the Court . . . extend[ing] its control for a decade or more . . . [by] put[ting] George W. Bush into the White House" (Ackerman 2001). Prophetic or exaggeration, Ackerman's statement has been borne out in fact: at this writing (April 2008), the Supreme Court is dominated by GOP appointees, with Bush's two justices completing a five-member conservative majority bloc.

Bush had no opportunity to nominate a Supreme Court justice during his first term, but, if Ackerman is to be believed, it scarcely mattered; his time would come. Bush's time came in July 2005, with Sandra Day O'Connor's announcement that she would be retiring with the end of the term. Her importance as a pivotal centrist on the Rehnquist-led bench— she was "a court of one" (Rosen 2001) due to the decisiveness of her vote and doctrinal formulations for so many polarizing issue areas—cannot be overemphasized (Maveety 2008).

After much prognostication by court watchers and by the administration itself, Bush announced the nomination of federal appeals court judge John Roberts, who had long been on the administration's short list of suitable candidates for a Supreme Court slot. Even Democrats admitted that his legal credentials were impeccable, though his status as a conservative jurist was clear. Despite his being the replacement for a divided Court's "swing" justice, he was personable and affable in his early interviews with senators, and "conventional wisdom on the Hill was that it would be an extraordinarily difficult task to demonize Judge Roberts" (Silverstein 2007,

211). Shortly after consideration of Judge Roberts began, another event occurred that changed the entire appointment dynamic: Chief Justice William Rehnquist, who had been ill for a long time and whose retirement announcement was expected, died in the late summer of 2005. Initially appointed by Richard Nixon in 1971 as an associate justice, Rehnquist had been elevated to the chief's chair by Ronald Reagan in 1986. Rehnquist had been a consistent conservative, though less of a crusading ideologue than a jurist committed to certain principles of limited government, like states' rights federalism. Having already stated that she would not retire until her successor was confirmed, O'Connor formally postponed her retirement so as not to leave the Court suddenly shorthanded, and Bush renominated Roberts for the chief justice position.

Roberts had clerked for then-Justice Rehnquist and was considered a fungibly conservative replacement for the recently deceased chief justice. As such, and given the reality—even to Democrats in the Senate—that "George Bush had won the election" in 2004, Roberts's confirmation was never really in doubt. This was even more apparent after the charmingly self-effacing performance he gave during his Senate confirmation hearings, in which he appeared as the witty and intellectually engaging poster boy of judicial restraint. His own ideological past, including service in the Reagan and Bush administrations—which had complicated his lower federal court confirmation hearing in 2003—was fodder for only a few liberal members of the Senate Judiciary Committee. The committee's chair, Senator Arlen Specter, a moderate Republican, was nevertheless committed to a fair but thorough investigation of Roberts's credentials, and a positive recommendation by a majority of the committee seemed inevitable. In the end, Roberts was confirmed by a vote of 78 to 22, and he took the center seat as chief justice when the next court term began in October 2005.

Several appointment factors discussed in the first section of this chapter explain Roberts's successful confirmation by the 109th Congress and also show that his nomination was classically low risk for President Bush. Probably the most important factor was nominee ideology in conjunction with the balance of power on the Supreme Court. Roberts was essentially a "wash," the replacement of one conservative justice with another by a Republican president. Bush lowered the risk of the Senate's strategic calculation further by selecting an extremely well qualified candidate, professionally and legally speaking, who was a known conservative but not a particularly *well*-known one—who could easily turn out to be a moderate conservative. Whether Bush knew "the truth" about Roberts and his Reagan/Bush administration credentials and paper trail of internal White House documents was irrelevant: Roberts was essentially a stealth-*y* candidate who offered at best an ideological compromise, at worst an expected and begrudgingly legitimate one-for-one trade.

The year before Roberts's nomination and confirmation became a reality, judicial appointments scholar David Yalof had predicted that a "simultaneous vacancies scenario" would increase the expectations of ideological compromise on Bush's part, even as it would multiply his transformative possibilities for the Supreme Court. He wrote that, "in 2005 or 2006, the presence of two vacancies at the same time will put the administration under considerable pressure to balance an extreme ideologue with a more moderate, highly-esteemed conservative. If so, the Democrats may actually benefit from the . . . scenario" (Yalof 2005, 20). Assuming Roberts is the "moderate, highly-esteemed conservative," then Bush was freed to nominate whomever he wanted for his other Supreme Court vacancy. The problem there was that it was the seat held by the moderate centrist and court pivot, Associate Justice Sandra Day O'Connor, and it was also one of the two "female" seats on the court. Democratic senators who might have given Bush a pass on Rehnquist's replacement were less likely to do so when court majority power hung in the balance. Republicans, moreover, still lacked a filibuster-proof majority in the Senate, and liberal Democrats on the Senate Judiciary Committee, including Edward Kennedy, Patrick Leahy, Charles Schumer, and Russell Feingold, could be counted on to aggressively confront any dubious Bush candidate.

That candidate turned out to be more dubious than expected, but to an unexpected constituency: GOP conservatives, both senators and party activists. The Bush choice for a second Supreme Court appointment seemed to be Bush's alone. It was White House counsel and longtime political friend and Texas crony Harriet Miers. She had no practical background or professional experience in constitutional law; put bluntly, her public career was defined by service to her patron. With no paper trail and slim credentials at best, Miers produced anxiety for senators of both parties, with Bush essentially asking committed conservatives to trust his judgment as to her conservative credos.

Silverstein (2007, 214) argues that Bush's perception of a diminishing supply of political capital was the most plausible explanation for the Miers nomination. Two *Washington Post* reporters speculated that religion and, specifically, the appeal to evangelical Christians was behind her selection, since Bush knew her as and represented her as a member of a conservative and pro-life church (Baker and Babington 2005). Initial assessments agreed that Bush was not going to choose anyone for the High Court who would surprise him or history, nor did he wish to spark a divisive partisan fight that would highlight the disarray then facing his administration over issues such as the federal government's Hurricane Katrina response and administrative figures' involvement in "outing" a CIA operative to punish her husband's political outspokenness on the Iraq war policy. In the wake of the Senate Republicans' threatened "nuclear option" and the compromise position of the Senate's centrist "Gang of Fourteen," Bush was attempting to stay within acceptable boundaries, get a confirmable conservative, and minimize risk.

But in his Miers gamble, he miscalculated badly. Her slender credentials and unknown status presented too many doubts for conservatives— or, as liberal Democratic senator Kennedy characterized the situation, "the extreme right-wing of the Republican Party . . . have a litmus test, and Harriet Miers didn't pass" (from Bumiller and Hulse 2005). As a result of the scorn piled on her by the conservative blogosphere and talk radio, by televangelist and cable talking heads (Comiskey 2006), Miers withdrew as a nominee. She and the administration evoked the convenient, executive-privilege impasse that had been developing over augmenting her almost nonexistent paper record with documents she produced during her service in the White House.

After the disastrous Miers selection, Bush named long-serving federal appellate judge Samuel Alito—the ideologue as safe choice. While not quite a "stealth" candidate in the mode of George H. W. Bush's David Souter, Alito, with his long record of acceptably conservative decisions in the federal circuit court, was neither as visible nor as high powered as other well-known conservative judges. Like Roberts, he was a palatable conservative whose professional credentials and shy, quiet manner made him difficult to challenge. Even if the combustible mix of replacing the Court's swing seat and Alito's clearly conservative bona fides did produce a partisan showdown and a possible filibuster, some observers predicted that Bush would win either way: either with a usefully distracting, protracted, but ultimately winnable battle, or with outright albeit glum Senate approval. Alito's evidence of and record in supporting, if not enhancing, the unilateral power of the executive branch was cited by Democrats as both a reason for his nomination and a reason to grill the nominee (*New York Times* editorial 2006).

In the end, Alito's confirmation hearing was devoid of real tension, with the few fireworks being provided by Senator Kennedy's badgering of the nominee over his 1972 membership in the admittedly retrograde organization Concerned Alumni of Princeton, which opposed admission of women to the previously all-male (and largely white) university. But given his "well-qualified" rating by the ABA and his party-line endorsement by the Judiciary Committee, his appointment was almost certain. Even after Judiciary Committee chair Patrick Leahy's speech putting forth his opposition—arguably to make a campaign issue of Alito's decisions on the Court *if* he was confirmed—Senate Democrats could not bring themselves to take responsibility for blocking another Bush nominee (Nagourney, Stevenson, and Lewis 2006; Romano and Ellperin 2006). A short-lived attempt by twenty-five Democratic senators to filibuster the Alito nomination on the floor fizzled, although forty-one Democrats did vote "no" on his confirmation. Bush's second, and much more significant Supreme Court appointee in terms of the balance of court power, was confirmed on a 58-to-42 vote and seated in the final days of January 2006.

It is clear that in the Alito episode, Bush benefited from Democratic fumbling and internal infighting if not outright bungling in the bid to define the nominee. Many Democrats "didn't have the stomach for a fight *they would probably lose*" (Romano and Ellperin 2006; emphasis added). Out-chickened by President Bush, Democratic senators contented themselves with voting against the Alito nomination and expecting the worst—craven opposition combined with a filibuster fight on principle. After the debacle of the Miers selection, Bush's risk-adverse Alito selection paid confirmation dividends even though Senate opponents were fully cognizant of the policy risk of this political appointment. But the combination of qualifications and demeanor that diffused the nominee's ideologically objectionable nature, the reality of a GOP Senate majority, and the lingering controversy over and ambiguity about the minority filibuster tactic rendered Bush's second choice a first-rate "low risk, big ambition" judicial appointment.

Still, Democrats were left feeling the sting of having been outmaneuvered and sensing potentially dire implications for the future. One commentator saw in both Bush Supreme Court confirmations "the increasing[ly] partisan nature of Senate votes on nominees" that "probably imprints upon" the newly selected justices "a stronger partisan identity than they had prior to nomination" (Wittes 2006, 9). Much as Clarence Thomas was said to have been traumatized and hardened in his reactionary jurisprudential commitments by his bruising confirmation experience, Roberts and especially Alito may have become more firmly ensconced in the conservative camp by their branding as unacceptable ideologues. If there is truth in these assertions about the impact of the confirmation experience (although the process and not the president is responsible for this dynamic), Bush's judicial appointment legacy will be one of further politicization of both the process and the appointees.

The Bush Constitution

Any discussion of the Bush impact on the judicial branch would be incomplete without some analysis of the Bush administration's efforts to influence the development of constitutional law on executive power. In this area, his two Supreme Court appointees would appear to be loyal supporters of the theory of the "unitary executive." This theory asserts that the Constitution's grants of power to each branch, particularly Article II's "vesting clause," accord a high degree of presidential self-sufficiency and exclusivity in the exercise of power (Skowronek 2008; Calabresi 1994; Calabresi and Rhodes 1992). Developed and elaborated by movement conservatives such as Terry Eastland (1992) and John Yoo (2005), the theory of the unitary executive also claimed an independent share of constitutional interpretation authority for the president (Nather 2007b), particularly in construing and performing the admittedly vague and potentially expansive powers of the executive in Article II.

It was presidential power in prosecuting the post-9/11 war on terror that would be the major occasion for an aggressive defense of presidential prerogatives in the forum of the federal judiciary. Immediately after 9/11, Congress on September 14 passed a resolution authorizing the president to "use all necessary and appropriate force against those nations, organizations, or persons *he determines* planned, authorized, committed, or aided the terrorist attacks that occurred" (emphasis added). The Authorization for the Use of Military Force Act seemed to give President Bush broad discretion and choice of means in protecting national security, which he soon acted upon. Following the October 2001 commencement of the war against the Taliban government and al-Qaida forces in Afghanistan, Bush issued an executive order authorizing the use of military tribunals to try foreign nationals apprehended in the war on terrorism. His order was not specific as to the circumstances under which the tribunals would be used or the procedures they would follow. In 2002, when the military began to incarcerate "enemy aliens" captured in Afghanistan at U.S. Naval Station Guantanamo Bay in Cuba, the constitutional questions surrounding

Bush's executive detention actions began to crystallize. In federal cases brought by detainees regarding their due process rights, Bush's attorneys would aggressively press for unilateral executive authority in a wartime context. As constitutional scholar Sue Davis notes, "The Bush administration's claims regarding the inherent power of the president in his capacity as commander in chief to take action in the absence of authorization from Congress and without review from the judiciary . . . are consistent with a theory, known as the 'unitary executive,' which posits that the president has broad authority to act in wartime without checks by Congress or the courts" (Davis 2008, 195).

While the Supreme Court would repudiate these claims in two cases on the legitimacy of executive-ordered detention of "enemy combatants," conservative justice Clarence Thomas defended a broad and plenary stewardship role for the executive in his dissenting opinions. In the case of *Hamdi v. Rumsfeld* (542 U.S. 507 [2004]), he was the only member of the Court to accept the Bush administration's argument for presidential authority to detain and hold American citizens deemed to be enemy combatants without formal charges and access to counsel. It is "antithetical to our constitutional structure," he continued in his dissent in *Hamdan v. Rumsfeld,* for the Court "to pass on the 'military necessity' of the Commander in Chief's decision to employ a particular form of force against our enemies" (548 U.S. ___ [2006]). Bush appointee Samuel Alito joined Thomas in dissent in the case, which rejected Bush's assertion of the power to convene military commissions without specific congressional authorization. And Bush appointee Roberts had shown that he, too, was sympathetic to expansive executive power claims, voting to support the military tribunals at issue in the *Hamdan* litigation while he was a circuit court judge on the DC Court of Appeals. Because of his participation in the case in the lower court, Roberts recused himself from the Supreme Court–level proceedings.

Bush's response to the juridical defeats in *Hamdi* and *Hamdan* was to secure the passage of the Military Commissions Act (MCA) of 2006. This legislation was consistent with two key Bush administration claims: first, that the prisoner-of-war treatment standards of the Geneva Conventions, a set of international treaties to which the United States is a party, did not apply to terrorism suspects; and second, that the federal courts could not interfere with executive decisions regarding the detainment of such suspects. The law was challenged as violating the Constitution's prohibition of the suspension of habeas corpus except in times of rebellion or invasion.

Bush would suffer another constitutional setback in the 2008 ruling on *Boumediene v. Bush* (553 U.S. ___ [2008]), which concerned the application of the MCA to the detainees at the Guantanamo Bay facility. These detainees were suspected terrorists, all noncitizens, who had neither been arrested in nor held in the United States. Guantanamo was leased from Cuba under a 1903 treaty and so was not actually U.S. territory, yet there was no tradition of applying Cuban law there. The detainees were being held at this facility because the Bush administration's lawyers were confident that, under the Supreme Court's precedent, they would not enjoy constitutional rights, including the right to a court hearing to challenge the legality of their incarceration. What the choice of Guantanamo demonstrated, according to one contemporaneous commentator, was "the profoundly legalistic way" in which Bush's anti-terror policies were designed. "Using the law itself," writes Noah Feldman, "the lawyers in the Bush administration set out to make Guantánamo into a legal vacuum" (Feldman 2008).

The Supreme Court repudiated such legal sophistry in *Boumediene*, arguing that for constitutional purposes, the Guantanamo facility was in the United States and that the detainees there had the same rights as those held on home soil. Justice Kennedy's majority opinion for the divided court rejected what the Bush administration claimed to be the rule that noncitizens held outside the United States were not entitled to constitutional protection. What most offended the *Boumediene* majority about Guantanamo was "*precisely* the effort by the executive branch, with the approval of Congress, to make Guantánamo into a place beyond the reach of any law" (Feldman 2008; emphasis added). For the four conservative dissenting justices (again, including Bush appointees Roberts and Alito)—all of whose views closely tracked those of the Bush administration—the matter was one of the president and Congress, acting together, enjoying the constitutional power to acquire and govern a territory outside the reach of federal courts if they so chose.

In a further setback for Bush's policies and postscript to the *Boumediene* Supreme Court case, on October 7, 2008, a federal district judge ordered the release into the United States of seventeen foreign-national detainees at Guantanamo, arguing that the government had provided no proof that they were enemy combatants or security risks. "Separation-of-powers concerns do not trump the very principle upon which this nation was founded—the unalienable right to liberty," said Judge Ricardo Urbina, rebuking the administration for the indefinite detention without cause (Wilber 2008).

In his self-assumed role as constitutional arbiter of executive branch powers, President Bush exhibited the big ambitions of the unitary executive theory espoused by his White House lawyers. In presenting this argument to a GOP-dominated Supreme Court whose controlling majority came to include two of his own appointees, Bush's constitutional assertions arguably were also low risk. In spite of their poor performance before the high bench, the Bush administration's claims about executive prerogatives during "war" enjoyed a house advantage in the 2007–2008 Supreme Court term. The reality of a closely divided Supreme Court with a conservative bloc that clearly favors the Bush vision of executive power overshadowed the specific setbacks suffered by the "Bush Constitution."

The Bush Bench?

His presidency may not be remembered fondly, with its Bush Doctrine of preemptive interventionism (Bell 2008) and executive branch imperialism, but Bush's presidency is likely to be well remembered—if only for its successful imprinting of his policy preferences on the federal judiciary. His two Supreme Court appointees are already remaking constitutional law in certain issue areas, such as abortion rights, race-conscious diversity policies, and campaign spending regulation. Because they complete a conservative majority coalition on the Court and because their relative youth means that they are likely to serve for decades, Roberts and Alito help constitute a "Bush Bench" that will extend far beyond the Bush presidency. Having had a similar impact on the composition of the lower federal courts, George W. Bush unquestionably leaves a personal policy legacy and an enviable record of presidential managerial success with respect to judicial staffing. "This administration," concluded Nan Aron of the Alliance for Justice on the eve of the 2008 presidential election, "has cemented a transformation of our federal judiciary begun by Ronald Reagan" (from Eggen 2008).

Bush's biggest and seemingly least likely "big ambition" recognized and took advantage of low-risk action and was his crowning achievement in an otherwise risky, costly, and overreaching presidential agenda. Yet the ultimate product of his ambitions for the judicial branch is like that of his other ambitious presidential projects: division and divisiveness. The Supreme Court is clearly a battleground, politically and constitutionally, at the close and in the wake of the Bush presidency.

Economic and Foreign Policy

PART IV

12

RIDING THE TIGER

Bush and the Economy

JOHN FRENDREIS and
RAYMOND TATALOVICH

I f peace and prosperity are the twin pillars of presidential popularity (Kernell 1978), then there is little wonder that the presidency of George W. Bush concluded with widespread dissatisfaction with his performance as president. Not only were his years in office marked by a long war with uncertain prospects for success, but his presidency was also distinguished by periods of economic downturn at both the beginning and end of his eight years as president. From his peak job approval rating of more than 90 percent shortly after 9/11, President Bush's popularity eroded steadily, ending at 22 percent, the lowest rating of any president at the close of his term since polling began (Frankovic 2009).

During the first four years of the Bush presidency, the tribulations of the economy were overshadowed by national security events and concerns. President Bush entered office just as the longest period of economic expansion in U.S. economic history was drawing to a close. Even before 9/11, the economy was slowing, and the economic consequence of the terrorist attacks was an economy pushed into a period of contraction. However, the traditional "rally 'round the flag" effect caused public confidence in the president to surge.

The 2002 midterm elections showed how national security fears can overwhelm concerns about the economy. Apart from the historical trend—that the presidential party had lost House seats in all (but three) midterm elections since 1860—was the economic record. Between the presidential inauguration and the midterm elections, the value of the Standard & Poor's 500 Stock Index suffered a steeper decline under Bush (31.8 percent) than under any president except Herbert Hoover (33.7 percent), during the Great Depression (Norris 2002). Twenty years earlier the Democrats had exploited the weak economy, attacked Reaganomics, and gained twenty-six seats in the House of Representatives, but this time the Democrats had difficulty getting any political traction based on economic issues. This was not because they failed to make economics the issue, since congressional Democratic candidates across the nation attacked GOP plans to privatize Social Security, claimed that the North American Free Trade Agreement (NAFTA) shifted jobs to Mexico, and promised more job growth. In the election aftermath, it was obvious that the Democrats made a strategic blunder by allowing President Bush and the GOP to monopolize the issue of domestic terrorism and homeland security.

The central portion of the Bush presidency—the period between the 2002 midterm election and the 2006 midterm election—marked the high point of economic performance on President Bush's watch. Politically, national discourse during this period focused more on the Iraq war and national security concerns than on traditional economic concerns. While dissatisfaction with the war was increasing, Bush was able to ride the relatively strong economy and the remaining public support for strong national security measures to a narrow victory in his 2004 reelection bid. However, by 2006, public dissatisfaction with the war led to a major victory for the opposition Democrats in the midterm elections, returning control of both the House and Senate to the Democrats for the first time in twelve years.

The 2008 presidential race commenced shortly after the midterm election. Initially, it appeared that the Iraq war would again dominate the public agenda—and the respective races for the parties' nominations and the general election. However, the decaying economic performance in the final eighteen months of the Bush presidency shifted public attention back to traditional economic concerns—not eliminating national security as an issue but refocusing the public's evaluations of the 2008 presidential candidates to emphasize their potential to restore economic prosperity to the nation. At the same time, the erosion of economic performance further diminished the public's regard for President Bush and promised to tarnish his legacy.

Seen from the vantage point of 2009, the Bush presidency's performance in managing the economy seems less purposeful and more reactive. The dramatic shift toward national security—and the subsequent wars in Iraq and on terror—shifted the focus of the administration and potential critics away from economic policy. Only in the closing eighteen months did the consequences of this benign neglect come forward in the form of a burst housing "bubble," collapse of the credit and mortgage markets, and a sustained and serious economic downturn. In the final six months of the Bush presidency, the administration struggled to manage successive crises and hurriedly developed plans for addressing these crises. These plans marked a sharp break with the prevailing Republican ideology of avoiding governmental intrusion into private markets.

The State of the Bush Economy

The five-member Business Cycle Dating Committee of the National Bureau of Economic Research (NBER), which tracks the business cycle, reported that in March 2001 the economy fell into a recession that lasted eight months before beginning to subside in November 2001. For the next six years, throughout the bulk of the Bush presidency, the U.S. economy was in a period of expansion. This expansion ended in December 2007, and the final thirteen months of the Bush presidency marked the onset of a relatively severe and lengthy (by post–World War II standards) recession. In a comparative sense, the "Bush expansion" of seventy-three months was fairly lengthy—well above the long-term (thirty-eight months) and postwar (fifty-seven months) U.S. averages, although it was only fourth among the nine postwar expansions. (See http://www.nber.org/cycles.html for a complete listing.)

Of course, the terms "expansion" and "contraction" describe general trends rather than continuous periods of improvement or decay; the business cycle does not display the smooth, perfect shape of a sine curve. This is readily apparent in figure 12.1, which shows the quarterly change in real gross domestic product (GDP) throughout the Bush presidency. For a large, developed economy, economists would regard a 4 percent real annual growth rate to be solid growth, while annual growth of less than 2 percent would be considered anemic. Thus, in figure 12.1, the most relevant dividing points for *quarterly* growth are above 1 percent (strong), 0.5 to 1 percent (moderate), and below 0.5 percent (weak); a decline in real

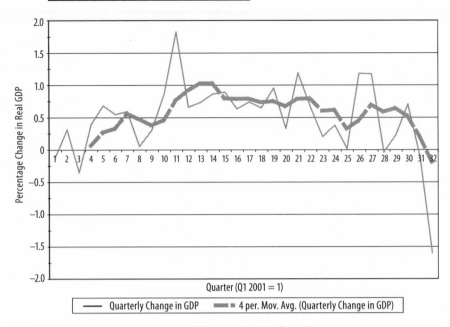

Figure 12.1. Quarterly change in real GDP during G. W. Bush presidency

GDP for two consecutive quarters is the formal definition of a recession. To smooth out quarterly variability, figure 12.1 also contains a plot of the four-quarter moving average.

The data on GDP growth conform to the general pattern noted above: an initial contraction followed by a long period of economic expansion, with a pronounced decay in the final year. Until the sharp drop in the final two quarters, the low point was the third quarter of the Bush presidency (July–September in 2001), while the strongest economic performance was approximately twelve to fourteen quarters into the Bush presidency (late 2003 into mid-2004). In terms of GDP growth, the economy staged a modest rebound in early 2007, although this was quickly followed by a sharp decline. Perhaps most significantly, even the broad middle period of economic expansion falls mainly in the range of moderate growth. The relatively few quarters with quarterly growth above 1 percent were always followed by quarters with far smaller growth rates, and the general rate of annual growth during the broad expansion was about 3 percent, which is a low rate of growth during a long expansion by recent standards.

Another dimension of economic performance during the Bush presi-

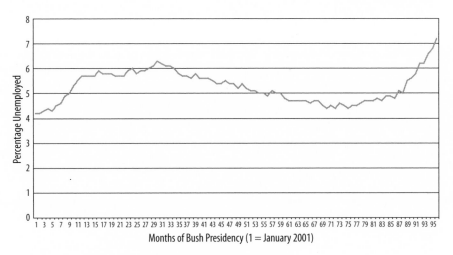

Figure 12.2. Monthly unemployment rate during Bush presidency

dency is displayed in figure 12.2, which shows the monthly rate of unemployment throughout these years. Since unemployment lags economic growth, the overall pattern resembles the pattern in figure 12.1, but with peaks and valleys occurring at later points. The best monthly unemployment rate of the entire Bush presidency (4.2 percent) occurred in the first month (January 2001), as the long Clinton-era expansion drew to a close. Even before 9/11, unemployment began to rise, and unemployment continued its rise following the attacks, peaking at 6.3 percent in July 2003 (month 30), several quarters after the GDP growth rate showed sustained economic expansion. Following this peak, unemployment slowly but steadily fell into the 4.5-to-5-percent range for much of the remaining Bush years, until it began to rise again during late 2007 and into 2008. The final three months of the Bush presidency witnessed the highest rates of unemployment of the entire eight-year period, rising to rates of 6.6, 6.8, and 7.2 percent. Overall, the unemployment levels of the Bush presidency reflect fairly good performance, ranging between 4 and 6 percent for nearly all of his years in office, a bit better than most postwar presidential terms and much better than the levels during much of the 1970s and 1980s. The Bush period unemployment thus looked anemic only to voters recalling the boom years of the late 1990s. However, the Bush presidency is unique in that the best performance was found in his first month in office, while the worst was seen in his last.

Along with the unemployment rate, the rate of inflation is another aspect of economic performance watched closely by the public. For the first seven years of the Bush presidency, yearly inflation was moderate to low, averaging about 2.5 percent. Not surprisingly, the lowest annual rates were in 2001 (1.6 percent) and 2008 (1.1 percent), both years of economic downturn. The highest annual rate was in 2007 (4.1 percent); because this surge in prices occurred at the same time the economic slowdown began, it raised briefly the specter of "stagflation," the pernicious pattern of economic contraction coupled with price inflation that proved so difficult to address during the 1970s. However, by mid-2008, the developing recession slowed and then reversed the pattern of price increases, in part because of a dramatic drop in oil prices once demand contracted as part of the slowing of the global economy.

Up to this point we have examined the performance of the economy during the Bush presidency largely in absolute terms. It is also instructive to examine it in the context of other recent presidential terms. Table 12.1 provides a comparison of all presidential terms since World War II, the modern era in which presidents are expected to be managers of national economic prosperity. This presidential economic scorecard shows economic performance for each presidential term for five economic indicators: unemployment, inflation, economic growth, productivity, and the current account balance (balance of trade). This scorecard updates an earlier version (Dolan, Frendreis, and Tatalovich 2008, 258) through the end of Bush's second term.

Among all fifteen of the postwar presidential terms, the two George W. Bush terms do not fare well, ranking eighth and twelfth. However, there is a secular trend for later terms to be less favorable than earlier terms, and the first George W. Bush term was, in fact, the second strongest presidential term since 1972, trailing only the second Clinton term. The initial George W. Bush term was particularly strong with respect to the rates of inflation and productivity gains. However, during the second Bush term, most aspects of the economy worsened, with only the unemployment rate and the economic growth rates showing modest improvements. Meanwhile, both productivity gains and inflation worsened, and the current account balance reached record levels of deficits. In fact, the two George W. Bush terms are the two worst postwar presidential terms with respect to trade deficits, reaching deficit levels (as percentages of the GDP) that are substantially greater than the previous record levels of the second Reagan and Clinton terms.

Table 12.1. Presidential economic scorecard

	Unemploy-ment	Inflation	Economic growth	Productivity	Current account balance*	Overall rank
Truman	4.4% (3.5)	2.7% (6)	4.9% (2)	3.6% (1)	0.05% (6)	2.5
Eisenhower I	4.2% (2)	0.8% (1)	3.2% (7.5)	1.9% (9.5)	0.12% (5)	4
Eisenhower II	5.5% (7.5)	1.9% (3)	2.7% (11)	2.5% (5.5)	0.36% (3.5)	5.5
JFK/Johnson	5.8% (9)	1.2% (2)	4.6% (3)	3.5% (2)	0.76% (1)	1
Johnson	3.9% (1)	3.3% (9)	5.1% (1)	3.0% (4)	0.36% (3.5)	2.5
Nixon	.0% (5.5)	4.6% (12)	3.0% (10)	2.2% (7)	-0.10% (7)	7
Nixon/Ford	6.7% (14)	8.2% (14)	2.6% (12)	1.9% (9.5)	0.50% (2)	10.5
Carter	6.5% (12.5)	10.4% (15)	3.3% (6)	0.6% (15)	-0.28% (8)	14
Reagan I	8.6% (15)	5.1% (13)	3.1% (9)	1.7% (12)	-0.96% (9.5)	15
Reagan II	6.5% (12.5)	3.4% (10)	3.8% (5)	1.7% (12)	-2.95% (12)	10.5
GHW Bush	6.3% (11)	4.2% (11)	2.1% (14.5)	2.1% (8)	-0.96% (9.5)	13
Clinton I	6.0% (10)	2.8% (7.5)	3.2% (7.5)	1.2% (14)	-1.54% (11)	9
Clinton II	4.4% (3.5)	2.3% (4.5)	4.2% (4)	2.5% (5.5)	-2.97% (13)	5.5
GW Bush I	5.5% (7.5)	2.3% (4.5)	2.1% (14.5)	3.3% (3)	-4.61% (14)	8
GW Bush II	5.0% (5.5)	2.8% (7.5)	2.2% (13)	1.7% (12)	-5.44% (15)	12
Average	5.6%	3.7%	3.3%	2.2%	-1.18%	
Republicans	5.9%	3.7%	2.8%	2.1%	-1.56%	
Democrats	5.2%	3.8%	4.2%	2.4%	-0.60%	

Sources: Bureau of Labor Statistics and Bureau of Economic Analysis.

Note: Parenthetical figures indicate rank order performance among the presidencies included in this table.

* Measured as a percentage of the GDP.

Taken as a whole, the Bush presidency is one of relative prosperity for the middle years, bracketed by periods of economic distress at the beginning and the end. Even the central period of economic growth was moderate by recent standards, both in duration and in the level of economic plenty. Of course, politically, the central portion of the Bush presidency was dominated by national security concerns, particularly the war in Iraq. Economic issues are at the forefront of the public agenda only in the period before the 9/11 attacks and in the last year of the Bush presidency.

This is not to say that the Bush presidency was devoid of activity with respect to economic policy. Much activity occurred in the areas of trade, tax policy, and monetary policy. Overshadowing all of these areas, however, is the sharp decline in the economy during the final year of the Bush presidency, representing the onset of a relatively severe and lengthy recession, triggered initially by the bursting of a housing bubble, which led to a credit squeeze and a near collapse of the global financial sector.

Economic Advisory Team

The Bush administration retained the formal economic advisory system created during the Clinton administration, consisting of the Treasury Department, the National Economic Council (NEC), and the Council of Economic Advisers (CEA). However, there were two key differences between the operations of these institutions in the Clinton and Bush administrations. First, the Bush economic advisers never reached the stature (or stability) of the Clinton advisers. After a promising start (barely four months after Bush's inauguration, Congress approved his proposed income tax cuts, the largest in twenty years), missteps led to unflattering comparisons with Clinton's sure-footed economic team, headed by Treasury Secretary Robert E. Rubin. The lesser stature of Bush's team was also reflected in somewhat greater turnover during his administration, particularly in positions in the Executive Office of the President. During his eight years as president, Bush appointed four chairs of the NEC and five chairs of the CEA, one more in each case than during the Clinton administration.

A second, and more important, difference between the NEC and CEA operations during the two administrations is that the efforts of the economic advisers to formulate policy were subordinate to the key political advisers surrounding President Bush. One early issue where the economic advisers lost the debate to political operatives was the March 2002 decision to impose tariffs on imported steel. It prompted Treasury Secretary Paul H. O'Neill to remark, before the Council on Foreign Relations, something to the effect that he opposed steel tariffs because the United States should be a leading free-trade nation, a remark that was "an unusual indiscretion in an administration that prides itself on loyalty" (Rosenbaum 2002). It was not long before O'Neill would resign. Within a year, two newly appointed economic advisers, Treasury Secretary John Snow and NEC chair Stephen Friedman, faced the task of rallying legislative support for a new round of proposed Bush tax cuts that neither had a role in formulating. One news account made the point that "the current staff turnover has had little effect on the economic stimulus package Mr. Bush is to announce" because that "economic plan was hammered out months ago by a small core of still-in-place presidential advisers—Vice President

Dick Cheney, Karl Rove, Andrew H. Card, Jr. and Joshua Bolten—who control all domestic policy in an administration where power is ever more tightly held at the White House" (Bumiller 2003).

What complicated the work of the economic advisers was that they had to compete for influence against a well-entrenched group of White House political insiders. Both O'Neill and Snow were disadvantaged because they were not intimate friends of President Bush and, more importantly, they were subordinate to Karl Rove, Bush's political adviser and deputy chief of staff, in the advisory system. Another formidable player was Vice President Dick Cheney, who, with White House experience as chief of staff for President Gerald Ford, wanted to consolidate his influence within the Bush administration. It was Cheney who promoted the 2003 package of tax cuts to jump-start the economy despite warnings from Federal Reserve chair Alan Greenspan and Treasury Secretary O'Neill that the tax cuts would fuel huge deficits. In fact, O'Neill's strong opposition led to Cheney's strong urging that O'Neill resign (Becker and Gellman 2007). Cheney was especially interested in economic policy. He chaired a weekly luncheon meeting of Bush's economic team, and he also consulted with a network of economic experts from outside the government. Cheney endorsed supply-side arguments that tax cuts would generate higher revenues despite lowering taxes. Whereas tax policy usually originates in the Treasury Department, in the Bush administration it was formulated in the vice president's office. One account quoted John H. Makin, an informal adviser to Vice President Cheney, as saying that President Bush "appears to want to have Treasury take the orders from the White House" (from Becker and Gellman, 2007).

In sum, the political insiders who dominated Bush's economic advisory system spoke with one voice on the need for tax cuts. Even when President Bush reached outside the White House for economic advice, he did not ask the opponents of tax cuts. In January and April 2003, for example, President Bush held two meetings with private sector economists to rally support for his third round of income tax cuts. Observed Ethan S. Harris of Lehman Brothers, "Basically 90 percent of the people are kind of preaching to the choir, and maybe they have one or two middle-of-the-road people. They really don't seem to want to hear opposing views" (from Altman 2003).

This pattern of subordinating the economic advisory team to political advisers without strong economic credentials persisted until the final year of the Bush administration, when events moved economic concerns to the top of the public's and the president's agendas. During 2008, two figures, Federal Reserve chair Ben Bernanke and Treasury Secretary Henry Paulson, took center stage in efforts to prevent or soften the effects of the series of crises that buffeted the economic sector. By this time, however, Karl Rove had left the White House, and Vice President Cheney's unpopularity had reduced his apparent role in responding to economic events.

Business (Mainly) as Usual, 2001–2007

The Bush administration maintained a basic consistency in its approach to fiscal policy: a deep-seated attachment to reducing tax rates. One of the principal legislative victories in the first few months of the Bush presidency was a package of $1.35 trillion in tax cuts over ten years, which President Bush signed into law on June 7, 2001. The reductions represented the first broad reduction in tax rates in twenty years and included reductions of the marginal rates in each tax bracket. However, several of the tax cuts, including reductions in estate taxes, were set to expire in 2010 unless made permanent by Congress. The Bush administration displayed the same supply-side faith in tax cuts shown by the Reagan administration. And, as with the Reagan experiment, the Bush tax cuts quickly drove the budget out of balance. The fiscal year 2001 budget surplus of $128 billion was replaced by a FY2002 deficit of $158 billion, which ballooned to $413 billion by FY2004 in the wake of spending on the Iraq war and the emergency response to Hurricane Katrina. The economic expansion of the middle years of President Bush's tenure helped shrink the deficit to $318 billion in FY2005, to $248 billion in FY2006, and to $162 billion in FY2007. But the onset of recession in December 2007 drove up the federal deficit to an estimated $389 billion for FY2008. In President Clinton's last year in office, the total federal debt represented 58 percent of GDP, which is the value of all goods and services produced in the American economy. If the estimate for FY2008 is accurate, the size of the total federal debt at the time represented 68 percent of GDP. The federal budget was unbalanced in every fiscal year during the Bush tenure, and the continued deficits—through periods of economic expansion as well as recession—suggest that the federal budget is structurally unbalanced, that is, there will be continuing deficits under any reasonable assumptions about the state of the economy.

On February 3, 2003, President Bush sent to Congress his thirteen-pound, three-thousand-page budget for FY2004 (which began October 1, 2003), which recommended total expenditures of $2.23 trillion and a

multibillion-dollar economic growth plan based on eliminating individual taxes on dividends as well as accelerating and making permanent the
2001 tax cuts. After a lengthy legislative battle, on May 28, 2003, President
Bush signed legislation that allocated $20 billion to fiscally strapped states
plus $12 billion to aid low-income families and that afforded $318 billion
in income tax cuts, increased child tax credits, reduced rates on capital
gains and dividends, and tax breaks for small business. All told, the package would cost $350 billion over ten years, but its price tag would more
than double if the various tax provisions are not allowed to expire in 2010.
Critics charged that this latest round of tax cuts would balloon the federal
deficit and do little to stimulate the economy, but President Bush was undeterred. "By ensuring that Americans have more to spend, to save and to
invest, this legislation is adding fuel to an economic recovery," Bush said
at the signing ceremony (from Stevenson 2003). The second Bush term
was a continuation of the first, with no basic changes made to either tax
laws or the pattern of federal spending. During the multiyear period of
economic expansion during the middle years of the Bush presidency, rising revenues slowly reduced the annual federal deficit, which fell from
$413 billion in FY2004 to $162 billion in FY2007.

Although the main plot about macroeconomic policy revolves around
the income tax cuts and deficits in the hundreds of billions of dollars,
the administration made other moves that had economic consequences.
When the Bush administration began, the reality of recession prompted
the executive and legislative branches to enact an extension of unemployment benefits for people who had exhausted their jobless aid. So-called
"supplemental unemployment assistance" was integrated into the White
House's 2002 economic stimulus package, and later, on January 8, 2003,
President Bush signed a second extension of unemployment benefits for
roughly 2.5 million Americans, an extension that ran through May. When
those benefits expired, Congress approved yet a third $7.4 billion exten-
sion for nearly a million unemployed people. At that time (May 2003), the
unemployment rate was 6.0 percent, and this quick approval by the GOP
Congress was intended to deflect Democratic criticism of its $350 billion
package of tax cuts mainly for middle- and upper-income Americans.

One early legislative achievement came when President Bush signed
the Corporate Responsibility Act of 2002, which passed Congress with
huge bipartisan majorities. This was the response to an avalanche of corporate scandals that began when the Houston-based energy-trading giant
Enron filed for bankruptcy in December 2001 and was followed by the

financial collapse of telecommunications conglomerate WorldCom in June 2002, as well as filings for bankruptcy protection by Adelphia Communications and Global Crossing. Amid a culture of insider trading and accounting practices that hid financial liabilities, corporate executives had made extraordinarily high profits while ordinary investors, company employees, and pensioners faced financial ruin. According to one reporter, "Rarely has an issue caught such instant bipartisan fire in Washington. This one was fueled by nearly daily disclosures of corporate fraud, the plummeting stock market and politicians' concerns that voters would hold them responsible" (Bumiller 2002). The Corporate Responsibility Act established the Accounting Oversight Board to register accounting firms and set accounting standards, and it also authorized the Securities and Exchange Commission to formulate conflict-of-interest regulations.

The enactment of these additional regulatory requirements represented an exception to a general commitment to deregulation and lax enforcement of existing regulations by the Bush administration. In this regard, the Bush administration marked the culmination of a thirty-year trend that began with President Carter, a Democrat, and continued through both Republican and Democratic administrations (Calmes 2008). Ironically, the zeal with which the Bush administration accepted these new regulations was reminiscent of the Reagan administration's ideological denigration of government regulation, which was part of the supply-side economics approach. The weakening of regulatory oversight in the economic sphere was part of a general stance on government regulation that extended to other areas, such as the environment, health care, and product safety (Calmes 2008). In the economic sphere, however, these deregulatory and antiregulatory impulses eventually contributed to the series of financial problems that surfaced during the final eighteen months of the Bush presidency.

Another important development in economic policy was Congress's renewal of "fast-track" trade authority in the Trade Act of 2002. This authority was first delegated to President Ford in 1974, but it lapsed in 1994 when President Clinton was unable to persuade Congress to approve its renewal. Passage of the Trade Act of 2002 was a major legislative victory, because President Bush was authorized to negotiate trade agreements that Congress can approve or reject but cannot change. Free trade was a cornerstone of economic policy in the Bush administration, and after 2004, bilateral trade agreements were implemented with Australia, Bahrain, Chile, Morocco, Singapore, El Salvador, Nicaragua, Honduras, Guatemala, and the Dominican Republic. The last five nations made up the Central America Free Trade Agreement area, which the Bush administration hoped to expand into the Free Trade Area of the Americas to integrate thirty-four nations of North and South America into one free-trade bloc. Prior to his trip to Africa (when he promised massive U.S. aid to fight AIDS), President Bush urged Congress to extend beyond 2008, its termination date, the African Growth and Opportunity Act of 2000, which gave thirty-five African nations duty-free access to American markets.

Free trade has become a partisan issue in recent decades, however, particularly for Democrats who represent "Rust Belt" districts in the North. Election year politics during 2008 stalled legislative action on a free trade agreement with Colombia, which President Bush had submitted to Congress in April. Speaker Nancy Pelosi (D-California) blocked a vote in the House of Representatives to protect the reelection prospects of her Democratic colleagues. Informed observers believed the Colombia trade pact would have easily passed with solid Republican and southern Democratic support. As of early 2009, the agreement with Colombia was still pending action in Congress because the political backlash against free trade only worsened during the 2008 presidential campaign. Both Democratic presidential contenders, Senators Hillary Rodham Clinton (D-New York) and Barack Obama (D-Illinois) had attacked the North American Free Trade Agreement (NAFTA) as a cause of lost manufacturing jobs and threatened to renegotiate that trade pact with Mexico and Canada.

During his first term, President Bush also briefly abandoned his free-trade principles by pandering to steelworkers and steel companies in West Virginia, Ohio, and Pennsylvania. In March 2002, President Bush took arguably the biggest protectionist action in decades by imposing tariffs of nearly 30 percent on many types of steel imported from Europe, Asia, and South America. While there is no doubt that the U.S. steel industry was in deep trouble, protectionism is a double-edged sword because other domestic industries such as automobile manufacturing rely on cheap steel imports. Moreover, other nations might begin a trade war. In reaction to the steel tariffs, the European Union petitioned the World Trade Organization (WTO), and in July 2003, the WTO issued its ruling that those steel tariffs were illegal. Previously, the Bush administration had repeatedly failed in its appeals before the WTO, having lost thirteen of fifty cases brought against the United States (Becker 2003). In August 2002, the Bush administration suffered another setback when the WTO ruled that the European Union could impose $4 billion in penalties against the United

States for allowing business tax breaks designed to foster American exports. This penalty was the largest imposed on any nation since the WTO was created in 1995 (Andrews 2002b).

Another unusual, though not entirely unprecedented, action on the economic front came about when President Bush imposed an eighty-day cooling-off period under the Taft-Hartley Act of 1947; he was the first president to do so since President Nixon halted a 1971 longshoremen's strike. Bush's invoking of Taft-Hartley to open twenty-nine West Coast seaports that had been shut down for eleven days due to a labor-management dispute came just one month before the 2002 midterm congressional elections.

One intractable economic problem that the Bush administration did not confront during its eight years in office was the stagnant growth of family income. Income distribution in the United States always has been less equitable than in Europe, but the situation has gotten worse. The Congressional Budget Office in 2004 determined that households in the lowest quintile (20 percent) saw their "real" income rise by only 2 percent since 1979. The next quintile had an 11 percent real increase, compared to a 15 percent increase for the middle quintile and a 23 percent increase for the next highest quintile, but a 63 percent increase in "real" income for the top 20 percent of all households (Lowenstein 2007). And the gap between the super-rich and the rest of society has widened to the point that the highest 1 percent of income earners derived 8 percent of total pre-tax income in 1980 compared to their 17 percent take in 2005 (Samuelson 2007).

After the Democrats won control of the House and Senate in the 2006 midterm elections, Congress passed legislation increasing the federal minimum wage over a two-year period, from $5.15 to $7.25 an hour. President Bush signed this increase in the federal minimum wage, which was the first increase in nearly a decade, despite the fact that inflation had eroded the purchasing power of the minimum wage to its lowest level in fifty years. Although increasing the minimum wage is no solution to the long-term growth in income inequality or even the short-term stagnation in wages, this problem was not a priority for the Bush administration. It was not until January 2007 that President Bush publicly acknowledged a problem: "I know some of our citizens worry about the fact that our dynamic economy is leaving working people behind. . . . Income inequality is real" (from Ip and McKinnon 2007). Credit for this political reversal was attributed to the new treasury secretary, Henry Paulson, since White

House political advisers did not consider income inequality to be a serious problem.

Federal Reserve Activism

President Clinton was entirely willing to accommodate Alan Greenspan, chair of the Federal Reserve Board, but there was speculation over whether President Bush would reappoint Greenspan when his term expired in June 2004. Greenspan's flip-flopping on the issue of tax cuts was later criticized when huge deficits materialized and the financial crisis hit Wall Street during 2008. Greenspan supported the initial 2001 tax cuts, but by early 2003, he was warning Congress about further tax cuts because of the uncertainty over whether the Iraq war would pose an obstacle to economic growth; he testified that further tax cuts should be offset by spending reductions. Greenspan also challenged the supply-side assumptions of the Bush administration, saying he doubted that economic growth would be sufficient to recover revenues lost from the tax cuts (Crutsinger 2003). The resulting swirl of political controversy caused Greenspan to back-track when he appeared a few days later before another congressional committee. This time he supported the Bush proposal. Having gotten signals from the White House that he would be reappointed as Fed chair, Greenspan did not restate any opposition to the 2003 package of tax cuts. "I would prefer to find the situation in which spending was constrained, the economy was growing, and that tax cuts were capable of being initiated without creating fiscal problems," said Greenspan in July before a congressional committee (from Weisman and Berry 2003).

Whatever misgivings Greenspan might have had about deficits, monetary policy was entirely compatible with fiscal policy during his tenure. The Bush administration repeatedly advocated cutting taxes, and the Federal Reserve Board obliged with an aggressive strategy of cutting interest rates to historic lows. On June 25, 2003, the Fed reduced its federal funds rate (the interest rate banks charge each other on overnight loans) from 1.25 to 1.0 percent, the lowest level since 1958. It was the thirteenth rate cut since January 2001. Though historically the Fed has been more concerned about price stability than joblessness, during Bush's first term the Fed was concerned less about inflation than about the sluggish economy yielding falling price levels (deflation), something the United States has not experienced since the Great Depression.

However, the Federal Reserve Board eventually returned to its anti-inflation stance and allowed interest rates to climb. By June 2006, the federal funds rate stood at 5.25 percent, a level at which it remained for more than fourteen months, until September 2007. But then the Fed began a new round of interest rate cuts in an effort to confront new and more complicated threats to the economy. This time the man in charge of monetary policy was Ben S. Bernanke, a former Princeton University economics professor who was acknowledged to be a top-drawer expert in monetary policy (Lowenstein 2008). Unlike Alan Greenspan, who dominated the Fed and was known for his use of rhetorical obfuscation and decision-making based on experience and instinct, Bernanke preferred a collegial style of consultation within the Fed and was enamored with economic modeling. It was said that Bernanke would have preferred to base monetary policy on some relatively firm guidelines so that business and consumers would be able to anticipate future growth in the money supply.

However, when confronted with a trio of crises in the housing, credit, and financial markets, Bernanke took unprecedented steps to infuse liquidity into the credit and financial markets. Testifying before the Joint Economic Committee of Congress in April 2007, Bernanke gave a pessimistic economic prognosis and said that a recession was possible. To head off an economic downturn, the Fed shifted its attention from curbing inflation to fighting recession by lowering key interest rates to stimulate economic activity. Beginning in September 2007, the federal funds rate of 5.25 percent was lowered ten times until, in December 2008, it was targeted to the range of 0 to 0.25 percent, the lowest level in a half century.

The housing bubble and the credit crisis were related and prompted extraordinary action by the Fed. The underlying problem was that bankers and financiers created a variety of a new and complicated types of home mortgages that allowed buyers to purchase homes beyond their means. The financial roots of these actions were easy credit policies and a lax regulatory environment to support greater home ownership, both of which began during the Clinton administration and picked up steam during the Bush administration. The financial problems of the "subprime" mortgage market (so-called because these riskier, less credit-worthy borrowers were charged rates of interest higher than "prime" borrowers) were aggravated because the mortgages were too complicated for inexperienced borrowers to understand. Not only were there hidden costs but also, after the short-term "teaser" rates ended, the monthly house payments escalated due to the accumulation of interest charges. There was also duplicity by some lenders who misled buyers and falsified their income records so that people with unworthy credit ratings still were able to purchases homes. Traditional practices regarding credit, income, and background checks on potential borrowers were often waived in the competitive rush to increase the volume of mortgage money being lent.

These creative methods of financing mortgages increased the percentage of home ownership from 64 percent in the mid-1990s to just over 69 percent by late 2004, and the underlying problems did not surface so long as the value of homes increased, meaning that distressed borrowers could either refinance or sell their properties at a profit. This increasingly unstable housing bubble exploded once the prices of homes began to fall. Prices began to decline across the country in 2007, forcing many marginal homeowners into bankruptcy and forcing banks to foreclose on homes now worth less than the cost of their mortgages. Since these risky mortgages were "packaged" and sold as investments, those banks, insurance companies, and other investors holding those investments also faced huge losses.

As bank losses mounted, banks became less willing to lend money to other banks, to commercial borrowers, and to individuals, creating a severe liquidity and credit crisis. By the summer of 2007, the Fed began to act, although its actions often seemed more reactive to events and the equity markets than proactive. Until then, the Fed had resisted lowering interest rates, fearing that inflation still posed a bigger threat to the economy than slowed growth. In response, investors stopped financing the risky types of commercial debt, the stock market plummeted, and the availability of credit began shrinking. During its regularly scheduled August 2007 meeting, the Fed again refused to lower interest rates, but ten days later the Fed reversed course. It held an unscheduled meeting and announced that banks could take short-term loans from its "discount window" and use their risky home mortgages as collateral. In December 2007, the Fed met again, but lowering its federal funds rate by a quarter of a point disappointed Wall Street and the stock market plunged again. The next day the Fed announced a new "Term Auction Facility" by which any financial institution would be able to bid for one-month loans not exceeding $20 billion, and banks were permitted to pledge their mortgage-backed securities as collateral. This program was expanded to $60 billion per month in January 2008 and $100 billion a month in March.

On March 7, 2008, Bernanke said the Fed would infuse an extra $100 billion into the credit markets through its "open-market" operations (the Fed adds to the money supply when it buys government securities from investors). A few days later, the Fed took another unorthodox step, creating a "Term Securities Lending Facility" to provide even more liquidity. One casualty from the burst bubble in the housing market was the venerable Wall Street investment bank of Bear Stearns Corporation. On March 14, the Fed provided a twenty-eight-day loan to JPMorgan Chase to assist Bear Stearns, but, with the bankruptcy of Bear Stearns looking imminent, two days later the Fed provided JPMorgan Chase with a $30 billion loan to buy Bear Stearns.

The Fed had delayed its action because of a concern over rising inflation, which rose to its highest annual rate during the Bush administration (4.1 percent) during 2007. Indeed, for much of 2007 the specter of stagflation, which ravaged the economy during the 1970s, was considered a serious possibility. Nevertheless, Bernanke eventually chose to target the developing recession as the Fed's primary economic concern, with the hope that inflationary pressures would not be aggravated. This strategy seemed risky during mid-2007, when oil prices climbed toward an eventual peak of $140 a barrel, but by 2008, the traditional effects of the economic slowdown halted and then reversed the rise in prices. In December 2008, the Fed took its boldest action, the cutting of the overnight federal funds rate to between 0 and 0.25 percent. Under "normal" conditions, the Fed might consider raising interest rates to prevent reigniting inflationary pressures, given the infusion of massive federal funds on bailouts, but what prompted this extraordinary Fed action was the greater likelihood of deflation than inflation. The day before the Fed took this action, the federal government reported that the Consumer Price Index fell 1.7 percent in November, the sharpest monthly decline since the federal government began tracking price levels in 1947. Deflation is linked to recession, and the Fed now acknowledged that recessionary trends were worse than it had anticipated, saying, "Labor market conditions have deteriorated, and the available data indicate that consumer spending, business investment and industrial production have declined. Financial markets remain quite strained and credit conditions tight. Overall, the outlook for economic activity has weakened further" (from Andrews and Calmes 2008).

The Crises of 2007–2008 and Their Aftermath

The final fiscal act of the Bush presidency was played out against the backdrop of an economic contraction during a hotly contested presidential election year. The crisis in the housing, credit, and financial markets fueled worries about recession. During 2007, the lead player in dealing with those economic trouble spots was the Fed, but by early 2008, the Bush administration moved to augment "loose" monetary policy with increased fiscal stimulus. In early February 2008, President Bush presented to Congress his final annual budget proposal (for FY2009, beginning October 1, 2008). Once again, he proposed making permanent the capital gains and dividend tax cuts set to expire in 2010, along with expanded spending for the military and foreign aid. While claiming a projected balanced budget for 2012, his proposal projected deficits of more than $400 billion in each of the next two years, bringing the cumulative increase in the national debt during the two terms of the Bush presidency to $4 trillion, a total federal debt of $9.7 trillion versus the $5.7 trillion debt in place when President Bush took office (Rogers 2008).

Even as this budget was being prepared, however, President Bush was also proposing an emergency stimulus package of $145 billion to head off an impending contraction in the economy. The package consisted largely of business incentives and one-time direct payments to individuals (Stolberg 2008a). Acting with unaccustomed speed and bipartisanship, Congress quickly passed (in four weeks) and President Bush signed a stimulus package costing $168 billion over two years. The plan was essentially a classic Keynesian maneuver of pumping dollars into the economy in hopes of stimulating consumer spending. While most economists regarded the one-time tax rebates as valuable remedies for a downturn (Herszenhorn 2008), the business incentives were seen as much less beneficial.

The public increasingly came to associate the economic downturn with President Bush. The housing bubble and the credit crisis were partly blamed on a failure of government oversight. In response, the Bush administration proposed the most comprehensive reform of how federal agencies regulate financial institutions since the Great Depression. In March 2008, Treasury Secretary Henry Paulson unveiled the "Blueprint for a Modernized Financial Regulatory Reform," a plan to allow the Federal Reserve Board to examine the bookkeeping of brokerage firms, hedge funds, commodity-trading exchanges, and any other financial institution that poses a threat to the overall stability of the financial markets. The problems in the subprime mortgage market that led to the collapse of banking giant Bear Stearns were not caused by the hodgepodge of regulatory agencies, but Paulson agreed that the complexity of the federal regulatory regime was a complicating factor. His proposal would have merged the Commodity Futures Trading Commission, which regulates the commodities market, with the Securities and Exchange Commission, which regulates the stock and bond markets. And the Office of Thrift Supervision, which regulates small thrift banks, would be eliminated and its authority shifted to the Office of the Comptroller of the Currency. Paulson also proposed a new Mortgage Origination Commission to evaluate state regulation of mortgage brokers and consumer protection. One controversial aspect of the plan would establish federal regulation of insurance companies, which historically have been regulated by the states. The primary objective of Paulson's plan was to streamline the regulatory system so that American business would not be at a disadvantage in global competition. So bold was this proposal that it was guaranteed to generate criticism from financial experts, insurance companies, state regulators, members of Congress, and employees of the federal bureaucracy. Secretary Paulson left office without any implementation of his proposal, and even his admirers speculated that it would take many years before Congress would so radically reorganize the federal regulatory system.

The Paulson proposal was a long-term remedy, but, despite the opposition of the Bush administration to bailouts, what forced the federal government to take extraordinary measures was a wave of threatened bankruptcies in the financial sector. It began in March 2008 when Bear Stearns nearly collapsed before the Fed and Treasury orchestrated its purchase by JPMorgan Chase at a bargain-basement price. Then, in July, the Bush administration came to the rescue of Fannie Mae and Freddie Mac, two government-sponsored enterprises (GSEs) that either own or guarantee mortgages whose total value was more than $5 trillion or nearly one-half of all mortgages issued in the United States. To prevent their insolvency, which would have been a financial disaster of catastrophic proportions, the Fed made funds available through a short-term lending program, and Treasury asked Congress to approve a $300 billion line of credit for the two GSEs.

Turmoil in the financial markets reached a crescendo in September 2008. Early that month, Bernanke and Paulson made the decision to allow the Wall Street firm of Lehman Brothers to go bankrupt and the larger Wall Street firm of Merrill Lynch to be sold to Bank of America. Then the Fed bailed out American International Group (AIG), the insurance conglomerate, with an $85 billion loan. In an effort to shore up confidence, the Fed announced before dawn on September 19 its plan to infuse $180 billion into the financial markets through lending programs operated by the European Central Bank and the central banks of Canada, Japan, Britain, and Switzerland. But that action did not calm the global financial markets, forcing the Fed to infuse yet another $100 billion in order to stabilize the federal funds rate at the Fed's target of 2 percent. But none of these individual bailouts calmed Wall Street, as individuals and institutional investors sold stocks and the Dow Jones Industrial Average (DJIA) continued its sharp decline. On October 9, 2007, the DJIA had closed at 14,164.53, its all-time high, but then steadily fell to historic lows. On September 15, 2008, when Lehman Brothers filed for bankruptcy, the DJIA lost more than 500 points and closed below 11,000. Only six months later, on March 5, 2009, the DJIA closed at a twelve-year low of 6,594.44. In other words, the DJIA lost more than half its value over a seventeen-month period.

The loss of confidence in the financial markets continued despite the bailouts and federal interventions. For its part, Congress had little choice but to follow the leadership of Treasury Secretary Paulson and Fed chair Bernanke. Public policy turned a corner when Paulson and Bernanke decided that the current ad hoc bailouts had to yield to a more systematic infusion of federal funds to provide liquidity in the capital markets and calm the mortgage and financial sectors. The result was the Emergency Economic Stabilization Act of 2008. Signed into law on October 3, 2008, it established a $700 billion Troubled Assets Relief Program (TARP), whose original purpose was to purchase distressed assets, especially mortgage-backed securities, and infuse desperately needed funds into the banking system. The law immediately authorized the treasury secretary to access $250 billion; then an additional $100 billion could be authorized by President Bush. The last $350 billion installment needed the acquiescence of Congress, however. (Congress did not supply that final installment until President Barack Obama took office.)

This legislation has been criticized in many quarters. Conservatives opposed both the price tag and the government's intervention in the marketplace. Liberals opposed using taxpayer funds to bail out financiers and bankers rather than help ordinary citizens keep their homes. Budgetary experts worried about the impact on federal indebtedness and the debt burdens being put on future generations of Americans. Financiers saw no obvious way to calculate the costs and benefits of those distressed assets, meaning that the federal government risked overpaying or underpaying. And opinion polls indicated that the American people were not thrilled about this bailout plan. One overarching concern was that the treasury secretary had unilateral authority to spend $700 billion without any meaningful oversight. In the final bill, the treasury secretary was required to consult with the Federal Reserve Board of Governors, the Federal Deposit Insurance Corporation, the comptroller of the currency, the director of the Office of Thrift Supervision, and the secretary of housing and urban development. A congressional oversight panel was also created within Congress, but how much influence these advisers will have in directing the day-by-day decisionmaking of the treasury secretary remains an open question at this writing.

Although TARP funds were supposed to be targeted to ailing financial institutions and banks, it was not long before other industries faced insolvency due to the worsening recession. In December 2008, the Bush administration came to the rescue of General Motors Corporation and Chrysler LLC with $17.4 billion in loans. (Ford Motor Company did not request federal aid.) In return, GM and Chrysler had to produce a restructuring plan by February 17, 2009, and a progress report by March 31, 2009, or they would have to pay back the loans (which undoubtedly would result in the bankruptcy of both automakers).

In the final analysis, despite all the criticism, Paulson's bailout plan was the nexus of efforts to deal with the financial meltdown. And, as further testimony to its significance, the basics of the Paulson bailout plan have not been radically changed by the Obama administration. Indeed, the financial markets were not reassured when newly confirmed Treasury Secretary Timothy Geithner first met with the press on February 10, 2009, to explain his use of the remaining $300 billion in TARP funds (Labaton and Andrews 2009). Confusion reigned because he did not detail how he would purchase toxic assets from banks and infuse liquidity into the financial markets.

Earlier, during congressional deliberations on Secretary Paulson's $700 billion bailout, some prominent Democrats, including House Speaker Nancy Pelosi, argued that Congress should also enact a massive stimulus package to jump-start the economy, which was obviously in recession. Although the idea of a massive stimulus package gained widespread support among economists (Uchitelle 2009), the Bush administration opposed any additional federal spending until the massive financial bailout plan had time to work. However, President-elect Obama quickly signaled his support for a stimulus package, which became the number-one legislative priority of the new Obama administration. In mid-February 2009, the Democratic-controlled 111th Congress passed a $787 billion economic stimulus bill, which Republicans charged was riddled with pork spending and would not create enough jobs. Despite several attempts by President Obama to secure bipartisan support, including the inclusion of substantial tax cuts as part of the package, the legislation received no Republican votes in the House of Representatives and only three Republican votes in the Senate.

The 2008 crisis in the housing, credit, and financial markets occurred during the tenure of President George W. Bush, so he is ultimately accountable. But is he entirely responsible? Informed commentators believe that there is plenty of blame to go around. The relaxation of oversight and easy credit policies designed to stimulate home ownership began during the Clinton administration. Some criticize Fed chair Alan Greenspan, saying that he aggravated the bubble in the housing market by keeping interest rates too low for too long after the economic recession began in 2001. Those low interest rates encouraged bad loan practices by both lenders and borrowers. By promoting an "ownership society," the Bush administration praised the expansion of home ownership as a positive goal, even though too many of these first-time borrowers were in precarious financial positions. Of course, a lion's share of the blame belongs with those bankers and financial institutions that ignored or manipulated the creditworthiness of applicants seeking home mortgages. Others point the finger at Fannie Mae and Freddie Mac for fostering the spread of subprime mortgages. When the Bush administration called for greater oversight of Fannie Mae and Freddie Mac, the Democratic-controlled Congress refused to act.

Regardless of who is to blame—either in the public's mind or in reality—the final year of the Bush presidency witnessed a sea change in longstanding elements of economic policy. The federal government engaged in attempts to shore up the financial industry that were so massive as to ignite a public discussion about the advisability of nationalizing significant parts of the financial services sector. A conservative Republican administration proposed a new, more vigorous financial regulatory regime and an unscheduled Keynesian stimulus. And Democrats and Republicans alike set aside (albeit perhaps only temporarily) any concern with deficits to embrace financial commitments of unprecedented size and scope to stimulate the economy and save key businesses. The aftermath of these unexpected reactions to economic challenges may well set the stage for a new era of government involvement in the economy—and a new phase of partisan conflict over this involvement.

A New Era of Partisan Economics?

This chapter began with the observation that peace and prosperity are the twin pillars of presidential popularity. There are political incentives, therefore, for presidents to follow a "general problem solving" approach to economic policymaking (Kernell 1997, 230–37). That is, presidents should not play partisan politics with the economy but should instead address the salient economic problem confronting the nation, because most Americans, regardless of their party affiliation, will recognize the same economic problem, be it unemployment or inflation. There is supporting evidence for this argument. For one thing, the American public has accurately perceived adverse economic conditions and excessively high unemployment rates over each presidential term since Truman (Dolan, Frendreis, and Tatalovich forthcoming). Moreover, trend data on the "most important" problem nicely tracks actual economic conditions, and public perceptions of inflation as the "most important" problem, for example, occur during periods of hyperinflation rather than during economic downturns (Smith 1980). There is a contrary argument (Hibbs 1987, 183–84) that Democrats and Republicans will pursue different economic priorities because they are sensitive to different "class" constituencies in the electorate. Although there is evidence showing that Republican administrations are overly concerned about inflation while Democratic administrations overemphasize the problem of unemployment (Frendreis and Tatalovich 2000), these findings do not necessarily mean that Republican and Democratic voters have dissimilar views of prevailing economic conditions.

However, public opinion surveys during the tenure of President George W. Bush suggest that partisanship may now be affecting public perceptions of the economy. Polls by Gallup and Pew reported how many people rated the economy as "excellent" or "good" (rather than "only fair" or "poor"), and the trends from 1992 to early 2006 show a dramatic change (Pew Research Center for the People and the Press 2006). In 1992, fewer than 10 percent of Democrats but about 20 percent of Republicans viewed the economy positively, but that partisan difference virtually disappeared from 1994 through 1998. A small partisan difference arose going into the 2000 election, but a significant partisan cleavage emerged beginning in 2001 and only got worse after the 2004 reelection of President Bush. By January 2006, overall 34 percent of respondents told Pew that the economy was excellent or good, but that question yielded a thirty-three-point difference between Republicans (56 percent saying so) and Democrats (23 percent). Thus, Pew concludes that partisanship affects how people assess the economy.

This problem may be unique to the George W. Bush presidency. Other trend data also document a huge partisan divide, beginning in January 2001, between Republican and Democratic levels of approval for Bush's handling of the economy (Jacobson 2007). But the fact that partisanship also affected public evaluations of how President Bush handled terrorism and Iraq, for example, led to the conclusion that President Bush had become "the most divisive occupant of the White House in at least 50 years" (Jacobson 2007, 13). An alternative explanation by political columnist Michael Barone (2008) suggests that the problem may not be entirely unique to the Bush presidency. According to Barone, the median-age voter in 1960 (born roughly in 1915) would have keen memories of the Great Depression and the median-age voter of 1992 (born around 1947) would have experienced the stagflation of the 1970s, but the median-age voter of 2008 would have been born around 1963. This generation of voters, therefore, has lived their entire adult lives with an economy in which low inflation and growth are taken for granted. For that reason, Barone believes that voting behavior or party loyalty are stronger influences on our economic perceptions than vice versa. If this pattern of polarized partisanship continues into the next presidency, one unhappy legacy of President George W. Bush would be that the very concept of prosperity has become a contested value in American politics.

13

THE FOREIGN POLICY OF THE BUSH ADMINISTRATION

Terrorism and the Promotion of Democracy

JAMES M. McCORMICK

D uring the 2000 presidential campaign, George W. Bush announced that he would pursue a "distinctly American internationalism" in foreign policy (Bush 1999a), largely in contrast to the liberal internationalism of the Clinton administration. He initially sought to have a foreign policy that placed greater emphasis on American national interests than on global interests. The 9/11 attacks quickly changed both the content of the administration's foreign policy and the process by which American foreign policy was made. As a result, the administration pursued a foreign policy that was universal in scope and that viewed virtually all international actions as affecting American interests. The efforts to build a "coalition of the willing" to find and defeat "terrorists and tyrants" on a worldwide scale illustrated the universal nature of this policy, but the difficulties that the invasion and occupation of Iraq created also demonstrated the limitation of this policy approach. At the beginning of its second term, the Bush administration reiterated its commitment to de-

A substantial portion of this chapter is drawn from James M. McCormick, "American Foreign Policy after September 11: The George W. Bush Administration," chap. 6 of *American Foreign Policy and Process*, 5th ed. (Belmont, CA: Cengage Learning Wadsworth, 2009).

mocratization worldwide as yet another way to combat global terrorism, and it initiated some actions toward that goal. Yet the Bush administration's foreign policy efforts were largely overshadowed by the continuing occupation of Iraq and the failure to bring that war to an end.

The Bush administration's foreign policy employed several approaches over its two terms—one used prior to 9/11, one adopted after 9/11, and one at the beginning of the second term, when the administration attempted to modify its most recent approach. The first approach was informed by the Bush administration's assumptions and policy positions and its initial commitment to classical realism. After 9/11, the administration moved toward defensive realism and idealism in foreign policy, as enunciated in the Bush Doctrine. The Bush Doctrine underwent an apparent modification at the beginning of the second term with the introduction of a "democracy initiative." Each approach has left its impact on the future of American foreign policy.

An important point of departure for understanding the initial foreign policy approach of the George W. Bush administration is to consider the foreign policy legacies that he inherited from the Clinton administration and from his father's (George H. W. Bush) administration. Both of those previous administrations experienced the seismic foreign policy shock that the end of the cold war wrought, and both administrations sought to put their own stamp on the new American foreign policy that would replace the anti-Soviet and anti-communist principles that had informed U.S. policy for so long. One stamp left the imprint of political realism, while the other left the imprint of liberal internationalism. Neither administration was wholly successful in setting the United States on a new foreign policy course, and, in this sense, both left different kinds of legacies for the George W. Bush administration.

An Initial Belief in Classical Realism

Because the George W. Bush administration was more inclined toward a foreign policy approach closer to that of his father's administration, the Clinton foreign policy legacies were generally not welcomed by the new Bush administration. Indeed, those legacies were a target of attack by candidate Bush and his foreign policy advisers since they represented a more universal and multilateral approach than the new Bush administration envisioned. Instead, George W. Bush was initially more inclined toward a foreign policy of classical realism.

Classical realism originates in several important assumptions about states and state behavior that had direct implications for the Bush administration's initial foreign policy approach. First, classical realists assume that states are the principal actors in foreign policy and that actions *between* states would trump any efforts to change behaviors *within* states. In this sense, the quality of relations between states is the major way in which to evaluate a country's foreign policy, and American policy would focus principally on state-to-state relations. Second, a state's "interests are determined by its power (meaning its material resources) relative to other nations" (Zakaria 1998, 8–9). As a state's relative power increases, it would seek to expand its political influence, albeit based upon a careful cost/ benefit analysis. In this regard, American power can and should be used to restrain states that could clearly harm the United States and its interests, but American power should be used carefully and selectively. Third, classical realists focus upon managing relations among the major powers, since these states are the ones that are likely to be the major threats in the international system. A guiding principle for realists is that no great power, or coalition of great powers, should dominate or endanger a nation or a group of nations. In this sense, the United States should focus on strengthening its alliances and on challenging some states, but it should do so in a highly prudent and selective manner.

These assumptions largely informed the types of policies that the George W. Bush administration initially supported or opposed when it took office in 2001. First of all, George W. Bush came to office as a particular kind of internationalist, one who sought to develop a "distinctly American internationalism." What that phrase implied was a much narrower definition of the American national interest than that of his immediate predecessor and even of his father's presidency (Bush 1999a). Second, candidate Bush made clear that a top priority of his administration would be to refurbish America's alliance structure around the world as a tangible manifestation of managing great power relationships. Europe and Asia would be the highest foreign policy priorities, since those regions contain longtime allies—and potential rivals. Third, Russia and China would be viewed in a more skeptical way than the Clinton administration had done, and American military capacity would be important for exercising American influence with these nations. Fourth, "hard power" would be preferred over "soft power" for dealing with the international system (Bush 1999b). Hard power refers to the utility of military capacity, sanctioning behavior, and threat behavior, among other coercive measures, as ways to influence the behavior of nations. Soft power relies upon the appeal of American culture and American values to enable the United States to influence the behavior of other states. Fifth, in concert with refurbishing alliances and the use of hard power, the remaking and strengthening of the American military would be a top priority for the new administration, both in terms of increased military pay and increased military spending.

The assumptions of classical realism also pointed to the policies that the Bush administration initially opposed. Most fundamentally, the new administration, largely in contrast to the Clinton administration, sought to narrow the number of American actions around the world and focus only on strategically important ones. First, the United States would not be as involved in trying to change other states internally or create political democracy within other countries. As Bush stated, "We value the elegant structures of our own democracy—but realize that, in other societies, the architecture will vary. We propose our principles, but we must not impose our culture" (Bush 1999a). Second, Bush opposed American humanitarian interventions without a clear strategic rationale for being involved in such missions. The American military, Condoleezza Rice stated, is neither "a civilian police force" nor "a political referee" in internecine and communal conflicts (Rice 2000, 53). Indeed, during the 2000 election campaign, Bush and others demonstrated this position by indicating a willingness to pull back from American involvement in Middle East discussions and, later, by deciding to move away from negotiations with North Korea during the administration's first months in office. Third, the Bush administration eschewed involvement with international institutions and opposed several key international agreements—rejecting the Kyoto Protocol to control global warming, opposing the Comprehensive Test Ban Treaty, and indicating its willingness to withdraw from the 1972 Anti-Ballistic Missile (ABM) Treaty in order to deploy national missile defense. Fourth, the Bush administration was not inclined to afford much influence to Congress or America's allies in the conduct of foreign policy. Instead, executive power in foreign affairs would be reasserted.

Reviving Wilsonianism after 9/11

Much as December 7, 1941, was a "day of infamy" for an earlier generation of Americans, September 11, 2001, became such a day for the millennial generation. Indeed, it is one of those days that has prompted every American to remember forever where they were and what they were doing when they first heard about the attacks on the World Trade Center and the Pentagon. From an analytic point of view, the events of that day represent one of those rare and spectacular political events that can change the mind-set or the image of the public and its leaders regarding foreign policy. Such "watershed" events are rare indeed, as one political scientist noted many years ago, but when they do occur, they can reverse or change the views of a whole generation or even several (Deutsch 1966, 5–26). Yet 9/11 appears to rank at the top end of these spectacular events not only because of its pervasive effect on the generation being socialized to politics at the time but also for the leveling effect it had on foreign policy beliefs across generations.

The 9/11 attacks had such a profound effect for at least three reasons. First, they were the first substantial attack upon the American continental homeland since the burning of Washington in the War of 1812. The American public had always assumed the security of the U.S. homeland, and these events shattered that assumption. Second, 9/11 was fundamentally an attack upon American civilians, not military personnel (although, to be sure, military personnel were killed at the Pentagon). Even the attack on Pearl Harbor had been directed primarily at military personnel. Third, and importantly, the terrorist attack was the deadliest in American history—costing almost three thousand lives and surpassing the total at Pearl Harbor by almost one thousand deaths. In all, then, 9/11 had a profound and pronounced effect, whether measured by the changed attitudes among the American public toward foreign policy, the changed agenda within Congress and new levels of support for the president on foreign policy issues, or the changed nature of the presidency itself.

Effects on the President

While the impacts on the public and Congress certainly merit attention and analysis and have been analyzed elsewhere (McCormick 2006), the effects on George W. Bush and his foreign policy approach are the focus here. Indeed, the impact of these events was evident at both the personal and policy levels. At a personal level, for instance, President Bush dictated for his diary on the night of those tragic events that "the Pearl Harbor of the 21st century took place today" (from Woodward 2002, 37). With that assessment, the president appeared to realize that "he was now a wartime president," as Bob Woodward (2002, 37) noted, with all the implications of that judgment for his leadership. Fred Greenstein (2004), a longtime scholar of the presidency, argues that Bush's cognitive style and his effectiveness with the public were the areas most affected by the events of that day. His emotional intelligence was strengthened in that Bush was able to face this national tragedy, and his political skills were sharpened by his need to try to put together a coalition against terrorism. Thomas Preston and Margaret Hermann reach a similar conclusion: "[Bush's] normal lack of interest in foreign affairs and desire to delegate the formulation and implementation of foreign policy to others, which had been the dominant pattern within his advisory system before the terrorist attacks, was forced to give way to his current, more active and involved pattern" (Preston and Hermann 2004, 370). Political psychologist Stanley Renshon, too, argues that 9/11 was a transforming moment for President Bush: "Those moments [on 9/11] changed the public's view of the Bush presidency, the president's view of the presidency, and, crucially, the president himself." Those events helped Bush find "his place and his purpose," Renshon writes, and Bush then "turned his efforts toward transforming America's place in the world and the world in which America has its place" (Renshon 2008, 386).

Effects on Policy

Indeed, the Bush administration's approach to foreign policy and its content changed almost overnight. While 9/11 ironically confirmed some of the administration's assumptions about the world and its approach (e.g., the importance of hard power over soft power and the need for enhanced military preparedness), they also suggested the limitations of the Bush administration's commitment to classical realism. While the administration did not do a volte-face in its policy, it did change from classical realism to what we would describe as "defensive realism," yet it also incorporated a distinct form of idealism into its approach.

While defensive realism makes many of the same assumptions as classical realism, it differs in one important aspect: the importance of "insecurity" as the motivating force for state actions. Fareed Zakaria summarizes the fundamental difference when he compares defensive realism and classical realism: "While the latter implies that states expand out of confidence, or at least out of an awareness of increased resources, the former maintains that states expand out of fear and nervousness. For the classical realist, states expand because they can; for the defensive realist, states expand because they must" (Zakaria 1998, 8–9). The new threatening environment after 9/11 thus propelled the Bush administration to change some of its foreign policy assumptions and actions—and eventually to create a new security strategy statement that incorporated elements of defensive realism rather than classical realism.

245

Combined with this new defensive realism, the Bush administration also embraced a form of idealism in foreign affairs, especially as it related to combating international terrorism in the post-9/11 era. A nation pursuing an idealistic foreign policy approach is motivated by a moral imperative in its actions and seeks to promote common values within and across states. In this sense, foreign policy became more than state-to-state relations among the strong for the Bush administration, which instead began seeking to advance universal norms. That is, the Bush administration sought to promote a worldwide imperative against terrorism, even as it also pursued greater global democratization. As such, it became increasingly concerned about the actions of all states (and groups) and the internal composition of many states, especially their attitude toward terrorism. Put somewhat differently, the administration appeared to embrace the more idealistic Wilsonian tradition in American foreign policy, albeit an idealism driven rather singularly on the imperative of combating international terrorism and doing so in a particular way (for a critique, see Dorrien 2003).

This change in approach—and the Bush administration's combining of realism and idealism—could be described as essentially the adoption of the key assumptions of what Francis Fukuyama (2006) labeled the "neoconservative legacy." The administration came to accept that the "internal characteristics of regimes matter" in the conduct of foreign policy, that American power and capabilities can and should be used for moral purposes even within states, and that international institutions and international law should be viewed skeptically in the conduct of foreign policy. At the same time, the Bush administration continued to view with suspicion any social engineering undertaken by governments (Fukuyama 2006, 48–49). In another analysis, Walter Russell Mead (2005) labels the Bush administration adherents of these views as "Revival Wilsonians." That is, they supported the spread of democracy and the goodness of American intentions and actions, albeit without the embrace of international law and institutions, as Wilson initially proposed. Hence, a revamped Wilsonianism is the result, driven fundamentally by domestic American values and implemented primarily by American power and American unilateralism.

With this change in approach after 9/11, three initial foreign policy assumptions were changed. First, and perhaps most significantly, the Bush administration moved from a narrow or particularistic foreign policy approach to a more universal one. That is, it moved from a focus on narrowing American national interests to a focus on broadening them to combat international terrorism. Second, the Bush administration initially moved away from its rather narrowly defined unilateralist approach to American foreign policy and toward a greater multilateral effort, albeit a multilateralism with a unilateralist option for the United States. While the United States sought to pursue multilateral goals, President Bush threatened to act unilaterally if multilateral support did not develop—much as the initiation of the war against Iraq would demonstrate. Third, the administration moved from its reliance on a starkly realist approach to foreign policy—without much concern about the internal dynamics of states—to a version of idealism—with a clear concern about the internal dynamics of *some* states. In this regard, humanitarian interventions, peacekeeping efforts, and peacemaking actions within states had now become part and parcel of the Bush foreign policy approach, which was not unlike that of his immediate predecessor.

Several administration actions provide evidence of these changes in assumptions. President Bush addressed a joint session of Congress shortly after 9/11 and called for a new universalism. Instead of embracing a "distinctly American internationalism," President Bush now adopted what might be called a "comprehensive American globalism," albeit defined and animated by the moral outrage against the attacks on the World Trade Center and the Pentagon. President Bush committed the United States to fight terrorism and states that support terrorism, and he outlined the nature of the global struggle in stark and dichotomous terms—in words reminiscent of the Truman Doctrine. The struggle, he noted, was now between the way of terror and the way of freedom, between states that support terror and those that do not, and between an uncivilized and a civilized world (Bush 2001a).

At the same time, President Bush conveyed the initial multilateral impulse of this new foreign policy approach and took several steps to implement such an approach against al-Qaida and the Taliban in Afghanistan. The administration adopted a coalitional approach to taking on al-Qaida and the Taliban effort, put the coalition together quickly, and incorporated an array of participants (U.S. Department of State 2001a).

By the time that military operations commenced in Afghanistan on October 7, 2001, several allied countries (Britain, Canada, Australia, Germany, and France, among others) pledged to assist with the operation. And more than forty nations, by that time, had approved American overflights and landing rights (U.S. Department of State 2001a; 2001b; U.S.

Embassy Islamabad 2002). These expressions of assistance came from the several continents and regions (Middle East, Africa, Europe, and Asia). In all, "Operation Anaconda" in Afghanistan eventually included contributions from some twenty countries. It quickly proved successful in breaking the Taliban's control in Afghanistan, and that country made progress toward democracy and reconstruction for a time. By 2007 and 2008, however, the Taliban was resurgent and posed an increasing problem for the outgoing Bush administration and the incoming Obama administration.

The Bush administration also undertook actions regarding communal and regional conflicts. While the decision to focus upon the internal situation in Afghanistan is hardly surprising in light of 9/11, the extent to which the administration committed itself to changing or to assist in changing the *domestic* situations in a series of other countries was surprising. Examples ranged from the effort to challenge the "axis of evil" countries—Iran, Iraq, and North Korea—to the commitments of sending personnel for military training as well as advisory units to several countries throughout the world—the Philippines, Yemen, Georgia—and to efforts to use American naval power around Somalia to block possible escaping al-Qaida fighters. Furthermore, the administration initiated some efforts at conflict resolution in the Middle East and between India and Pakistan and also opened up discussions with North Korea. At the same time, the administration was willing to look past some internal issues in other nations (e.g., China, Russia, and Pakistan), especially their human rights conditions, since their cooperation in the war on terrorism was more important than the differences that this Bush administration initially expressed about them.

In sum, the new approach, quickly labeled the Bush Doctrine, sought to hunt down terrorists, and those that supported terrorists, on a worldwide scale. While cooperation and support from other countries would be sought, the United States would go it alone if necessary. The globalism of this effort and the motivation for its actions represent the major transformations of the policy approach of the Bush administration after 9/11.

Formalizing the Bush Doctrine in
the National Security Strategy Statement

While its statements and actions conveyed the new foreign policy approach, the Bush administration issued a fuller rationale for its policy direction almost exactly one year after 9/11. "The National Security Strategy Statement of the United States of America" (2002) postulated that the fundamental aim of American foreign policy was "to create a balance of power that favors freedom." To create such a balance, the administration asserted that the United States "will defend the peace by fighting terrorists and tyrants[,] . . . will preserve peace by building good relations among the great powers[,] . . . [and] will extend the peace by encouraging free and open societies on every continent." The statement demonstrates how much American actions would now be motivated by the new threatening environment, much as defensive realism would postulate. The policy statement also conveyed the idealist and universal nature of this proposed foreign policy agenda with its concerns for the internal make-up and operations of states and groups. The United States, it noted, "is now threatened less by conquering states than we are by failing ones . . . less by fleets and armies than by catastrophic technologies in the hands of the embittered few," but it also recognized and accepted the fact that the United States "possesses unprecedented—and unequaled—strength and influence in the world" and acknowledged that "this position comes with unparalleled responsibilities, obligations, and opportunity."

The Bush administration outlined seven courses of action to promote this fundamental goal of promoting freedom and advancing the "nonnegotiable demands of human dignity." These included seeking to rally nations and alliances around the world to defeat terrorism (and relying on a broad array of actions to do so); addressing (with the goal of resolving) regional conflicts to reduce their impact on global stability; and focusing on those "rogue states" and terrorists who might gain access to weapons of mass destruction (WMD). The administration indicated, moreover, that it would seek to lead a broad coalition—"as broad as practicable"—to promote a balance of power in favor of freedom (National Security Strategy 2002). This coalition would consist not only of traditional American allies but also Russia, India, and China as well as others. In addition, the national security strategy statement included U.S. commitments to ignite global economic growth, fundamentally through free trade initiatives but also through increased development assistance and an expansion of the number of global democracies. Finally, the document called for transforming national security institutions at home. The priorities were to improve the military and the intelligence communities and strengthen homeland security to meet the demands of defending peace at home and abroad. While there was a brief mention of improving diplomacy and the Department of State, the emphasis was more on the "hard power" agencies than the "soft power" ones.

In what became the most controversial statements in the document, the Bush administration asserted first that the United States must have available "the option of preemptive actions to counter a sufficient threat to our national security." In addition, the statement concluded by emphasizing the commitment of the Bush administration to act unilaterally if collective efforts fail: "In exercising our leadership, we will respect the values, judgment, and interests of our friends and partners. Still, we will be prepared to act apart when our interests and unique responsibilities require" (National Security Strategy 2002). These statements concerning preemption and the unilateral option would ultimately gain most of the critical attention at home and abroad and would soon undermine the administration's initial effort to produce a "grand strategy" against terrorism with broad support.

America's allies, friends, and even adversaries initially supported the Bush administration's new foreign policy approach after 9/11. The acknowledgment that the Bush administration needed other states to fight terrorism, its initial turn to international institutions, and the recognition of multiple actors in the international arena undoubtedly struck a responsive chord. Furthermore, the concern with the internal dynamics of some states and the need to address festering regional and communal conflicts also met with some receptivity in Europe and elsewhere. After all, Article V of the NATO pact ("an armed attack against one . . . should be considered an attack against . . . all") was invoked for the first time in the history of the fifty-year alliance, immediately after 9/11, and virtually all European nations agreed to provide some assistance against al-Qaida and the Taliban in Afghanistan.

This international receptivity, however, was short lived. The 2002 State of the Union address, in which President Bush identified the "axis of evil" nations and appeared to foreshadow actions against one or more of them, caused some immediate alarm. As the French foreign minister, Hubert Védrine, noted at the time, "We are currently threatened by a simplified approach which reduces all problems of the world to the mere struggle against terrorism." Javier Solana Madariaga, the European Union's minister for foreign affairs, warned about the "dangers of global unilateralism," and the German foreign minister, Joschka Fischer, called the "axis of evil" notion a concept "not in accordance with our political ethos" (from Schwarz 2002). In the ensuing months of 2002, as Iraq, one of the axis of evil nations, increasingly drew the attention of President Bush and key American policymakers, further concerns were expressed over the di-

250

rection of American policy, both at home and abroad. Although Saddam Hussein's regime had used chemical and biological weapons against its own people in the past and had started a nuclear program, Iraq's links to terrorists were seemingly tenuous.

By summer 2002, the issue of Iraq had set off a pitched debate within the administration. Some key advisers supported quick and unilateral action to remove Saddam Hussein, while others, most prominently Secretary Colin Powell and his deputy, Richard Armitage, argued that this approach had "risks and complexities" that needed more analysis (Purdum and Tyler 2002). Such discussion of war against Saddam also alienated Republican allies in Congress and officials from previous administrations, notably former secretary of state Henry Kissinger and former national security adviser Brent Scowcroft. While these officials supported the need to remove Saddam Hussein, they were concerned that the administration's approach risked "alienating allies, creating greater instability in the Middle East, and harming long-term American interests" (Purdum and Tyler 2002). Indeed, the Europeans, too, were becoming increasingly leery of America's future intentions and its policy.

Iraq and the Bush Doctrine

A series of actions that began in the fall of 2002 only accelerated these domestic and international concerns and ultimately moved the Bush administration toward unilateral action against Iraq. First, the national security strategy statement of September 2002, with its use of preemption and the "go it alone" language, quickly alarmed many. Second, President Bush (2002a) issued a challenge to the international community at the United Nations to address the issue of WMD in Iraq and hinted that the United States would act alone if necessary. To be sure, the UN Security Council passed Resolution 1441 unanimously on November 8, 2002, finding Iraq in "material breach" of previous UN Resolution 687, but it also called for more international inspections. Over the next several months, the chief inspectors provided reports to the UN Security Council on the status of the inspections and the disarmament activities. In all, these reports indicated that Iraq was not fully complying with the resolution and with the inspectors. The inspectors requested more time from the Security Council to continue their work. As a result, real divisions emerged among the UN Security Council members on how to address the Iraq issue. Third, with the White House's support, Congress passed a sweeping resolution that authorized the president to use American military forces against Iraq "as he determines to be necessary and appropriate" to defend the national security of the United States and to enforce "all relevant United Nations Security Council resolutions regarding Iraq." Fourth, and very importantly, by March 2003, the Bush administration's patience had run out on the failure of the UN Security Council to act against Iraq. At the urging of the Prime Minister Tony Blair of Great Britain, the United States, Britain, and Spain circulated another draft UN resolution to once again find Iraq in "material breach" and, implicitly, to get approval for military action to enforce UN Resolution 1441. This resolution never reached a vote, since several nations on the UN Security Council, led principally by French opposition and the potential use of its veto, indicated that they would not support it.

As a result, President Bush issued an ultimatum to Iraq and its leadership on March 17, 2003: "Saddam Hussein and his sons must leave Iraq within 48 hours. Their refusal to do so will result in military conflict, commenced at a time of our choosing" (Bush 2003b). When the Iraqi leadership refused to comply with the ultimatum, the United States attacked a command bunker in Baghdad, and the war, called "Operation Iraqi Freedom," had begun. The president took this action without another UN resolution and instead relied upon the congressional resolution passed in October 2002 and his constitutional authority as commander in chief. To be sure, the administration put together a "coalition of the willing" (some forty-two nations initially), much as the national security strategy statement of a few months earlier had implied. Yet the United States and the United Kingdom carried out the principal military action, with some assistance from Australia and a few other countries. In all areas, the Bush administration was willing to act alone (or with an informal coalition) in addressing the issues of tyrants and terrorists and in implementing its national security strategy.

The war campaign went well and progressed quickly for the United States and Great Britain, with the loss of relatively few lives. The United States gained control of Baghdad by April 9, only three weeks after the war's initiation, and President Bush declared "major combat operations" over on May 1. Still, "winning the peace" and establishing a stable democratic government proved extraordinarily difficult. Indeed, Americans continued to be wounded and killed over the following months as Iraqi resistance remained—and increased. Equally challenging was the effort to uncover clear evidence of the existence of weapons of mass destruction, the fundamental rationale for the war. As a result, the Bush administration's foreign policy quickly came under greater scrutiny and criticism by the summer of 2003.

Criticism of the Bush foreign policy approach arose from the bureaucracy and Capitol Hill at home and from several sources abroad. At home, some charged that the administration had skewed intelligence data to support its desire to pursue the war against Iraq or had pressured intelligence analysts to provide supportive estimates (see Pillar 2008). And the Pentagon was accused of developing its own "hard-line view of intelligence related to Iraq" to justify American military actions there (see, e.g., Schmitt 2003). While the Bush administration denied such charges, skeptics remained, and Congress initiated inquiries into these matters. By July 2003, the administration was forced to admit that a passage in the president's State of the Union address regarding Iraq's efforts to obtain uranium from an African nation was not supported by American intelligence (see Sanger and Risen 2003). In general, the integrity of the Bush administration's policymaking was called into question, and the Senate Intelligence Committee called hearings to investigate. By this time, too, foreign policy arose in the incipient 2004 presidential election campaign. Representative Richard Gephardt, for example, charged the president with "stunning incompetence" in the area of foreign policy (from Beaumont 2003), and Senator John Kerry, the eventual Democratic nominee in 2004, accused the administration of failing to have a plan to "win the peace" in Iraq and pointed to the "arrogant absence of any major international effort to build what's needed" in Iraq (from Balz 2003, A6).

Abroad, allies and adversaries alike continued to criticize Bush administration policy. Critics disliked the administration's pursuit of unilateral policies without considering the views of other states. Arguably, these criticisms accelerated after two particular actions the American government pursued during this period. The first action was the holding of "enemy combatants" at Guantanamo Bay, Cuba, in solitary confinement, without access to counsel and without charges. These prisoners were denied basic rights, critics charged, seemingly in violation of the Geneva Conventions. Furthermore, these prisoners were subject to vigorous interrogation measures that constituted torture or bordered on it. The second action was the revelation in April 2004 of the appalling treatment of Iraqi prisoners at Abu Ghraib. Photographs showed American military members humiliating Iraq prisoners by requiring them to parade naked, making them pose with nooses around their necks, and using dogs to frighten them.

The Bush administration sought to deflect some of these criticisms by engaging in diplomatic initiatives on other pressing regional and international problems during 2003 and 2004. First, and perhaps most importantly, the administration issued its "roadmap for peace" between the Israelis and the Palestinians in April 2003 and promptly began to work on implementing it; President Bush traveled to the Middle East to give impetus to this road map. Second, in May 2003, the Bush administration won approval of UN Security Council Resolution 1483, which lifted sanctions against Iraq and encouraged other nations and international institutions to assist with the reconstruction of that nation. Third, President Vladimir Putin of Russia and President Bush exchanged instruments of ratification for another strategic arms reduction treaty in June 2003, signaling continued cooperation with a nation that had opposed the Iraq war. Fourth, and also in June 2003, President Bush met with European leaders at the G-8 summit (and most notably with French president Jacques Chirac) to begin to repair the rift with alliance partners that the war against Iraq had created. Finally, President Bush went on a five-day trip to Africa in July 2003, becoming only the third American president to visit that continent, to promote his AIDS/HIV initiative and to demonstrate a broader foreign policy agenda than the war on terrorism had connoted.

None of these actions, though, reflected a fundamental shift in policy approach by the Bush administration from the one adopted after 9/11. Indeed, terrorist incidents in Saudi Arabia and Morocco in the spring of 2003 (and attributed to al-Qaida) and the Madrid train bombings of March 11, 2004, only reinforced the administration's stance. The mounting criticism at home and abroad of the administration's unilateral and ideological approach appeared to introduce a more cautionary note in considering further military responses, whether against North Korea, Iran, or another entity. And presidential popularity had declined to the levels of prior to 9/11, and support for the Iraq war was beginning to wane by late 2004. Still, the policy slogan was "stay the course." That slogan applied to the policy in Iraq, but it applied equally to the unique combination of defensive realism and limited idealism that the Bush administration had adopted in the post-9/11 period.

A New Foreign Policy Approach for the Second Term?

George W. Bush was able to obtain a narrow victory in the 2004 presidential election, and his anti-terrorist foreign policy stance contributed to that success. In the aftermath of that election victory, though, the Bush administration initially sought to alter its foreign policy approach, including the war on terrorism. The initial hint of a change in approach came in a meeting with Prime Minister Tony Blair shortly after Bush's reelection. At the end of that meeting, President Bush declared that "[in] my second term, I will work to deepen our trans-Atlantic ties to nations of Europe." He also declared that stronger ties between Europe and America were vital to the "promotion of worldwide democracy" (from Stout 2004, 1, 4; see also McCormick 2006 for some of the themes developed in this section).

The Democracy Imperative

President Bush more fully signaled a modified approach in his second inaugural address and in his State of the Union address a few weeks later. In the inaugural address, for example, he directly tied America's well-being to the expansion of freedom and liberty around the world. America and the world would be secure only by promoting these ideas and by reconstructing the international system with them. "The survival of liberty in our land," he declared, "increasingly depends on the success of liberty in other lands. The best hope for peace in our world is the expansion of freedom in the world." Later in that address he added, "It is the policy of the United States to seek and support the growth of democratic movements and institutions in every nation and culture, with the ultimate goal of ending tyranny in the world" (Bush 2005a).

In his State of the Union address a short time later, President Bush continued to link America's well-being at home and the promotion of freedom abroad. A principal goal for his administration, he declared, would be "to pass along to our children all the freedoms we enjoy—and chief among them is freedom from fear." Key passages from this address convey these sentiments: "Pursuing our enemies is a vital commitment of the war on terror . . . [but] in the long term, the peace we seek will only be achieved by eliminating the conditions that feed radicalism and ideologies of murder. If whole regions of the world remain in despair and grow in hatred, they will be recruiting grounds for terror, and that terror will stalk America and other free nations for decades. The only force powerful enough to stop the rise of tyranny and terror, and replace hatred with hope, is the force of human freedom" (Bush 2005b).

Furthermore, President Bush emphasized that this transformational foreign policy would not be imposed from abroad or implemented by military means. Instead, this change would need to be evoked, or encouraged, by the global community.

At her Senate confirmation hearings in early 2005, Condoleezza Rice, too, was quick to outline some new central themes of the administration: to unite, strengthen, and spread democracies around the world and to do so through diplomacy. In her words, "We must use American diplomacy to help create a balance of power in the world that favors freedom. And the time for diplomacy is now" (U.S. Congress 2005). To be sure, such themes were not entirely new for the Bush administration. After all, the notion of creating "a balance of power favoring freedom" is seemingly straight out of the national security strategy statement (2002), and promoting democracy was a theme that President Bush enunciated in his visit to Britain in November 2003, when he called for the "global expansion of democracy" to be a key pillar of American security (Bush 2003d).

What was new, however, was the initial effort that President Bush and Condoleezza Rice, the new secretary of state, undertook to try to assuage allies, particularly the Europeans. Secretary Rice's "peace offensive" to several European capitals was one such step. It was generally well received, and it continued from there. By one analysis, Secretary Rice visited forty-nine countries in her first year as secretary of state and "nearly 70 percent of Rice's time abroad in 2005 was spent in Europe" (Gordon 2006, 81). President Bush, too, sought to send a different signal to the Europeans in 2005 by visiting NATO and European Union headquarters and by having long meetings with two key European skeptics of the Bush approach adopted after 9/11: French president Jacques Chirac and German chancellor Gerhard Schroeder.

Changes in Personnel and Policy Actions

The administration also made changes in foreign policy personnel at home as part of this seemingly new direction. Key neoconservatives (Paul Wolfowitz and Doug Feith at Defense and John Bolton at State) left, and new pragmatists and foreign policy realists took their places (Gordon 2006, 81–82). In particular, Robert Zoellick was appointed deputy secretary of state, Nicholas Burns assumed the number-three position as undersecretary of state for political affairs, and Christopher Hill became assistant secretary of state for East Asian and Pacific affairs (and eventually the lead American negotiator with North Korea).

Multilateral diplomatic initiatives were also established or restarted toward two "axis of evil" countries: Iran and North Korea. Partly as a result of President Bush's trip to Europe in 2005, the "EU-3"—France, Germany, and Great Britain—agreed to work with the United States on a diplomatic initiative with Iran to forestall the country's potential development of nuclear weapons. This initiative ultimately led to a series of economic sanctions against Iran and to considerable unity among these key allies and the United States over the next three years. This multilateral diplomatic approach remained the principal foreign policy vehicle for the Bush administration during the balance of its second term, despite some of the administration's rhetoric to the contrary.

By mid-2005, too, the "Six-Party Talks" over North Korea's development of nuclear weapons were resurrected, even though the North Koreans had declared several months earlier that they were "indefinitely suspending" them. Indeed, by mid-September 2005, all parties reaffirmed that the goal of the talks should be the "verifiable denuclearization of the Korean Peninsula in a peaceful manner" (U.S. Department of State 2008). While the Six-Party Talks experienced ups and down over the next three years (including UN-imposed sanctions over a North Korean nuclear test), the talks ultimately resulted in an agreement in 2007 about the phased shutdown, and eventual dismantlement, of North Korean nuclear facilities. The timely implementation of these agreements, however, eluded the Bush administration. Nonetheless, the Bush administration largely followed this diplomatic course with this "axis of evil" state.

Finally, several other modest changes in the Bush administration's foreign policy approach near the beginning of the second term, and more recently, suggested a slightly different course. Some changes were made in the administration's position on foreign aid, especially in providing more aid for Africa, and on climate change, including a statement that it was "largely a man-made problem." Halting steps of change were also evident in the administration's working with international organizations; there were some favorable actions vis-à-vis the International Criminal Court and UN efforts to solve the Darfur problem in Sudan (Gordon 2006, 83). In 2007 and 2008, the Bush administration made a new drive to prompt some headway in Middle East peace negotiations between the Palestinians and the Israelis, although these efforts were largely stalled after the Israeli invasion of Gaza in January 2009. The administration also worked collectively with NATO allies for expansion of that organization once again, although it did not succeed in getting all the new members desired. Still, by 2008, the administration was gaining unanimous support from the European NATO allies for the placement of a missile shield in Poland and the Czech Republic, even in the face of repeated Russian protests, fueled in part by the Russian incursion into South Ossetia in August 2008.

Declining Support for Bush's Foreign Policy

Despite these modifications in personnel and policy actions, sharp doubts continued to arise among foreign leaders and publics about the Bush administration and its policy approach. In turn, a majority of the American public and numerous members of Congress raised doubts about the direction of foreign policy, especially as reflected in the Iraq war.

Continuing Criticism from Abroad

Skepticism about any real change in direction by the Bush administration was largely driven by the continued unpopularity of the Iraq war (and the unilateralist approach that it reflected), but it was also driven by Bush's rhetoric and personal unpopularity. Any goodwill generated after 9/11 among the European public, for example, quickly dissipated in the prelude to the Iraq war, and it did not rebound for the remainder of Bush's presidency. In March 2003, just before the start of the Iraq war, only 48 percent of the public in Britain, 34 percent in Italy, 25 percent in Germany, 31 percent in France, and 14 percent in Spain expressed a favorable view of the United States (Pew Global Attitudes Project 2003, 19). Three years later, and more than a year into President Bush's second term (April 2006), the favorable perception percentages of the United States had improved only slightly among key European allies; 56 percent of Britons, 39 percent of the French, 37 percent of the Germans, and 23 percent of the Spanish expressed favorable opinions of the United States. This skepticism or downright opposition, of course, was not confined to Europeans. In the 2006 Pew survey of global attitudes toward the United States, in only three countries of the ten surveyed outside Europe did a majority of the publics view the United States favorably; these were Japan, India, and Nigeria. The rest (Russia, Indonesia, Egypt, Pakistan, Jordan, Turkey, and China) had favorability ratings of the United States ranging from 12 percent positive in Turkey to 47 percent positive in China (Pew Global Attitudes Project 2006, 1).

President Bush's personal unpopularity undoubtedly continued to cloud any change in policy direction. In a BBC World Service poll (2005), in only three countries (out of twenty-two surveyed) did a majority or a plurality view Bush's reelection positively; these were India, the Philippines, and Poland. The rest, including five European countries, viewed the reelection of Bush as "negative for peace and security for the world."

This skepticism of key European publics (and others) was also mirrored at the governmental level. Only a few European states were willing to provide much assistance in the effort to stabilize Iraq. Even among those that did, they later withdrew or announced their intention to withdraw their forces, often because of opposition at home. Still, some of the states most critical of the United States over initiating the Iraq war have been willing to train Iraqi security personnel (e.g., Germany) and have provided some resources for reconstruction (e.g., France). Yet there clearly were barriers to how far they would go to endorse the Bush administration's foreign policy approach. With new leaders elected in Germany in November 2005 (Angela Merkel) and in France in May 2007 (Nicolas Sarkozy) and with the selection of Gordon Brown to replace Tony Blair as prime minister in Britain during 2007, President Bush had a new set of leaders who were generally more willing to cooperate with the United States than those (except for Blair) at the height of the Iraq war. Nonetheless, the Iraq war hovered over other nations moving too close to the United States—and it continued to impinge upon any enthusiastic alliance support for the administration.

Emergent Criticism at Home

Although the Bush administration was able to win the White House and keep Republican control of Congress in the 2004 elections based in part on its antiterrorism policy, domestic support for the president and his Iraq policy quickly began to erode by mid-2005. Indeed, public approval of the president dropped significantly after the initiation of that war, and by 2008, it hovered at about 30 percent. Since March 2005, when Bush's approval rating dropped to 45 percent, there were only two instances in the weekly Gallup tracking polls (April 4–7, 2005, and May 2–5, 2005) when the president's approval rating was at 50 percent. Instead, the trend was consistently downward from March 2005, with a low (up to that time) of 31 percent in the polling of May 5–7, 2006 (Gallup poll 2008b). With the full formation of the Iraqi government and the killing of Abu al-Zarqawi, al-Qaida's leader in Iraq, in 2006, President Bush's approval rating inched back up a bit to the high-30 percent level and even to 42 percent, but it eroded to 29 percent in July 2007 and, in April 2008, it dropped to 28 percent (Newport 2008). In all, a majority of the public throughout most of Bush's second term disapproved of his job performance—and much of that disapproval, of course, was related to foreign policy, specifically, to Iraq.

The number of people who thought that sending troops to Iraq was a good idea steadily eroded during Bush's second term, and by its con-

259

clusion, a large majority believed it to have been a mistake. As early as June 2004, a majority of the public in Gallup tracking polls judged that the United States "made a mistake in sending troops to Iraq." Over the next year, though, a slim majority usually disagreed with this statement, but, after June 2005, a majority of the public consistently viewed the action as a "mistake," with only an exception or two (Newport 2006). By April 2008, 58 percent of the public viewed the Iraq war as a mistake, and public disapproval remained at about that level through the balance of the Bush term. In this sense, while majority opposition to Iraq policy was probably more recent than many might believe, the level of popular belief that the invasion was a mistake remained quite stable from 2005 through 2008. Moreover, in his comparison of the Iraq, Vietnam, and Korean wars, political scientist John Mueller reports that the most striking aspect is how much more quickly domestic support for the Iraq war faded (Mueller 2008, 116).

David Broder (2006), the dean of the Washington press corps, summarized the problems facing the administration by putting himself in the president's position and asking himself how the world looked from this vantage point. His answer was a single word: "trouble." Indeed, across the foreign policy horizon in 2006—from Mexico and Canada in the Western Hemisphere; to China, North Korea, and Russia in Asia and Europe; and to Iraq, Iran, Israel, and Lebanon in the Middle East—the administration was encountering trouble in pursuing its foreign policy objectives. More importantly, as Broder noted, the administration seemed to lack good ideas for addressing these festering challenges around the world.

In an intriguing analysis in the same period, political scientist Steven Schier (2006) points to the Iraq war to account for why things went so badly for the administration. That is, he charted the number of positive and negative events, whether discretionary events (where the president had an impact) or nondiscretionary events (where he had no direct impact), and found, not surprisingly, that the Iraq war was a clear turning point for the administration. What is so compelling, though, is the dramatic decline in the ratio of positive to negative events before and after the initiation of the war. Overall, discretionary events were at a 4-to-1 ratio (positive to negative) from 2001 to 2005, but the number of positive events declined from 2003 onward. The nondiscretionary events were at a 1-to-4 ratio (negative to positive) over the time period. The important message is how costly the Iraq war was for the administration both in events that it could affect and those that it could not. The "soft power" of the United

States (to borrow Joseph Nye's felicitous phrase) declined at home and abroad as a consequence of the Iraq war.

.During this same time period, congressional criticism of the Bush administration's Iraq policy began to escalate on both sides of the aisle. Two military veterans in Congress dramatized the changing nature of the political environment and epitomized the growing opposition in that body. In late November 2005, Representative John Murtha (D-Pennsylvania), the ranking Democrat on the House Subcommittee on Appropriations, a former marine, and a supporter of the Iraq war, broke with the Bush administration and called for the withdrawal of American troops from Iraq within six months: "The military has done everything that has been asked of them. The U.S. cannot accomplish anything further in Iraq militarily. It is time to bring the troops home" (from Nather 2005a, 3120). On the Republican side, Senator Chuck Hagel (R-Nebraska), a Vietnam veteran and a media favorite because of his outspokenness on the Bush administration's postwar Iraq policy (Nather 2005b, 2834), became an increasingly vocal critic. One profile of Hagel characterized his determination on the Iraq issue in this way: "He did not let up, despite extreme pressure from party leaders to cool it" (*CQ Weekly Online* 2006, 2926). These members of Congress were not alone, and Congress's push for greater White House accountability on the Iraq war escalated in 2005 and 2006. As a result, the 2006 congressional elections quickly became a referendum on Iraq policy specifically and the Bush approach to foreign policy more generally.

A Change in Course?

In a news conference the day after the 2006 congressional elections, President Bush characterized the results as a "thumping" for his party. Republicans lost six seats in the Senate and thirty seats in the House, and both chambers changed from Republican to Democratic control. In short order, Secretary of Defense Donald Rumsfeld resigned, a new commander was appointed in Iraq, and the president considered a new Iraq strategy. A month later, the Iraq Study Group, an independent, bipartisan group led by former secretary of state James Baker and former congressional representative Lee Hamilton, issued its report, which contained seventy-nine recommendations outlining "the way forward in Iraq." The thrust of these recommendations was a call for the United States to launch "a new diplomatic initiative to build an international consensus for stability in Iraq and the region" and to "adjust its role in Iraq to encourage the Iraqi people to take control of their own destiny." The U.S. military "should evolve into one of supporting the Iraqi military," the report concluded, with the principal responsibility left to the Iraqis themselves. Furthermore, the American government "should work closely with Iraq's leaders to support the achievement of specific objectives . . . on national reconciliation, security, and governance" (Baker and Hamilton 2006). In short, the Iraq Study Group called for new diplomatic initiatives toward Iraq's neighbors, reduced American military involvement within Iraq except for training and some embedded units, enhanced Iraqi progress in internal reconciliation among religious groups, and improved national governance.

While President Bush indicated that he would carefully review the Iraq Study Group's recommendations, he rather quickly moved in a different direction. In early 2007, the president embraced a new Iraq strategy prepared by General David Petraeus, the coalition commander in Iraq. Popularly called the "surge strategy," this new approach called for sending an additional twenty-one thousand American troops to Iraq in an effort to quell the sectarian violence and thus provide the Iraqi government with time to make progress on internal political reconciliation. This policy change provoked sharp criticism from Congress. Senator Hagel, for example, called the president's speech about the surge strategy "the most dangerous foreign policy blunder in this country since Vietnam" (from Nather 2007a, 170). The House of Representatives subsequently passed a nonbinding resolution disapproving surge, although the Senate failed to follow suit.

In the ensuing months of 2007, the Democratic majority made various attempts to cut off funding for Iraq and to set a date for American withdrawal, all in response to the president's action and as part of its perceived election mandate. One supplemental Iraq war funding measure was passed by Congress in late April 2007 with language requiring the withdrawal of troops if certain "benchmarks" were not achieved. President Bush quickly vetoed this bill on May 1, 2007, and the House upheld his veto a day later (Higa and Donnelly 2007; Clarke 2007). While the veto pen proved important, the president successfully staved off congressional actions for other reasons as well. President Bush was largely able to maintain the support of his Republican colleagues in the House and Senate, even in the face of rather united Democratic opposition. The rules in the Senate require sixty votes of that body to end filibuster on controversial matters, and that procedure also aided the president. Furthermore, the threat of a presidential veto for any Iraq legislation also supported Bush's position. Finally, and importantly, Democrats (and Republicans) had to face the real difficulty of cutting off funds for the troops in the field and also to gauge the political backlash that such action might create among their constituents back home.

Although the surge strategy proved successful in dampening sectarian violence in 2007 and into 2008, the Iraqi government's progress on fostering national reconciliation among the competing sectarian groups was markedly slow, as documented in an independent assessment by the U.S. Government Accountability Office (GAO) and as confirmed by General Petraeus's testimony to Congress on two different occasions. By April 2008, moreover, because of some increase in Iraqi violence, General Petraeus was forced to ask for a "pause" in the draw-down of the surge forces for a year to consolidate the progress that had been achieved. Such actions, along with the continuing loss of American lives in Iraq, made foreign policy, and specifically the Iraq war, a central issue in the 2008 presidential campaign. In this sense, more than five years after the start of the war, Iraq cast a long shadow over those contending for the highest office in the land and over American foreign policy more generally.

Even as Iraq was moving toward stability by the end of 2008, the situation in Afghanistan had taken a turn for the worse. The increase in the number of killings, the expansion of civil unrest, and the limited territorial control by the central government reflected a deteriorating situation. Both the outgoing Bush administration and the incoming Obama administration were looking to increase the number of American troops in Afghanistan and were reviewing new strategies for dealing with the situation. In this sense, the initial site of success in the war on terrorism was now somewhat in doubt.

The Foreign Policy Legacies of the Bush Years

What, then, are the principal foreign policy legacies of the George W. Bush administration across its two terms? How did its foreign policy actions impact the United States and the rest of the world? What policy challenges does it leave for future administrations? In large measure, of course, the Bush administration's response to 9/11 and to Iraq and the Iraq war shape the nature of its legacy in foreign policy.

The Bush administration came to office committed to creating a "distinctly American internationalism" in which it sought to limit American involvement abroad and to pursue a narrower interpretation of the national interest than the Clinton administration had used. In effect, this approach was a commitment to classical realism where relative capabilities largely shaped actions abroad and relations with major powers dominated the agenda. With 9/11, however, the Bush administration jettisoned its classical realist approach and embraced defensive realism, where foreign policy actions were driven primarily by the threat environment. When terrorism intensified the threat environment, the administration was compelled to pursue a more globalist strategy than it initially envisioned. This new environment, too, saw the administration embrace elements of idealism by pursuing regime change abroad, most notably reflected in the wars in Afghanistan and Iraq, and by providing military support to several states threatened by internal (and terrorist) insurgencies (e.g., the former Soviet republic of Georgia and the Philippines).

The 9/11 attacks had a profound effect on several dimensions of American foreign policy. On the policymaking side, 9/11 enhanced the authority of the president, increased the degree of congressional deference to the executive, rallied public opinion behind the actions of the president, and, in a sense, narrowed America's foreign policy agenda. On the content side, 9/11 altered some initial foreign policy assumptions that the Bush administration brought to the office (e.g., opposition to humanitarian interventions and a global strategy) and confirmed others (e.g., the greater need for hard power over soft power; the importance of security issues over political and economic issues). At the same time, 9/11 also seemingly afforded the Bush administration the opportunity to forge a "grand strategy" of foreign policy for the years ahead. That strategy was grounded in the belief that terrorism and rogue states were the major adversaries of the United States and that a "coalition of the willing" should be developed worldwide to isolate and defeat those adversaries. Importantly, too, the United States reserved the right to act alone if necessary and to engage in preemptive actions, especially when weapons of mass destruction were in the hands of adversaries. The actions against the Taliban and al-Qaida in Afghanistan and the war with Iraq illustrate differing dimensions of this new strategy.

The post-9/11 approach of the George W. Bush administration represents a determined effort to restore a more consistent, coherent, and universal foreign policy approach, an approach that more closely resembled that of the early years of his father's immediate predecessor, Ronald Reagan, than of any other recent president. Although the contexts were markedly different in the early 1980s and the early years of the new century, the ideology and universal nature of American actions during each of these administrations—one staunchly anticommunist, the other, staunchly anti-terrorist—are strikingly similar for each administration. Both were strongly committed to setting a clear course to direct American actions abroad, and both were willing to act alone and use America's military capacity, if necessary.

The Iraq war dramatically affected the transformative foreign policy that the Bush administration initiated after 9/11. The contested rationale for the Iraq invasion over the existence of weapons of mass destruction in the hands of a rogue state, the failure of reconstruction planning and implementation after the initial invasion, and the difficulties of bringing democracy to a country fraught with sectarian divisions brought into serious question the transformative nature of Bush's foreign policy approach. Furthermore, the largely unilateral nature of the Iraqi invasion—despite the "coalition of the willing" veneer—the opposition of key allies, and the failure to gain the endorsement of the United Nations further tarnished America's image abroad and weakened its attractiveness in the international community. In short, the transformative foreign policy that the administration attempted to undertake was largely left fallow by actions and events surrounding Iraq and the Iraq war. More than five years after that invasion, America's global reputation remained weakened, and the administration's vision of promoting both a grand strategy against international terrorism and wide-ranging democracy had been seriously compromised.

To be sure, the administration sought to recast its foreign policy approach at the beginning of its second term to focus on promoting democracy and eliminating tyranny worldwide. The administration undertook an effort to modify its approach—by removing or having key neoconservative advisers resign, by reaching out to the Europeans, and by initiating a number of multilateral diplomatic efforts toward the other "axis of evil" states—Iran and North Korea—and toward other international concerns, such as Darfur and the Middle East. Yet these new initiatives were largely lost because of the deteriorating situation in Iraq, the "stay-the-course" approach, and the administration's continued embrace of the rhetoric of the immediate post-9/11 period. Because of the dominance of the Iraq issue and the caricatured way in which the president was portrayed, the Bush administration, and the United States more generally, had a difficult time exercising international influence. In this sense, America's global reputation was yet another casualty of the Iraq war.

The reliance on unilateralism and preemptive action by the Bush administration (along with its strident rhetoric in these areas) had the effect of tarnishing American images abroad and, more generally, eroding its "soft power"—the attractiveness of its values and culture and the ability to influence international actions more indirectly. Changes in these two areas by the Obama administration—and some important policy changes as well—would likely have the important benefit of improving America's global reputation and restoring its policy influence. Indeed, in the early days of the new administration, President Obama sought to do just that. He issued an executive order seeking to close the prison at Guantanamo Bay, Cuba, within one year and met with his top military officers to discuss ending America's combat role in Iraq within sixteen months. Further, the economic meltdown in the United States and worldwide at the end of 2008 and into 2009 also required a nation more engaged multilaterally to address these shared economic problems. In all, a changed image—and the appeal of America's values and culture—will likely enhance the prospects of the promotion of democratic values abroad, but the Obama administration should harbor no illusions regarding the challenges of advancing democracy in other countries, as the U.S. experience in Iraq and Afghanistan so dramatically reveals.

14

NATIONAL SECURITY AND THE BUSH DOCTRINE
A Legacy of the George W. Bush Presidency

STANLEY A. RENSHON

oreign policy provides the most likely source of an enduring legacy for George W. Bush's presidency. That may seem less than obvious in the immediate aftermath of his time in the White House, but it is not unusual for a president's historical reputation to change with the perspective allowed by distance. At the end of a presidency, analysts, pundits, and partisans scour the historical record to find evidence that supports their views and provides lessons for the issues we now face. It is particularly difficult to give a fair, balanced assessment of a president's policies when those policies are controversial and the president himself is reviled in some quarters and widely viewed as ineffective in others. Such is the case with George W. Bush's foreign policy legacy, the major innovation of which was the Bush Doctrine.

The Bush Doctrine grew out of the 9/11 attacks and represented President Bush's response to what he and his advisers saw as the key issues and lessons to emerge from those attacks. Those attacks reframed the Bush administration's view of the most serious problems it faced and what to do about them. The potential for the linkage between catastrophic terrorism and weapons of mass destruction (WMD) raised the national security stakes enormously for the United States, or so the Bush administration thought, and it acted accordingly.

For a brief moment after 9/11, the country and many in the world were united in their rhetorical support of the United States. Many allies, and even those who had not been America's friends, offered various kinds of help, whether out of fear or solidarity, to bring the perpetrators to justice. But Bush had more serious concerns than revenge. A sophisticated, ruthless, and deadly enemy had pulled off a stunning and severely damaging attack on American soil against major national symbols, destroying the World Trade Center and seriously damaging the Pentagon. Either the White House or the Capitol was also targeted and escaped devastation only because of the heroic Americans who gave their lives so that one hijacked plane could not complete its mission. There was widespread and genuine fear of another attack that might inflict even greater damage on America.

The Bush administration put into place a large set of policies designed to prevent another, more deadly terrorist strike. These policies were controversial both domestically and abroad. As a result, their nature and contributions to national security remain underappreciated. It is partially on the basis of those controversies that Barack Obama ran for and was elected to the presidency. Thus, an interesting question we can then pose regarding Bush's national security legacy is to what extent the new Obama administration has changed—or preserved—the national security architecture that it inherited from the Bush administration.

Upon his inauguration, the new president faced many national security questions for which the Bush Doctrine cannot and was not developed to give answers. What does one do about a resurgent Russia? What should the president do about the loose alliance of dictatorships that is gathering momentum and linking South America, parts of Eastern Europe, East Asia, and Southeast Asia? What policies are best suited to handle "revisionist" powers? Should the United States intervene in genocidal wars, like the one raging in Darfur, and, if so, in what circumstances? However, the new Obama administration still faces a number of the same national security questions that faced the Bush administration after 9/11. Obama's initial answers, as we will see, are suggestive of the potential foreign policy legacy of the Bush administration.

The cold war that Presidents Truman, Eisenhower, Kennedy, Nixon,

Carter, and Reagan confronted was urgent and consequential, but except for President Truman's basic decision to opt for the policy of containment, each of these presidents further developed what seemed to be a successful policy rather than putting a brand-new one into place. By contrast, the audacity and success of the 9/11 attacks were unanticipated, unprecedented, and extremely consequential. In forging his response, President Bush was much more in the position of President Truman than of those who followed. Like Truman, Bush had to develop and begin to implement a new strategic paradigm applied to a wholly new set of circumstances—the dangers of catastrophic terrorism. Also like Truman, Bush's may have been underestimated by his critics. Bush's early insights into the meaning and implications of the 9/11 attacks may prove to be one of the signal accomplishments of his presidency and the foundation of any legacy that survives him.

When the first of the hijacked airplanes slammed into the World Trade Center, President Bush was in a classroom at a Florida elementary school. His chief of staff, Andrew Card, entered the room and whispered in the president's ear, "A second plane has hit the tower, America is under attack" (Bush 2001c). Shortly thereafter, the president left the room and said, "We're at war. Get me the Vice President and get me the director of the FBI" (from American Enterprise Institute 2001).

Let us briefly consider the attacks and the president's response to them in that moment. The "who" and "why" were not clear, but it was obviously an act of war and President Bush treated it as one. A war is a struggle between adversaries in which the full measure of their resources is used to vanquish or mortally wound the other. Limited responses, be they military, legal, or diplomatic, would not suffice.

What was also clear is that the attacks represented an audacious act of lethal intention, careful planning, and ruthless execution undeterred by American power and the retaliation that was certain to follow. In those respects, 9/11 was a set of signals indicating profound danger to the United States. It is worth considering the frames other than war that President Bush could have used (Renshon 2004, 104–5). He could have framed 9/11 as just an attack and limited his response to bombing Afghanistan, the country that had provided sanctuary to the culprits. However, that would not have addressed the larger strategic threat that terrorists with demonstrated determination, skill, resources, and worldwide reach represented. Nor would limited counterattacks carry much weight as deterrence measures, and it could reasonably be argued that a limited response would embolden future attacks. Finally, there is the question of exactly what targets would have been available in Afghanistan and whether those limited targets would satisfy the emotional, strategic, and political need for a strong response.

President Bush could also have framed the attacks as essentially a legal issue. This, however, would have been incommensurate with the nature, scope, and gravity of the attacks, and there was no reason to think such a frame would have been effective either as punishment or prevention. The FBI had, after all, caught the perpetrators of the first World Trade Center attack in 1993 and they were tried and convicted, but that did not deter the 9/11 attacks. Moreover, subsequent experience has shown that the United States has had enormous trouble establishing military tribunals for terrorist suspects, and those difficulties would have been magnified if terrorists had been brought to the United States for trial, as some Democrats argued ought to have been done (see Gentile 2008; Zeleny 2007).

President Bush could also have framed the issue as a diplomatic one. That strategy would have entailed demanding that the United Nations pass a resolution condemning the attacks as acts of aggression. But aggression by whom? Technically, the government of Afghanistan was complicit, but it might well have argued that it was not directly responsible. Many UN members might well have asked for proof of that government's direct and operational involvement. How would this have been obtained? Moreover, the United Nations is premised on the interaction of states, not nonstate actors like al-Qaida. What punishment would the UN have called for in these circumstances, and who would carry it out?

In short, all three alternative frames of analysis and action would have been inadequate responses to the attacks. They would be not have been fitting either emotionally, psychologically, politically, or strategically. And, most importantly, they would not have put in place the wide array of institutional responses that became essential parts of the Bush Doctrine.

The 9/11 attacks transformed Bush into a wartime president scrambling to deal with an unprecedented attack in two major American cities and the threat that those attacks were a harbinger of even more devastating assaults, possibly nuclear or biological, in the future. The 9/11 attacks required from the president, his advisers, and top American political leaders, regardless of party affiliation, a rapid and accurate understanding of the nature of the attacks, their implications, and a timely and comprehensive strategic response. All of these necessities were reflected in the development and deployment of the American response under the framework of the widely criticized and misunderstood Bush Doctrine.

The Bush Doctrine was a logical and supportable response to the critical set of questions that the 9/11 attacks raised. That response, with its early and essential insight about the nature of the new threat, and the policy architecture developed as a direct result represent the signal contributions of the Bush presidency to American national security. They constitute Bush's real leadership legacy.

The war in Iraq, its misunderstood and mischaracterized foundations, and the choices that were made about how it was fought have damaged Bush's reputation and obscured the importance of his larger contributions. In many critics' minds, the Iraq war is synonymous with the Bush Doctrine. Yet the Iraq war was an outgrowth of the doctrine, the scope of which extends far beyond the single case of Iraq.

Recalling the doctrine's origins helps make that point. The Bush Doctrine grew most directly out of the 9/11 attacks and the strategic questions that it raised. First, there were groups who were capable of launching major terror strikes against the United States and its allies and who intended to do so with nuclear, chemical, or biological weapons if at all possible. This fact added weight to another—that certain foreign leaders hostile to the United States were motivated by grandiose regional aspirations, murderous proclivities, and a drive for power that was permeated by ruthlessness, revenge, and in some cases a sense of messianic religious entitlement.

It was hard to envision a strategy of containment or deterrence that would work well in the face of such leadership psychologies. Worse, because of isolation and few internal or external checks on their psychologies, these kinds of leaders also tend to show poor judgment. Ordinarily, a purely rational calculation would lead decisionmakers to avoid being associated in any way with terrorists who wanted to launch a major attack against the United States. Afghanistan was a case in point. As rational actors, the regime's leaders should have avoided any complicity. But whether they misjudged the likely American response or did not care, they harbored the culprits and then refused to turn them over. As a result, the Bush administration made the judgment that there were some leaders for whom the assumption of rationality was a poor national security risk.

In response to the assumption-shattering 9/11 attacks, the Bush administration faced five major questions, which now also face the Obama administration:

1. How can the United States and its allies avoid being the victim of another major terrorist attack, possibly with weapons of mass destruction?

2. What roles can the doctrines of prevention, preemption, containment, and deterrence play, given the range of threats with which the United States and its allies must now contend?

3. How can the United States resolve the dilemma of needing the cooperation of allies to address common threats, while having to deal with allies' different priorities and understandings of these very threats that may require the United States to occasionally act without their help?

4. How can the United States balance the need for international institutions to further develop a liberal democratic world order with the fact that some members of the "international community" are not democratic, liberal, or supportive of the assumptions that underlie the liberal international order?

5. How can the United States address the challenge of a fervent and aggressive religious ideology, some of whose elements are potentially attractive to billions of followers worldwide?

Failure to consider the strategic context represented by these questions has led to frequent misunderstandings of the underpinnings of the Bush Doctrine. Some of these misapprehensions can be corrected immediately. As two Bush Doctrine critics, Ivo H. Daalder and James Lindsay, have noted, "The Bush Administration is right to see the trinity of terrorists, tyrants and technology as the principal threat to national security" (Daalder and Lindsay 2003a, 135). Similarly, through that new post-9/11 prism, the Bush administration saw Saddam Hussein in a new and more dangerous light. The doctrine itself calls on the United States to assess the dangerousness of particular situations, but it does not require any particular conclusion regarding any country, group, or leader. It does, however, require consideration of specific cases in the context of the new strategic situation the country faces.

The Bush Doctrine is also not synonymous with instituting democracy at the point of a gun, as is often thought. Rather, it begins with the recognition that democratic pluralism, open institutions, and accessible political processes are an important hedge against the rise of radical ideologies that can build on political, cultural, economic, or religious discontent. The Iraq war was waged because the Bush administration judged that Saddam Hussein was dangerous, not to install democracy. Democracy was the answer to the question, What should replace Saddam's tyranny? It was *not* the answer to the question, On what basis should we consider removing him from power?

Additionally, it is important to keep in mind that the Bush Doctrine may be correct in its major foundational premises, yet, at the same time, it is possible for the administration to have carried out their own policies poorly and at times even disastrously. The second statement does not necessarily invalidate the first.

With these caveats in mind, we can now turn to the answers that the Bush Doctrine proposed for the set of national security questions that emerged after the 9/11 attacks. In reality, the Bush Doctrine is not one single policy, like preventive war or unilateralism. It is, rather, a set of policies that reflect five related strategic elements. These are: American primacy, assertive realism, stand-apart alliances, a new internationalism, and democratic transformation.

One basic premise of the Bush Doctrine is American primacy, a tenet that has been held by every modern presidential administration with the possible exception of Jimmy Carter before the Soviet invasion of Afghanistan. It is not synonymous with empire, although it is often confused with it. It is a strange empire indeed when the citizens of this "hegemonic power" would generally prefer to go about their own business and not that of other countries. It is stranger still when many countries demand the attention of the United States and complain when they do not get enough of it.

Of course, much of the world prefers American involvement so long as it is on their own terms. America's international role, therefore, is bound to be controversial and conflicted. America's allies expect it to live up to what they think of as its international responsibilities. Yet they forget that the United States, while being the major world power now, has its own national security interests in addition to its worldwide responsibilities. It is often forgotten that these worldwide national security interests and the power necessary to sustain them are a direct result of responsibilities that others cannot shoulder.

Consistent with its intellectual origins in cold war realism, the Bush Doctrine was premised on looking hard facts in the eye and acting accordingly. I am not arguing that the administration always saw things clearly; they certainly did not. But in this new and more dangerous world, the arguments on behalf of the Bush Doctrine about danger, risk, and uncertainty are certainly plausible.

Once dangers are understood, the question becomes what to do about them. Assertive realism has a second element—a preference when it comes to critical national security problems for an offensive stance, rather than a defensive crouch. The Bush administration's judgment was that when it comes to catastrophic terrorism, the best defense is a strong offense. Offense, it should be emphasized, is not synonymous with military action. Indeed, military force may have nothing to do with active, assertive policies meant to forestall damage to American national interests. The Bush Doctrine's National Strategy to Secure Cyberspace (2003, five years before the Latvia cyberattack and the NATO response to it) and its Strategy for Homeland Security and National Intelligence are cases in point. They are assertive because they seek to develop and shape new security architecture in these areas, assertively filling in dangerous gaps with appropriate programs.

The third element of the Bush Doctrine is a focus on strategic, standapart alliances, most notably encapsulated in the phrase "coalition of the willing." Realists may disagree about many things, but there is one matter on which they concur: international cooperation is extremely difficult because states are always tempted to go their own way and there is little to stop them from doing so.

Institutionalists respond that even if international actors are egotistic and live in an anarchic world where self-help is prevalent and no authorities can enforce the rules, cooperation can and does occur. That is true. However, many of their examples are economic, and it is perfectly reasonable to suppose that the domains of national security and international economics operate according to different rules.

In reality, a number of criticisms of the Bush Doctrine in this area are overblown. President Bush's rhetorical stance that "you're either with or against us" belies the fact that the administration had to address a far more complex reality and that it did so with some success. We are in alliance with *parts* of the governments in Pakistan and Saudi Arabia, while other parts of those governments continue to pursue interests that are unhelpful and may even be damaging to American and western interests. The United States tolerates this because it has to. These two countries (plus others) are central to American and wider western security concerns. It is certainly true that the administration's assertive stance toward retaining its options can be easily seen in its views on the Kyoto Protocol, the International Criminal Court, and the ABM Treaty. But that is not the whole story.

The Bush Doctrine is fundamentally concerned with how, exactly, American national security policy should engage international institutions. The Bush Doctrine views these institutions as not currently structured or operating in a way that allows them to effectively fulfill their important roles. Certainly, the United States cannot depend on them when concerns of vital national security arise. The question is then what to do.

President Bush's efforts with international institutions often went unnoticed. The administration attempted to transform existing institutions and their practices, including the United Nations, the World Bank, foreign aid, and NATO, to name just a few. The Bush administration took the lead in developing new international institutional initiatives, including the Proliferation Security Initiative; a new international climate pact among the United States, Japan, Australia, China, India, and South Korea that provides an alternative to the Kyoto accords; and possible alternative multilateral structures such as the 2000 Community of Democracies initiative. I term this activity the "New Internationalism," and whether one agrees with the policies or not, they hardly represent the leadership of a unilateralist hegemon. They are the possible foundations of a new post-9/11 liberal world order.

Finally, there is the issue of spreading democracy. The Bush Doctrine emphasizes expanding democracy, often in difficult and inhospitable places. It is here that the Bush Doctrine departs most directly from its mainly realist heritage. How to push, how far to push, and when to push for democracy are not easy questions to answer. Democratic transformation is almost always a process that is most prudently measured in decades, and there is little solid knowledge about why or how such transitions occur or can be brought about. It is very clear that trying to develop democracy after an invasion and occupation, as Iraq and Afghanistan have demonstrated, is a costly, brutal, and uncertain undertaking.

Yet, in championing democracy, the Bush administration was following a well-worn path in American diplomatic and strategic traditions. Admittedly, crusades to "make the world safe for democracy" are dangerous, but again, it is important to note that the Bush administration did not remove Saddam Hussein to install democracy but because he was believed to be dangerous.

Regardless of the solutions to these foreign policy dilemmas that Bush's critics may have preferred, most people would agree that for the foreseeable future, the United States is likely to be actively engaged, with its allies, in a worldwide security struggle unparalleled even during the cold war. These efforts are bound to be contentious and will be played out before skeptical domestic and international audiences.

It may be that alternative strategic doctrines might, with development, provide their own more effective, comprehensive answers to the questions that faced the Bush administration after 9/11. Yet, to date, critics of the Bush Doctrine have offered broad generalities, like being more responsive to the concerns of our allies, or being more willing to talk with our enemies and adversaries, or deepening our involvement in international institutions. These are all useful pieces of advice in some circumstances, but they do not address the hard questions that the Bush administration faced after 9/11 and which the Obama administration will also have to answer.

There is no doubt that the war in Iraq and its enormous costs have negatively affected assessments of the Bush Doctrine. That war presented the administration with many choices, a number of which proved to be critical, and none of which was without substantial risk. Should we use more troops, which would remove the element of surprise and likely stimulate anti-American nationalism, or should we go with smaller numbers and rely on the Iraqis at the earliest possible date? We went in light, and it came to pass that local political forces did not lend themselves to quick turnover. Should we have allowed members of the Ba'ath Party to regain power, or should we have tried to develop new democratic institutions untainted by the murderous rule of that party the U.S. occupation displaced? Should we have brought in and installed our own preferred Iraqis, or should we have allowed the possibilities of a more truly democratic system to unfold?

These were questions to which there were no obvious and easy answers. Moreover, there is no doubt our military was unprepared with either an effective counterinsurgency doctrine, sufficient numbers of troops to implement such a doctrine, or effective military commanders to deal with the insurgency that took root and caused such brutal carnage over several years. As a result of these errors, support for the war—and for the doctrine and president associated with it—plummeted.

With a new and apparently more effective strategy and a new set of field commanders in place, the situation improved. If, in the years to come, Iraq emerges as a relatively stable, pro-western, more democratic than dictatorial country, the costs of that war will have been somewhat redeemed. But it will always remain a difficult and divisive war that will not redeem President Bush's historical reputation. In the best case, what a successful conclusion to the war will mean for Bush's legacy is the possibility that his larger national security contributions might emerge from behind the cloud of the brutal war that obscured them.

One key test for the legacy of the Bush Doctrine is whether Bush's presidential successors find it useful and keep some or all of its elements in place. So far, the new Obama administration seems to be caught between an acknowledgment that the doctrine has useful elements that should be kept and the fact that Obama won office in part by emphasizing his national security disagreements with the Bush administration.

President Obama quickly signed executive orders setting out a time frame for closing the prison facility at Naval Station Guantanamo Bay (Executive Order 2009b), requiring all interrogations to be conducted according the procedures laid out in the U.S. Army Field Manual (Executive Order 2009a), and reviewing detainee policy (Executive Order 2009c). These three presidential directives led one *Washington Post* correspondent to declare on page one, "Bush's War on Terror Comes to a Sudden End" (Priest 2009).

Perhaps. But each of those directives contained caveats whose importance are yet to be determined (Bellantoni 2009). On interrogations, a task force was created to study whether harsher methods might be needed in some cases. President Obama's directives also keep in place the controversial policy of "extraordinary renditions," the secret abductions and transfers of prisoners to countries that cooperate with the United States, so long as it is done on a "'short-term' basis" (Miller 2009). Obama's Justice Department appears to be continuing the Bush administration's practice of urging domestic courts to throw out civilian cases involving rendition and torture allegations on the grounds of "state secrets" (Starks 2009; Lake 2008). It also applied for an emergency stay motion at the Ninth Circuit, asking it to freeze a district judge's order in a lawsuit challenging the legality of President Bush's warrantless surveillance program (Perine 2009; Gerstein 2009). Elena Kagan, Obama's choice to represent his administration before the Supreme Court, told a key Republican senator during hearings that she believed the government could hold suspected terrorists, without trial, as war prisoners (C. Savage 2009). The new administration has also continued the Bush administration policy of using remotely piloted aircraft to attack militants within Pakistan's borders (Oppel 2009) and has even expanded the target list (Mazzetti and Sanger 2009). Given all of these apparent parallels, it is not surprising that a *New York Times* article reviewing these developments was headlined, "Obama's War on Terror May Resemble Bush's in Some Areas" (C. Savage 2009).

As to some of the more basic strategic premises that are the foundation of the Bush Doctrine, the new president appears to be adopting them, too. On "unilateralism," President Obama has been very clear that he places a high value on working with allies, but he has also said this about American national interests and the international community: "And it is important that we don't provide veto power to the United Nations or anyone else in acting in our interests" (from CNN 2008c).

As to the United States' potentially most dangerous state adversary, Iran, it is clear that President Obama hopes that direct talks will succeed, even though talks between the EU and Iran have not. Yet Obama has laid down a very strong rhetorical gauntlet. In his first campaign debate with Senator John McCain, on September 26, 2008, he said, "Senator McCain is absolutely right, we cannot tolerate a nuclear Iran. It would be a game changer" (from CNN 2008b). This is a tough, direct statement and not too dissimilar in tone or substance to what President Bush and many Democrats said about Saddam Hussein before and after 9/11. The question is, What actions will follow?

What of the other, more basic levels of President Obama's strategic worldview? Are these, too, similar to those embedded in the Bush Doctrine? On American primacy and world leadership Obama has said this: "I reject the notion that the American moment has passed. I dismiss the cynics who say that this new century cannot be another when, in the words of President Franklin Roosevelt, we lead the world in battling immediate evils and promoting the ultimate good" (Obama 2007). Apparently, like his predecessor, President Obama does believe that there is evil in the world, and sometimes Americans must confront it. He has also said that "America cannot meet the threats of this century alone, but the world cannot meet them without America" (Obama 2007), which sounds very similar to the Clinton's administration's version, in which the primacy of America was "indispensable."

What of force used unilaterally? Obama had this to say: "no President should ever hesitate to use force—unilaterally if necessary—to protect ourselves and our vital interests when we are attacked or imminently threatened" (Obama 2007).

What of the Bush Doctrine's premise that when it comes to addressing the issue of catastrophic terrorism, the best defense is a good offense? Of that, Obama has said that he wants "a 21st century military to stay on the offense, from Djibouti to Kandahar," and, further, that "the ability to put boots on the ground will be critical in eliminating the shadowy terrorist networks we now face" (Obama 2007). That does not read as being too far removed from the Bush administration's National Security Strategy Statement, which said, "We must be prepared to stop rogue states and their terrorist clients before they are able to threaten or use weapons of mass destruction against the United States and our allies and friends" (National Security Strategy 2002, 14). When one considers President Obama's strong statement regarding Iran's efforts to develop WMD, the distance between the presidents' positions lessens considerably.

There is always the danger that Barack Obama's statements only reflect "what he and his advisers think Americans want to hear" (Kagan 2007). But they do stand as markers against which his national security policies and legacy will be judged.

It is clear that the Obama administration does not believe that the war on terror is over. President Obama so far has not dismantled the basic national security architecture developed by the Bush administration. What is not clear is how the new administration will respond to the key strategic challenges that it faces, what its strategic worldview and premises are, and how risk acceptant the administration will be when confronted with assessing any differences between its operational premises and the hard national security circumstances that it will face.

The question of whether the Bush Doctrine has helped increase or decrease threats to American national security cannot be answered with a simple yes or no. There are at least three strategically related but distinctive questions that must be addressed. Does the Bush Doctrine and its general set of policy premises provide a sound template for addressing the major concerns of America's post-9/11 security dilemma? Have the doctrine and its associated policies helped to secure the American homeland from further attack? And, finally, have the foreign policies pursued by the Bush administration, most notably the war in Iraq and the push for democratization, helped the national security position of the United States? At this point, the answers to all three questions must remain provisional, but let us at least begin to address them.

The question of whether the Bush Doctrine provides a viable framework for addressing American post-9/11 security concerns is a vital one. If it does not, the policies conducted under its rubric begin with a basic and perhaps irremediable flaw. I have argued throughout this chapter that the Bush Doctrine has strong conceptual framing and policy answers to the very basic post-9/11 strategy questions. No other "grand theory" put forward as a successor to the Bush Doctrine comes close to providing such a comprehensive framework. More importantly, no other theory provides plausible answers to the most bedeviling questions that face America with regard to its strategic policy. "Selective engagement" does not tell us where to draw the line and under what circumstances. Neo-isolationism is a dangerously passive policy when our enemies have vowed to continue their attacks.

Realist accommodation also has its dangers when your sworn enemies threaten to obliterate one of your primary allies—Israel—to gain hegemony over the vital Middle East region. None of the replacement strategies suggested really answers the question of when you should employ preventive or preemptive strategies, build policy-specific coalitions, or even go it alone. Of course, talk is preferable to fighting, when possible. Having many allies is preferable to having fewer allies. And having the respect and appreciation of the world community is preferable to its opposite, though not if obtained at the cost of being vulnerable. To date, replacement strategies for the Bush Doctrine have not advanced concrete policies that tell us how they will address, much less resolve, these issues.

On the second question, there can be little doubt that the United States is better prepared today than before the 9/11 attacks to respond to an unprecedented set of threats. That fact is a direct result of the Bush Doctrine and the policies developed as a result of it. This is not an argument that nothing more needs to be done; no defense is foolproof. However, the Bush administration put into operation a wide variety of initiatives designed to protect Americans at home. These included centralizing security efforts in the Department of Homeland Security, creating the position of national director of intelligence, improving security at airports and ports, and enhancing domestic surveillance of suspected terrorists.

And what of the Iraq war and democratization? Has the pursuit of those policies increased or decreased the overall threat to the United States? The very first step in answering this question is to ask whether it was prudent to remove Saddam Hussein instead of tolerating or trying to contain him. There is ample evidence that sanctions against him were eroding, and there was little international appetite for even more stringent policies. Moreover, a very strong case can be made for assessing Saddam Hussein as an extremely dangerous tyrant on psychological and strategic grounds and with regard to his poor judgment. So there remains a strong case for removing him that is difficult to measure factually against optimistic scenarios of containment.

The next question that arises is whether the Iraq war and efforts to develop a democratic government there after the removal of Saddam Hussein have increased or decreased the threat to the United States. Has the invasion of Iraq made matters worse? Some think so. Their view is that the Iraq war has diverted resources that could have been used to fight terrorism, that it has become a rallying cause for radical recruitment, that it inflamed elements of world opinion against the United States, and that it proved to be a theater of training for al-Qaida and allowed the movement to reconstitute itself.

Several counterarguments can be made to these. Under Bush, America and its allies dramatically bolstered their efforts against al-Qaida worldwide, even while fighting in Iraq. Any action against al-Qaida, whether centering on Iraq or not, would have been used against the United States for propaganda purposes. World opinion may well have been inflamed by anything short of American quiescence. Further, every terrorist effort, whether in Bali, Madrid, London, or elsewhere, provides terrorists with operational experience. Reconstitution, by replacing dead leaders and searching for new safe havens, is what groups do when they suffer losses during war. Such efforts demonstrate determination on their part and the need for equal determination on our part and are by no means a sign that we have "failed." All the admitted costs of battling al-Qaida and other insurgent groups in Iraq also must be seriously weighed against the costs of defeat.

There is no question that the war in Iraq and, to some degree, the Bush Doctrine in general have led to strong differences over American policy among some U.S. allies and inflamed Muslim sensibilities. They are also no doubt related to the continued erosion of the American image. Yet it is not at all clear that the presidency of Barack Obama will automatically make American national interests and those of its allies synonymous. One editorial noted that "at least three-quarters of people surveyed by the *Financial Times* in Britain, France, Germany, Italy and Spain (including 93 percent in France) believe that the new president will have 'a positive impact on international relations'" (*Washington Post* editorial 2009). Some anticipate a new American stance toward the world because Obama, during his campaign for president, repeatedly promised one. Some took this to mean that the new administration would abandon what they consider the various crusades of President Bush, among them his focus on expanding democracy's reach, the war against terror, and his skeptical stance toward international organizations and agreements.

Yet that same editorial noted that, "in Europe and elsewhere, there is a disconnect between Mr. Obama's popularity and receptiveness to his likely policies" (*Washington Post* editorial 2009). Just one example concerns the United States' repeated request to some of its NATO allies to increase their troop commitments in Afghanistan and change their rules of engagement to allow more robust offensive actions. A two-day meeting of NATO defense ministers produced no further commitments for President Obama than previous entreaties had produced for President Bush (Cienski 2009). It is an error to assume that harsh criticisms directed against U.S. policy during the Bush administration are almost all his fault.

The Iraq war has also contributed to the American public's fatigue at the early stages of what promises to be a long struggle, and it has also increased the partisan divisions underlying our efforts. It has fueled resentment and thus recruitment among the extremist Muslim elements in the Middle East, Western Europe, and elsewhere. And finally, the war has resulted in thousands of American soldiers being killed or wounded and cost billions of dollars in war-related expenditures. These are substantial and sobering costs.

However, while the situation in Iraq remains fragile, there is general agreement that in finally finding the right combination of effective doctrine, sufficient troop strength, and competent military commanders, American policy on Iraq has turned a corner. There is now a distinct possibility that Iraq will become a relatively moderate, pro-western ally, with no aspirations for regional hegemony at the expense of its neighbors, and a partner for the United States and its allies in the Middle East. This too must be added into the assessment.

One final element of President Bush's national security legacy that may emerge in time is the way that he endured and persisted under the most difficult of circumstances—a war that was not going well, the view that military setbacks were a direct result of decisions made by the administration with little patience for the fact that the alternative choices were also likely to result in grave difficulties, a collapse of public support, the united opposition of opponents in government and other major institutions at home and abroad, and the savage personal attacks of his many enemies. Throughout all of this, Bush kept his composure and his focus. He did not give up. He did not search for face-saving measures to cover over what he thought failure would cost America in terms of security. He made strong use of the shrinking set of political tools available to him as public support eroded and Democrats took over both houses of Congress. And by his maneuvering, he ensured that the new strategy put into place in Iraq would have some time to prove its merit.

It is doubtful that George W. Bush will ever be considered a great president. The Iraq war has simply been too costly and divisive. However, it certainly is possible that he will be seen as a consequential president. And it is even possible that the various elements of the Bush Doctrine will be seen more clearly and appreciated for the major and important contribution to American national security policy they represent.

If all of that happens, it just might be possible for Bush to emerge historically in a new narrative, as the president who—though despised by his enemies and abandoned by much of the public—determinedly carried on in the face of daunting setbacks to secure fundamental American national security interests and who was, in the long run, vindicated.

CONCLUSION
Bush's Legacy and the Limits of Ambition

STEVEN E. SCHIER

T he preceding chapters have revealed the George W. Bush presidency as unusual in the wide scope of its ambitions. The Bush administration's redefinition of foreign policy, spurred by 9/11, led to an audacious doctrine of preempting likely terrorist threats overseas and prosecution of an initially successful war with Iraq in 2003. Domestically, the White House voiced the agenda of its partisan base in pressing for successive tax cuts, even in the face of growing budget deficits, and conservative stands on judicial appointments and social issues such as same-sex marriage and abortion. In an attempt to expand his supportive coalition, Bush tacked toward the center in his approach to education, prescription drugs for seniors, and immigration. Just as Bush's innovations in foreign policy altered basic parameters of international relations, his approach to taxing and spending reshaped the politics of fiscal policy. These far-reaching changes are broadly consistent with the major project of the administration: the entrenchment of a Reagan-style conservative regime of military hawkishness and supply-side economics within the major institutions of national politics.

Did this big project succeed? The administration initially proved more successful in achieving its policy and electoral goals than most observers predicted at the time of Bush's inauguration. Still, many impediments stood in Bush's way. Several of the features of contemporary politics I mentioned in this volume's introduction served to frustrate Bush's plans. Many characteristics of "institutional thickening," in Stephen Skowronek's phrase, curbed Bush's ambitions. In this situation, according to Skowronek, "more has to be changed to break from the past, and those adversely affected by the changes will be able to put up more formidable resistance" (Skowronek 1997, 56).

Three aspects of institutional thickening were very prominent when Bush took office. First, party power was weaker than during the times of successful regime reconstruction (Lincoln and Franklin Roosevelt) or orthodox innovation (Polk and Theodore Roosevelt). At the beginning of the twenty-first century, it is much more difficult to install a durable political regime through long-term changes in mass party identification. The lasting success of any party's "governing team" is less electorally certain now. A major impediment to such aspirations is the large number of political independents whose allegiance seems beyond secure control of either party. These independents split evenly between Bush and his opponents in 2000 and 2004 but shifted strongly against Bush's party in the 2006 midterm elections (Abramson, Aldrich, and Rohde 2007, 280). Independents also voted Democratic in the 2008 presidential and congressional elections (Cable News Network 2008a; 2008b). Second, there was an even partisan balance in the House and Senate, which impedes ambitious legislative programs unless a president can command virtually unanimous support from congressional partisans. Bush was able to do this with his tax cuts and judicial nominees but failed notably at this on immigration and Social Security reform. Third, the proliferation of thousands of interest groups in Washington (Rauch 1999) complicates presidential initiatives in domestic policy to no end. Interest group battles over proposed oil drilling in the Arctic National Wildlife Refuge and the administration's faith-based initiative proposals in 2003, for example, stymied progress on these fronts for the Bush administration. Similar interest group conflicts scuttled immigration reform during Bush's second term.

Given these impediments, the scale of Bush's early political and policy successes is impressive. He benefited, as John J. Coleman and Kevin S. Price note in their chapter, from several GOP electoral victories beginning in 1994, which created opportunity for realignment into majority party status in the early twenty-first century. The GOP's ascendancy in the Senate in 2002 gave the party control of Congress (albeit narrowly), and, as Bertram Johnson notes in his chapter, Bush made much of this opportunity. Bush's sway over Congress from 2001 through 2006 was, arguably, broader than Bill Clinton ever enjoyed. Though Clinton in 1993–1994 had a Democratic-controlled Congress, his relations with Democratic lawmakers were continually rocky during his presidency. Several authors here attest to the strategic and tactical dexterity of the Bush administration in extending its political control in Washington during the early years of Bush's presidency.

The George W. Bush presidency frequently was tactically preemptive. John J. Coleman has defined preemptive tactics this way: "The preemptive president seeks to occupy a middle ground largely defined by the priorities of his opponents, but with enough independence from these opponents and his own party to put his distinctive stamp on policy" (Coleman 2000, 153). But Bush's tactical preemption was always partisan, not personal like Clinton's, as John F. Harris explains in his chapter. Moreover, it followed a series of GOP preemption tactics in election campaigns in the late 1990s in which the party effectively blurred the lines on differences with Democrats on key electoral issues like health care, the environment, and education. GOP candidates fought on the other party's turf because swing voters care about certain Democratic issues. By presenting their own answers to education reform and Medicare prescription drug coverage for seniors, Republican congressional candidates effectively neutralized their vulnerability on these issues with key voting groups. Bush did the same as president, proposing his own education and health care initiatives in order to blunt Democratic attacks.

Bush's success at tactical preemption waned as his presidency proceeded, for two reasons. First, the major issues of his presidency—the Iraq war and his economic policies—became the grounds for harsh partisan contestation, well described here by John J. Pitney Jr. Bush was never able to rise above the noise of this battle in order to change America's long-standing political alignments. Second, the Bush administration's own miscues, notably regarding the Iraq occupation and the response to Hurricane Katrina, became cannon fodder for his entrenched and emphatic opponents. As John F. Harris notes, Bush's partisan style left "too narrow a margin of support when events and political fortunes go astray." Because of this, Bush's mistakes imposed great political costs on his presidency.

Preemptive tactics, however, were not central to the Bush project of conservative regime restoration. Rather, they were concessions in order to win the wider war over the role of government, a war initially declared by Ronald Reagan. One strategically vital initiative of the Bush presidency concerned this project. A repeated resort to tax cuts fueled the GOP base. It also deprives the national government of funds for further spending expansion, a strategy attributed to the Reagan administration in the early 1980s (Schick 2003, 6). It also reflected the supply-side economic thinking that characterized much of the Reagan administration's economic policymaking. As I mentioned in my introduction, George W. Bush sought to be even more supply-side than Reagan or Bush's father by pressing for additional tax cuts in a time of growing budget deficits. A second strategically vital initiative involved stocking the federal courts with reliably conservative jurists. This was a top priority for Bush, his father, and Reagan, given the long-term impact of such appointments on the course of legal and constitutional interpretation. It was of high priority as well among the GOP base, particularly among social conservatives, as James L. Guth notes in this volume. George W. Bush can claim some success regarding both initiatives.

Less successful was Bush's innovation in foreign policy. Bush's highlighting of military power and its use reflected Reagan's consistent emphasis on "peace through strength," and it attracted strong support from fellow GOP partisans. The administration's military involvements in Iraq and Afghanistan, however, proved far more lengthy and costly in lives and dollars than did those of Reagan and Bush's father. His embrace of unitary executive theory from the Reagan administration in his conduct of wartime duties embroiled him in conflicts with Congress and in the federal courts, noted here by Peri E. Arnold and Nancy Maveety. Perhaps, as Stanley A. Renshon suggests in his chapter, Bush's policies in response to international terrorism will constitute a strong, innovative legacy of his presidency. The difficulties he encountered with his foreign policy, well documented in James M. McCormick's chapter, nevertheless imposed immediate political costs.

By appealing to groups of swing voters and keeping the conservative GOP base energized over judicial appointments, social conservatism, and economic and foreign policy, the Bush presidency pursued lasting conservative dominance of national politics. Operating, in Nicol C. Rae's terms, as a "partisan president in a partisan era" was a difficult undertaking, one that could have succeeded only in the context of more favorable conditions, both foreign and domestic. In part due to the administration's own performance, that context turned against Bush over the course of his presidency.

The Issue Context

Economic issues posed serious risks for the Bush presidency. After a 9/11-induced downturn in 2001–2003, the economy grew moderately and unemployment declined steadily from 6 percent in 2003 to 4.6 percent in 2007. Despite this, public support for Bush's economic management remained modest, due to partisan disapproval from Democrats and stagnation in real income growth (Joshi 2006; Greenhouse and Leonhart 2006). Throughout this time, Bush's preferred growth policy involved federal tax cuts. At the end of President Clinton's time in the White House, it seemed that balanced budgets had become the unquestioned basis of domestic economic policy, reducing policy debate to middle regulatory issues regarding health care, trade, and the environment (Schier 2000; Coleman 2000). The Bush presidency has turned that conventional wisdom upside down. Sluggish economic growth spawned budget deficits early in Bush's tenure. As John Frendreis and Raymond Tatalovich note in their chapter here, George W. Bush responded not by making a balanced budget the signal goal, as did his father, but by focusing on economic growth via supply-side tax cuts. The great likelihood, however, was that additional tax cuts would perpetuate lasting budget deficits. So it proved.

Large, persistent deficits limited the spending prospects for other policies, a boon for conservatives who had long sought to limit the size of the public sector (Hacker and Pierson 2007). The deficits were not accompanied by an overall reduction in government size but rather a redirection of spending to national defense, given the costs of the wars in Afghanistan and Iraq. Budget constraints also helped to prevent new spending desired by the Bush administration. The Bush administration's ambitious and expensive plan to partly privatize Social Security proved all but politically impossible in an era of already large deficits (Fletcher 2002). Perhaps the terror war will maintain political support for expansive defense spending, but the longer that large deficits persist, the more pressure will build on all federal spending, even by the Pentagon. A looming explosion in entitlement spending as baby boomers retire after 2010 will put great pressure on all forms of federal expenditures.

Orthodox innovators like Bush run the risk of innovating in a fashion that disrupts the partisan coalition that brought them to power: "The characteristic challenge is to mitigate or assuage those factional ruptures within the ranks of the establishment that will inevitably accompany even the most orthodox of innovations and agenda adaptations" (Skowronek 1997, 41). Bush's second round of tax cuts might at first glance seem among the "most orthodox" of innovations, deriving from the supply-side theories in vogue during the Reagan administration. The Republican coalition, however, includes traditional fiscal conservatives for whom a balanced budget is a primary goal. Bush's aspiring GOP successor, Senator John McCain of Arizona, voted against both Bush tax cuts on the grounds that they did not involve enough spending cuts. The Newt Gingrich–led Republican revolution in the 1995 Congress strongly pushed for a balanced budget, coming within one Senate vote of approving a balanced budget amendment to the Constitution. Those sentiments will die hard in the face of persistent deficits. The consequences of Bush's fiscal ambitions portend problems for the GOP coalition down the road.

The 9/11 attacks permanently altered the issue context of American foreign policy and, as crises do, handed President Bush a great political opportunity. The immediate response to the crisis made partisanship temporarily unfashionable in Washington and lessened institutional combat between the White House and the Democratic-controlled Senate over how to address the threat of international terrorism. Bush used this opportunity to define threats to national security and how to address them, an undertaking Bill Clinton had avoided during his eight years in power (McCormick 2000). Some of what Bush articulated then remains widely accepted in Washington politics: his views on the gravity of the threat and the need for enhanced domestic security and increased military spending. Far more controversial today, however, is the administration's emphasis on preempting potential terrorist threats in other nations, epitomized by the invasion of Iraq in 2003. James M. McCormick in this volume terms this approach "defensive realism": protecting America's national security interests through unprecedented military initiative. The record of the Iraq war—no weapons of mass destruction discovered, four thousand American lives lost and thousands more wounded, and an occupation far longer and more expensive than predicted by the Bush administration—makes the future of the Bush Doctrine of threat preemption quite doubtful.

Unilateralist premises underlie this approach to national security. Ivo Daalder and James Lindsay define the core assumption of the administration's foreign policy this way: "American primacy in the world is the key to securing America's interests—and that it is both possible and desirable to extend the unipolar moment of the 1990s into a unipolar era" (Daalder and Lindsay 2003b, 6). The administration's unipolar orientation proved domestically unpopular for Bush as the Iraq occupation continued. International diplomatic costs also became quite evident. The administration received international disparagement for its abandonment of the Kyoto global warming agreement, International Criminal Court, and Anti-Ballistic Missile Treaty. Opposition to the Iraq war by France, Russia, and Germany reflected their rejection of this expansive American foreign policy doctrine. The "coalition of the willing" in the Iraq war contained only three nations with significant military forces—the United States, Great Britain, and Australia—and worldwide opinion polls revealed that the Bush approach to the war was widely unpopular (Pew Research Center the People and the Press 2003). Bush himself, later in his presidency, regretted his peremptory manner in rejecting the Kyoto treaty as "too abrupt, too defiant and too negative without offering an alternative" (from Baker 2007).

Orthodox innovators often tap "the strength of the established regime most effectively when asserting American power in international affairs" (Skowronek 1997, 245). So it proved in Bush's case. The public had long viewed Republicans as more competent in the stewardship of foreign and defense policy, and Bush initially strengthened the conservative regime by "playing to type" after 9/11. The administration recognized prosecution of the terror war as crucial for regime legitimacy, but it also offered great political opportunities. Therefore, during the 2002 congressional elections, the administration highlighted national security issues, on which they had a great polling advantage, and did so with impressive results. By the end of Bush's tenure, however, Iraq and America's low international popularity had erased the GOP polling advantage on national security and foreign policy (Pew Research Center for the People and the Press 2008). Ultimately, successful negotiation of the international and domestic economic environment was the indispensable ingredient for restoration of the conservative regime with which Bush affiliated. In meeting these challenges, Bush encountered strong domestic and international opposition, and by 2008, his regime ambitions had suffered greatly.

The Two Pillars

In earlier works, I identified two pillars underlying the American political situation: global geopolitical hegemony and domestic economic prosperity (Schier 2000; 2004). In the period since George W. Bush took office in 2001, both pillars have been shaken, rearranging America's politics. The 9/11 attacks revealed international dangers far more clear and present than most commentators had imagined. The international politics of American security are far more central to presidential governance than they appeared before 9/11. With terrorism the larger threat, the Bush administration deemphasized the multilateralist approach of the Clinton administration. This pattern pre-dated 9/11; by that time, the administration had already withdrawn from the Kyoto accord on global warming and the International Criminal Court (Daalder and Lindsay 2003b).

Whether the Bush administration's deemphasis of multilateralism will be carried over into future administrations depends on whether Bush's political legacy and the progress of the war on terror improve over time. These two fates are entangled. By 2003, the Bush administration had achieved considerable public approval through its aggressive response to the terror threat in Afghanistan and Iraq. The troublesome military occupation of Iraq, however, eroded popular support for Bush's foreign policy. Whatever the costs of his foreign policy in terms of international diplomacy and domestic public opinion, Bush did solidify his domestic political coalition around this approach. But that coalition dwindled to include only a majority of fellow GOP partisans by 2008, as John Kenneth White and John J. Zogby demonstrate in their chapter. Bush's experience made multilateral talk and action a far more likely priority for his presidential successor.

The second pillar, domestic economic prosperity, is far less stable than it appeared to be in 2000. At that time, healthy levels of economic growth produced a booming stock market and a federal government bulging with budget surpluses. Real GDP growth slowed after 2000 and unemployment rose to more than 6 percent by mid-2003. Bush, in response, was as bold as in foreign policy. In his recurrent advocacy of tax cuts, he sought to rearrange parameters of fiscal policy discussion as dramatically as he transformed foreign policy. The priority of tax cuts downgraded traditionally hallowed budget balancing as a policy goal. A successful economic stimulus through additional tax cuts proved tactically brilliant for the 2004 election, but the ensuing deficits left unsolved the looming problem of growing entitlement spending obligations for the future. Despite reductions in unemployment and steady economic growth during most of his presidency, Bush received little credit from the public for his economic stewardship. Democrats challenged his policies with zest following their takeover of Congress in 2006. A drastic economic slump in 2008, entailing the collapse of the financial and housing sectors, derailed GOP prospects for retaining the White House. Bush was unable to establish a political superiority for the GOP in the realm of economic policy. Instead, his presidency ended by ushering in the largest economic downturn in decades.

George W. Bush's presidency will ultimately be judged by how well the president took control of the events that transpired on his watch. This administration's definition of "control" was a very expansive one. The goal was the resurrection of "political time" through the installation of a lasting conservative political regime. This sort of restoration has not achieved completion since FDR entrenched the New Deal coalition during the 1930s. It is a historically big task. Bush ran the risk of fracturing his own coalition, as many regime articulators have done before, his own father and Lyndon Johnson among them in recent history. George W. Bush managed to keep his GOP coalition together during his presidency but notably failed to expand it. Meanwhile, his ambitious, controversial, and problematic foreign and economic policies energized his Democratic opponents and helped engender their victories in the 2006 and 2008 elections.

Bush thus proved not to be on top of his "political time," thus raising the question of whether any president can so succeed. Perhaps we are in an era of "permanent preemption" in which scrappy survival is the best outcome a president can hope for. Or maybe the GOP reversals of recent years portend a "disjunction" involving "a president affiliated with a set of established commitments that have in the course of events been called into question as failed or irrelevant responses to the problems of the day" (Skowronek 1997, 39), as was the case with Herbert Hoover and Jimmy Carter. If political time has persisted, it has not been kind to Bush's leadership, and Democrats have a stellar chance to become America's majority party for years to come. At this writing, the emergence of such a durable majority coalition seems less likely than an extended period of even partisan balance coupled with "sticky" national institutions resistant to the construction of any lasting partisan regime. In Skowronek's terms, permanent preemption, not political time, seems to be with us. If political time has vanished, George W. Bush's fate is one that many of his successors—Democrat and Republican—will share.

WORKS CITED

ABC News/*Washington Post* poll. 1991. October 24–29.

———. 2001. September 25–27. http://www.pollingreport.com.

———. 2007. January 16–19.

Abraham, Henry A. 1999. *Justices, presidents, and senators: A history of the U.S. Supreme Court appointments from Washington to Clinton.* Lanham, MD: Rowman & Littlefield.

Abramson, Paul R., John H. Aldrich, and David W. Rohde. 2007. *Change and continuity in the 2004 and 2006 elections.* Washington, DC: Congressional Quarterly Press.

Ackerman, Bruce. 2001. The court packs itself. *American Prospect,* February 12.

Aldrich, John H. 1995. *Why parties? The origins and transformation of party politics in America.* Chicago: University of Chicago Press.

Aldrich, John H., and David W. Rohde. 1997. The transition to Republican rule in the House: Implications for theories of congressional politics. *Political Science Quarterly* 112, no. 4: 541–67.

———. 2000. The consequences of party organization in the House: The role of the majority and minority parties in conditional party government. In *Polarized politics: Congress and the president in a partisan era,* ed. J. R. Bond and R. Fleisher. Washington, DC: CQ Press.

Allen, John L. 2003. In Rome, Novak makes case for war. *National Catholic Reporter,* February 21.

Allison, Wes, and Anita Kumar. 2005. What Terri's Law cost the Republicans in Congress. *St. Petersburg Times,* December 18, 1A.

Altman, Daniel. 2003. Divided economic advice and the lure of politics. *New York Times,* April 12.

American Bar Association. 2006. Task force on presidential signing statements and the separation of powers doctrine. August. http://www.abanet.org/op/signingstatements/.

American Enterprise Institute. 2001. A discussion with Karl Rove. December 11. Transcript.

American Research Group poll. 2007. November 9–12.

Andrews, Edmund L. 2002a. White House aides push for 50% cut in dividend taxes. *New York Times*, December 25, A1.

———. 2002b. Steel tariffs put G.O.P. on the spot in campaigns. *New York Times*, August 24.

———. 2006. Interior official assails agency for ethics slide. *New York Times*, September 14, 1.

———, and Jackie Calmes. 2008. In a bold action, Fed cuts key rate to virtually zero. *New York Times*, December 17.

Antle, W. James. 2006. Exit stage right: Democratic votes, conservative victories? *American Conservative*, October 23. http://www.amconmag.com/2006/2006_10_23/article1.html.

Apple, R.W., Jr. 2000. The 43rd president. *New York Times*, December 14.

———. 2001. President seen to gain legitimacy. *New York Times*, September 16.

Arnold, Peri. 1998. *Making the managerial presidency: Comprehensive executive reorganization, 1904–1996*. Lawrence: University Press of Kansas.

Associated Press/IPSOS. 2008. April 7–9. http://www.pollingreport.com.

Auster, Elizabeth. 2002. Bush aide always rushing, but job gives him a rush. *Cleveland Plain Dealer*, March 3.

Ayers, Edward L. 1992. *The promise of the New South: Life after Reconstruction*. New York: Oxford University Press.

Babington, Charles. 2007. More Bush-Congress court fights likely. Associated Press, *New Orleans Times-Picayune*, August 6.

Baer, Kenneth S. 2000. *Reinventing Democrats: The politics of liberalism from Reagan to Clinton*. Lawrence: University Press of Kansas.

Baker, James A., III, and Lee H. Hamilton. 2006. *The Iraq Study Group report*. New York: Vintage Books.

Baker, Peter. 2007. In Bush's final year, the agenda gets greener. *Washington Post*, December 29, A01.

———, and Charles Babington. 2005. Role of religion emerges as an issue. *Washington Post*, October 13.

———, and Jim VandeHei. 2005. Bush's political capital spent, voices in both parties suggest. *Washington Post*, May 31, A2.

———. 2006. More White House staff changes coming; Bolten plans overhaul to widen Bush's circle, tighten West Wing operations. *Washington Post*, April 1, A06.

Balz, Dan. 2003. Kerry raps Bush policy on postwar Iraq. *Washington Post*, July 11, A1, A6.

———. 2005. Social Security stance risky, Democrats told. *Washington Post*, March 8, A3.

Barber, James David. 1992. *The presidential character: Predicting performance in the White House*. 4th ed. Upper Saddle River, NJ: Prentice Hall.

Barnes, James A. 2001. Bush's insiders. *National Journal,* June 23.

Barone, Michael. 2001. *The almanac of American politics.* Washington: National Journal Group.

———. 2002. Whose majority? *National Review* 54 (December 9): 30–34.

———. 2008. It's the partisan economy, stupid. *The American,* January 23.

———, and Richard E. Cohen. 2005. *The almanac of American politics.* Washington, DC: National Journal Group.

Barshay, Jill. 2001. Bush starts a strong record of success with the Hill. *Congressional Quarterly Weekly Report* 60:110–12.

———. 2003. Can tax cuts pay their way? *Congressional Quarterly Weekly Report,* January 11, 67.

———, and Alan K. Ota. 2003. White House tax cut package gets a wary reception. *Congressional Quarterly Weekly Report,* January 11, 68.

Barstow, David. 2008. Behind analysts, Pentagon's hidden hand. *New York Times,* April 20.

Bartels, Larry. 1998. Where the ducks are: Voting power in a party system. In *Politicians and party politics,* ed. John Geer. Baltimore: Johns Hopkins University Press.

———. 2005. Homer gets a tax cut: Inequality and public policy in the American mind. *Perspectives on Politics* 3, no. 1: 15–32.

Bartlett, Bruce. 2006. *Impostor: How George W. Bush bankrupted America and betrayed the Reagan Legacy.* New York: Doubleday.

Baumgartner, Jody C. 2007. *The American vice presidency reconsidered.* Westport, CT: Praeger.

———, Peter L. Francia, and Jonathan S. Morris. 2008. A clash of civilizations? The influence of religion on public opinion of U.S. foreign policy in the Middle East. *Political Research Quarterly* 61:171–79.

BBC World Service Poll. 2005. http://www.pipa.org/OnlineReports/BBCworldpoll/Analysis01_19_05pdf.

Beaumont, Thomas. 2003. Gephardt takes aim at Bush. *Des Moines Register,* July 14, 1B.

Becker, Elizabeth. 2003. W.T.O. rules against U.S. on steel tariff. *New York Times,* March 27.

Becker, Jo, and Barton Gellman. 2007. A strong push from backstage. *Washington Post,* June 26.

Bell, Jeffrey. 2008. The politics of a failed presidency. *Weekly Standard,* March 17.

Bellantoni, Christina. 2009. Obama's exec orders have loopholes. *Washington Times,* February 2.

Bendavid, Naftali. 2007. *The thumpin': How Rahm Emanuel and the Democrats learned to be ruthless and ended the Republican revolution.* New York: Doubleday.

Benedetto, Richard. 2006. GOP: "We were wrong" to play racial politics. *USA Today,* July 14. http://www.usatoday.com/news/washington/2005-07-14-GOP-racial-politics_x.htm.

Berke, Richard L. 1998. The Gore guide to the future. *New York Times Magazine,* February 22, 47.

——, and Frank Bruni. 2001. Crew of listing Bush ship draws Republican scowls. *New York Times,* July 2.

Berry, Jeffrey. 1999. *The new liberalism: The rising power of citizen groups.* Washington, DC: Brookings Institution Press.

Binder, Sarah A., and Steven S. Smith. 1997. *Politics or principle: Filibustering in the United States Senate.* Washington, DC: Brookings Institution Press.

Black, Amy E., Douglas L. Koopman, and David K. Ryden. 2004. *Of little faith: The politics of George W. Bush's faith-based initiatives.* Washington, DC: Georgetown University Press.

Blogger Central. 2008. Top 100 blogs. May 1. http://technorati.com/pop/blogs.

Bork, Robert. 1989. Foreword to *The fettered presidency: Legal constraints on the executive branch,* ed. L. Gordon Crovitz and Jeremy Rabkin. Washington, DC: American Enterprise Institute.

Brant, Martha. 2002. West Wing story: More than a war of words. *Newsweek Online,* April 12. http://archives.newsbank.com.

Brinkley, Douglas. 1998. *Unfinished presidency: Jimmy Carter's journey beyond the White House.* New York: Viking.

Broder, David. 2006. For Bush, a world of worry; abundant trouble, but few solutions. *Washington Post,* July 13.

Brooks, David. 2003. Democrats go off the cliff. *Weekly Standard,* June 30.

Brownstein, Ronald. 2001. Bush's legislative strategy: No concessions upfront; style mirrors the approach he used with lawmakers in Texas. *Milwaukee Journal Sentinel,* January 8, 4A.

——. 2002. Loyal to the core, Bush knows how to play to the crucial outsiders. *Los Angeles Times,* May 27. http://www.latimes.com/la-000037395may27.column.

——. 2003. Bush moves by refusing to budge: Seen as a centrist while governor of Texas, he is testing the limits of consensus as president. *Los Angeles Times,* March 2.

——. 2007. *The second civil war: How extreme partisanship has paralyzed Washington and polarized America.* New York: Penguin.

Bumiller, Elisabeth. 2001. Bush keeps a grip on presidential papers. *New York Times,* November 2.

——. 2002. Bush signs bill aimed at fraud in corporations. *New York Times,* July 31.

——. 2003. The president's team changes some players but not its game plan. *New York Times,* January 5.

——. 2007. *Condoleezza Rice: An American life.* New York: Random House.

——, and Carl Hulse. 2005. Bush Court choice ends bid after attack by conservatives. *New York Times,* October 28.

Burke, John P. 1992. *The institutional presidency.* Baltimore: Johns Hopkins University Press.

————. 2004. *Becoming president: The Bush transition, 2000–2003.* Boulder, CO: Lynne Rienner, 2004.

Burnham, Walter Dean. 1970. *Critical elections and the mainsprings of American politics.* New York: Norton.

————. 1996. Realignment lives: The 1994 earthquake and its implications. In *The Clinton presidency: First appraisals,* ed. Colin Campbell and Bert A. Rockman. Chatham, NJ: Chatham House.

Bush, George W. 1999a. A distinctly American internationalism. Speech delivered at the Ronald Reagan Presidential Library, November 19. http://www.georgew bush.com/speeches/foreignpolicy/foreignpolicy.asp.

————. 1999b. A period of consequences. Speech delivered at The Citadel, September 23. http://www.georgewbush.com/speeches/defense/citadel.asp.

————. 2001a. Address to a joint session of Congress and the American people. September 20. http://www.whitehouse.gov/news/releases/2001/09/20010920-8 .html.

————. 2001b. President's remarks at National Day of Prayer and Remembrance. September 14. http://www.whitehouse.gov/news/releases/2001/09/20010914-2 .html.

————. 2001c. Remarks at a town hall meeting in Orlando, Florida. December 4. *Weekly Compilation of Presidential Documents,* 37: 49, 1743–54. Washington, DC: Government Printing Office.

————. 2001d. Speech at the ruins of the World Trade Center, New York City. *Weekly Compilation of Presidential Documents,* September 14. Washington, DC: Government Printing Office.

————. 2002a. President's remarks at the United Nations General Assembly. September 12. http://www.whitehouse.gov/news/releases/2002/09/2002/09.

————. 2002b. Statement on signing the Bipartisan Campaign Reform Act of 2002. *Weekly Compilation of Presidential Documents,* March 29. Washington, DC: Government Printing Office.

————. 2003a. The president discusses the future of Iraq. February 16. http//www . whitehouse.gov/news/releases/2003/02.

————. 2003b. President says Saddam Hussein must leave Iraq within 48 hours. March 17. http://www.whitehouse.gov/news/releases/2003/03/20030317-7.html.

————. 2003c. Remarks at the 2003 President's Dinner. *Weekly Compilation of Presidential Documents,* May 21. Washington, DC: Government Printing Office.

————. 2003d. Remarks by the president at Whitehall Palace, London, England. http://www.whitehouse.gov/news/releases/2003/11/20031119-1.html, accessed February 12, 2006.

————. 2005a. President sworn-in to second term. http://www.whitehouse.gov/ news/releases/2005/01/print/20050120-1.html.

————. 2005b. State of the Union address. http://www.whitehouse.gov/news/ releases/2005/01/print/20050202-11.html.

————. 2006. Statement on signing Department of Defense emergency supplemental appropriation. *Weekly Compilation of Presidential Documents*, January 2. Washington, DC: Government Printing Office.

———. 2007. Remarks following a meeting with the House Republican Conference. *Weekly Compilation of Presidential Documents*, January 26. Washington, DC: Government Printing Office.

———. 2008a. Interview with Charles Gibson, ABC News. December 1.

———. 2008b. President Bush discusses Iraq. April 10. http://www.whitehouse.gov.

Cable News Network. 2008a. National presidential exit poll. http://www.cnn.com/ELECTION/2008/results/president/.

———. 2008b. U.S. House national exit poll. http://www.cnn.com/ELECTION/2008/results/polls/#USH00p1.

Calabresi, Steven G. 1994. The vesting clauses as power grants. *Northwestern University Law Review* 88:1377–1405.

———, and Kevin Rhodes. 1992. The structural Constitution: Unitary executive, plural judiciary. *Harvard Law Review* 105–6:1153–1216.

Calmes, Jackie. 2008. Both sides of the aisle see more regulation. *New York Times,* October 14. http://www.nytimes.com/2008/10/14/business/economy/14regulate.html?_r=1&scp=1&sq=Both%20sides%20of%20the%20aisle%20see%20more%20regulation&st=cse.

Campbell, David E., ed. 2007. *A matter of faith: Religion in the 2004 presidential election*. Washington, DC: Brookings Institution Press.

Carnes, Tony. 2000. A presidential hopeful's progress. *Christianity Today,* October 20.

Carp, Robert A., Kenneth L. Manning, and Ronald Stidham. 2005. The decision-making behavior of George W. Bush's judicial appointees: Far-right, conservative, or moderate? In *Judicial politics: Readings from* Judicature, ed. E. Slotnick. Washington, DC: CQ Press.

Carter, Jimmy. 1979. Address to the nation. Washington, DC, July 15.

———. 2005. *Our endangered values: America's moral crisis*. New York: Simon and Schuster.

Carville, James, Stan Greenberg, and Robert Shrum. 2002. Re: Enron. Democracy Corps memorandum, January 28. http://www.greenbergresearch.com/articles/1618/1413_Enron_report.pdf.

CBS News exit poll. 1976. November 2.

———. 1980. August 2–7.

———. 2003. April 11–13. http://www.pollingreport.com.

———. 2008. March 28–April 2. http://www.pollingreport.com.

Ceaser, James W. 1979. *Presidential selection: Theory and development*. Princeton: Princeton University Press.

———, and Andrew E. Busch. 2001. *The perfect tie: The true story of the 2000 presidential election*. Lanham, MD: Rowman & Littlefield.

———, Andrew E. Busch, and John J. Pitney Jr. 2009. *Epic journey: The 2008 elections and American politics*. Lanham, MD: Rowman & Littlefield.

Chafee, Lincoln. 2008. *Against the tide: How a compliant Congress empowered a reckless president.* New York: Thomas Dunne.

Chait, Jonathan. 2007. *The big con: The true story of how Washington got hoodwinked and hijacked by crackpot economics.* New York: Houghton Mifflin.

Cheney, Richard. 2002. Dangers and opportunities. Speech delivered before the Veterans of Foreign Wars convention, Nashville, TN, August 26. http://www.nationalreview.com/document/document082702.asp, accessed May 7, 2009.

———. 2005. Vice president's remarks to the traveling press. http://www.whitehouse.gov/news/releases/2005.

Cienski, Jan. 2009. NATO allies spurn US troops plea. *Financial Times,* February 19.

Clarke, David. 2007. Search for a supplemental compromise. *CQ Weekly,* May 7, 1348.

Clausewitz, Carl von. 1976. *On war.* Trans. and ed. Michael Howard and Peter Paret. Princeton: Princeton University Press.

Clayton, Cornell. 2005. The Bush presidency and the New Right constitutional regime. *Law & Courts Newsletter* 15 (winter): 6–14.

Clyne, Meghan. 2005. President Bush is "our Bull Connor," Harlem's Rep. Charles Rangel claims. *New York Sun,* September 23. http://www2.nysun.com/article/20495?page_no=1.

CNN. 2008a. Broadcast, November 29.

———. 2008b. Transcript of first presidential debate. September 26. http://www.cnn.com/2008/POLITICS/09/26/debate.mississippi.transcript/, accessed February 10, 2009.

———. 2008c. Transcript of second McCain-Obama debate. October 7. http://www.cnn.com/2008/POLITICS/10/07/presidential.debate.transcript/#cnnSTCText, accessed February 1, 2009.

CNN/Opinion Research Corporation poll. 2008. December 19–21.

CNN/*USA Today*/Gallup poll. 2005. July 22–24.

Cochran, John. 2002. Bush readies strategies for legislative success in 2003. *Congressional Quarterly Weekly Report,* December 14, 3235–39.

Coleman, John J. 2000. Clinton and the party system in historical perspective. In *The postmodern president: Bill Clinton's legacy in U.S. politics,* ed. Steven E. Schier. Pittsburgh: University of Pittsburgh Press.

Collier, Kenneth E. 1997. *Between the branches: The White House Office of Legislative Affairs.* Pittsburgh: University of Pittsburgh Press.

Comiskey, Michael. 2004. *Seeking justices: The judging of Supreme Court nominees.* Lawrence: University Press of Kansas.

———. 2006. The Supreme Court appointment process: Lessons from filling the Rehnquist and O'Connor vacancies. Paper presented at the annual meeting of the American Political Science Association, Philadelphia, PA, August 31–September 3.

Commission on Presidential Debates. 2000. The second Gore-Bush presidential debate. October 11. http://www.debates.org/index.html.

Confessore, Nicholas. 2003. Welcome to the machine. *Washington Monthly*, July–August.

Congressional Quarterly Almanac (2003). 2004. Partisanship defines the session. Washington DC: CQ Press.

Congressional Research Service. 2008. Report to Congress. The cost of Iraq, and the global war on terror operations since 9/11. February 8.

Cook, Charlie. 2001. The phases of Bush. *National Journal*, December 18.

———. 2007. The coming challenge. *National Journal*, October 9.

Cooper, Philip J. 2002. *By order of the president: The use and abuse of executive direct action*. Lawrence: University Press of Kansas.

Corrado, Anthony, and Katie Varney. 2007. The role of national party committees in financing congressional campaigns. Washington, DC: Campaign Finance Institute. http://cfinst.org/books_reports/pdf/Corrado_Party-2006_Final.pdf.

Corzine, Jon. 2006. Governor Corzine delivers weekly radio address. February 28. http://www.democrats.org/a/2006/02/governor_corzin.php.

Cottle, Michelle. 2007. Liddy's fall from grace. *New Republic*, February 19–26, 8.

CQ Weekly. 2008a. 2008 vote studies: Presidential support. December 15, 3322.

———. 2008b. Presidential position votes rise. January 14, 135.

———. 2008c. Presidential support background. January 14, 137.

CQ Weekly Online. 2006. 2008 White House contender: Chuck Hagel. November 6, 2926. http://library.cqpress.com/cqweekly/weeklyreport109-000002398071, accessed August 23, 2008.

Crabtree, Susan. 2003. Rove vows to GOP: No triangulation. *Roll Call*, February 3.

Crutsinger, Martin. 2003. Speculation rises on Greenspan's future. *Washington Times*, February 16. http://customwire.ap.org/dynamic/stories/G/GREENSPANS_FUTURE?SITE=DCTMS&SE.

Cummings, Jeane. 2006. Redistricting: Home to roost. How Republicans' gerrymandering efforts may have backfired. *Wall Street Journal*, November 10, A6.

Daalder, Ivo H., and James Lindsay. 2003a. Bush's foreign policy revolution. In *The George W. Bush presidency: Early appraisals*, ed. Fred I. Greenstein. Baltimore: Johns Hopkins University Press.

———. 2003b. The Bush revolution: The remaking of America's foreign policy. Paper presented at the conference "The George W. Bush Presidency: An Early Assessment," Woodrow Wilson School, Princeton University, April 25–26.

———. 2003c. *America unbound: The Bush revolution in foreign policy*. Washington, DC: Brookings Institution Press.

Dahl, Robert A. 1990. The myth of the presidential mandate. *Political Science Quarterly* 105, no. 4: 355–72.

Davies, Philip John. 2003. A new Republican generation? *Contemporary Review* 282 (March): 139–46.

Davis, Sue. 2008. *Corwin and Peltason's* Understanding the Constitution. 17th ed. Belmont, CA: Thomas Wadsworth.

DeFrank, Thomas M. 2009. Ex-VP Cheney outraged Bush didn't grant "Scooter" Libby full pardon. *New York Daily News*, February 17.

———, and Kenneth R. Bazinet. 2006. GOP set to unlock the vault; vote machine even knows your beer. *New York Daily News,* October 27, 26.

DeGregorio, William A. 1997. *The complete book of US presidents.* 5th ed. New York: Random House.

Democratic National Committee. 2006. DNC launches new ad campaign for "tough and smart" immigration reform. April 19. http://www.democrats .org/a/2006/04/dnc_launches_ne_7.php.

Derby, Samara Kalk. 2004. Blue state of mind: Area therapists are flooded with post-election depression. *Capital Times* (Madison, WI), November 13, 1A.

Desmond, Joan Frawley. 2006. The war room: What we have learned about confirming good judges. *Crisis,* September, 22–31.

Deutsch, Karl W. 1966. External influences on the internal behavior of states. In *Approaches to comparative and international politics,* ed. R. Barry Farrell. Evanston, IL: Northwestern University Press.

Dewar, Helen, and Dan Balz. 2001. Democrats fault Bush tactics on tax cut. *Washington Post,* March 10, A4.

DeYoung, Karen. 2006. *Soldier: The life of Colin Powell.* New York: Vintage.

Dingell, John. 2002. Who helped Cheney? *New York Times,* January 24.

Dionne, E. J., Jr. 2000. The Republicans' stealth agenda. *Washington Post,* October 27.

———. 2001. Harder than McKinley. *Washington Post,* April 2. http://www .washingtonpost.com/wp-dyn/A4875-2002Apr.

———, and William Kristol, eds. 2001. *Bush v. Gore: The court cases and the commentary.* Washington, DC: Brookings Institution Press.

Dolan, Chris J., John Frendreis, and Raymond Tatalovich. 2008. *The Presidency and economic policy.* Lanham, MD: Rowman & Littlefield.

———. Forthcoming. A presidential economic scorecard: Performance and perception. *PS: Political Science & Politics.*

Domke, David. 2004. *God willing? Political fundamentalism in the White House, the "war on terror," and the echoing press.* London: Pluto Press.

———, and Kevin Coe. 2008. *The God strategy: How religion became a political weapon in America.* New York: Oxford University Press.

Dorrien, Gary. 2003. Axis of one. *Christian Century* 120 (March 8): 30–35.

Dorval, Chris, and Andrea LaRue. 2006. Immigration fails as wedge issue for GOP: Succeeds in expanding base for Democrats. November 8. http://www .immigration2006.org.

Draper, Robert. 2007. *Dead certain: The presidency of George W. Bush.* New York: Free Press.

Dubose, Lou, Jan Reid, and Carl Cannon. 2003. *Boy genius: Karl Rove, the brains behind the remarkable political triumph of George W. Bush.* New York: Public Affairs.

du Pont, Pete. 2006. Bleak house. *Opinion Journal* (online). October 24.

Easterbrook, Gregg. 2008. Life is good, so why do we feel so bad? *Wall Street Journal,* June 13, A15.

Eastland, Terry. 1992. *Energy in the executive: The case for a strong presidency.* New York: Free Press.

Edison Media Research and Mitofsky International. 2004. Exit poll, November 2.

———. 2008. Exit poll, November 4.

Edsall, Thomas B. 2002. GOP touts war as campaign issue. *Washington Post,* January 19, A02.

Edwards, George C., III. 1989. *At the margins: Presidential leadership of Congress.* New Haven: Yale University Press.

———. 2007. *Governing by campaigning: The politics of the Bush presidency.* New York: Pearson Longman.

Eggen, Dan. 2008. Bush stresses judicial nominations. *Washington Post,* October 7.

Eisgruber, Christopher L. 2007. Umpires, ideologues, and justices: How to evaluate Supreme Court nominees. Paper presented at the workshop for the Program in Law and Public Affairs, Woodrow Wilson School, Princeton University, April 2.

Epstein, Lee, and Jeffrey A. Segal. 2005. *Advice and consent: The politics of judicial appointments.* New York: Oxford University Press.

Evans, Roland, and Robert D. Novak. 1968. *Lyndon B. Johnson: The exercise of power.* New York: New American Library.

Executive Order: Ensuring Lawful Interrogations. 2009a. January 22. http://www .whitehouse.gov/the_press_office/EnsuringLawfulInterrogations/, accessed January 30, 2009.

Executive Order: Review and Disposition of Individuals Detained at the Guantánamo Bay Naval Base and Closure of Detention Facilities. 2009b. January 22. http://www.whitehouse.gov/the_press_office/ClosureOfGuantanamoDetentionFacilities/, accessed January 30, 2009.

Executive Order: Review of Detention Policy Options. 2009c. January 22. http:// www.whitehouse.gov/the_press_office/ReviewofDetentionPolicyOptions/, accessed January 30, 2009.

Fagan, Amy. 2003. Estimates on Medicare hit $2 trillion; prescription-drug benefit promises "huge costs." *Washington Times,* December 9, A1.

———, and Stephen Dinan. 2006. DeLay declares "victory" in war on budget fat. *Washington Times,* September 14, A1.

Farhi, Paul, and James V. Grimaldi. 2004. GOP won with accent on rural and traditional. *Washington Post,* November 4, A01.

Federal Document Clearing House. 2000. Vice President Gore and Governor Bush participate in second presidential debate sponsored by the Presidential Debate Commission. *Federal Document Clearing House Political Transcripts,* October 11.

Feldman, Noah. 2008. When judges make foreign policy. *New York Times Magazine,* September 25.

Fineman, Howard. 2003. Bush and God. *Newsweek,* March 10.

Fiorina, Morris P., Samuel J. Abrams, and Jeremy C. Pope. 2005. *Culture war? The myth of a polarized America.* New York: Pearson Longman.

————. 2006. *Culture war? The myth of a polarized America.* 2nd ed. New York: Pearson Education.

Fletcher, Michael A. 2002. Social Security changes put on the back burner. *Washington Post,* November 11. http://www.washingtonpost.com/ac2/wp-dyn/A36577-2002Nov10?la.

————. 2005. Bush immigration plan meets GOP opposition. *Washington Post,* January 2, A6.

Foner, Eric. 2006. He's the worst ever. *Washington Post,* December 3.

Ford, Gerald R. 1974. Address to the nation. Washington, DC, September 8.

Fortier, John C., and Norman J. Ornstein. 2003. Congress and the Bush presidency. Paper presented at the conference, "The Bush Presidency: An Early Assessment," Woodrow Wilson School, Princeton University, April 25–26.

————, eds. 2007. *Second-term blues: How George W. Bush has governed.* Washington, DC: American Enterprise Institute and Brookings Institution Press.

Fournier, Ron. 2006. Approval ratings plunge for Bush, Republican Party. Associated Press, May 6. http://www.boston.com/news/nation/washington/articles/2006/05/06/approval_ratings_plunge_for_bush_republican_party/.

Frankovic, Kathleen. 2009. Bush's popularity reaches historic lows. CBSNews.com, January 15. http://www.cbsnews.com/stories/2009/01/15/opinion/pollpositions/main4724068.shtml?source=search_story.

Frendreis, John, and Raymond Tatalovich. 2000. Accuracy and bias in macroeconomic forecasting by the administration, the CBO, and the Federal Reserve Board. *Polity* 32 (summer): 623–32.

Froomkin, Dan. 2005. A polling free-fall among blacks. *Washingtonpost.com,* October 13. http://www.washingtonpost.com/wp-dyn/content/blog/2005/10/13/BL2005101300885.html.

Frum, David. 2003a. It's his party. *New York Times,* January 5.

————. 2003b. *The right man: The surprise presidency of George W. Bush.* New York: Random House.

————. 2008. *Comeback: Conservatism that can win again.* New York: Doubleday.

Fukuyama, Francis. 2006. *America at the crossroads: Democracy, power, and the neoconservative legacy.* New Haven: Yale University Press.

Gallup poll. 1952. February 9–14.

————. 1968. August 7–12.

————. 1973. August 2, October 5–8.

————. 1974. August 16–19, September 27–30.

————. 1977. February 4–7.

————. 1979. June 1–4.

————. 1991. February 28–March 3.

————. 1992. October 22–23.

————. 2008a. Majority still favors timetable for troop withdrawal. Princeton, New Jersey: Gallup poll. http://www.gallup.com/poll/104398/Majority-Still-Favors-Timetable-TroopWithdrawal.aspx?version=print.

————. 2008b. Comprehensive presidential approval ratings for the modern

presidency. Specific figures available at http://www.gallup.com/poll/1723/
Presidential-Job-Approval-Depth.aspx?version=print.

Garbus, Martin. 2003. How the Federalist Society is capturing the federal courts. *American Prospect,* March 1. http://www.prospect.org/cs/articles.

Gellman, Barton. 2008. *Angler: The Cheney vice presidency.* New York: Penguin.

———, and Jo Becker. 2007. A different understanding with the president. *Washington Post,* June 24.

Gentile, Carmen. 2008. Six suspects will be tried for a third time. *New York Times,* April 24.

Gershkoff, Amy, and Shana Kushner. 2005. Shaping public opinion: The 9/11-Iraq connection in the Bush administration's rhetoric. *Perspectives on Politics,* 3:3.

Gerson, Michael J. 2007. *Heroic conservatism: Why Republicans need to embrace America's ideals.* New York: HarperOne.

Gerstein, Josh. 2009. Obama defends Bush-era secrets. *Politico,* February 21.

Gillespie, Ed. 2006. Populists beware! The GOP must not become an anti-immigration party. *Wall Street Journal Online,* April 2. http://www.opinionjournal.com/editorial/feature.html?id=110008173.

Ginsberg, Benjamin, and Martin Shefter. 2002. *Politics by other means: Politicians, prosecutors, and the press from Watergate to Whitewater.* 3rd ed. New York: Norton.

Goldberg, Jeffrey. 2006. The believer. *New Yorker,* February 13–20, 56–69.

Goldman, Sheldon, Elliot Slotnick, Gerard Gryski, and Gary Zuk. 2001. Clinton's judges: Summing up the legacy. *Judicature* 78:28–34.

Goldman, Sheldon, Elliot Slotnick, Gerard Gryski, Gary Zuk, and Sara Schiavoni. 2005. W. Bush remaking the judiciary: Like father like son? In *Judicial politics: Readings from* Judicature, ed. E. Slotnick. Washington, DC: CQ Press.

Goldsmith, Jack. 2007. *The terror presidency: Law and justice inside the Bush administration.* New York: Norton.

Goldstein, Amy, and Dan Eggen. 2007. Immigration judges often picked based on GOP ties. *Washington Post,* June 11.

Goodstein, Laurie. 2002. Evangelical figures oppose religious leaders' broad antiwar sentiment. *New York Times,* October 5.

———. 2003. Divide among Jews leads to silence on Iraq war. *New York Times,* March 15.

Gordon, Michael R., and General Bernard E. Trainor. 2006. *Cobra II: The inside story of the invasion and occupation of Iraq.* New York: Pantheon Books.

Gordon, Philip. 2006. The end of the Bush revolution. 85 *Foreign Affairs* (July–August): 75–86.

Green, John C. 2006. Faithful voters. *Christian Century,* December 12, 9–10.

———. 2009. What happened to the values voter? Believers and the 2008 election. *First Things,* March, 42–48.

———, Lyman A. Kellstedt, Corwin E. Smidt, and James L. Guth. 2007. How the faithful voted: Religious communities and the presidential vote. In *A matter of faith: Religion in the 2004 presidential election,* ed. David E. Campbell. Washington, DC: Brookings Institution Press.

Greenhouse, Steven. 2006. Labor goes door to door to rally suburban voters. *New York Times,* October 8, 20.

———, and David Leonhart. 2006. Real wages fail to match a rise in productivity. *New York Times,* August 28, A1. http://www.nytimes.com/2006/08/28/business/28wages.html?_r=1&scp=1&sq=real+wages+fail+to+match+a+rise+in+productivity&st=nyt&oref=slogin.

Greenstein, Fred. 2002. The changing leadership of George W. Bush: A pre- and post-9/11 comparison. *Presidential Studies Quarterly* 32 (June): 387–96.

———. 2004. The changing leadership of George W. Bush: A pre- and post-9/11 comparison. In *The domestic sources of American foreign policy: Insights and evidence,* ed. Eugene R. Wittkopf and James M. McCormick. 4th ed. Lanham, MD: Rowman & Littlefield.

Guth, James L. 2000. Clinton, impeachment and the culture wars. In *The postmodern presidency: Bill Clinton's legacy in U.S. politics,* ed. Steven E. Schier. Pittsburgh: University of Pittsburgh Press.

———. 2004. George W. Bush and religious politics. In *High risk and big ambition: The presidency of George W. Bush,* ed. Steven E. Schier. Pittsburgh: University of Pittsburgh Press.

———. 2006. Religion and foreign policy attitudes: The case of the Bush Doctrine. Paper presented at the annual meeting of the Midwest Political Science Association, Chicago, April 20–22.

———. 2009. Religion in the 2008 election. In *The American elections of 2008,* ed. Janet Box-Steffensmeier and Steven E. Schier. Lanham, MD: Rowman & Littlefield.

———, Lyman A. Kellstedt, Corwin E. Smidt, and John C. Green. 2006. Religious influences in the 2004 presidential election. *Presidential Studies Quarterly* 36, no. 2: 223–42.

Hacker, Jacob S. 2006. *The great risk shift: The assault on American jobs, families, health care, and retirement—and how you can fight back.* New York: Oxford University Press.

Hacker, Jacob, and Paul Pierson. 2005a. Abandoning the middle. *Perspectives on Politics,* 3, no. 1: 33–53.

———. 2005b. *Off center: The Republican revolution and the erosion of American democracy.* New Haven: Yale University Press.

———. 2007. Tax politics and the struggle over activist government. In *The transformation of American politics: Activist government and the rise of conservatism,* ed. Theda Skocpol and Paul Pierson. Princeton, NJ: Princeton University Press.

Halperin, Mark, and John F. Harris. 2006. *The way to win: Taking the White House in 2008.* New York: Random House.

Hamburger, Tom, and Peter Wallsten. 2005. *One party country: The Republican plan for dominance in the 21st century.* New York: John Wiley and Sons.

Hamilton, Alexander, John Jay, and James Madison. n.d. *The Federalist*. New York: Modern Library.

Hargreaves, Mary W. M. 1985. *The presidency of John Quincy Adams*. Lawrence: University Press of Kansas.

Harper's Magazine. 2009. Harper's Index. January, 11.

Harris, Gardiner. 2007. Nominee for surgeon general testifies in Senate. *New York Times*, July 12.

Harris, John F. 2000. A clouded mirror: Bill Clinton, polls and the politics of survival. In *The postmodern presidency: Bill Clinton's legacy in U.S. politics*, ed. Steven E. Schier. Pittsburgh: University of Pittsburgh Press.

Harwood, John. 2003. Bush faces Republican fire on postwar costs for Iraq. *Wall Street Journal*, March 19. http://online.wsj.com/article/0,,capital_journal,00 .html.

———. 2005. Republicans splinter on Bush agenda. *Wall Street Journal*, April 7. http://online.wsj.com/public/article/SB111282698216100132-0GnQKkV_guNprR __U8NEr4aX3G8_20050507.html?mod=blogs.

Hayes, Stephen F. 2007. *Cheney: The untold story of America's most powerful and controversial vice president*. New York: HarperCollins.

Hecht, Marie B. 1972. *John Quincy Adams: A personal history of an independent man*. New York: Macmillan.

Hendra, Tony. 2006. A Thanksgiving prayer for Dick Cheney's heart—and a few other favorite things. Huffington Post, November 26. http://www.huffington post.com/tony-hendra/a-thanksgiving-prayer-for_b_34780.html.

Herszenhorn, David. 2008. Congress votes for a stimulus of $168 billion. *New York Times*, February 8.

Hibbs, Douglas A., Jr. 1987. *The American political economy: Macroeconomics and electoral politics*. Cambridge, MA: Harvard University Press.

Higa, Liriel, and John Donnelly. 2007. War supplemental heads to veto. *CQ Weekly*, April 30, 1266.

HillaryClinton.com. 2007. Accessed television commercial, September 11.

Hoogenboom, Ari. 1995. *Rutherford B. Hayes: Warrior and president*. Lawrence: University Press of Kansas.

Hook, Janet. 2003a. Bush plan to end dividend tax in for changes. *Los Angeles Times*, February 2, 30.

———. 2003b. Senate limits tax cut, triggers GOP feud. *Los Angeles Times*, April 12, 1.

———. 2007. Bush boxed in his congressional foes. *Los Angeles Times*, December 21. http://www.latimes.com/news/nationworld/nation/la-na-congress21dec21 ,0,6679238.story?coll=la-home-center.

Hoover, J. Nicholas. 2006. Democrats used databases in election wins over GOP. *Information Week*, November 15. http://www.informationweek.com/news/ showArticle.jhtml?articleID=194400260&subSection=.

Hudson, Deal W. 2008. *Onward, Christian soldiers: The growing political power of Catholics and evangelicals in the United States*. New York: Simon and Schuster.

Hunter, James D. 1991. *Culture wars: The struggle to define America.* New York: Basic Books.

iCasualties.org. 2009. http://icasualties.org/Iraq/index.aspx, accessed February 28, 2009.

Ip, Greg, and John D. McKinnon. 2007. Bush reorients rhetoric, acknowledges income gap. *Wall Street Journal,* March 26.

Jacobs, Lawrence R., and Robert Y. Shapiro. 2000. *Politicians don't pander: Political manipulation and the loss of democratic responsiveness.* Chicago: University of Chicago Press.

Jacobson, Gary C. 2000. Party polarization in national politics: The electoral connection. In *Polarized politics: Congress and the president in a partisan era,* ed. Jon R. Bond and Richard Fleisher. Washington, DC: CQ Press.

———. 2007. *A divider, not a uniter: George W. Bush and the American people.* New York: Pearson Longman.

———. 2008. *A divider, not a uniter: George W. Bush and the American people; The 2006 election and beyond.* New York: Pearson Longman.

Jelen, Ted. 2007. Life issues. In *Religion and the Bush presidency,* ed. Mark J. Rozell and Gleaves Whitney. New York: Palgrave Macmillan.

Jervis, Robert. 1976. *Perception and misperception in international politics.* Princeton, NJ: Princeton University Press.

Jones, Charles O. 2003. Capitalizing on position in the George W. Bush presidency: Partisan patterns and Congress in a 50-50 government. Paper presented at the conference, "The George W. Bush Presidency: An Early Assessment," Woodrow Wilson School, Princeton University, April 25–26.

Jones, Jeffrey. 2006. Ratings of Cheney, Rumsfeld sinking to new depths. Gallup poll, May 10. http://www.gallup.com/poll/22726/Ratings-Cheney-Rumsfeld-Sinking-New-Depths.aspx.

———. 2007. Low trust in federal government rivals Watergate era levels. Gallup poll, press release, September 26.

Joshi, Jitendra. 2006. Poor poll ratings vex Bush's economic czars. Agence France Presse, August 18.

Judis, John. 2002. Soft sell. *New Republic,* November 11, 12.

———, and Ruy Teixeira. 2002. *The emerging democratic majority.* New York: Scribner.

Kagan, Robert. 2007. Obama the interventionist. *Washington Post,* April 29, B07.

Kamarck, Elaine C. 2006. Assessing Howard Dean's fifty state strategy and the 2006 midterm elections. *The Forum* 4 (issue 3, article 5). http://www.bepress.com/forum/vol4/iss3/art5.

Kane, Paul. 2008. West Wing aides cited for contempt. *Washington Post,* February 15, A4.

Kasniunas, Nina T., and Jack E. Rossotti. 2007. President George W. Bush and judicial restraint: Accommodating religion. In *Religion and the Bush presidency,* ed. Mark J. Rozell and Gleaves Whitney. New York: Palgrave Macmillan.

Kaufman, Chaim. 2004. Threat inflation and the failure of the marketplace of ideas: The selling of the Iraq war. *International Security* 29:1, 4–48.

Keen, Judy. 2005. Why Bush wants personal retirement accounts. *USA Today,* February 3, A1.

Keller, Bill. 2003. The radical presidency of George W. Bush. *New York Times,* January 26.

Kelley, Christopher. 2005. Rethinking presidential power—The unitary executive and George W. Bush's presidency. Paper presented at the annual meeting of the Midwest Political Science Association, Chicago, April 7.

Kellman, Laurie. 2007. Senate subpoenas White House, Cheney's office. Associated Press, *New Orleans Times-Picayune,* June 28.

Kengor, Paul. 2004a. Cheney and vice presidential power. In *Considering the Bush presidency,* ed. Gary L. Gregg II and Mark J. Rozell. New York: Oxford University Press.

———. 2004b. *God and George W. Bush.* New York: Regan Books.

Kernell, Samuel. 1978. Explaining presidential popularity: How ad hoc theorizing, misplaced emphasis, and insufficient care in measuring one's variables refuted common sense and led conventional wisdom down the path of anomalies. *American Political Science Review* 72 (June): 506–22.

———. 1997. *Going public: New strategies of presidential leadership.* 3rd ed. Washington, DC: Congressional Quarterly Press.

Kessler, Glenn. 2001. House panel approves key part of Bush tax cut plan. *Washington Post,* March 2, A1.

———, and Dana Milbank. 2001. Tax cut compromise close enough, Bush says. *Washington Post,* April 7, A9.

Kessler, Ronald. 2004. *A matter of character: Inside the White House of George W. Bush.* New York: Sentinel.

Kettl, Donald F. 2003. *Team Bush.* New York: McGraw-Hill.

Key, V. O. 1955. A theory of critical elections. *Journal of Politics* 17:3–18.

———. 1959. Secular realignment and the party system. *Journal of Politics* 21:198–210.

Kirkpatrick, David D. 2006. Alito clears final hurdle for confirmation to Court. *New York Times,* January 31.

Kleppner, Paul. 1979. *The third electoral system, 1853–1892: Parties, voters, and political cultures.* Chapel Hill: University of North Carolina Press.

Kornblut, Anne. 2001. Tax cut bill wins final approval. *Boston Globe,* May 27, A1.

Krehbiel, Keith. 2000. Party discipline and measures of partisanship. *American Journal of Political Science* 44, no. 2: 206–21.

Krent, Harold J. 2008. From a unitary to a unilateral presidency. *Boston University Law Review* 88, no. 2: 523–560.

Krugman, Paul. 2008. Deliverance or diversion? *New York Times,* March 3. http://www.nytimes.com/2008/03/03/opinion/03krugman.html?_r=1&oref=slogin.

Kuo, David. 2006. *Tempting faith: An inside story of political seduction.* New York: Free Press.

Kurtz, Howard. 2005. Suddenly, everyone's a critic. *Washington Post,* October 3, C1.

———. 2008. Ad watch. *Washington Post,* October 17.

Labaton, Stephen, and Edmund L. Andrews. 2009. Bailout plan: $2.5 trillion and a strong U.S. hand. *New York Times,* February 11.

Lacy, Mark. 2001. Bush deploys charm on Daschle in pushing tax cut. *New York Times,* March 10, A7.

Lake, Eli. 2008. Small change. *New Republic,* March 4.

Lakoff, George. 2004. *Don't think of an elephant: Know your values and frame the debate; The essential guide for progressives.* White River Junction, VT: Chelsea Green.

Lambro, Donald. 2005. Social Security reform "on the table." *Washington Times,* June 6, A4.

Lancaster, John. 2001. Senate Republicans try to regroup. *Washington Post,* May 26, A18.

Langer, Gary. 2005. Poll: No role for government in Schiavo case. ABC News, March 21. http://abcnews.go.com/Politics/PollVault/story?id=599622.

———. 2008. Bush defeats Truman. ABC News, April 14. http://abcnews.go.com/PollingUnit/story?id=4652847&page=1.

Layman, Geoffrey. 2001. *The great divide: Religious and cultural conflict in American party politics.* New York: Columbia University Press.

Leal, David L., Stephen A. Nuño, Jongho Lee, and Rodolfo O. de la Garza. 2008. Latinos, immigration, and the 2006 midterm elections. *PS: Political Science and Politics* 41 (April): 309–17.

Lemonick, Michael. 2006. *Time* poll: Registered Republicans less enthusiastic about voting than Democrats. *Time,* November 5. http://www.time.com/time/nation/article/0,8599,1555024,00.html.

Leonnig, Carol D. 2006. Secret court's judges were warned about NSA spy data. *Washington Post,* February 9.

Lewis, Andrew. 2008. The role of the solicitor general in church-state cases within the Clinton and Bush administrations. Paper presented at the Fourth Biennial Symposium on Religion and Politics, the Henry Institute, Calvin College, April 24–26.

Lewis, Neil A. 2006. Bush blocked ethics inquiry, official says. *New York Times,* July 19, A14.

———. 2007. A prosecution tests the definition of obscenity. *New York Times,* September 28.

Lichtblau, Erich. 2006. Bush defends legality of domestic spy program. *New York Times,* January 2.

Lieberman, Robert C. 2000. Political time and policy coalitions: Structure and agency in presidential power. In *Presidential power: Forging the presidency for the twenty-first century,* ed. Robert Y. Shapiro, Martha Joynt Kumar, and Lawrence R. Jacobs. New York: Columbia University Press.

Lincoln, Abraham. 1861. First inaugural address. March 4. http://www.yale.edu/
  lawweb/avalon/presiden/inaug/lincoln1.htm.
Lindsay, D. Michael. 2007. *Faith in the halls of power.* New York: Oxford University
  Press.
Lithwick, Dahlia. 2007. Justice's holy hires. *Washington Post,* April 8.
Lloyd, Laura. 2008. Closet Catholic in the White House? *National Catholic
  Reporter,* May 2, 10.
Lochhead, Carolyn. 2006. Immigration bill faces tough foe. *San Francisco
  Chronicle,* May 27, A8.
Louis Harris and Associates poll. 1974. September 23–27.
———. 1988. November 11–14.
Lowenstein, Roger. 2007. The inequality conundrum. *New York Times,* June 10.
———. 2008. The education of Ben Bernanke. *New York Times Magazine,* January
  20.
Lowi, Theodore J. 1985. *The personal president: Power invested, promise unfulfilled.*
  Ithaca, NY: Cornell University Press.
Mahler, Jonathan. 2008. After the imperial presidency. *New York Times Magazine,*
  November 9.
Maltese, John Anthony. 1995. *The selling of Supreme Court nominees.* Baltimore:
  Johns Hopkins University Press.
———. 2003. Confirmation gridlock: The federal judicial appointments process
  under Bill Clinton and George W. Bush. *Journal of Appellate Practice and
  Process* 5:1–28.
Mann, James. 2004. *Rise of the vulcans: The history of Bush's war Cabinet.* New
  York: Viking.
Mann, Thomas, and Norman J. Ornstein, eds. 2000. *The permanent campaign
  and its future.* Washington, DC: American Enterprise Institute and Brookings
  Institution Press.
———. 2006. *The broken branch: How Congress is failing America and how to get it
  back on track.* New York: Oxford University Press.
Marcus, Robert D. 1971. *Grand Old Party: Political structure in the Gilded Age,
  1880–1896.* New York: Oxford University Press.
Marsh, Charles. 2007. *Wayward Christian soldiers: Freeing the gospel from political
  captivity.* New York: Oxford University Press.
Massaro, John. 1990. *Supremely political: The role of ideology and presidential
  management in unsuccessful Supreme Court nominations.* Albany: State
  University of New York Press.
Maveety, Nancy. 2008. *Queen's court: Judicial power in the Rehnquist era.* Lawrence: University Press of Kansas.
Mayer, Jane. 2008. *The dark side: The inside story of how the war on terror turned
  into a war on American ideals.* New York: Doubleday.
Mayer, William G. 1998. Mass partisanship, 1946–1996. In *Partisan approaches to
  postwar American politics,* ed. Byron E. Shafer. Chatham, NJ: Chatham House.

————. 2001. The presidential nominations. In *The election of 2000,* ed. Gerald Pomper. New York: Chatham House.

Mayhew, David R. 2002. *Electoral realignments: A critique of an American genre.* New Haven: Yale University Press.

————. 2005. Wars and American politics. *Perspectives on Politics* 3, no. 3: 473–94.

Mazzetti, Mark, and David E. Sanger. 2009. Obama expands missile strikes inside Pakistan. *New York Times,* February 21.

McCarty, Nolan, Keith T. Poole, and Howard Rosenthal. 2006. *Polarized America: The dance of ideology and unequal riches.* Cambridge, MA: MIT Press.

McCormick, James M. 2000. Clinton and foreign policy: Some legacies for a new century. In *The postmodern presidency: Bill Clinton's legacy in U.S. politics,* ed. Steven E. Schier. Pittsburgh: University of Pittsburgh Press.

————. 2006. The war on terror and contemporary U.S.-European relations. *Politics and Policy* 34 (June): 426–50.

McCormick, Richard P. 1975. Political development and the second party system. In *The American party systems: Stages of political development,* ed. William Nisbet Chambers and Walter Dean Burnham. 2nd ed. New York: Oxford University Press.

McDonald, Forrest. 1994. *The American presidency: An intellectual history.* Lawrence: University Press of Kansas.

McManus, Doyle. 2003. The world casts a critical eye at Bush's style of diplomacy. *Los Angeles Times,* March 3.

McQuilken, Marisa. 2009. A shocking look at Bush's civil rights boss. *Legal Times,* January 19. http://www.law.com/jsp/article.jsp?id=1202427625817.

Mead, Walter Russell. 2005. *Power, terror, peace and war: America's grand strategy in a world at risk.* New York: Vintage Books.

Meyerson, Harold. 2002. Dems in the dumps. *American Prospect* 13 (December 16): 22–24.

Mieczkowski, Yanek. 2001. *The Routledge historical atlas of presidential elections.* New York: Routledge.

Milbank, Dana. 2001. *Smashmouth: Two years in the gutter with Al Gore and George W. Bush.* New York: Basic Books.

————, and Ellen Nakashima. 2001. Bush team has "right" credentials; conservative picks seen eclipsing even Reagan's. *Washington Post,* March 25, A1.

————, and Eric Pianin. 2001. Energy task force works in secret. *Washington Post,* April 16.

Milkis, Sidney. 1993. *The presidents and the parties.* New York: Oxford University Press.

————, and Michael Nelson. 1999. *The American presidency: Origins and development, 1776–1998.* Washington, DC: CQ Press.

Miller, Greg. 2009. Obama lets CIA keep controversial renditions tool. *Chicago Tribune,* January 31.

Moe, Terry M., and William G. Howell. 1999. The presidential power of unilateral action. *Journal of Law, Economics & Organization* 15, no. 1: 132–79.

Mollison, Andrew. 2001. House finds "common ground" on education. *Atlanta Journal and Constitution,* March 23, 12A.

Moore, David W. 2001. Top ten Gallup presidential approval ratings. Gallup press release, September 24. http://www.gallup.com/poll/releases/pr030701.asp.

Morin, Richard, and Claudia Deane. 2006. In Abramoff case, most see evidence of wider problem. *Washington Post,* January 10, A7.

Morris, Dick. 2003. W's triangulation. Front Page Magazine.com, June 25.

Mueller, John. 2008. The Iraq syndrome. In *The domestic sources of American foreign policy: Insights and evidence,* ed. Eugene R. Wittkopf and James M. McCormick. 5th ed. Lanham, MD: Rowman & Littlefield.

Muirhead, Russell, Nancy L. Rosenblum, Daniel Schlozman, and Francis X. Shen. 2005. Religion in the 2004 presidential election. In *Divided states of America: The slash and burn politics of the 2004 presidential election,* ed. Larry Sabato. New York: Longman.

Mulkern, Ann. 2004. When advocates become regulators. *Denver Post,* May 23.

Murphy, Cullen, and Todd S. Purdum. 2009. Farewell to all that: An oral history of the Bush White House. *Vanity Fair,* February.

Murray, Shailagh. 2005. Storms show a system out of balance; GOP Congress has reduced usual diet of agency oversight. *Washington Post,* October 5, A21.

Nagel, Paul C. 1997. *John Quincy Adams: A public life, a private life.* New York: Knopf.

Nagourney, Adam. 2003. Bush, looking to his right, shores up support for support in 2004. *New York Times,* national ed., June 30, A1.

———. 2006a. Democrats try to use Katrina as G.O.P. used 9/11. *New York Times,* April 22. http://www.nytimes.com/2006/04/22/us/22dems.html.

———. 2006b. Democratic hard chargers try to return party to power. *New York Times,* April 30. http://www.nytimes.com/2006/04/30/washington/30dems.html.

———. 2006c. In campaign ads for Democrats, Bush is the star. *New York Times,* September 17. http://www.nytimes.com/2006/09/17/us/politics/17ads.html.

———. 2007. A year still to go, and presidential politics have shifted already. *New York Times,* November 4.

———, and Janet Elder. 2006. Foley scandal is hurting GOP's image, poll finds. *New York Times,* October 9. http://www.nytimes.com/2006/10/09/us/politics/10pollcnd.html.

———, and Richard W. Stevenson. 2003. Bush's aides plan late sprint in '04. *New York Times,* April 22, A1.

———, Richard W. Stevenson, and Neil A. Lewis. 2006. Glum Democrats can't see halting Bush on courts. *New York Times,* January 15.

Nather, David. 2001a. Conferees make little headway on biggest issues in education bill. *CQ Weekly,* August 4, 1926.

———. 2001b. Education bill passes in House with strong bipartisan support. *CQ Weekly,* May 26, 1256.

———. 2005a. War of words intensifies. *CQ Weekly Online,* November 21, 3120.

http://library.cqpress.com/cqweekly/weeklyreport109-000001975373, accessed August 23, 2008.

———. 2005b. GOP nominee 2008: Let the speculation begin. *CQ Weekly Online,* October 24, 2834. http://library.cqpress.com/cqweekly/weeklyreport109 -000001925236, accessed August 23, 2008.

———. 2007a. Waging war on the surge. *CQ Weekly Online,* January 15, 170–77. http://library.cqpress.com/cqweekly/weeklyreport110-000002428775, accessed August 23, 2008.

———. 2007b. New handshake, same grip. *CQ Weekly,* December 16.

———, and John Cochran. 2002. Still-thin edge leaves GOP with a cautious mandate. *CQ Weekly,* November 9, 2888–93.

National Conference of State Legislatures. 2008. Same sex marriage, civil unions, and domestic partnerships. October. http://www.ncsl.org/programs/cyf/ samesex.htm.

National Security Strategy Statement of the United States of America. 2002. September 17. http://www.whitehouse.gov/nsc/nss.html.

NBC. 2006. Transcript of *Meet the Press.* June 11.

Neal, Terry. 2000. Bush anticipates an "emotional moment." *Washington Post,* July 30, A20.

Nelson, Michael. 1988a. Choosing the vice president. *PS: Political Science and Politics* 21 (fall): 858–68.

———. 1988b. *A heartbeat away.* Washington, DC: Brookings Institution Press.

———. 1998. Bill Clinton and the politics of second terms. *Presidential Studies Quarterly* 28, no. 4: 786.

———. 2001. The election: Ordinary politics, extraordinary outcome. In *The elections of 2000,* ed. Michael Nelson. Washington, DC: CQ Press.

Neustadt, Richard E. 1990. *Presidential power and the modern presidents: The politics of leadership from Roosevelt to Reagan.* New York: Free Press.

Newport, Frank. 2006. Americans continue to call Iraq involvement a mistake. July 28. http://www.gallup.com/poll/23923/Americans-Continue-Call-Iraq -Involvement-Mistake.aspx.

———. 2008. Bush job approval at 28%, lowest of his administration. Gallup Online, April 11. http://www.gallup.com/poll/106426/Bush-Job-Approval-28 -Lowest-Administration.aspx.

New York Times. 2000. Transcript of debate between Vice President Gore and Governor Bush. October 4, A30.

———. 2009. President Bush's final news conference. January 12.

New York Times editorial. 2001. Environmental rollbacks. April 8.

———. 2006. Senators in need of a spine. January 26.

Nie, Norman H., Sidney Verba, and John R. Petrocik. 1979. *The changing American voter.* Enlarged ed. Cambridge, MA: Harvard University Press.

Nitschke, Lori. 2001. The elusive middle ground. *CQ Weekly,* March 3, 467.

Nixon, Richard M. 1969. Inaugural address. Washington, DC, January 20.

———. 1974. State of the Union address. Washington, DC, January 30.

———. 1991. *In the arena.* New York: Pocket Books.

Nohlgren, Stephen. 2005. As words change, so does public opinion. *St. Petersburg Times,* February 4, 1A.

Noonan, Peggy. 2008. Breaking up is hard to do. *Wall Street Journal,* January 25.

Norris, Floyd. 2002. Bush facing 2 challenges: S.E.C. choice and economy. *New York Times,* November 7.

Novak, Robert D. 2005. Bush: Winning ugly. April 4. http://www.townhall.com/columnists/RobertDNovak/2005/04/04/bush_winning_ugly.

Obama, Barack. 2007. Remarks to the Chicago Council on Global Affairs. April 23. http://www.thechicagocouncil.org/dynamic_page.php?id=64, accessed March 1, 2009.

———. 2008. Acceptance speech. Democratic national convention, Denver, August 28.

Oldmixon, Elizabeth, Beth Rosenson, and Kenneth Wald. 2005. Conflict over Israel: The role of religion, race, party and ideology in the U.S. House of Representatives, 1997–2002. *Terrorism and Political Violence* 17:407–26.

Olson, Laura R., and Adam L. Warber. 2008. Belonging, behaving, and believing. *Political Research Quarterly* 61:192–204.

Opinion Research Corporation poll. 2007. March 9–11.

Oppel, Richard A., Jr. 2009. Strikes in Pakistan underscore Obama's options. *New York Times,* January 24.

Ornstein, Norman J. 2001. Relations with Congress. *PS: Political Science and Politics* 35, no. 1: 47–50.

Ota, Alan K. 2003. Tax cut package clears amid bicameral rancor. *Congressional Quarterly Weekly Report,* May 24, 61:1245–49.

Page, Susan. 2001. Cheney takes "backseat" in a strong way. *USA Today,* November 16.

Parmet, Herbert S. 1997. *George Bush: The life of a Lone Star Yankee.* New York: Simon & Schuster.

Pear, Robert, and Robin Toner. 2003. House Committee approves drug benefits for Medicare. *New York Times,* June 18, A1.

People for the American Way. Right wing organizations. http://www.pfaw.org/pfaw/general/default.aspx?oid=4287, accessed July 20, 2008.

Perine, Keith. 2009. Justice Department again defends Bush on state secrets. *CQ Politics,* February 20.

Peters, Ronald M., Jr. 1990. *The American Speakership: The office in historical perspective.* Baltimore: Johns Hopkins University Press.

Peterson, Mark. 1990. *Legislating together: The White House and Capitol Hill from Eisenhower to Reagan.* Cambridge, MA: Harvard University Press.

Pew Forum. 2003. Different faiths, different messages. Pew Forum on Religion and Public Life, Washington DC, March 19.

———. 2008. U.S. religious landscape survey. Pew Forum on Religion and Public Life, Washington DC, June 23.

Pew Global Attitudes Project. 2003. Views of a changing world: June 2003. Washington, DC: Pew Research Center for the People & the Press.

———. 2006. America's image slips, but allies share U.S. concerns over Iran. Washington, DC: Pew Research Center for the People & the Press.

Pew Research Center for the People and the Press. 2003. America's image further erodes, Europeans want weaker ties. http//people-press.org/reports/display .php3/ReportID=175.

———. 2006. Economy now seen through partisan prism. News release, January 24.

———. 2008. Survey report: Obama has the lead, but potential problems, too. http://people-press.org/reports/display.php3?PageID=1259.

Pew Research Center poll. 2008. December 3–7.

Pfiffner, James P. 2007. George W. Bush and the abuse of executive power. Paper prepared for presentation at the American Political Science Association Convention, Chicago, August 29–September 2.

Pianin, Eric. 2001. Tax cuts may bust budget. *Washington Post,* May 26.

Pillar, Paul R. 2008. Intelligence, policy, and the war in Iraq. In *The domestic sources of American foreign policy: Insights and evidence,* ed. Eugene R. Wittkopf and James M. McCormick. 5th ed. Lanham, MD: Rowman & Littlefield.

Pious, Richard M. 1979. *The American presidency.* New York: Basic Books.

Pitney, John J., Jr. 2000. Clinton and the Republican Party. In *The postmodern presidency: Bill Clinton's legacy in U.S. politics,* ed. Steven E. Schier. Pittsburgh: University of Pittsburgh Press.

Pollich, Diana. 2002. A divided electorate. *CBSNews.com.* November 6. http:// www.cbsnews.com/stories/2002/11/06/politics/main528295.shtml.

Pollster.com. 2008. http://www.pollster.com/polls/us/jobapproval-bus.php, accessed December 28, 2008.

Ponnuru, Ramesh. 2006. How to win by losing. *New York Times,* September 13, A23.

———. 2007. One term, with feeling. *National Review,* October 24.

Preston, Thomas, and Margaret G. Hermann. 2004. Presidential leadership style and the foreign policy advisory process. In *The domestic sources of American foreign policy: Insights and evidence,* ed. Eugene R. Wittkopf and James M. McCormick. 4th ed. Lanham, MD: Rowman & Littlefield.

Price, Kevin S. 2002. The partisan legacies of preemptive leadership: Assessing the Eisenhower cohorts in the U.S. House. *Political Research Quarterly* 55 (September): 609–32.

Priest, Dana. 2006. Rethinking embattled tactics in terror war. *New York Times,* July 11, A1.

———. 2009. Bush's war on terror comes to a sudden end. *Washington Post,* January 23, A01.

Purdum, Todd S., and Patrick E. Tyler. 2002. Top Republicans break with Bush on Iraq strategy. *New York Times,* August 16. http://www.nytimes.com.

Rae, Nicol C. 1998. *Conservative reformers: The Republican freshmen and the lessons of the 104th Congress.* Armonk, NY: M. E. Sharpe.

————. 2000. Clinton and the Democrats: The president as party leader. In *The postmodern presidency: Bill Clinton's legacy in U.S. politics,* ed. Steven E. Schier. Pittsburgh: University of Pittsburgh Press.

————, and Colton C. Campbell. 2004. *Impeaching Clinton: Partisan strife on Capitol Hill.* Lawrence: University Press of Kansas.

Rauch, Jonathan. 1999. *Government's end: Why Washington stopped working.* New York: Public Affairs.

Ray, Julie. 2003. Gallup brain: Opinions on partial-birth abortions. Gallup poll, July 8. http://www.gallup.com/poll/8791/Gallup-Brain-Opinions-PartialBirth-Abortions.aspx.

Reagan, Ronald. 1980. Acceptance speech. Republican national convention, Detroit, July 17.

Remini, Robert V. 1999. *Andrew Jackson.* New York: HarperCollins.

Renshon, Stanley A. 1998. *The psychological assessment of presidential candidates.* New York: Routledge.

————. 2004. *In his father's shadow: The transformations of George W. Bush.* New York: Palgrave Macmillan.

————. 2008. Assessing the personality of George W. Bush. In *The domestic sources of American foreign policy: Insights and evidence,* ed. Eugene R. Wittkopf and James M. McCormick. 5th ed. Lanham, MD: Rowman & Littlefield.

Rice, Condoleezza. 2000. Promoting the national interest. *Foreign Affairs* 79 (January–February): 45–62.

Richert, Catharine. 2008. Party unity: United we stand opposed. *CQ Weekly,* January 14, 143.

Robinson, Carin, and Clyde Wilcox. 2007. The faith of George W. Bush: The personal, practical, and political. In *Religion and the American presidency,* ed. Mark J. Rozell and Gleaves Whitney. New York: Palgrave Macmillan.

Rogers, David. 2008. Bush unveils new $3.1 T budget. Politico.com, February 4. http://www.politico.com/news/stories/0208/8298.html.

Rohde, David W. 1991. *Parties and leaders in the postreform House.* Chicago: University of Chicago Press.

Romano, Lois, and Juliet Ellperin. 2006. Republicans greased path to Supreme Court for Alito. *Washington Post,* February 6.

Roosevelt, Franklin D. 1933. First inaugural address. March 4. http://www.yale.edu/lawweb/avalon/presiden/inaug/froos1.htm.

Rosen, Jeffrey. 2001. A majority of one. *New York Times,* June 3, 32.

Rosenbaum, David. 2001. Congress agrees on final details of tax cut bill. *New York Times,* May 26, A1.

————. 2002. No strong voice is heard on Bush's economic team. *New York Times,* July 21.

————. 2003. Bush signs law to cover drugs for the elderly. *New York Times,* December 9, 1.

————. 2005. Few see gains from Social Security tour. *New York Times,* April 3, 24.

Rossiter, Clinton. 1957. *The American presidency.* London: Hamish Hamilton.

Rozell, Mark J. 2004. Executive privilege in the Bush administration: The conflict between secrecy and accountability. In *Considering the Bush presidency,* ed. Gary L. Gregg II and Mark J. Rozell. New York: Oxford University Press.

Rudalevige, Andrew. 2006. The decline and resurgence and decline (and resurgence?) of Congress: Charting a new imperial presidency. *Presidential Studies Quarterly* 36, no. 3: 506–24.

Rutenberg, Jim. 2007. Ex-aide says he's lost faith in Bush. *New York Times,* April 1.

———. 2008. On his way out, Bush leads others in. *New York Times,* December 6.

Saad, Lydia. 2008. Disapproval of Bush spans the issues. Gallup Online, February 20.

Saloma, John. 1984. *Ominous politics: The new conservative labyrinth.* New York: Hill and Wang.

Samuelson, Robert J. 2007. The rich and the rest. *Washington Post,* April 18.

Sandler, Michael. 2006. House GOP schedules forum on immigration. *CQ Weekly Report,* September 11, 2394.

Sanger, David E., and James Risen. 2003. C.I.A. chief takes blame in assertion on Iraqi uranium. *New York Times,* July 12, A1, A5.

Savage, Charlie. 2005. Court backs Cheney on secrecy. *Boston Globe,* May 11.

———. 2007a. Scandal puts spotlight on Christian law school. *Boston Globe,* April 8.

———. 2007b. *Takeover: The return of the imperial presidency and the subversion of American democracy.* Boston: Little, Brown.

———. 2009. Obama's war on terror may resemble Bush's in some areas. *New York Times,* February 18.

Savage, David G. 2008. Conservative courts likely to be Bush legacy. *Los Angeles Times,* January 2.

———. 2009. Solicitor general nominee says "enemy combatants" can be held without trial. *Los Angeles Times,* February 11.

Schick, Allen. 2003. Bush's budget problem. Paper presented at the conference "The George W. Bush Presidency: An Early Assessment," Woodrow Wilson School, Princeton University, April 25–26.

Schier, Steven E. 2000. *By invitation only: The rise of exclusive politics in the United States.* Pittsburgh: University of Pittsburgh Press.

———. 2004. Introduction: George W. Bush's project. In *High risk and big ambition: The presidency of George W. Bush,* ed. Steven E. Schier. Pittsburgh: University of Pittsburgh Press.

———. 2006. Events haven't gone Bush's way since start of Iraq. *The Hill,* June 27.

Schlesinger, Robert. 2001. Senate committee puts Bush's education plan on fast track. *Boston Globe,* March 7, A6.

Schmitt, Eric. 2001. The vice president: Out front or low profile, Cheney keeps powerful role. *New York Times,* October 7.

———. 2003. Aide denies shaping data to justify war. *New York Times,* June 5. http://www.nytimes.com.

Schmitt, Gary, and Abraham Shulsky. 1987. The theory and practice of separation of powers: The case of covert action. In *The fettered presidency: Legal constraints on the executive branch,* ed. L. Gordon Crovitz and Jeremy Rabkin. Washington, DC: American Enterprise Institute.

Schrader, Ann, and Mike Soragher. 2001. Initial reviews strong for Bush speech. *Denver Post,* September 23.

Schwartz, Frederick A. O., Jr., and Aziz Huq. 2007. Where's Congress in this power play? Brennan Center for Justice of New York University Law School, April 1. http://www.brennancenter.org/content/resource/wheres_congress_in_this_power_play/.

Schwarz, Peter. 2002. European foreign ministers attack Bush's policy. World Socialist Web site. http://www.wsws.org/articles/2002/feb2002/euro-f15.shtml.

Shane, Scott. 2005. Increase in the number of documents classified by the government. *New York Times,* July 3.

Shenon, Philip. 2007. Justice Department chief is facing test in Minnesota. *New York Times,* November 13.

———. 2008. *The Commission: The uncensored history of the 9/11 investigation.* New York: Twelve.

Shepard, Scott. 2001. Bush, GOP fight for tax cut. *Atlanta Journal and Constitution,* April 6, 1A.

Sievers, Harry J. 1968. *Benjamin Harrison, Hoosier president: The White House and after.* Indianapolis: Bobbs-Merrill.

Silverstein, Mark. 2007. *Judicious choices: The politics of Supreme Court confirmations.* 2nd ed. New York: Norton.

Simon, Richard. 2006. Business groups woo Democrats. *Los Angeles Times,* October 27, A16.

Sinclair, Barbara. 1995. *Legislators, leaders, and lawmaking: The House of Representatives in the postreform era.* Baltimore: Johns Hopkins University Press.

———. 2006. *Party wars: Polarization and the politics of national policy making.* Norman: University of Oklahoma Press.

Singer, Paul. 2005. Roberts and the religious right—and left. *National Journal,* August 13, 2610.

Skowronek, Stephen. 1993. *The politics presidents make: Leadership from John Adams to George Bush.* Cambridge, MA: Harvard/Belknap.

———. 1997. *The politics presidents make: Leadership from John Adams to Bill Clinton.* Cambridge, MA: Harvard University Press.

———. 2003. Presidential leadership in political time. In *The presidency and the political system,* ed. Michael Nelson. 7th ed. Washington, DC: CQ Press.

———. 2008. *Presidential leadership in political time: Reprise and reappraisal.* Lawrence: University Press of Kansas.

Slavin, Barbara. 2002. Cheney rewrites role in foreign policy. *USA Today,* July 29.

Smith, Mark A. 2000. *American business and political power: Public opinion, elections and democracy.* Chicago: University of Chicago Press.

Smith, Tom W. 1980. America's most important problem: A trend analysis, 1946–1976. *Public Opinion Quarterly* 44 (summer): 164–70.

Socolofsky, Homer E., and Allan B. Spetter. 1987. *The presidency of Benjamin Harrison.* Lawrence: University Press of Kansas.

Sosnik, Douglas B., Matthew J. Dowd, and Ron Fournier. 2006. *Applebee's America.* New York: Simon and Schuster.

Sproat, John G. 1968. The best men. In *Liberal reformers in the Gilded Age.* New York: Oxford University Press.

Stanley, Harold W., and Richard G. Niemi. 2008. *Vital statistics on American politics, 2007–2008.* Washington, DC: CQ Press.

Starks, Tim. 2009. Intelligence policy: New perspectives of familiar approach. *Congressional Quarterly,* February 16.

Steigerwalt, Amy, and Lori A. Johnson. 2005. Judges, courts, and policy in President George W. Bush's second term. Paper presented at the conference "The Second Term of George W. Bush: Prospects and Perils," Villanova University, January 22.

Stevenson, Richard W. 2001. Bush projections show sharp drop in budget surplus. *New York Times,* August 23.

———. 2003. Bush signs tax cut bill, dismissing all criticism. *New York Times,* May 29, A18.

Stiglitz, Joseph E., and Linda J. Blimes. 2008. *The three trillion dollar war.* New York: Norton.

Stolberg, Sheryl Gay. 2008a. Bush proposing $145 billion plan to spur economy. *New York Times,* January 19.

———. 2008b. In glimpses, Cheney contemplates his legacy. *New York Times,* August 31.

Stonecash, Jeffrey M. 2000. *Class and party in American politics.* Boulder, CO: Westview Press.

———. 2005. *Political parties matter: Realignment and the return of partisan voting.* Boulder, CO: Lynne Rienner Publishers.

———, Mark D. Brewer, and Mack D. Mariani. 2003. *Diverging parties: Social change, realignment, and party polarization.* Boulder, CO: Westview Press.

Stout, David. 2004. Bush vows to improve ties with Europeans. *International Herald Tribune,* November 13, 1, 4.

Strahan, Randall. 1998. Thomas Brackett Reid and the rise of party government. In *Masters of the House: Congressional leadership over two centuries,* ed. Roger H. Davidson, Susan Webb Hammond, and Raymond W. Smock. Boulder, CO: Westview Press.

Stutts, Phillip. 2006. Did microtargeting hurt or help GOP's voter turnout efforts? *Human Events,* November 14. http://www.humanevents.com/article.php?id =18033.

Sullivan, Amy. 2006. Not as lame as you think. *Washington Monthly,* May. http://www.washingtonmonthly.com/features/2006/0605.sullivan1.html.

———. 2008. *The party faithful: How and why Democrats are closing the God gap.* New York: Scribner.

Sullivan, Andrew. 2007. Goodbye to all that. *The Atlantic,* December.

Suskind, Ron. 2004. *The price of loyalty: George W. Bush, the White House, and the education of Paul O'Neill.* New York: Simon and Schuster.

Tanner, Michael D. 2007. *Leviathan on the right.* Washington, DC: Cato Institute.

Taylor, Sara. 2004. Deputy strategist, Bush 2004 reelection campaign. Telephone interview with Steven Schier. November 20.

Teixeira, Ruy. 2003. Deciphering the Democrats' debacle. *Washington Monthly,* May.

Tipton, Steven M. 2007. *Public pulpits: Methodists and mainline churches in the moral argument of public life.* Chicago: University of Chicago Press.

Toner, Robin. 2005. It's "private" v. "personal" in debate over Bush plan. *New York Times,* March 21, A16.

———, and Robert Pear. 2003. Compromise seen as harder to find on Medicare drugs. *New York Times,* July 13. http://www.nytimes.com/2003/07/13/politics/13MEDI.html.

Toobin, Jeffrey. 2002. Ashcroft's ascent. *New Yorker,* April 15.

———. 2005. Blowing up the Senate. *New Yorker,* March 7.

———. 2007. *The nine: Inside the secret world of the Supreme Court.* New York: Doubleday.

Tulis, Jeffrey K. 2003. The two constitutional presidencies. In *The presidency and the political system,* ed. Michael Nelson. 7th ed. Washington, DC: CQ Press.

Tumulty, Karen. 1993. Bob Dole is back on top of Hill. *Los Angeles Times,* May 2, A12.

Uchitelle, Louis. 2009. Economists warm to government spending but debate its form. *New York Times,* January 6. http://www.nytimes.com/2009/01/07/business/economy/07spend.html?_r=1.

Unger, Craig. 2007. *The fall of the house of Bush.* New York: Scribner.

U.S. Congress. 1987. Committee Investigating Iran Contra. The Iran Contra report. 100th Congress, 1st session.

———. 2005. Senate Committee on Foreign Relations. Secretary of State nomination. 109th Congress, 1st session, January 18.

U.S. Department of Justice. 2006. Legal authorities supporting the activities of the National Security Agency described by the president. January 19.

U.S. Department of Justice. Office of Legal Counsel. 1986. Samuel Alito, Memorandum, to Litigation Strategy Group. February 5. http://www.archives.gov/news/samuel-alito/accession-060-89-269/.

———. Office of Legal Counsel. 2001a. Memorandum for William J. Haynes, December 28. http://www.usdoj.gov/ofc/warpowers.

———. Office of Legal Counsel. 2001b. The president's constitutional authority to conduct military operations against terrorists and nations supporting them. September 25. http://www.usdoj.gov/ofc/warpowers9/25.

U.S. Department of State. 2001a. Operation Enduring Freedom overview. October 1. http://www.state.gov/s/ct/rls/fs/2001/5194.htm.

———. 2001b. The United States and the global coalition against terrorism, September–December 2001: A chronology. December 31. http://www.state.gov/r/pa/ho/pubs/fs/5889.htm.

———. 2008. Background note: North Korea. http://www.state.gov/r/pa/ei/bgn/2792.htm.

U.S. Embassy Islamabad. 2002. Fact sheet: Coalition contributions to the war on terrorism. May 25. http://usembassy.state.gov/post/pk1/wwwh02052502.html.

U.S. Marine Corps. 1994. *Warfighting.* New York: Doubleday, Currency.

University of Connecticut. Department of Public Policy. 2005. National polls of journalists and the American public on First Amendment and media released. May 16.

VandeHei, Jim. 2003. Decision on tax cut left open in GOP budget deal. *Washington Post,* April 11, A2.

———. 2006. Democrats closing fundraising gap with Republicans. *Washington Post,* June 11, A1.

———, and Mike Allen. 2005. In GOP, resistance on Social Security. *Washington Post,* January 11, A1.

———, and Jonathan Weisman. 2006. Republicans split with Bush on ports. *Washington Post,* February 23, A1.

Van Natta, Don, Jr. 2001. The sporting life at the White House. *New York Times,* September 9.

Venkataraman, Nitya, and Jonann Brady. 2008 Cheney cites "major success" in Iraq. ABC News, March 19. http://abcnews.go.com/WN/Vote2008/story?id=4481249&page=1.

Washington Post editorial. 2009. The world reacts. January 26.

Wattenberg, Martin P. 1984. *The decline of American political parties, 1952–1980.* Cambridge, MA: Harvard University Press.

Weber, Max. 1970. *From Max Weber: Essays in sociology,* ed. H. H. Gerth and C. Wright Mills. London: Routledge and Kegan Paul.

Weisberg, Jacob. 2008. *The Bush tragedy.* New York: Random House.

Weisman, Jonathan. 2006. Divide is sharpening among Republicans. *Washington Post,* May 15, A4.

———, and John M. Berry. 2003. As budget deficit grows, Greenspan speaks softly. *Washington Post,* July 20. http://www.washingtonpost.com/wp-dyn/articles/A17138-2003Jul19.html.

Wells, John B., and David B. Cohen. 2007. Keeping the charge. In *Religion and the Bush presidency,* ed. Mark J. Rozell and Gleaves Whitney. New York: Palgrave Macmillan.

White, John Kenneth. 1997. *Still seeing red: How the cold war shapes the new American politics.* Boulder, CO: Westview Press.

———, and John J. Zogby. 2004. The likeable partisan: George W. Bush and the transformation of the American presidency. In *High risk and big ambition: The presidency of George W. Bush,* ed. Steven E. Schier. Pittsburgh: University of Pittsburgh Press.

White House. 2003. National Strategy to Secure Cyberspace. February. http://www.dhs.gov/xlibrary/assets/National_Cyberspace_Strategy.pdf, accessed March 1, 2009.

Wilber, Del Quentin. 2008. Chinese Muslims ordered released from Guantanamo. *Washington Post,* October 8.

Wildavsky, Aaron. 1975. The two presidencies. In *Perspectives on the presidency,* ed. Aaron Wildavsky. Boston: Little, Brown.

Wilentz, Sean. 2006. The worst president in history? *Rolling Stone,* April 21.

Williams, Rhys H. 1997. *Cultural wars in American politics.* New York: Aldine de Gruyter.

Wittes, Benjamin. 2006. *Confirmation wars: Preserving independent courts in angry times.* Lanham, MD: Rowman & Littlefield.

Wood, Gordon S. 1992. *The radicalism of the American revolution.* New York: Knopf.

Wood, Graeme. 2007. Classify this. *Atlantic* 300, no. 2 (September).

Woodward, Bob. 2002. *Bush at war.* New York: Simon and Schuster.

———. 2004. *Plan of attack.* New York: Simon and Schuster.

———. 2006. *State of denial.* New York: Simon and Schuster.

———. 2008. *The war within: A secret White House history, 2006–2008.* New York: Simon and Schuster.

Yalof, David A. 1999. *Pursuit of justices: Presidential politics and the selection of Supreme Court nominees.* Chicago: University of Chicago Press.

———. 2005. On lame ducks, election spoils, and the incredible shrinking term. *Law and Courts Newsletter* 15:18–21.

Yoo, John. 2005. *The powers of war and peace: The Constitution and foreign affairs after 9/11.* Chicago: University of Chicago Press.

Zabarenko, Deborah. 2008. Bush last-minute rules cement environmental legacy. Reuters, December 9. http://www. reuters.com.

Zakaria, Fareed. 1998. *From wealth to power: The unusual origins of America's world role.* Princeton, NJ: Princeton University Press.

Zeleny, Jeff. 2007. Democrats hope to expand rights at Guantánamo. *New York Times,* June 6.

Zeller, Shawn. 2008. Votes studies: Party unity—parties dig in deep on a fractured Hill. *CQ Weekly,* December 15, 3332.

Zogby, John J. 2007. President George W. Bush and U.S. Congress register record-low approval ratings in new Reuters/Zogby poll. Press release, September 19.

Zogby International poll. 2007a. August 23–27.

———. 2007b. May 17–20.

———. 2008. December 10–13.

CONTRIBUTORS

Peri E. Arnold is professor of political science at the University of Notre Dame and specializes in the presidency, executive organization, policy formation, and American political development. He is the author of numerous articles and book chapters as well as *Making the Managerial Presidency*, which won the 1987 Louis Brownlow Book Award of the National Academy of Public Administration. He is also the author of *Remaking the Presidency* (University Press of Kansas, 2009), a book investigating the presidency and presidents of the Progressive Era.

John J. Coleman is professor and chair of the Political Science Department at the University of Wisconsin–Madison. He is the author and co-editor of several books and numerous articles on political parties, elections, public knowledge, Congress and the presidency, and campaign finance. His current research includes projects on campaign spending, party accountability in elections, and the relationship between income distribution and voter turnout.

John Frendreis is professor of political science at Loyola University Chicago. He is co-author, with Chris Dolan and Raymond Tatalovich, of *The Presidency and Economic Policy* (Rowman & Littlefield, 2008) and has written for such leading journals as the *American Political Science Review, American Journal of Political Science,* and *Political Research Quarterly*.

James L. Guth is William Kenan Jr. Professor of Political Science at Furman University. He has written extensively for scholarly and popular publications on religion's role in American and European politics. In 2008, he received the American Political Science Association's Paul J. Weber Award for the Best Paper on Religion and Politics, presented at the 2007 annual meeting, for his work on religious influences on congressional voting. He is a co-editor of and contributor to the forthcoming *Oxford Handbook of Religion and American Politics.*

John F. Harris is the founder and editor in chief of Politico.com. His book *The Survivor: Bill Clinton in the White House* (Random House, 2005) was named a "Notable Book of the Year" by the *New York Times.* His most recent book (with Mark Halperin) is *The Way to Win: Taking the White House in 2008* (Random House, 2006).

Bertram Johnson is associate professor of political science at Middlebury College. He joined the faculty in 2004 and teaches courses in American politics, money in politics, the media as a political institution, and federal, state, and local politics. Johnson is a co-author of *America's New Democracy,* 5th edition (Longman, 2007). His research interests include intergovernmental relations, state and local politics, interest groups, and campaign finance.

Nancy Maveety is professor of political science at Tulane University. She is the author of *Queen's Court: Judicial Power in the Rehnquist Era* (University Press of Kansas, 2008) and other books and articles on the U.S. Supreme Court and judicial decisionmaking.

James M. McCormick is professor and chair of the Political Science Department at Iowa State University. He is the author of *American Foreign Policy and Process,* 5th edition (Wadsworth/Cengage Learning, 2010) and numerous journal articles on U.S. foreign policy. He has twice received Fulbright fellowships, to New Zealand in 1990 and to the Philippines in 2003, and was an American Political Science Association Congressional Fellow in 1986–1987.

Michael Nelson is the Fulmer Professor of Political Science at Rhodes College in Memphis, Tennessee. Nelson has published twenty-two books, including *How the South Joined the Gambling Nation: The Politics of State Policy Innovation,* with John Mason (Louisiana State University Press, 2008), which won the 2009 V. O. Key Award from the Southern Political Science Association. He has published numerous articles in scholarly journals such as the *Journal of Politics* and *Political Science Quarterly* and in periodicals such as *Newsweek,* the *New York Times,* and *Virginia Quarterly Review.*

John J. Pitney Jr. is professor of government at Claremont McKenna College in Claremont, California. He is the author of *The Art of Political Warfare* (University of Oklahoma Press, 2001), among other works.

Kevin S. Price is chief investment officer at Interlake Capital Management, LLC. He received his PhD at the University of Wisconsin–Madison and has taught at the University of Washington. His research and teaching interests are in the fields of presidential and party politics, with an emphasis on American political development.

Nicol C. Rae is professor of politics and international relations and senior associate dean for liberal arts at Florida International University. He is the author of *The Decline and Fall of the Liberal Republicans* (Oxford University Press, 1989), *Southern Democrats* (Oxford University Press, 1994), and *Conservative Reformers: The Republican Freshmen and the Lessons of the 104th Congress* (M. E. Sharpe, 1998), among other books.

Stanley A. Renshon is professor of political science at the City University of New York and a psychoanalyst. He is the author of thirteen books, among them *In His Father's Shadow: The Transformations of George W. Bush* (Palgrave Macmillan, 2004).

Steven E. Schier is Dorothy H. and Edward C. Congdon Professor of Political Science at Carleton College in Northfield, Minnesota. He has written or edited twelve books, including *The Postmodern Presidency: Bill Clinton's Legacy in U.S. Politics* (University of Pittsburgh Press, 2001), which won a *Choice* Outstanding Academic Book award. He was a Fulbright senior lecturer at York University in Toronto in 2002. His most recent book is *Panorama of a Presidency: How George W. Bush Acquired and Spent His Political Capital* (M. E. Sharpe, 2008).

Raymond Tatalovich is professor of political science at Loyola University Chicago. He specializes in the American presidency, co-authoring with Chris Dolan and John Frendreis *The Presidency and Economic Policy* (Rowman & Littlefield, 2008). He also co-authored with Thomas S. Engeman *The Presidency and Political Science: Two Hundred Years of Constitutional Debate* (Johns Hopkins University Press, 2003).

John Kenneth White is a professor of politics at Catholic University of America. He has written extensively on the presidency and American political parties. His latest book is entitled *Barack Obama's America: How New Conceptions of Race, Family, and Religion Ended the Reagan Era* (University of Michigan Press, 2009).

John Zogby is president and CEO of Zogby International, a worldwide research and marketing firm based in Utica, New York, with offices in Washington, DC. He writes a column for *Politics* magazine and has had pieces published on the opinion pages of the *New York Times*, the *Wall Street Journal*, the *Financial Times*, the *Christian Science Monitor*, the *Philadelphia Inquirer*, *Newsday*, and the *Boston Globe*. He has taught at the State University of New York, Utica College, and Hamilton College's Arthur Levitt Public Affairs Center.

INDEX

Note: Figures and tables are indicated by "f" or "t," respectively, following page numbers.